The politics of Latin American development

The politics of
Latin American
development

GARY W. WYNIA

ASSOCIATE PROFESSOR OF POLITICAL SCIENCE
UNIVERSITY OF MINNESOTA

CAMBRIDGE UNIVERSITY PRESS

CAMBRIDGE

LONDON   NEW YORK   MELBOURNE

Published by the Syndics of the Cambridge University Press
The Pitt Building, Trumpington Street, Cambridge CB2 1RP
Bentley House, 200 Euston Road, London NW1 2DB
32 East 57th Street, New York, NY 10022, USA
296 Beaconsfield Parade, Middle Park, Melbourne 3206, Australia

First published 1978

Printed in the United States of America
Typeset, printed and bound by Vail-Ballou Press, Inc.,
Binghamton, New York

Library of Congress Cataloging in Publication Data
Wynia, Gary W   1942–
The politics of Latin American development.
Includes bibliographies.
1. Latin America – Politics and government – 1948-
2. Latin America – Economic policy. I. Title.
JL960.W9   320.9'8'003   77–87395
ISBN 0 521 21922 1   hard covers
ISBN 0 521 29310 3   paperback

Contents

Contents

Preface

Latin America is an enduring source of fascination to the student of politics. Within the territory that lies between the Rio Grande and Tierra del Fuego there exist exceptionally diverse forms of political life ranging from the very traditional to the revolutionary. Fundamental issues of politics, economic development, and social justice are still intensely debated throughout the region, and governments continue to experiment with competing forms of political rule and public policy. But Latin America is also a source of frustration to those who try to comprehend its public affairs. Its immense variety and diversity defy simple description, and the behavior of its leaders repeatedly confounds observers. It is no wonder many students of the region prematurely abandon their quest soon after they have begun, convinced that the analysis of Latin America's intrigues should be left to the expert or those involved in its daily affairs.

Some of this frustration is justified, of course. Latin America is a vast region where 316 million people of European, Indo-American, African, and Asian heritage occupy an area larger than the United States. Its politics is complex, the motives of its leaders often obscure, and its range of experience great. Yet, it is the thesis of this book that Latin American politics, though complex, is comprehensible and that a few basic tools of analysis, consistently applied, can take us a long way toward the development of understanding. To begin with, despite their diversity, the Latin American nations do have many things in common that facilitate systematic analysis. They have, for example, shared a long colonial experience that has had a lasting impact on their social values, economic structures, and political institutions. Most also gained their independence at the same time and spent their formative years struggling with similar nation-building problems. And most important to the student of the contemporary scene, they now share several conditions, including widespread poverty, uneven and irregular economic growth, and heavy dependence on the more affluent industrialized nations, which provide markets for their exports and financial capital and technology for their development.

There is no better place to begin to develop an understanding of Latin American politics and public policy than with these last three conditions and the ways governments have dealt with them. A rich and diverse array of measures has been tried in recent times. You can still find a few traditional autocrats who endeavor to hold back the forces of change even though self-imposed isolation is no longer possible. There are others who have placed their faith in democratic politics, hoping change will come peacefully through citizen participation in the resolution of development problems. Still others have rejected democracy, claiming that their citizens cannot accept responsibility for self-governance or that a firm authoritarian hand is needed to impose the kinds of growth-stimulating policies that can overcome the region's underdevelopment. And some have decided that only through a revolutionary transformation of their societies under the direction of a mass-based political party can development and social justice be achieved.

The purpose of this book is to introduce you to these governments and to give you some of the intellectual tools needed to analyze their conduct and assess the effects of their decisions on the welfare of Latin Americans. When you complete it, you will not only have become familiar with the different ways governments have dealt with poverty, inadequate economic growth, and dependency, but you will also have acquired some of the skills needed to explore the world of Latin American politics on your own.

A book of this kind cannot be written without drawing on the research of others who have studied Latin American politics and economic life. I am especially indebted to the path-finding work of Charles W. Anderson, William Glade, Celso Furtado, Albert Hirschman, Helio Jaguaribe, Guillermo O'Donnell, and Kalman Silvert. Of course, I alone am responsible for the way their ideas have been interpreted and joined in this book. I have spared the reader footnotes and instead have listed at the end of each chapter the principal English language monographs that were consulted. It is my hope that these brief bibliographies will also serve as points of departure for readers interested in pursuing each topic further. Most of the works cited contain excellent bibliographies of relevant material available in Spanish, Portuguese, and English. In addition, maps of Latin America are provided at the end of this Preface, and data describing each nation's economic and social conditions are included in the Appendix.

This undertaking is the product of several years of teaching Latin American politics to university undergraduates. It represents the culmination of successive attempts to meet the challenge laid down each year by students who insist that they be taught how to understand the

Preface

political behavior of the Latin Americans who share the hemisphere with them. Had they been less demanding, this project never would have been begun. I have also gained immensely during the past fifteen years from the wisdom of the Latin American public officials and private citizens with whom I have discussed the region's affairs during my visits to their countries. I can only hope that this book faithfully communicates their insights.

Several colleagues have read the manuscript and contributed to its improvement. In particular I thank Roger Benjamin, Peter Johnson, and Sue Matarese of the University of Minnesota, along with Sue Brown, who typed the many drafts. I am also grateful to Professors Lawrence Graham of the University of Texas, Richard Clinton of Oregon State University, and William Garner of Southern Illinois University, who gave much needed criticism and advice at each stage of the project's development. Finally, I owe my greatest debt to my teacher, colleague, and friend, Charles W. Anderson, whose intellectual influence on this project is greater than either of us cares to admit.

G. W. W.

Latin America

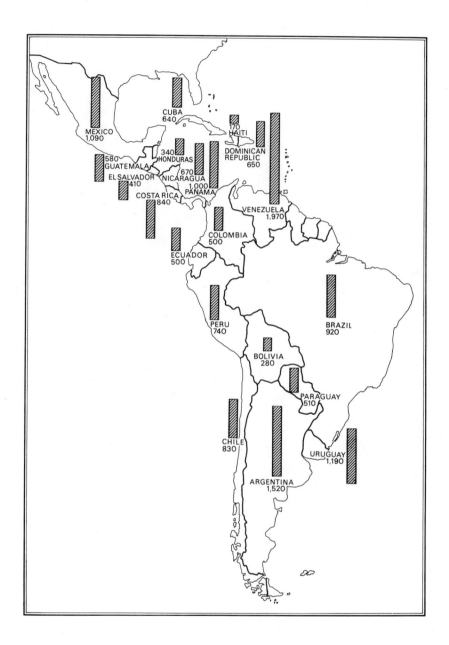

Per capita gross national product of Latin American nations, 1974, measured in U.S. dollars. (*Source:* Overseas Development Council. *The United States and World Development: Agenda 1977.* New York: Praeger, 1977, Table A-3.)

Part I

The analysis of Latin American politics

1. The Latin American condition

Introductions to Latin American politics usually begin with descriptions of the land, people, and history of the region. Then its political institutions and processes are described and analyzed. In this book, however, a different method will be used to introduce you to Latin America. Because we are concerned primarily with how Latin American governments have responded to the challenge of development in recent years, we will begin our investigation with the region's underdevelopment and its causes.

Our guide will be a fictional Latin American president who was elected to office after campaigning on a platform that promised economic and social reform. We will accompany him as he reviews his country's heritage, examines its current difficulties, and drafts proposals to deal with them. Our fictional leader does not represent all Latin American presidents; no one could. Despite their similarities, Latin American nations differ from one another in many ways, and no single example can capture their diversity. What follows, then, is one view of the Latin American condition that draws attention to some of the problems and issues Latin American leaders have faced during the postwar era. In reading the report you should pay particular attention to explanations of the region's underdevelopment and proposals for overcoming it in the face of existing political and economic obstacles.

DEVELOPMENT PROBLEMS AND PROSPECTS: A PRESIDENTIAL REPORT

A brief description of our country is presented in Table 1-1. We have approximately 20 million inhabitants, most of whom are *mestizos* or mixed-bloods (Hispanic and Indian), though 10 percent are Negro or mulatto, 10 percent are still classified as Indians, and approximately 5 percent are descendants of European and Asian immigrants. If you divide our gross national product by the number of inhabitants, we have a per capita product of $500, just below the Latin American average.

As you can see from Table 1-1, we are primarily an agrarian nation, though mining and industry are important to our economy. We depend very heavily on the export of a few products – primarily coffee, sugar, cotton, and iron

3

Table 1-1. *Country profile*

Population: 20 million	
Size: 500,000 square miles	
Ethnic composition	Literacy: 50%

Ethnic composition
  Mestizo: 75%
  Negro: 10%
  Indian: 10%
  European: 5%

Gross national product: $10 billion[a]
Per capita product: $500

Class structure

		Land tenure
Upper stratum:	5%	Richest 5% owns 60% of land
Upper middle stratum:	20%	Middle 20% owns 30% of land
Lower middle stratum:	25%	Poorest 75% owns 10% of land
Lower stratum:	50%	

Distribution of gross national product
  Agriculture: 35%
  Industry: 25%
  Mining: 10%
  Services: 30%

Trade patterns

Exports to		Imports from	
United States:	40%	United States:	50%
West Germany:	20%	Japan:	20%
Japan:	10%	West Germany:	10%
Great Britain:	10%	Great Britain:	10%
Latin America:	8%	Latin America:	5%
Others:	12%	Others:	5%

[a] American billion.

ore – to the industrialized nations, especially the United States. Our principal domestic industries are food processing, textiles, and clothing, although in recent years we have added some chemical and pharmaceutical industries. Most of our public utilities are owned by the state, having been nationalized by the government over the past thirty years. But we have also welcomed foreign investors in areas where we lack technology and capital. Today, foreign companies are majority shareholders in two of our banks, our iron mines, retail fuel companies, and chemical and pharmaceutical firms. Since the early 1950s we have accepted loans and grants from international agencies and the United States government to finance our development programs. By the end of last year we had received $600 million in loans, which we are now repaying with some difficulty, and $100 million in grants. Through the use of such assistance, we have tripled the length of our paved roads, modernized our ports, built a hydroelectric facility, improved our telecommunications, built new schools, constructed hospitals, and financed several domestic industries. Yet there is still much to be done if we are to provide our citizens with a decent life, as the following review of our social and economic conditions will demonstrate.

Social conditions

Undeniably the structure of our society has changed a great deal since the beginning of this century, especially under the impact of postwar industrialization and urbanization. Nevertheless, one thing has been constant throughout our modern history: the continued concentration of wealth and power. In contrast to the more industrialized Western European societies, where the wealthiest 20 percent of the population receives approximately 40 percent of the national income, our wealthiest 20 percent receives 70 percent of our national income. Rural poverty remains a major problem for us, as does increasing urban poverty as a result of rural-to-urban migration and population growth.

Because census information is incomplete, our social structure cannot be described in great detail. Nevertheless, we know enough to make some rough estimations. At the top there is an "upper stratum" of approximately 5 percent of the population; this includes what is left of the landed elite as well as the owners of the country's largest commercial and industrial firms, banks, and import-export businesses. The next 20 percent, or "upper middle stratum," includes managers in industry and commerce, professionals (e.g., doctors, lawyers, and engineers), the larger commercial farmers, top government bureaucrats and technicians, and high-ranking military officers. Below them comes the 25 percent that makes up the "lower middle stratum" of unionized laborers, along with schoolteachers, lower bureaucrats, noncommissioned military officers, and small farmers. Finally, there is the remaining 50 percent of our population, composed of urban and rural poor. Although this group is quite diverse in its composition, its members share the condition of poverty. It includes seasonal rural workers, subsistence farmers, peasants who work on landed estates as sharecroppers, part-time menial laborers and vendors, and domestic servants.

Clearly this last group has benefited the least from our economic development and now requires the greatest attention if we are to increase economic production and improve social welfare. At present these persons neither take much from nor contribute much to our national economic and political life. Their concerns are local and conditioned by a preoccupation with survival in a usually hostile world. Although most of the urban and rural poor tend to be passive politically, accepting the status quo as something that is beyond their power to change, we know from the experiences of some of our neighbors as well as our own past that their frustrations can sometimes be manipulated by ambitious political leaders for revolutionary causes. If we are to promote sustained economic growth and create a durable democratic order, we cannot afford to ignore this marginal population, for if it is left outside the modern sector it may become a willing collaborator of those who would use more violent methods to reform our society.

Before we can discuss the development problems raised by our present social structure and suggest ways we can deal with them, some understanding of that structure's origins and persistence throughout our history is required. There are, of course, hazards in looking to our past to explain our present condition, for we are tempted to take an oversimplified view of our Iberian and Indian heritage that assigns it responsibility for our underdevelopment. Undeniably, we have inherited a great deal from our forefathers, including much of our culture and many of our social values, economic structures, and political institutions. Yet, even though the remnants of our colonial past are still present in our society, I do not believe they constitute insurmountable obstacles to the creation of a more productive and just society.

Until early in the twentieth century our society was characterized by the domination of the masses by a small agro-exporter elite. The origins of this condition can be traced back to the conquest of the New World. The first *conquistadores* brought with them social values that had been formed during the last stages of the reconquest of the Iberian peninsula from the Moors during the fourteenth and fifteenth centuries. The reconquest was a long and bitter struggle that had a lasting impact on Iberian society and heavily influenced Iberian rule in the New World.

The reconquest required daring and determination. A premium was placed on military skills, and the heroic military leader became the model against which all leadership was judged. For their efforts, the valiant warriors of the reconquest were rewarded not only with the glory of military victory but also with power and wealth, most commonly in the form of property, which the Crown disbursed in large quantities to those who had expanded its domain. For future generations the lesson of the reconquest was clear: The quickest route to fame and fortune was through heroic deeds on behalf of the Crown. Opportunities for such deeds were extended by the exploration of the New World at the beginning of the sixteenth century. Hernán Cortés, Francisco Pizarro, and the other ambitious adventurers who explored the New World were determined to serve God and the king and to get rich. Most came from poor families in a society where rank and social distinction were derived from the ownership of land and the command of peasant laborers. They knew that if they conquered new territories and discovered precious metals they would become wealthy and powerful men. If there was no more land in Spain for distribution, they would be given title to the lands they had found in the New World. There they would replicate the social system that had been created in the Iberian peninsula during the reconquest by making the conquered Indians the new peasantry and the clergy, civil servants, and themselves the new elite.

The *conquistadores* also brought with them the patrimonial political values that had taken root in the Iberian peninsula during the reconquest. Their approach to politics was uncompromisingly authoritarian, stressing hierarchy and ordered relationships between governors and the governed. Authority moved in only one direction, from the monarch downward to his or her subjects. Individual citizens were not free agents who could seek out any place they chose in the political order; with few exceptions, they had to accept the station into which they were born. According to the Iberian view, authority was not delegated by the people to public officials; rather the people alienated their rights to those who by heritage or conquest had come to prevail in society. This approach to politics differs sharply from the contemporary liberal democratic concept of political authority, which calls for the selection of leaders by the citizens they govern. To the sixteenth-century Iberian elite such a practice would have been incomprehensible. Citizens were subjects who were denied the right to withdraw their consent whenever they wished because in theory they had already accepted the monarch as their sovereign. Only the administration of the laws was subject to appeal, but even that had to be done through courts controlled by the Crown.

The New World proved fertile ground for the transplanted reconquest values and institutions. Military victories over the Aztecs, Incas, and other indigenous peoples came with relative ease; precious metals were found and shared with the Crown; and thousands were converted to Catholicism. Through the institution of the *encomienda,* a right granted by the Crown to landowners that allowed them to extract labor or tribute from Indians within their domain, the new nobility created a system of large landed estates, called *latifundios,* which they used to generate wealth, social prestige, and political power.

The *latifundio* system was very different from the mode of land tenure developed in North America outside the Deep South. In Latin America land was distributed by the Crown immediately after the conquest. Even though many areas remained unoccupied until the late nineteenth century, most of the best land had been distributed through royal grants long before our Independence. What made the *latifundio* possible was the availability of conquered laborers. In North America, in contrast, much of the farmland was secured after Independence and distributed gradually in relatively small parcels by the government to immigrant farmers after indigenous populations had been liquidated or moved. As a result, except for slavery in the plantation agriculture of the South, labor was scarce, forcing farmers to limit themselves to what they could farm by themselves. For them, land was primarily a means to a modest livelihood; for us it became not only a source of production for domestic and foreign markets but also the basis of prestige and power. It made possible the creation of a privileged class who believed it deserved economic and political power by right. From it, we inherited a rural society composed of landed aristocrats and peasants, whereas North America escaped the legacy of both.

The institutions, values, and social structures we inherited from the colonial era have not survived unmolested since our Independence. On the contrary, despite the intensity of their struggle to prevail, they could not resist the forces of change, especially after the turn of the century. With the expansion of commerce and trade in the late nineteenth century came the rise of social groups that were part of neither the traditional elite nor the rural masses. It was they who eventually formed what we earlier described as the upper and lower middle class, ranging from professionals, merchants, and bureaucrats down to the organized laborers, whose number increased rapidly after 1930. What we now find is neither the simple two-class society we inherited from the colonial era nor a completely transformed society dominated by the values of a modern middle class. Today, remnants of the traditional society coexist with the institutions of a more modern one. In the countryside one still finds some traditional *latifundios* and plantations as well as productive market-oriented family farms. But there are also thousands of landless peasants as well as small farmers who subsist on relatively few acres. In the cities we find descendants of our traditional elite alongside foreign-trained technicians and aggressive merchants and industrialists. But there also exist thousands of poor who live in slums and survive precariously through their unskilled labor and petty commerce and services. It is a world in which the old tolerates the new and the modern coexists with the traditional. It would be satisfying to conclude that we are swiftly moving from one stage of development to another and that the vestiges of traditional society are giving way to the modern, but we cannot be so sure. Instead, we seem to have become stuck somewhere in midtransition and now realize that we may not be going through a series of developmental stages at all, but have become trapped between our past and our future.

This brings us back to the problems I mentioned at the outset of this survey of our social condition. Our contemporary problem is not the lack of economic growth and modernization per se, for we can proudly point to the transformation of our cities into modern metropolises, the growth of manufacturing, and the rise of something resembling a middle class as evidence that we are indeed making progress. Our problem is the failure to extend the benefits of modernization to a majority of our citizens. For those with easy access to the culture and skills of modernity, life is changing rapidly, and new opportunities are continually arising. But for others, who begin without such advantages, there still appears little hope of sharing in these opportunities. Instead, they are trapped within a vicious circle of poverty that has not been broken by the kind of economic progress we have enjoyed in recent years. Nearly 50 percent of our citizens lack the skills and capital needed to escape their very low level of productivity; their low output, in turn, brings them little income with which to purchase goods and services in our economy. Thus they neither contribute much to our economic growth nor gain much from it. Our economic transformation will not be complete, however, until they are included in it, and to that end our economic development program must be dedicated.

Economic underdevelopment and its causes

Since colonial times we have been primarily an agrarian nation devoted to the production of commodities for export and domestic consumption. As we have seen, landed estates were granted to the *conquistadores*, who used them to build local empires, which they governed paternalistically but harshly. Our economy began as an extension of an Iberian imperial system that ruled us through its stifling bureaucracy. Throughout the colonial era we were mere consumers, confined to the cultivation of indigo, sugar, cacao, and other cash crops; the extraction of silver and gold for the Crown; and the raising of cattle on unpopulated plains. With Independence at the beginning of the nineteenth century, we finally escaped the grasp of the Spanish Crown. Yet, instead of seeking out new lines of production, we stayed with what we knew best – the production of agricultural goods. We relapsed into the classic export economy, producing commodities for world markets and exploiting our principal assets – land and labor. In the place of our Spanish rulers we welcomed foreign investors, especially Englishmen, who brought with them much-needed capital and entrepreneurial skill and supplied us with manufactured goods. Our agriculture continued to be dominated by the *latifundio* and the plantation, both of which were strengthened by Independence and the end of Spanish controls. And, not unexpectedly, the *latifundistas,* bankers, and traders who had managed our economy during colonial times became the new ruling class after Independence.

The principal impetus to economic growth during the late nineteenth century came from the increased commercialization of cash crops such as coffee and cotton under the leadership of ambitious rural entrepreneurs and traders. With the growth of our export economy came the expansion of our ports, the construction of railroads by foreign investors, the extension of internal commerce, and the gradual modernization of our cities. In the early twentieth century more export products were added, tying us even closer to the world economy. Those who led the country in those days were proud of their accomplishments, for through our participation in the international trading system we greatly increased our national product, expanded our urban areas, and provided a good standard of living for those fortunate enough, and they were admittedly few (perhaps 20 percent), to participate in the export economy or in internal commerce.

Agricultural development and the growth of the export economy in the mid-nineteenth century had several effects on our society. There were still many large estates that used archaic farming methods, and most of our political and religious leaders were still recruited from the rural elite. Yet, as a result of economic growth and export diversification, there arose a new corps of commercial farmers, merchants, bankers, and traders. We still had our sugar plantations and with them a rural work force, descended from African slaves and *mestizos,* who remained poor and dependent on seasonal plantation labor for their survival. But we also had many medium-sized farms that produced coffee and cotton and provided seasonal employment to our rural poor. Finally, there remained many subsistence farmers, descendants of Indians, *mestizos,* and freed slaves. They composed approximately 40 percent of the country's population, but contributed little to its economic growth. Because of their dispersion throughout the countryside, their subservience to the landowning class, and their preoccupation with physical survival, they remained isolated from the political mainstream and were largely ignored by our political leaders.

Our economy continued to change slowly during the early twentieth century. First came the discovery of iron ore in interior mountains around 1910. There had been some mining during colonial times, but this was the first major discovery since then. With the mines came foreign investors, who exploited our minerals after making sizable capital investments and shared a small portion of their profits with the government, while giving employment to several thousand former peasants. Like coffee, mining also contributed to an expansion of internal commerce, transportation facilities, and banking, so that by the 1920s we could take pride in the fact that our small capital had become a modern city of 500,000 inhabitants enjoying many of the conveniences and entertainments found in Europe. Though in comparison with the industrial nations of Europe and North America we were still a poor country, especially if one looked at our per capita income of only $200, we had changed significantly from colonial days, and our business, farm, and political leaders could take credit for these transformations.

Unfortunately, our self-satisfied leaders never recognized the precariousness of the economic edifice they had constructed. To be sure, there had been occasional economic crises in the past, such as the one brought on by the interruption of trade during World War I, but on the whole such crises were accepted as temporary interruptions that could be tolerated in a system that had otherwise performed well. But in 1929 our leaders were shocked from their complacency by a worldwide depression that made clear the costs of relying entirely on commodity exports for our economic development. There we were, suddenly without markets for our agricultural products and cut off from the suppliers of the manufactured goods our urban consumers had come to rely on. At first we did little but adapt ourselves to hard times, as there seemed no feasible alternative but to continue with the system that had served the significant few so well for so long. Gradually, however, we came to recognize that some modification of our course was called for.

The solution to our problems, it seemed, rested with industrialization. It was neither an easy nor an uncontroversial choice. Those who argued for industrialization were opposed by the producers of export commodities, who feared that the growth of domestic manufacturers would displease our traditional trading partners and prevent the renewal of bilateral trade once the depression-induced economic crisis had subsided. Nevertheless, others, convinced of industrialization's necessity, struggled on, using governmental regulations and economic policies wherever possible to stimulate greater industrial growth during the 1940s and 1950s.

Where have these changes left us today? I would like to conclude that our economic transformation has been completed, that we are no longer dependent on the export of agricultural commodities and minerals for our economic survival, and that we now supply nearly all the manufactured goods we consume domestically. Unfortunately, we cannot make such a claim. The past three decades have, in fact, been difficult ones. Although our economy has changed a great deal and our industries now produce almost as much of our gross national product as does agriculture, we still find ourselves faced with widespread poverty, slow and irregular economic growth, and periodic balance-of-payments and inflation crises. Many of the development issues that divided us in the past are still subjects of controversy. Our per capita income, admittedly an inadequate measure of welfare because it ignores distribution of wealth, is only $500 in contrast to $3,500 in industrialized Great Britain, $6,600 in the United States, and $1,500 even in other industrializing nations like Argentina. To the credit of past governments, 50 percent of our adult population is now literate. Although insufficient education remains a concern, especially in rural areas, we are now faced by another problem: how to create jobs for the new literates who are flooding our cities in search of work.

What we now need is rapid economic growth and the creation of new employment opportunities for our citizens. But that is easier said than done. If one looks at our past record of economic growth superficially, it is impressive. Between 1945 and 1965, for example, our gross national product grew by an annual average of 5.5 percent – as fast as that of some industrial nations. However, such gross figures can be misleading. Our population has also been growing rapidly during this period, increasing by an annual average of 3 percent, making our per capita growth rate only 2.5 percent. That rate might be acceptable in a society that is already affluent, but it is unacceptable where nearly half the population exists at or just above the subsistence level and where thousands of new jobs must be created each year to absorb the rapidly increasing work force. If we continue at this pace, we will not only fail to achieve the standard of living of the industrial nations, but we will continue to be plagued with even larger pockets of poverty.

Political life: past, present, and future

We have already noted the influence of the colonial experience on our political values. Until Independence we were governed by the Crown and its colonial representatives in an authoritarian manner. Our only escape from colonial administrators came from their inability to enforce all their laws in every corner of the empire. Even though we considered ourselves loyal to the Crown, we did not hesitate to ignore its more troublesome laws whenever we thought we could get away with it. Our disobedience to colonial law eventually reached the point of political rebellion in the early nineteenth century, when we took advantage of the defeat of the Spanish Crown by Napoleon to declare our independence. Although our wars of liberation freed us from the Crown, we have not abandoned our habit of ignoring laws we find unjust or inconvenient. However, this tradition, which served us well when used against dictatorial governments, now threatens the implementation of progressive legislation that is opposed by vested interests.

Those who led our revolt against Spain were motivated by many things, the most notable being their desire for greater autonomy from the colonial trading system, the termination of arbitrary and harsh rule by the Crown's administrators, and a desire for some form of constitutional government similar to that founded by the American Revolution. But however one interprets the achievements of Independence, one fact is inescapable: The Independence struggle may have freed us from the Crown, but it did not liberate us entirely from Iberian political values and social institutions. Nor should such a dramatic transformation have been expected, for the signing of constitutions creating republican governments, no matter how noble and well intended, could not by itself reconstruct our way of life overnight. What Independence did was impose the idea of the "social contract" onto our tradition of hierarchical political authority. By severing our ties to the Crown we had hoped to open the door to the creation of government based on popular consent. Yet, what we achieved was not the construction of democratic government, but only the superimposition of a democratic veneer over a traditional, autocratic political system in which our leaders gained their authority more from their social-economic status and military might than from popular will.

Despite some valiant efforts to make democracy work, post-Independence governments were overthrown with regularity as local leaders and their private armies contended for the right to govern us. These local leaders, called *caciques,* or *caudillos* when they controlled large regions, dominated politics for fifty years after Independence. Their objective was the preservation of local autonomy in the face of central government efforts to create a unified nation-state. Some wore military uniforms, called themselves generals, and fought continuously with the government and other *caudillos.* The more ambitious ones eventually defeated their rivals and seized the government for themselves, often ruling through brutality and intimidation while imposing an order that lasted until they were deposed by their rivals. However, little changed during the rule of the *caudillos,* for despite frequent upheavals, they and their supporters in the landowning elite held onto their property and privileges throughout.

By the 1860s political parties began to appear. Initially, we had only two parties, one calling itself the Conservative party and the other the Liberal party. However, these were not parties in the modern sense; rather, they were elite cliques that created no constituency organizations and made no effort to appeal directly to the masses. At the time, our politics was dominated by a system of patron-client relationships in which individuals of lower status used those with higher status to gain access to resources under the latter's control. Peasants, for example, relied on landowners; the landowners depended on local *caudillos;* and they, in turn, depended on national political leaders. From the landowner the peasant received access to land and protection against natural and human enemies in exchange for deference, cheap labor, and support for the landowner's political causes; similarly, landowners received physical protection from *caudillos* in return for financial tribute and political support. Our interest in this nineteenth-century system of patron-client politics would be only academic were it not for the fact that its legacy still haunts our political life. Today, patron-client relationships pervade our political parties and heavily influence the operation of the state bureaucracy. Upward mobility within the political process still depends heavily on patronage, and survival in office requires that one serve as a broker between clients and the state institutions that provide the resources and regulations needed by industrialists, farmers, union leaders, peasants, and the like. Any development strategy we choose will have to take these realities into account.

Given the elitist nature of nineteenth-century politics, it is not surprising that there were few differences between the Conservative and Liberal parties. The Conservatives, as their name implies, favored the traditional social order, the economic status quo, and the dominance of the Roman Catholic Church in society. The Liberals, though also elitist, were anticlerical and promoted the opening of economic opportunities through policies that encouraged the production of agricultural exports and foreign investment. It was under the rule of the Liberals during the late nineteenth and early twentieth centuries that our economy began to grow at a steady pace through the foreign-financed construction of railways and ports used to transport our coffee, cotton, and iron ore to foreign markets. It was also during this period that the state seized most of the Church's landholdings, as well as those of our Indians, and redistributed them to opportunistic rural entrepreneurs, who quickly put them into the production of exportable commodities.

This is not the place to assess the contributions of Liberal governments to our development, though we cannot ignore the gradual economic changes their policies encouraged. The Liberals did give us unprecedented political stability, holding five consecutive elections without violent interruptions. Of course, only 10 percent of our adult population participated in those elections, as the franchise was limited to literate male property owners; moreover, those who did vote were often the victims of threats and other forms of intimidation. What the Liberals failed to do was create any sense of nationhood among our people. We were taught that it was our function to supply the rest of the world with food and minerals and leave public affairs to a small elite and their foreign allies. For most of our people, there was no distinct nation to identify with, but only a village or region that from time to time was harassed by a distant central government.

We have already discussed how the 1929 world depression undermined our export economy and prompted efforts to industrialize. The drive for industrialization coincided with the birth of nationalism and the emergence of new political forces that challenged the traditional elite and its monopoly over economic and political power. In less than two decades our political process was transformed from one in which a few political leaders settled all policy questions among themselves to one in which the representatives of industrial, professional, and labor groups became actively involved in the policy-making process.

The transition had actually begun around the turn of the century. With the growth of our foreign trade and domestic commerce had come a dramatic increase in the number of merchants, lawyers, and white-collar employees. Simultaneously, there arrived on our shores several hundred thousand immigrants from Europe. Many founded new lives as farmers and merchants, and some, inspired by European socialism and anarchism, organized our first labor unions. It was not long before these new groups demanded admittance to our political process; although some were incorporated into an expanded Liberal party, many others formed their own political parties and campaigned for electoral reforms that would give them competitive advantages. However, it was the military, not the new political parties, that finally ended the elite monopoly over public office. Frustrated by the Liberal party's inability to deal with the economic collapse and social protests that followed in the wake of the 1929 depression, the military reluctantly seized the government, ending five decades of civilian rule by the agro-exporter elite. Although it tried to remain neutral, the military did much to promote the growth of our industries by nationalizing railroads and several public utilities, creating an industrial development bank, and raising tariffs on imported goods that were produced domestically. At the same time, however, it ignored the rural economy, leaving its management to the *latifundistas* and commercial farmers who had dominated it for the past fifty years.

After World War II our politics became even more complicated. The military was now in politics to stay. Even though it has returned the government to civilians after its interventions, it continues to influence the way the country is governed. Our political party system has also changed. In addition to the Liberal and Conservative parties, there are small Socialist and Communist parties and my own Popular Democratic party, which we created in the late 1930s. In 1936 the military held an election that was won by the Liberals; however, amid charges of corruption and incompetence it removed them again in 1944. When elections were held again in 1950, my party won for the first time. But when we hastily enacted an agrarian reform program and nationalized the foreign-owned mines, we alienated several political forces who persuaded the military to depose us in 1953. Now after several years of military rule, we have won another election and will try once again to implement our reform program. This time we will have to be more cautious, as we received only 45 percent of the popular vote compared with the Liberals' 25 percent, the Conservatives' 15 percent, and the Socialists' 10 percent, and are just short of a majority in both houses of Congress.

New interest groups have been added to our political process as a result of the economic and social changes of the past forty years. The Roman Catholic Church, now divided between progressive and conservative factions, *latifundistas,* commercial farmers, exporters, bankers, and foreign investors have been joined by large and small industrialists, labor unions, and peasant leagues. Some of these groups, such as bankers and foreign investors, are well organized and financed and enjoy great influence, whereas others, like the peasant leagues, are grossly underrepresented in the policy-making process. Their respect for democratic institutions varies considerably, depending on how well such institutions serve their particular interests. It is not uncommon for some groups, especially the more conservative ones, to urge military intervention whenever their interests are seriously threatened by the government. My party has tried hard to secure the support of some of these groups, especially the new peasant associations and the labor unions, but our campaigns have been only partially successful because many peasants still submit to landlord pressure to vote for the Liberals or Conservatives, or do not vote at all, and some of the laborers prefer the Socialist party to ours. An even more difficult problem is the one raised by the hostility of many powerful interests to our reform program. Foreign investors are very concerned about our nationalization proposals, landowners are fearful of our plans to expropriate inefficient estates, bankers oppose our desire for government control over the allocation of credit, and industrialists do not agree with our plans to create more state industries. If we are to succeed, we must somehow overcome the threats posed by such formidable opponents, who will undoubtedly try to block passage of our program and obstruct its implementation through the use of the many resources at their disposal.

Finally, there is the question of our ability to sustain the democratic process in a country that has frequently rejected constitutional government. The democratic rules of the game have served my party well because our ability to organize large numbers of voters has earned us the opportunity to rule. Others have not been served as well by the democratic process and, therefore, have less reason to support it than we do. For conservative political and economic groups representative democracy has always posed a threat because it offers an avenue through which representatives of the masses can deprive them of their resources. At the other extreme, those peasant and labor groups who were denied their rights under our traditional system of elite rule have come to view democracy as nothing more than window dressing for a system of domination of the poor and powerless by the rich and powerful. We therefore are caught in the middle between those who fear we might do them harm and others who are convinced we will do nothing at all for them. The more we fulfill the fears of the first and the expectations of the second, the more difficult it will be to sustain democratic rule.

What can we do?

The task that lies ahead is not an easy one. We must alleviate poverty as much as possible, increase our national economic independence, and build a solid foundation for our political democracy. In order to prepare for the task of governing this country, I have, with the assistance of my economic advisors, prepared the following report on the economic reforms we plan to implement as well as an assessment of the obstacles we will face once we have begun.

Economic reforms. We begin by recognizing that we are still a long way from the industrialization of our economy. We continue to import some consumer goods and nearly all our iron, steel, machinery, and electrical goods. We also suffer from what Dr. Raúl Prebisch of the United Nations Economic Commission for Latin America (ECLA) has called adverse terms of trade with the industrial nations, which has forced us to expend increasing amounts of our commodities to pay for the same quantity of imported industrial goods simply because the prices of manufactured goods have risen faster than those of sugar, coffee, cotton, and other primary commodities. This is precisely why we must continue to push hard for as much industrialization as we can afford.

But industrialization will not come easily because we are still plagued by a shortage of financial capital. There are several reasons for this. First, we lack domestic savings. Savings derive primarily from individual savings accounts in financial institutions and from government taxation. Private savings are relatively scarce because nearly half our population is too poor to save. Those who can – property owners, merchants, professionals, and skilled laborers – do so at a lower rate than their counterparts in industrial nations because of well-founded fears that our persistent inflation will reduce the value of their savings. Under such precarious conditions they prefer to consume goods today rather than save now and then purchase the same goods at higher prices later. They also prefer to put their money in foreign banks or to exchange it for foreign currencies and gold. Despite repeated government efforts to restrict such capital flight, it continues.

The shortage of private capital leaves the government as financier of last resort. Through its taxes, it can force private entrepreneurs and wage earners to contribute to national savings by taking income from them and transferring it through government banks and investments to industrial activities. Unfortunately, this works better in theory than in practice. Traditionally, our government has relied primarily on import and export taxes for public revenues because of the ease of their collection. Only after 1945 did we initiate income and capital gains taxes. Both are still resisted even though their rates are less than half what they are in Western Europe and the United States. In fact, tax evasion permeates our society. We estimate that only about 30 percent of the taxable income is declared annually; unfortunately, we can do little to prevent tax evasion because our bureaucrats lack the skill and technology needed to tighten tax collections. Consequently, the forced savings that might be captured by the public sector continue to escape our grasp.

Another obstacle to industrialization is the small size of our national market. We cannot achieve economies of scale in our manufacturing as long as half our population is outside the market economy. In a sense we are a victim of our own underdevelopment and the poverty of our rural sector. Gradually our agrarian reforms and rising urban employment will expand our domestic markets, but until they do our industrial growth will be constrained. There is, however, another way to deal with our market problem in the short term. Here again Dr. Raúl Prebisch and his colleagues at ECLA have come to our rescue by proposing regional economic integration as a way to deal with the difficulties that arise when underdeveloped countries try to industrialize in isolation from one another. Separately, each of us faces the problem of too little domestic demand, but collectively we can overcome this by allowing one another free access to our domestic markets. To succeed, we must first agree to a division of labor and specialization in our industrial output in order to avoid duplication of effort and then integrate our markets through regional agreements that abolish tariffs on goods traded within our region and increase the free movement of labor and capital among member nations. We are cautiously optimistic that we can create some kind of common market among the Latin American countries that will help solve our problems of insufficient demand in the short term. Of course, we recognize that in order to succeed we must overcome many obstacles, not the least of which are traditional rivalries and distrust among our neighbors as well as the costs of industrial specialization, which will necessitate our closing some industries.

Regional economic integration may help with our market problems, but we are still left with the problem of capital shortage. If domestic private investors and the state cannot supply what is needed, we must borrow abroad or encourage foreign investors, often in the form of multinational corporations, to finance our industrialization. That, of course, raises an issue that greatly concerns my administration: the danger of excessive reliance on foreign suppliers of capital and technology. There is nothing unique about our turning to foreigners for assistance with our development; other nations have done it with much success, as have we in the past. Foreigners built our railways, constructed our ports, financed some of our industries, and made it possible to import advanced technology. What concerns us now are the political and economic effects of increasing our dependence on foreigners in the decades ahead.

We know from past experience that with foreign capital comes foreign intervention into our domestic affairs, if only to protect investments. Moreover, as our debts to outsiders increase, so do the outsiders' demands that we change our financial policies so we can devote more resources to repaying our debts. We must guard against a process of "denationalization" that transfers control over important domestic economic decisions from individuals and organizations loyal to our nation to those who are loyal to other nations or to multinational corporations. If we do not, we will find that in exchange for the benefits of foreign capital and technology we have relinquished control over the course of our development. In particular we must guard against foreign control over industries, like mining, whose exports are critical to our national development. Whatever arrangement we decide on should leave our citizens in the dominant position, to assure that foreigners do not use their economic power against us. We must also develop regulations that curb the export of profits from foreign investments. Although the stockholders of such corporations merit a return on their investments, we must encourage the reinvestment of profits within our economy, channeling them into areas where they can be most productive without threatening national sovereignty. There are so simple solutions to the problem of denationalization. Common sense tells us that we require some foreign investment and technology in order to continue our program of industrialization; yet a desire to control our own destiny dictates that we regulate foreign capital closely, assuring that it serves our purposes as well as those of its suppliers.

Finally, we must recognize that industrialization alone will not solve our development problems. It is imperative that we expand our rural production as well. We are still plagued by many inefficient farms, including the remnants of the *latifundios* that have survived since colonial times; moreover, two-thirds of our rural population still works at or just above the subsistence level. New taxes that penalize farmers who leave their land idle or exploit it inefficiently are essential to encourage higher productivity. But if we are going to improve the condition of the rural poor, something more than tax reform is needed. We must also implement an agrarian reform program that expropriates land from the larger, less efficient producers and transfers it to landless peasants. With adequate technical assistance the latter should increase their productivity, improve our food supply, and raise their personal incomes. And with their higher incomes they will become consumers of the goods produced elsewhere in our economy, thus contributing to economic development generally.

We are faced with a challenging assignment. We have seen how our economy has developed during the past two centuries and are aware of its many deficiencies. Our growth rate is not sufficient to meet the needs of our expanding population as well as the aspirations of most of our citizens for an improved standard of living. We have tried to free ourselves from our dependence on an agricultural economy and its raw product exports through a gradual and costly process of industrialization. We are now less dependent on the importation of consumer goods than ever before; yet we must still import fuels and other raw products to operate our industries. We are also becoming increasingly dependent on foreign investors to complete our industrialization. Unfortunately, the postwar years have not always been smooth ones; despite an annual average gross national product growth rate of 5.5 percent, our annual rates have fluctuated widely, rising and falling with the market value of exports. Moreover, we have on occasion been plagued by inflation rates as high as 30 percent owing to a variety of causes, including unproductive government spending, the failure of our industries to meet the demands of urban consumers for particular goods and of our farmers to supply enough food to local markets, and occasional wage-price spirals touched off by unions trying to get ahead of prices and management trying to cover their costs. In order to deal with inflation, we must not only treat such symptoms as wages and prices, but also increase production so that enough foodstuffs and manufactured goods will be available to meet our growing consumer demand.

We must now implement policies that will reform our economic institutions and stimulate the growth of our rural and industrial economies. Our goal is not only rapid economic expansion, but the inclusion of greater numbers of our citizens in the modern economic sector where they can share the benefits of our growth. Should we fail to make such opportunities available to them, we will be plagued by an ever-increasing number of marginal poor who will threaten our economic progress and undermine any hope of achieving political stability through democratic means.

The obstacles we face. We are not so naive as to believe we can achieve our objectives without confronting significant opposition and overcoming many obstacles to economic reform. Our agrarian reform program, for example, will be opposed by the landowners whose property we propose to expropriate; the Liberal party, which is opposed to rural reform generally; and even the Communists and Socialists, who view our reforms as a threat to their campaigns for peasant support. There are many technical problems associated with agrarian reform as well. First, much of the peasantry, encased as it is in tradition, fear, and apathy, may not at first respond to our reforms; even when it does accept them, it may react less enthusiastically than we would like, especially in putting the new lands to productive use. Second, we face the question of which lands to include within our reforms. Should we, for example, encourage colonization of public lands or depend entirely on the expropriation of private ones? If the latter, should we expropriate land presently in production or only that not in use? And once it has been expropriated, how should it be reallocated: into individual family farms, cooperatives, or state farms? We must also come to grips with the fact that in trying to improve the welfare of the rural poor we may actually reduce production, at least in the short run, because it may take some time before peasant farmers, who lack technology and know-how, will be able to raise their productivity. There are no simple answers to these questions, but we will not get very far if we do not resolve them quickly.

Our tax reform program, which is aimed at ending tax avoidance and increasing the tax burden of the richest 20 percent of our population as well as of foreigners who invest and work in our country, can expect opposition from industrialists, professionals, landowners, and foreign investors. They will be helped by the fact that it will not be easy to administer our new tax laws. If we are to enforce them, we will have to end the practice of bribing public officials. We can no longer ignore the fact that many of our low-paid bureaucrats have succumbed to the temptation to accept bribes and other favors in exchange for ignoring those who avoid the law. Unless we can seriously reduce this practice, we will never end the cynical abuse of our tax laws.

Nor will it be easy to operate the foreign-owned mines we plan to nationalize. Of course, we are not without precedents in this area, as our military governments nationalized foreign-owned railways and telephone companies in the 1940s. But in extending state ownership from utilities to extractive enterprises we are embarking on a new and risky course, one that will threaten foreign investors in other fields. As they have done elsewhere, the mining companies will exert pressures on foreign banks who have lent us money and on foreign governments who supply us with development assistance in an effort to persuade them to punish us if we go ahead with our plans. Our vulnerability to such pressures is well known. Our dependence on foreign loans and technology is what makes it so difficult for us to chart our own economic course. Here again we seem to be caught in a vicious circle, for the more we try to develop our economy, the more we must depend on foreign help; but the more we accept the latter, the more difficult it becomes to develop on our own terms.

Finally, we face the more general problem of how to hold on to public office in the face of likely attempts to bring our government down. Our party's first try at public office ended, it will be recalled, with our overthrow by the military at the urging of the other political parties. Conservatives and Liberals feared that our reforms would undermine their economic power; Socialists were concerned that our success might undercut their campaigns for popular support. What we have learned from that experience is that we cannot merely announce our programs in the expectation that everyone will step aside and let them take hold. Nor can we assume that our election under the democratic rules of the game will in itself prevent a military coup. We know we face a very difficult dilemma: If we move too swiftly we will encourage our opponents to block us in the legislature, obstruct the execution of our program, or encourage the military to overthrow our government. Yet, if we move too slowly, our supporters will become disillusioned and our reforms will not develop the momentum needed to carry us through. What we now need more than anything else is a plan of political action that will guide us through the many obstacles that lie ahead.

A CHALLENGE AND A PROMISE

You have just read the commentary of a hypothetical Latin American president-elect who is searching for ways to implement a program of reform and development in his country. The example we used happened to be that of a democratically elected, reform-oriented president, but we could just as easily have used a conservative, military, or revolutionary one. Whatever their motives and objectives, they would have to deal with some of the political and economic legacies just described in this case. There are no simple solutions to the problems they face or easy ways to overcome the obstacles. In each case hard decisions have to be made and high political risks taken.

Now the time has come to turn the tables and consider what you would do if you were in the position of our hypothetical president. How would you search the recent past for lessons that might help you implement a development program? Which political forces would you have to contend with and what are their chances of defeating your program? What would be your chances of serving out your term without a military coup? How would you deal with your opponents: by compromising with them, by ignoring them, or by repressing them? What would be the costs of compromise or repression to you and your program? Are the development problems you face solvable in the long term or is the country doomed to poverty and continued dependence on foreigners? And what about the chances for reform in general? Can you explain why so many reform governments in Latin America in recent years have ended in military dictatorships?

But wait a minute, you say; you are not prepared to deal with such questions after reading only one brief summary of the problems faced by the leader of a hypothetical country. Do not be discouraged; if you could answer them satisfactorily, you would have no need for this book. Our purpose in the chapters that follow is to discuss some ideas that will help you analyze Latin American political life. We offer no easy answers, but instead suggest how you can go about finding answers on your own. The remainder of this book is divided into two parts. In the first you will be introduced to the rules of the Latin American political game, the players who participate in it, and the economic strategies they use to affect its outcomes. In the second part you will learn how to apply these tools to the analysis of Latin American political systems. Examples of four different types of governments will be described in some detail. Our objective is to develop analytical skills while learning about the contemporary politics of several Latin American countries.

FURTHER READING

Arciniegas, German. *Latin America: A Cultural History.* New York: Knopf, 1967.

Furtado, Celso. *Economic Development of Latin America.* Cambridge: Cambridge University Press, 1970.

Glade, William P. *The Latin American Economies.* New York: Van Nostrand Reinhold, 1969.

Glassman, Ronald M. *Political History of Latin America.* New York: Funk & Wagnalls, 1969.

Griffin, Keith. *Underdevelopment in Spanish America.* London: Allen and Unwin, 1969.

Herring, Hubert. *A History of Latin America: From the Beginnings to the Present.* New York: Knopf, 1962.

James, Preston. *Latin America.* New York: Odyssey Press, 1969.

Lambert, Jaques. *Latin America: Social Structures and Political Institutions.* Berkeley: University of California Press, 1971.

Morse, Richard M. "The Heritage of Latin America," in Louis Hartz, ed., *The Founding of New Societies.* New York: Harcourt, Brace & World, 1964, pp. 123–77.

Odell, Peter R. *Economies and Societies in Latin America: A Geographical Interpretation.* New York: Wiley, 1973.

Olien, Michael D. *Latin Americans: Contemporary Peoples and Their Cultural Traditions.* New York: Holt, Rinehart and Winston, 1973.

Pike, Frederick B. *Spanish America 1900–1970: Tradition and Social Innovation.* London: Thames and Hudson, 1973.

Pebisch, Raúl. *Change and Development: Latin America's Great Task.* Washington, D.C.: Inter-American Development Bank, 1970.

Stein, Stanley J., and Barbara Stein. *The Colonial Heritage of Latin America: Essays on Economic Dependence in Perspective.* New York: Oxford University Press, 1970.

Tannebaum, Frank. *Ten Keys to Latin America.* New York: Knopf, 1962.

Urquidi, Victor. *The Challenge of Development in Latin America.* New York: Praeger, 1964.

Wagley, Charles. *The Latin American Tradition: Essays on the Unity and Diversity of Latin American Culture.* New York: Columbia University Press, 1968.

2. The rules of the Latin American political game

When you study the politics of another country and try to explain why a particular political event occurred, what questions do you ask? Most likely, you draw on what you have experienced in your own country and use it as a norm against which to compare the politics of other nations. Recall, for example, the last time you read about a coup in Argentina, terrorism in Mexico, the inauguration of a military president in Brazil, or police repression in Chile. When you tried to explain why these events occurred, did you first compare them with the politics of your own country, trying to discover how and why the Latin American events differed? You were not alone if you did, for many observers have approached Latin America in this manner. But what did such comparisons tell you? You probably concluded that Latin America is a region of unusual political phenomena, where the conventions of politics as you know them are frequently ignored. In contrast to the Anglo-American democracies, which pride themselves on their orderly, representative governments where elections are held on schedule and constitutional rules generally obeyed, Latin America seemed quite different, with its military coups, riots, demonstrations, and frequent unscheduled changes of government.

But have you really learned anything from such observations? Most likely, you discovered more about yourself and political life in your own country than about Latin America. Although there is nothing inherently wrong with asking how one nation's politics differs from another's, such comparisons, to be useful in building explanations of political behavior, require something more than an inquiry into what is "unusual" about another nation's politics. Instead, we must try to examine a country's politics on its own terms, asking why its leaders and citizens behave as they do, given the conditions they face. This does not mean we must relinquish our personal preferences for particular forms of government or refrain from judging others harshly; it means only that we must try to begin our inquiry with an open mind.

Currently there are many different ways to approach the study of Latin American politics. Each offers a point of view that generates insights. One of the oldest, for example, urges us to study constitutions

23

and governmental institutions, such as executives, legislatures, and judiciaries; another insists that we also study less formal institutions, such as political parties, the military, and various interest groups in order to discover who controls government and for what ends. We could also focus on the political culture of Latin America, searching for explanations of political behavior in elite and popular attitudes toward politics and in the ways they are passed from generation to generation. Others prefer to emphasize the social determinants of political behavior, paying particular attention to systems of class stratification and how they lead to the domination of one class by another through political and economic means. Still others claim that Latin American politics cannot be explained without taking into account the influence of foreign governments and investors on public officials. And there are those who prefer to understand Latin America as an example of the process of modernization through which traditional agrarian institutions are being transformed into modern industrial ones.

Each of these approaches is useful, for each draws attention to relevant parts of the larger political process. Despite the fact that they are often abused in practice, we cannot ignore constitutions and government institutions, and even though political parties may perform unusual functions or no apparent functions at all, they must be studied as well. Some awareness of political culture is also essential if we are to understand beliefs and codes of political behavior. And, of course, explanations of political life must also consider the influence of class structures and the intervention of foreigners. In sum, we cannot ignore any of these factors if we are to understand Latin American politics in its entirety. But how do we put them together? There is obviously no easy way. Nevertheless, if we adopt a point of view that raises questions general enough to incorporate many different aspects of the political process, yet specific enough to inform us about the similarities and differences among Latin American states, we can take an important step in that direction. And that is precisely what we will attempt to do.

THE LATIN AMERICAN POLITICAL GAME

We will begin by viewing Latin American politics as a kind of game, with rules, players, competitions, winners, and losers. The choice of the game concept is not meant to suggest that Latin American politics is frivolous or merely recreational; on the contrary, it is a deadly serious struggle that affects the physical as well as the political survival of those involved in it. Rather, we have chosen the game metaphor because it offers a useful model of the real world that draws on some familiar ideas about human conduct. Like most games, political systems operate according to rules. They may be quite formal rules that are spelled out in a constitution or they may be informal norms that instruct behavior. There may be a single set of rules that all members of the society agree upon or several competing sets struggling to prevail. Rules govern the conduct of political life and give a political system its particular character; therefore, to understand politics and public policy in different countries, we must first comprehend the rules that govern the political conduct of their citizens.

In addition to rules, political games involve players who seek to gain through their participation in the game. In some settings their gains may come only at the expense of their competitors; in others, cooperation may be possible, leading to simultaneous benefits for all. Players may be motivated by a desire for material gain, social status, the fulfillment of noble ideals, or many other things. But whatever their objectives, they have to cooperate or compete with others to satisfy their needs through the political process. In a country whose resources are monopolized by a small elite, the number of active players is quite small; in a nation that encourages open competition, nearly all sectors of society are represented by active players. As analysts, we must identify the principal players in each game, observe and explain their behavior, and then assess their impact on the lives of others. To guide us in this endeavor we need only apply some familiar concepts to the systematic analysis of Latin American politics.

The remainder of Part I of this book constitutes an introduction to the components of the Latin American political game. We will begin with some fundamental concepts and illustrations of how they may be used. In this chapter we will learn how to identify the rules of the game. In Chapters 3 and 4 we will meet some of the principal players, and in Chapter 5 we will examine four of the economic strategies Latin American players have used to direct the production and distribution of goods in their societies.

IDENTIFYING FORMAL AND INFORMAL POLITICAL RULES

When someone speaks of political rules, we think first of a constitution or public document that specifies how the government is organized, how public officials are selected, and how citizens are to be treated. We usually consider agreement on such rules to be essential to the creation and maintenance of a political society. But where do such rules come from? Their origins are as varied as their content. They may evolve slowly over time, commencing as local customs and later becoming formal laws. The ruling monarch of Saudi Arabia, for example, governs under rules that have evolved over the centuries. Rules may also arise from agreements on fundamental principles ratified by a nation's citizens, as in the case of the American Constitution. They may also be imposed by force. In the latter case, the majority may disagree with the prevailing rules but, nevertheless, obey them for fear of punishment for disobedience. In Czechoslovakia, Russian troops intervened in 1968 to restore a system of rules many Czechs had discarded; the Russians prevailed, not because of their popularity but through the use of physical force and their control over resources essential to the Czech economy. Similarly, throughout Latin America the military has frequently overthrown a popularly elected government and imposed a new order despite the opposition of a majority of citizens. In such cases, rules were imposed whether they were popular or not.

But are the rules contained in constitutions or other documents the only ones that guide political conduct in Latin America and, therefore, the only ones that should concern us? Obviously not. Our interest in formal rules should not be allowed to blind us to the many unwritten, informal ones that also influence the behavior of political activists. In some cases, informal rules develop simply because constitutions ignore important practices; most of the constitutions written in the eighteenth and nineteenth centuries, for example, did not address themselves to the regulation of either political parties or influential private interest groups. Informal rules also arise when formal ones are ignored or temporarily suspended, such as occurred frequently in colonial Latin America when local elites refused to obey Spanish and Portuguese laws that they regarded as unjust or inconvenient. Because they have assumed great importance in Latin American political life throughout the region's post-Independence history, informal rules must be studied closely by anyone seeking to understand how the political game is played.

The task before us is formidable, but certainly not beyond our reach. To demonstrate how you can identify informal rules and assess their influence, we will devote the remainder of this chapter to an examination of the rules that govern three areas of Latin American political life: first, those that influence how public office is won and lost; second, rules that shape presidential conduct; and third, those that govern the treatment of political opposition.

How public office is won and lost

Few questions have attracted more attention from political scientists through the ages than the one that asks how public officials should be chosen. Political experience teaches us that there are many different answers to this question. Today, diversity rather than uniformity characterizes the way nations select their leaders. Citizens in liberal democracies are guided by the principle of popular sovereignty, which holds that political authority is derived from the consent of the governed as expressed through some form of election. But liberal democracies are now the exception rather than the rule, a minority among the world's nations. In communist regimes, in contrast, popular consent comes not through elections, but via the creation of a collective consciousness, which has its origins in fundamental ideological principles. Another point of view, quite common among Third-World military regimes, justifies authority in terms of necessity rather than consent, arguing that strong authoritarian government is required to overcome internal racial, linguistic, ethnic, or economic conflicts. Still others stress the importance of tradition, claiming that public office should be passed from one member of the royal family to his descendants. Finally, public office can be won and held through the use of charismatic or personal appeals, so that citizens obey leaders because of personal affection or respect for them.

How have Latin Americans chosen among these various options when establishing the rules for the selection of their public officials? Not surprisingly, diversity is found in Latin America, just as in the rest of the world. If you had compared the Latin American countries at any time during the 1960s or 1970s, you would have discovered liberal democracies governed by political parties, traditional autocracies ruled by a small elite, military regimes that expressed little concern for popular consent, and even revolutionary regimes that sought to establish new foundations for legitimate government. But it is not just the diversity among Latin American nations that is intriguing. Of even greater interest is the fact that if we examine Latin American countries over time, we discover diversity not only among nations but within them as well. A nation that organized its politics along liberal democratic lines one year could be found under military rule the next. A country ruled by a conservative elite at one point would a few years later be under military rule and then a decade later governed constitutionally. Of course, not all Latin American governments have undergone such frequent changes, but the fact that many have and continue to do so raises some intriguing questions about the rules of the political game in these nations.

The diversity of political rules within many Latin American countries is primarily the product of a failure to solve the fundamental problem of political legitimacy that arises in all political systems. Political order and the governing of a nation are greatly facilitated if political authority is made acceptable to a nation's citizens. If citizens agree on the principles under which the government is organized and its occupants selected, it can be assumed that most citizens will play by the rules they have agreed to. Under such conditions authorities should not have to expend a great deal of time worrying about rule violators or much energy enforcing basic laws. But where agreement does not prevail, public authorities have to contend with such problems continually.

Disagreement on political rules was the norm rather than the exception throughout Latin America during the nineteenth century. When most of the region's nations achieved their independence around 1820, they adopted a set of constitutional rules modeled on those developed in the newly independent United States of America, which called for the regular election of public officials who would govern according to principles established in law. But the new post-Independence rules were not universally accepted. In fact, they were accepted by only a small minority. Most citizens were either unaware of the new rules or ignored them because they threatened their status and power. What resulted were not stable democracies but political systems in which traditional forms of localized power and authority contended with the newly imposed liberal democratic rules, often to the disadvantage of the latter. Neither the old Iberian values nor the new democratic ones gained enough popular legitimacy to prevail. Instead, there developed a strong and lasting habit throughout the region of using whichever set of rules gave greatest advantage to one's cause. As a result, Latin America has been plagued during much of its modern history by the kind of fundamental disputes over questions of political legitimacy and authority that many other nations resolved long ago.

If Latin Americans do not always agree on a single set of political rules, what determines the way the game is played? To answer this question we must look not to general principles but to those who participate in the game, the players. For our purposes, a "player" is defined as any individual or group that seeks to capture public office or influence public authorities. Over the past two centuries the number of players in the Latin American game has gradually increased until representatives of nearly every sector of society have become involved. Today, in the more developed Latin American countries one finds spokesmen for landowners of various kinds, industrialists, merchants and traders, labor unions, peasants, political parties, the Church, the military, students, multinational corporations, and foreign governments all trying in one way or another to influence public policy. How well each player does in the game depends in large part on his skill in using the political resources at his disposal.

Political "resources" are what you use to get public officials and political activists to do what you desire. Many different kinds of resources are used in politics. Economic and financial ones are the most familiar. Control over economic resources can be translated into political influence in several ways. For instance, those who produce coffee in a country where coffee is the principal export can use their strategic position to secure favorable tax, trade, and other policies; similarly, the managers of corporations that mine rare minerals can use their control over such resources to secure tax and other economic policy concessions. Wealthy individuals can buy official favors the poor cannot afford, and they can use their social status to influence upwardly mobile public officials by admitting the officials to their social circles.

A second political resource is the use of force. Throughout Latin America the military coup or the threat of a coup has become a powerful instrument for influencing the course of public affairs. But force is not a monopoly of the military. Civilian and paramilitary guerrillas have learned to use the tools of violence to their advantage as well. If not as influential as the military, they are nevertheless able to harass and occasionally undermine governments.

Normative resources, or the ability to use moral principles to influence others, are a third source of political power. The Roman Catholic Church, for example, has traditionally used its normative resources to influence political life. Even though the Church's influence over national affairs has declined significantly during the past century, the clergy to some extent can still shape the attitudes of their parishioners toward political groups and public policies. Normative resources, in the form of ideologies like nationalism, capitalism, and socialism, are also employed by civilian and military political leaders. By condemning policies as violations of an ideology or of principles held dear by citizens, they can undermine the implementation of those policies.

Fourth, there is the resource of numbers. Anyone who can mobilize a majority of his fellow citizens into a large political organization is in a good position to influence public policy. If democratic rules prevail, he can win elections, and if such rules have been suspended, he can mobilize his followers to demonstrate against the government. Modern political parties, labor unions, and peasant leagues all draw heavily on their large followings as a political resource.

Finally, there is the resource of expertise. With the growing complexity of public policy, especially in the application of economic planning techniques to the management of ambitious development programs, a premium has been placed on expertise in economic affairs. Not satisfied to depend entirely on foreign advisors, Latin American nations have, in recent decades, developed their own corps of technocrats, who manage public and private enterprises throughout the region. Presidents and legislators who in the past had little need for technical advisors now find themselves heavily dependent on them. Technocrats have acquired substantial influence over public policy by exploiting such dependence.

What makes Latin America unique is not the variety of resources used by its citizens to capture or influence government. Wealth, force, numbers, normative principles, and expertise are not peculiar to Latin America, but influence politics to some degree in political systems throughout the world. What makes Latin America different is the fact that resources are used not only to capture public office or influence policy, but also to undermine the formal rules of the political game. In the liberal democracies of Anglo-America and Western Europe the resource of numbers, or the ability to win elections, has become dominant through the application of a set of rules that places a premium on the electoral decision. To be sure, economic resources and expertise also influence policy, but it is the election, with all its imperfections, that governs the choice of political leaders. In communist regimes normative principles and force dominate the political process. But in much of Latin America no single resource or set of resources consistently determines the selection of public officials or the making of public policy. From time to time one may appear to have gained a foothold, but more often than not it is replaced by another instead of prevailing itself. Thus, if asked how public office is gained and held in Latin America, we would have to answer that several different ways are employed because no one of them has become definitive.

First, there are elections. The fact that modern Latin American history is littered with presidential elections might lead us to conclude that voting is the dominant mode of selecting public officials. However, on closer examination we discover that the results of elections

Table 2-1. *Modes of capturing public office in Latin America*

Process involved	Political resources employed
Election	Numbers of people, normative values, organization
Military coup	Force of arms, organization
Mass demonstration	Numbers of people, normative values
Insurrection	Force of arms, normative values
Economic pressure	Wealth, technical expertise, productive capacity

have not always been respected in Latin America. The mere fact of election is by no means a guarantee that an official will complete his term of office. On the contrary, the probability that an elected president will complete his term in most Latin American countries has been quite low. Survival depends not so much on the election itself as on who accepts the results of the election. For example, if powerful groups, let us say landowners or the military, opposed a candidate's election, they might employ the instruments of wealth and force to block his inauguration, thus nullifying the election.

A second way of taking office is the military coup. In contrast to elections, which require extensive campaigning, coups can be implemented quite swiftly. For those who have lost an election or strongly oppose a government and its policies, the coup becomes a political instrument of last resort. Few political groups in Latin America have resisted the temptation at one time or another to call on the military to bring down a government they oppose. Thus, it is not only the military's ambition for public office that makes the coup so common throughout the region, but also the civilians' practice of calling upon the military to use force against those whom they cannot defeat through other means.

Elections and military coups are not the only ways of winning public office in Latin America. There are several others that should be noted. One of the most familiar is the mass demonstration. Students are among the most notorious demonstrators, though urban workers are not far behind. The demonstration makes use of numbers and the concentration of effort within a specific locale where the protesters can confront the police, who defend the government. Very often it is led by individuals who seek to express the grievances of citizens ignored or abused by authorities. It is, however, more effective at forcing the government to consider an issue or a problem than at resolving the issue or bringing about a change in government. Nevertheless, demonstrations that have embarrassed governments by raising questions about their ability to maintain public order sometimes have undermined their authority and encouraged military intervention.

Insurrections and guerrilla warfare are also used to depose governments. Peasant uprisings aimed at evicting local ruling elites from their property and national political leaders from their offices have occurred several times in most countries since Independence. More recently, opponents of incumbent governments, inspired by the success of national liberation movements, especially in Asia, have organized small armed units and employed guerrilla tactics to undermine authorities by frustrating and humiliating the armies that try to protect them. Some operate in the countryside, where they seek to develop peasant support for their struggle; others go to the cities and use kidnapping, assassination, bank robberies, and the destruction of public facilities to promote a collapse of public authority.

Governments can also be changed through the efforts of powerful elites who use their resources to apply economic pressure on public officials. Farmers, bankers, and industrialists may slow production in order to damage the economy and thereby reduce public confidence in the government. Domestic groups are not, however, alone in such efforts. Foreign governments, international agencies, and multinational corporations, separately and together, may from time to time try to end the life of what they define as an undesirable government. By cutting off desperately needed loans, boycotting a country's exports in foreign markets, withdrawing investments, or supporting opposition groups, they can weaken a nation's economy and force the replacement of its government.

By now it should be apparent why most Latin American countries find it so difficult to live by a single set of rules. Groups and individuals who find that the prevailing rules favor others more than themselves may undermine the rules rather than obey them. Such players have certain preferred rules and will do all they can, including the creation of conflict and disorder, to see that their rules are adopted. The leaders of large political parties may prefer elections because they can mobilize large numbers of voters. But groups who do not have large followings may oppose elections, especially if the elections result in victories for parties that threaten the group's interests. For example, conservative economic elites may try to block elected governments through the use of their economic and technical resources, perhaps even provoking a military coup to depose the government. Similarly, labor unions persecuted by a conservative government may shut down critical industries or take to the streets to force a change in policy or bring down the government.

The diversity of political rules found in many Latin American countries is not a recent phenomenon, but, as we have seen, is a condition that has persisted since Independence. Latin America's political development, therefore, has not been characterized by steady progress toward a single form of political rule; instead, there has been continual conflict over different sets of rules. To be sure, there has been much political change during the region's modern history, but generally it has resulted in increased competition over different sets of rules rather than the creation of agreements on a single set. The most significant changes have come during the past fifty years as groups representing the urban and rural masses have entered the game, intensifying the competition for scarce resources and sometimes provoking hostile reactions from traditional power holders. Naturally, the rates and forms of political change have differed from nation to nation, depending on the prevailing social and economic conditions in each country at different periods in its history. In the more traditional polities like Paraguay, a very small minority continues to rule without much interference from other players. In most of the region, however, many new players have joined with traditional ones in contesting public office.

There are, of course, some exceptions to this pattern of additive political change. After seizing power, some players have eliminated others from the game. The elimination of a player involves something more than temporary repression. Military coups and other unscheduled changes in leadership have often led to the temporary suspension of political parties or the denial of political access to certain players, but seldom have they resulted in the permanent elimination of a player. The latter requires that a player be forced to relinquish not just his juridical status or political rights, but also his political resources. Landowners must be deprived of their property, the military of its arms, and political parties of their followers. When that occurs, subtractive rather than additive political change has been achieved.

The Mexican Revolution was one of the first successful efforts to achieve subtractive political change in Latin America in this century. Its leaders were determined to eliminate the Church, *latifundistas,* and foreign investors from the game. Though none were completely eliminated, their political resources were reduced substantially and their participation greatly circumscribed. In their place the Mexicans erected a new power structure using a revolutionary party supported by organized labor, peasants, and the emerging middle class. The regime they created has prevailed for sixty years, a notable achievement in a region characterized by political instability. The Cuban Revolution of Fidel Castro has eliminated players as well. Beginning in 1959 the Cuban revolutionaries expelled landowners, most of the urban middle class, and foreign investors in the process of enforcing a new set of rules drawn largely from Marxist-Leninist thought and practice. What remains is a political regime that shares little in common with its predecessors or with those in the rest of the hemisphere.

Since World War II Latin Americans have been making an unprecedented effort to create enduring sets of political rules to regulate their political games. They have taken ideas from many different sources and have sought legitimacy for widely disparate types of rules. During the 1950s and 1960s, for example, many tried to create reform-oriented constitutional democracies and make them invulnerable to popular insurrection as well as military coups. Their rise to power in several countries encouraged a belief that democratic rules had finally taken root in the region. However, with the violent overthrow of most democratic regimes after 1964, doubts about the viability of democracy in the region again prevailed. More recently the militaries of several countries have tried to impose new autocratic rules of their own. In Brazil civilian politics was brought to an abrupt halt by a military coup in 1964, and since then the military has governed the country using authoritarian methods and modern techniques of economic management. Though often tempted to restore some form of party democracy to the country, the military has refused to do so, fearing that democratic government would bring a return of the radicalized politics and indecisiveness that paralyzed the country in the early 1960s. Another military experiment was tried in Peru after civilian government was ended in 1968. By adopting a more reformist development strategy than did the Brazilians, the Peruvian military tried to create a new and lasting political order by increasing the power of the state and using it to implement a host of rural, educational, and industrial reforms. In sum, we find today in Latin America not a single set of political rules that prevails throughout the region, but several different ones that still contend for legitimacy. In a few countries very traditional rules continue to survive, and in a couple the old rules have been transformed radically and a new consensus created, but in the majority a lack of consensus contributes to continuous conflict between groups who support incompatible ways of playing the game.

How rules affect presidential conduct

Having examined how political rules affect the rise and fall of Latin American governments, we can now turn to the example of presiden-

tial conduct. What is intriguing about Latin American presidents is
not only the amount of power they enjoy, but also how they use their
power to cope with the uncertainty that arises when a consensus on
political rules is lacking. Traditionally, Latin American presidents
have been freer of legislative and judicial constraints than their North
American or European counterparts. Not only do their constitutions
assign them more authority over the initiation of legislation, the maintenance of public order, and the conduct of foreign affairs than do
most Western constitutions, but in actual practice Latin American
presidents have managed to dominate their nations' political life to a
greater degree than have their counterparts in constitutional regimes.
Throughout the nineteenth century, when the central political issues
were national unification and the expansion of the authority of the
state at the expense of the Church, it was the president who organized
the armies and maintained the peace. The legislature has always been
the weaker partner in this relationship, making checks and balances
among the different branches of government more a form than a
fact. Countries where legislatures have achieved significant strength,
such as Uruguay and Chile before 1973 and Costa Rica since 1948,
are the exception rather than the rule in Latin America.

What limits the exercise of presidential power is not only the constitution but also the ability of other players to constrain the president
by using their political resources against him. During the late nineteenth and early twentieth centuries, especially in the less developed
Latin American countries, the president assumed the role of the "man
on horseback," or strong-armed ruler, and employed physical force to
create and maintain political order. His approach to government re-
sembled that of a stern father who felt compelled to keep his children
in line more than that of a popularly elected democratic leader. Since
then, many other types of presidents have come and gone, ranging
from the very cruel and autocratic to weak leaders entirely dependent
on the support of other players. In each case presidential conduct was
affected as much by the power exercised by others as by the presidents' own initiatives. Some enjoyed immense latitude; others were
forced to struggle continually against powerful adversaries.

Presidential conduct is influenced by the status as well as the content of political rules. Where a single set of rules dominates, the president tends to be more secure and can exercise his power with a firmer
hand. But in countries where the rules are still debated and changed
from time to time, the president is less secure and to survive is forced
either to balance interests and rules or to use autocratic methods to
repress potential opponents. Why is this so? Little reflection on the
matter is necessary to appreciate that where the rules of the game are

well known and accepted, a president can follow them without fear that they will be breached by other players. When there is less uncertainty about how citizens will respond to the exercise of presidential authority, a president is less hesitant about using it. Under such conditions, presidential authority tends to be more institutionalized and better regulated, for as norms and practices become well established, presidents are increasingly reluctant to depart from them.

Examples of such well-institutionalized presidencies are few, but their strengths are readily apparent. Take Mexico, for example. The Mexican president is elected every six years to a single term. Since the late 1920s, Mexican elections have been held on schedule and without interruption. During those years the Mexican presidency has become the dominant institution in the country's political life, with its occupant functioning as both the leader of the ruling party and the head of government. The revolutionary tradition requires that the president be responsive to the interests of the party's constituent organizations and loyal to the goals of the revolution; yet to implement these objectives, it gives him immense control over the bureaucracy and the party organization. Whether he is an autocrat or a democrat is still intensely debated in Mexico, but regardless, it is apparent that the public acceptance of the Mexican rules of the game has made him a very powerful political leader.

The same is true, for somewhat different reasons, in contemporary Cuba. Undoubtedly Prime Minister Fidel Castro derives much of his power from the strength of his character and his leadership of the insurrection that ended the tyranny of Fulgencio Batista. But his authority is maintained not through personality alone but also through the organization of a new revolutionary power structure under the leadership of the Cuban Communist party. Castro and his associates are able to prevail because they have created a consensus of sorts on the way the country should be governed. Regardless of the means used to achieve the consensus, one cannot deny its effect in strengthening Cuban leadership.

There are nonrevolutionary examples of the strong presidency as well. Interestingly, they are found primarily in the more traditional countries that occupy the opposite end of the spectrum of political modernization. This should not surprise us, for it is in the very traditional society that a single set of rules tends to dominate. In Paraguay, which has been governed by General Alfredo Stroessner for over three decades, or Nicaragua, where the Somoza family has presided for nearly half a century, we find strong presidents who face few political constraints and little uncertainty over the rules that govern political life in their countries.

But what about the powers of the president in those countries that are plagued by lack of agreement on the rules of the game? Formally, the president in such a system claims as much authority as do his more secure neighbors. In practice, however, he often finds himself constrained by the uncertainties created by the lack of political consensus and his vulnerability to the use of political resources by his opponents. In contrast to a president in a consensual system, who knows how and in what form his critics will attack him, the less secure president does not know where his opponent will stop or which resources they will bring to bear against him. He is plagued by uncertainty, never knowing for sure when labor unions may riot to block his policies or when the military may implement a coup to depose him. Politics in such a society is often the politics of rumor and conspiracy, where a president spends most of his time consorting with his allies to disarm and isolate his critics.

An outstanding example of presidential insecurity and its manifestations is postwar Argentina. Even though it is one of the most affluent nations in Latin America, Argentina has been plagued by political instability, especially since 1955 when President Juan Perón was overthrown by the military. Since that date three presidents have been elected, but none has completed his term. Six military presidents have also come and gone, some yielding to elected governments and others being overthrown by military colleagues. Argentina's elected presidents, despite substantial constitutional authority, have faced repeated attacks on their leadership by civilian and military players. Among the former is a militant and well-organized labor movement that demands the government meet its welfare needs; the latter includes the highly factionalized military services. There is no easy escape from the dilemmas faced by Argentine presidents: When they resort to force to deter militant workers, they only provoke more illegal protests that threaten political order; yet when they yield to labor's demands, they often provoke the intervention of antilabor military officers. In the face of such competing pressures, the president can either try to bargain with each player in the hope of securing temporary compromises or retreat from the battle, conceding that he lacks the support required to lead the nation. The contrast between the vulnerable Argentine president and the very strong Mexican one is apparent. The formal constitutional authority of the two is quite similar, but the Argentine president has been forced by the lack of consensus on political rules to struggle, unsuccessfully, against his opponents, whereas the Mexican president has enjoyed the security of his well-organized and pervasive political organization.

We have seen that presidential power is a variable rather than a constant in the Latin American political game. Both the amount of presidential power and the manner of its use are heavily influenced by the content and status of the rules operative in each nation. Rules may give the president much latitude for governing the nation, or they may restrict his authority, forcing him to share it with others in the government. And where there is widespread agreement on the rules, the president is spared the insecurity that comes from the unregulated give and take of political warfare. In contrast, where there is no agreement on fundamental rules, there is little to protect him against his opponents except his use of force. One of our objectives in Part II of this book will be the comparison of the behaviors of presidents who operate under each of these sets of conditions.

How rules affect political opposition

One of the most critical relationships in politics is the one that exists between a government and its opponents. The rules that govern this relationship are a principal defining characteristic of a political system. Liberal democracy, for example, is defined in part by its toleration of political opposition; authoritarianism, in contrast, is distinguished by its intolerance. Most Latin American systems conform to neither of these idealized models. Instead, we usually find players who lend their support to public officials when it serves their needs and oppose the government when their vital interests are threatened, and governments that tolerate some opponents while repressing others. Policy making under these conditions is a dynamic process involving actions by authorities and critical reactions by other players. It also frequently involves intense conflicts between political ins and outs, especially when governments try to promote development by redistributing resources from one player to another. Those who find themselves threatened may not only try to block the execution of adverse policies but may also seek to bring down the government and end the threat it poses. At the same time, it is not unusual for authorities to anticipate such reactions and repress potential opponents before they can mobilize an attack.

The treatment and behavior of political opponents also affect the creation of a political consensus in a society. The more the rules give each player a sense that he is being treated fairly in the competition for public office and society's scarce resources, the more likely he is to accept them. On the other hand, the more the rules threaten his interests and deny him an opportunity to capture public office or influence public policy, the more he is forced to break the rules in order to protect himself from those in power. It is the latter circumstance that contributes to much of the extralegal protest behavior found in Latin America.

One cannot place all the responsibility for coups, riots, and demonstrations on governmental abuse of opponents, but it is not hard to understand why opposition players express themselves through such means when they feel ignored or abused. We have already seen how different players prefer to follow the rules most favorable to them rather than those selected by opponents who seek some advantage over them. When given a choice between living under a government that denies them influence over public policy and the opportunity to regain public office and continuing in a state of political uncertainty, many players prefer the latter, with all its obvious costs, simply because it appears to offer greater opportunities for blocking adverse government policies or recapturing public office.

Latin American governments have developed many different ways for dealing with political opponents, each of which reflects an application of different rules of the game. The most familiar is the conventional competitive process, modeled on the practices of Western democracy, in which groups strive openly to influence government policy, and political parties compete for public office in elections. Very few Latin American countries have fulfilled the requirements of this purest form of the competitive model for extended periods of time, though Uruguay from 1903 until 1973, Chile between 1932 and 1973, Venezuela since 1958, and Costa Rica since 1948 have come close. More common is a less conventional competitive system in which strikes, demonstrations, and military coups are used along with elections to create governments. It is not unusual to find public authorities in such systems using all legal means and some illegal ones to weaken their opponents in the hope of defeating them more easily in subsequent elections.

Another departure from the pure competitive system is the one in which the government coopts or incorporates its potential opponents into its regime, securing their temporary cooperation by sharing public authority with them. The most familiar mode of cooptation is through a coalition government in which the leaders of the ruling party invite other political parties to share cabinet posts and legislative leadership. Chilean governments during the 1940s and Venezuelan ones in the 1960s have used the coalition technique with some success. Its most impressive application, however, occurred in Colombia after 1958 when the country's two largest political parties ended a decade of bitter civil strife by agreeing to form a national front government in which for sixteen years the presidency was alternated between the two parties and all cabinet positions were divided among them. In essence, the Colombians agreed to suspend the normal competitive rules of the game, which had led to violent interparty conflicts during the 1950s, and substitute new ones, which froze the competition so that each of the dominant parties was assured a place in the government.

Cooptation and coalition building do not apply only to political parties in Latin America, but have also been used by governments seeking to control critical economic and social groups. The practice of linking private groups formally to the government has been quite common in Western societies, ranging from the schemes of the extremist fascist regimes of the 1930s to the contemporary industrial societies of northern Europe, where labor unions, farmers, and business groups are used by governments as instruments of political control and economic management. The cooptation of private groups has taken many different forms in Latin America. In some countries it involves only informal agreements between groups and public officials; in others, like contemporary Mexico, groups representing laborers and peasants are included in a corporatist-type ruling party. In each case the practice of cooptation represents an attempt by public authorities to alter the rules of the competitive game so that they can better coordinate and control its outcome. Their objective is to replace the open conflict of poorly regulated competitive processes with a system of well-defined channels of communication between authorities and private groups that the former can use to resolve conflicts before they get out of hand.

Two other sets of rules have been applied to political opposition throughout Latin America. Under one, the government's opponents are seen but not heard; the other seeks to eliminate them altogether. The first is found in countries where opposition parties exist, but are never allowed by the incumbent party to win public office. Mexico is again a good example of such politics. The Mexican government encourages the participation of opposition parties in elections and in the legislative process, while at the same time using all resources at its disposal, both legal and illegal, to limit the opposition's success. Though in many ways very different from Mexico, post-1964 Brazil offers another example of circumscribed opposition. Its military regime organized two political parties, one of which it has used to control the legislature and the other of which became a loyal but impotent opposition. Through complex electoral laws that favor the government party, the military sustains its control over its opponents. Thus, in both Mexico and Brazil political opposition is tolerated, but only up to a point; its criticisms of the government must be muted, its support for the governmental system complete, and its expectations of capturing the presidency or an electoral majority repressed.

Why is an opposition tolerated at all when a government has no intention of letting it capture important public offices? Some argue that the ritual of democracy is important to the leaders of such systems, even though the fact of democracy is not. First, it is necessary for external consumption, for placating those nations who insist on democratic institutions as a precondition for the maintenance of relations; second, it offers a means, albeit a crude one, through which opposition pressures can be channeled and controlled without doing harm to the regime and its policies; and third, the existence of a visible opposition is an effective tool in a government's campaign to mobilize supporters, for it provides a convenient target or common enemy against which to unite followers.

Oppositions are treated even more harshly in those systems where the government strives for political unanimity. The most notable example is Communist Cuba, where opposition parties are considered irrelevant to the needs of the Cuban Revolution. Fidel Castro candidly admits his preference for a one-party regime. He argues that there can be only one true revolutionary ideology and, therefore, only one party to interpret and enforce that ideology. Dissent over policy, if it occurs at all, should come from within the party and other official organizations. The communist regime is not the only one, however, that has sought to eliminate opposition parties. Some contemporary military regimes, like those that governed Argentina, Chile, and Peru in the mid-1970s, abolished political parties without creating any new ones in their place. To them, political parties were divisive forces that undermined social order and, therefore, served no useful purpose. Consequently, when they designed their new political systems, political party competition was deliberately omitted.

This brief review of political opposition and the rules that govern its behavior in Latin America would not be complete without mention of "antisystem" oppositions. Most of the opposition groups we have discussed thus far are ones whose principal political objective is to capture public office or to acquire political influence that can be used within the existing political game. But Latin America has a history of opposition groups whose aim is not playing the game but transforming it through revolutionary means. Both the Mexican and Cuban revolutionary groups were of this type before they conquered power. During the 1960s and 1970s antisystem groups proliferated throughout the region, often adopting the tactics of rural guerrillas or urban terrorists in order to harass and try to defeat the political elite and its military defenders. Though they have seldom succeeded in their campaigns since Fidel Castro's victory in 1959, antisystem revolutionaries remain active throughout the region. To deal with them, governments, which claim they must do whatever is required to defend the system from attack, have often resorted to the most brutal and repressive tactics.

ANALYZING POLITICAL RULES

You are now familiar with the concept of political rules and the role such rules play in the game of politics. We have discovered that they come in many forms and can be found in constitutional codes and informal norms that guide political expectations and behavior. They influence how political office is won, how presidents behave, and how political opposition is treated. The concept of political rules offers a useful point of departure in our quest to understand Latin American politics and public policy. It is a tool you can now use to study and compare individual Latin American political systems.

The study of political rules cannot provide all the answers we seek, but it does take us a long way toward asking the right questions. For example, henceforth when you examine a Latin American political system you can begin by asking: What are the current rules of its political game and who respects them? To what extent is a single set dominant and followed in practice? Are there informal rules that shape behavior? If so, what are they and what is their effect? And what about the consequences of the rules of the game? To whose advantage do they work and how do they affect the process by which development policy is made and implemented? More specifically, who benefits most and who benefits least from the way the game is played?

FURTHER READING

Adams, Richard Newbold. *The Second Sowing: Power and Secondary Development in Latin America*. San Francisco: Chandler, 1967.

Anderson, Charles W. *Politics and Economic Change in Latin America: The Governing of Restless Nations*. New York: Van Nostrand, 1967.

Burnett, Ben. G., and Kenneth Johnson, eds. *Political Forces in Latin America: Dimensions of the Quest for Stability*. Belmont, Calif.: Wadsworth, 1970.

Chilcote, Ronald H., and Joel C. Edelstein, eds. *Latin America: The Struggle with Dependency and Beyond*. Cambridge, Mass.: Schenkman, 1974.

Edelman, Alexander T. *Latin American Government and Politics: The Dynamics of a Revolutionary Society*. Homewood, Ill.: Dorsey Press, 1969.

Fagen, Richard R., and Wayne A. Cornelius. *Political Power in Latin America.* Englewood Cliffs, N.J.: Prentice-Hall, 1970.

Jaguaribe, Helio. *Political Development: A General Theory and a Latin American Case Study.* New York: Harper & Row, 1973.

Kling, Merle. "Toward a Theory of Power and Political Instability in Latin America." *Western Political Quarterly* 9(1):21–40, March 1956.

Lambert, Jacques. *Latin America: Social Structure and Political Institutions.* Berkeley: University of California Press, 1967.

Liss, Sheldon B., and Peggy Liss, eds. *Man, State and Society in Latin American History.* New York: Praeger, 1972.

Malloy, James M., ed. *Authoritarianism and Corporatism in Latin America.* Pittsburgh: University of Pittsburgh Press, 1977.

Mercier Vega, Luis. *Roads to Power in Latin America.* London: Pall Mall Press, 1969.

Needler, Martin. *Latin American Politics in Perspective.* New York: Van Nostrand, 1963.

  Political Development in Latin America: Instability, Violence and Evolutionary Change. New York: Random House, 1968.

  The Political Systems of Latin America. New York: Van Nostrand Reinhold, 1970.

Powelson, John. *Institutions of Economic Growth: A Theory of Conflict Management in Developing Countries.* Princeton: Princeton University Press, 1972.

Silvert, Kalman. *The Conflict Society: Reaction and Revolution in Latin America.* New York: American Universities Field Staff, 1966.

3. Players – I

If the participants determine how the Latin American political game is played, our inquiry cannot proceed without a more detailed introduction to the principal players. In Chapter 2 we defined them as individuals and groups who seek to capture public office or influence public authorities. They include political parties, economic elites, the military, peasants, labor unions, foreign governments, multinational corporations, and many others.

Most players are readily identifiable to even the most casual observer of the Latin American scene, but their political interests and influence are more obscure. There are several reasons why this is so. First, despite their impressive titles Latin American political groups are usually less well organized than similar groups in Europe or North America. Moreover, leaders who claim to represent large constituencies may actually enjoy little support. Even more important, the ways they try to influence public officials sometimes differ significantly from those of similar groups in other societies. In each case the political goals, strategies, and tactics of different players are shaped by the players' own histories, prevailing political structures, the strength and skills of other players, and existing economic and social conditions. Players are not static characters who remain unalterably the same; they change and adapt to the conditions around them. Our job is to observe and analyze them as they play the political game. And we can begin by setting aside any preconceptions we may have taken from other political systems.

To guide this introduction to the principal players in the Latin American game, we will ask four questions of each one. First, who are the people involved? What do they share in common and how united are they economically, socially, and politically? Second, what do they want from politics, if anything? We should acknowledge at the outset that most people in Latin America, as elsewhere, do not devote themselves to politics. Many are entirely disinterested; others expect their representatives to make decisions for them. Some players, in fact, want only to be left alone, free of public authorities who seek to tax, regulate, or otherwise deprive them. Others want favors or subsidies to secure advantages over their competitors. So instead of assuming

44

that they are active merely because they share in some objective political interest, we must inquire about their subjective interests and whether these lead to any form of political participation. Third, what resources does each player or group of players have at his disposal and how does he use them to influence the outcome of the game? The mere possession of resources does not assure that they will be put to effective use; they must be employed with skill and good timing to be effective. And fourth, which set of rules do players prefer and how successful have they been in determining which rules dominate the playing of the game? Because players are just as likely to do battle over the rules as over public policy, their influence over the way the game is played is even more important than their effects on its policy outcomes.

We shall now meet the principal players in the Latin American political game. Each description offered below represents only a very brief synthesis of the player's dominant characteristics. Obviously, not every player in every country conforms to the patterns described. We will, however, leave the discussion of variations in player behavior to the analysis of individual countries in Part II. For now, it will suffice to make only general introductory observations.

THE LANDED ELITE

Latin America's underdevelopment is frequently blamed on the *oligarquía.* The term has been applied to many villains, but to none more consistently than the landowners who have dominated the region's economic life throughout most of its history. At various times the landowning elite has been accused of brutally exploiting the peasantry, skillfully manipulating the Church and the military, and obstructing all efforts at social and economic progress. But are such characterizations any longer appropriate? After all, Latin American societies have changed a great deal since the halcyon days of elite rule in the nineteenth century. Modern cities have replaced muddy villages, transportation networks have been vastly expanded, and industry and commerce have absorbed much of the work force in many countries. How have these developments affected the rural elite? How has the elite responded to the changes forced upon it by the evolution of the Latin American economies? Has it survived with its power intact or has it been forced to yield to the new conditions?

The first thing one discovers when studying the landed elite is that it is not as monolithic as one might assume. Its members may still be powerful and dominate political life in a few of the region's less devel-

Table 3-1. *Synthesis of dominant traits of players*

	Latifundistas	Commercial farmers	Business elites
Composition	Owners of large landed estates more interested in traditional social and economic role than in maximizing production	Landowners dedicated to maximizing production using affordable modern technologies	Owners of large domestic industries, wholesale and retail firms, and financial institutions
Political objectives	To be left alone by national government and assisted by local law-enforcement agencies and courts Minimum of taxes and state regulation Repression of peasant organizations	Stable government Economic policies: Low taxes Easy credit Low tariffs High support prices Adequate infrastructure Repression of rural labor organizations	Stable government Economic policies: Low taxes Easy credit High tariffs Free market pricing Repression of militant labor unions
Political resources	Economic dependence of rural work force Wealth Social prestige Control of local law enforcement	Production of essential cash crops and commodity exports Wealth Personal and economic ties with commerce and industry	Control over critical economic activities Wealth Economic expertise

oped countries, but seldom does it act any longer as a cohesive political force. Instead, it is represented by many individuals and organizations that sometimes disagree among themselves on matters of policy and political strategy. Latin American landowners differ from one another in several ways, such as whether they produce primarily for the domestic or foreign market, the production processes in which they are engaged, the size of their operations, and the degree to which they are tied to traditional social values. There are also important differences among the landed elites of separate countries that

Table 3-1. (*cont.*)

Military	Bureaucrats	Multinational firms	United States government
Officer corps of army, navy, and air force	High-ranking civil servants and technocrats who staff government agencies and enterprises	Foreign-owned firms involved in manufacturing, mineral extraction, commerce, finance, and utilities	Agencies of U.S. government, such as: State Department Defense Department Central Intelligence Agency Treasury
Strong government able to maintain order and promote national development Anticommunism Financial and political support for military institution	Social status Political power Influence over content and execution of policy Personal wealth	Political and economic stability Easy access to labor, markets, and local raw products Minimal regulation by state Subordination of labor unions	Political and economic stability Anticommunist governments Cooperation in mutual security effort Access to resources and markets Support in international organizations
Force of arms Hierarchical organization Managerial skills	Bureaucratic authority Expertise Provision of goods and services	Investment capital Technology Access to foreign markets Creation of jobs	Military power Economic power Foreign assistance Covert action capability

have been caused by contrasting traditions, demography, resource availability, and government economic policy. We will explore some of the effects of these differences on the behavior of landed elites when we examine recent national experiences in Part II of this book.

Of the many ways of classifying landowners for analytical purposes, one of the most useful to the political analyst is the distinction between the *latifundistas* and the progressive commercial farmers. Within the *latifundista* category are grouped landowners who are more interested in traditional forms of social control than in economic gain. Although they usually own large tracts of land, they cultivate only small sections, leaving the rest idle or for use as unimproved pastures. *Latifundistas* employ very little modern technology, but rely instead on manual labor supplied by low-paid workers or sharecroppers. Their goal is the preservation of the *latifundio* as a social institution through their control over land and peasant laborers and the production of enough goods to sustain their aristocratic life style.

The progressive commercial farmer, on the other hand, is devoted primarily to the maximization of economic gain. His operation tends to be more capital intensive, as he makes use of all technologies that are profitable. Intensive commercial farming is not new to Latin America. Since colonial times there have been plantations and *haciendas* organized primarily for commerical purposes. But not until the twentieth century has intensive commercial farming come to dominate the rural economies of most Latin American countries. Of course, the analytical distinction we have made between the *latifundista* and the commerical farmer is quite imprecise. Those whom we have classified as *latifundistas* occasionally adopt modern modes of production, and some commercial farmers still rely on traditional technologies. Nevertheless, it is useful to distinguish among landowners on the basis of differences in their social values and economic goals because it helps explain their varied policy concerns and political activities.

The *latifundista* has been on the retreat throughout Latin America in recent decades. Some *latifundios* have been divided by inheritance; others have been transformed into productive commercial operations by a new generation of farm managers. But by far the biggest challenge to the *latifundio* has come from deliberate government efforts to implement land tenure reforms aimed at breaking elite control over the rural economy. In Mexico, Venezuela, Chile, Peru, and Cuba extensive holdings have been expropriated by the state and redistributed to peasants or reorganized as cooperative or state farms. Yet, as successful as these efforts have been in some parts of the region, the *latifundista* is not yet extinct. Many tradition-bound landowners still struggle tenaciously to withstand deliberate attacks on their way of life. Although they are now on the defensive, they can still use their wealth, family ties, and rural organizations to keep government reformers from encroaching on them.

What, in addition to his self-preservation, does the *latifundista* want from politics? Very little, actually, for besides high prices for his limited produce, he wants primarily to be left alone. He requires few government services and has little use for most of its regulations. Traditionally, he has taken advantage of his isolation from central government authority to establish his own political control at the local level. All he has wanted from the state is economic order and occasional protection against peasant organizers and other disrupters of the status quo. Since World War II, few *latifundistas* have sought public office, led political parties, or controlled the making of national development policy. They have relinquished such tasks to the urban professionals, party politicians, and military officers who now direct most government agencies. Instead, they have concentrated their attention on the bureaucracy and the courts, the implementers of the law. Through personal influence, bribes, and obstinacy, *latifundistas* have sought, often successfully, to escape laws aimed at depriving them of their wealth and power.

What about the political resources of the *latifundista?* Obviously, he has wealth and social prestige, especially if his family was part of the traditional ruling class. But how can wealth and social prestige be translated into power that will deter reform governments? We have already mentioned bribery, a practice that has proved effective in deterring tax collectors, land surveyors, and judges, among others. It also secures the protection of low-paid local police officers. Social status and familial ties also help secure favors from public officials, many of whom seek admittance to higher social circles. Traditionally, *latifundistas* have made excellent use of regional political bosses on whom the government sometimes depends for political control at the local level. The exchange of favors between landowners and local politicians builds mutual obligations that can be used to halt the enforcement of undesirable laws. At one time the landed elite also enjoyed the support of the military, but as the majority of officers have come to be recruited from the middle rather than the upper class, this natural bond has been disappearing. In sum, the *latifundista's* political strength lies at the local level. Though he is not without influence on the national scene, it is his ability to hold off enemies who try to intrude on his domain that sustains his survival. It takes a strong, well-organized, and determined bureaucracy to penetrate Latin America's local political systems; insecure governments, even if popular with large numbers of people, are seldom capable of making such an effort.

Finally, which rules of the game does the *latifundista* prefer? He sees little advantage in electoral democracy. Even though he can sometimes control votes within his region, the votes controlled by the rural elite are insufficient to defeat urban political parties. He can, of course, join with commercial farmers and urban elites to organize a conservative coalition, but such coalitions seldom receive more than one-third of the popular vote in most countries. The *latifundista* wants a set of rules that circumscribes reform-oriented mass-based political parties and, when the latter are elected, limits their power. He needs a government that is either disinterested in penetrating and reforming local power structures or too weak to do so. In practice, this means either an elite-controlled and elite-manipulated democracy, as was common in the late nineteenth century, or, in the contemporary age of activist popular classes, a weak reformist government or an autocratic one devoted to the maintenance of the rural status quo.

If our analysis of the landed elite were confined only to *latifundistas,* we would be guilty of ignoring a majority of those who wield power in the countryside. Gradually but steadily, commercial farming has been spreading throughout rural Latin America. Today, plantations and large family farms outnumber traditional *latifundios* in many countries. They are important not only to the welfare of those who own and manage them but to the national economy as well. Commercial agriculture includes units of all sizes, and it is, therefore, very difficult to draw an arbitrary line between the elite and the rest of the commercial farmers. We find a continuum rather than a sudden break between one group and the other; nevertheless, the large commercial farmer is economically important and politically influential and, therefore, is a distinguishable player within the rural sector.

But who exactly are these commercial farmers? Some are descendants of *latifundistas* who have transformed their estates into modern commercial enterprises; others are the sons and grandsons of the commercial farmers of the late nineteenth century who produced coffee, cattle, and other commodities for export. Some are descendants of immigrants, primarily from Europe but also from Asia, who came to Latin America after the turn of the century, began as colonists and tenant farmers, and gradually expanded their enterprises. Commercial farms come in many forms and operate with varying degrees of efficiency, ranging from well-organized plantations employing several hundred laborers to family farms engaged in mixed cropping. On the whole, commercial farmers are less prominent socially than the traditional rural elite, though many have achieved social status from their wealth. They are, however, not as isolated from other economic sectors as the *latifundistas;* some, in fact, are also deeply involved in food processing, banking, and commerce. Many of their enterprises are modern, efficient operations comparable to those of North America, although the majority operate at lower levels of efficiency, handicapped by the high cost of equipment, fertilizers, and seeds. In sum, Latin America's commercial farmers are a diverse and sizable group that includes, among others, the cattlemen and grain producers of Argentina, Uruguay, and southern Brazil; the coffee producers of Colombia, Brazil, and Central America; the truck gardeners that surround most large cities; the sugar barons of Brazil and the Caribbean; the banana producers of Ecuador and Central America; and the cotton farmers found throughout the region.

Commercial farmers want more from government than do *latifundistas*. First and foremost, as active participants in the modern economy, they want policies that promote high prices for their produce. They also want the government to regulate export firms to prevent their taking advantage of local producers and to provide price supports that guarantee a fair return on the farmers' investments and protection against widely fluctuating world prices. In addition, commercial farmers lobby for roads, railways, and storage facilities, and against land taxes and agrarian reform. Like farmers elsewhere they want to be protected against adversity but allowed to take advantage of opportunity. And as in Europe and North America, they have created organizations to represent them before government officials; some farmers' organizations join the producers of a single commodity; others follow regional lines. Although they are small and often inadequately staffed, they do carry on publicity campaigns, lobby in legislatures, and maintain close contacts with relevant bureaucracies. Commercial farmers covet membership on government boards and commissions as a means of gaining control over agricultural policy making. Though they do not eschew political parties, they prefer to deal directly with the officials who make policy, avoiding the broader political issues in favor of more narrow technical decisions.

Success in the political arena depends not only on organization and access to public authorities, but also on the resources one can bring to bear on particular issues. The commercial farmers' strength as a group derives from the economy's dependence on their products. Most Latin American economies rely heavily on the export of agricultural commodities for desperately needed foreign exchange. Any interruption in the flow of such commodities could have disastrous effects on the economy. Thus, no matter how hostile they may be to commercial farmers in principle, most governments are forced to rely on them. Critical to the farmers' political clout is their ability to use the government's dependence on them to influence its choice of public policies. They must convince officials that unless particular policies are adopted, agricultural production will decline and undermine the economy.

Finally, there is the question of farmers and political rules. Do commercial farmers have a preference for one set of rules over another? Latin American farmers, like farmers elsewhere, prefer stability in all things. There is already enough uncertainty in their world as a result of natural forces without the addition of political instability. Therefore, they desire a political game that offers few uncertainties and a government that is sympathetic to technical economic argument rather than only the demand of voters. It is not so much the form of the government that matters to the commercial farmers as its stability and performance. Like the *latifundistas,* they tolerate democratic government as long as it is orderly and not hostile to rural interests. On the other hand, they also accept autocratic government, especially if it is well managed and able to carry out supportive economic policies. As they are for most players, the rules are for the commercial farmers a means to an end rather than ends in themselves, and whichever set of rules secures their objectives is the one they are most likely to support.

It is evident that our four questions can generate some basic information about the way rural elites play the Latin American political game. Nevertheless, our task is not completed. The rural elite is quite complex; the behavior of its members varies regionally and according to background and training. Moreover, members often act as individuals covertly seeking personal favors from public authorities as well as in groups pursuing common policy objectives. These facts tell us that we must examine the behavior of *latifundistas* and commercial farmers with our eyes open to occasional deviations from the patterns just described. We cannot assume that an *oligarquiía* exists merely because this concept provides a comfortable explanation of the status quo; rather, we must seek it out, establish its identity, if in fact it does exist, and examine its conduct in the political game.

BUSINESS ELITES

Other citizens often lumped together with the rural elite to form the *oligarquía* are the industrial, commerical, and financial elites that, it is said, own and manage Latin America's urban economy. They are the descendants of the nineteenth-century entrepreneurs who were forced to take a back seat to the *latifundistas* and commercial farmers who dominated the region's economies until the 1930s. After the depression they were the prime movers behind the strategy of industrialization through import substitution, using high tariffs and easy credit to stimulate the development of domestic industry. As a result of their efforts, the larger Latin American countries like Brazil,

Argentina, and Mexico now boast dynamic industrial sectors that produce most of the goods consumed internally.

Who are these entrepreneurs and what do they want from politics? The immense diversity of industry, commerce, and finance in Latin America makes these questions difficult to answer. Here more than anywhere generalization is hazardous. For example, in any Latin American country the majority of industrialists and merchants operates small family firms, employing less than two dozen workers. Businessmen also come from a variety of backgrounds. Some are immigrants who took advantage of opportunities opened after the depression and the disdain of many natives for industrial enterprise. Others are the sons of wealthy rural families who left the farm for new conquests in business, small-business men who have grown into prosperous ones, government officials who have used their influence to create powerful commercial empires, and foreign investors from many different countries. Clearly, the business sector is even less monolithic than the rural sector. Not only are firms divided by size and function, they also differ in ownership, some being owned by nationals and others by foreigners. Even though the entire business sector supports common goals from time to time, it is plagued by rivalries between domestic and foreign investors, large and small firms, and commerce, banking, and industry.

What do businessmen want from politics and how do they try to get it? Those who got their start in an age of high tariffs and easy credit want such policies continued, especially if they feel themselves threatened by competition from larger, more efficient foreign firms. If anything unites Latin American businessmen, however, it is not their fiscal, monetary, and tariff policy preferences, but their opposition to militant labor unions. The more the government can contain labor's appetites, the happier businessmen seem to be. They also share an antipathy toward taxation and go to great lengths to avoid paying taxes. And they are among the first to speak out against price controls, something that is common in inflation-ridden Latin American countries. Businessmen and industrialists want advantages for their firms: If they can secure a monopoly over their markets, they do so; if not, they try to gain policy decisions that give them advantages over their competitors.

The political activities of businessmen are not unlike those of commercial farmers. They have organized interest groups that represent various elements of the commercial, financial, and industrial sectors before the government. Seldom do such groups work directly through political parties, though they do lobby before legislative bodies and participate as much as they are allowed to on government boards and commissions. But more than any other players, businessmen seek out public officials on their own, trying to secure favors for their individual firms, such as import privileges and tax exemptions. Unfortunately, the political activities of businessmen are among the most difficult to observe because they seldom occur openly, within public view.

It is not surprising that businessmen, like commercial farmers, use their importance to the economy to persuade authorities to meet their policy demands. When threatened by higher taxes or undesirable regulations, they warn the government of the economic calamity that will result. Whether officials believe them depends on the strength of their economic arguments and the seriousness of their threats. Bribery and other forms of financial influence are also quite common in Latin America. And family connections are used to secure favors, as they are in other areas of Latin American life. At the more general level, businessmen also use economic ideology to their advantage. Small industrialists seeking protection against foreign imports have championed nationalism, often to good effect in securing restrictions on foreign competitors. Foreign investors, on the other hand, have used free trade ideologies to convince economic authorities that their countries will develop only with the help of foreign capital. In both cases, technical and political arguments are used to justify development strategies that serve particular as well as general interests.

There is no consensus among businessmen on which rules of the game serve them best. Many small domestic firms, which believe they stand to gain most from the victory of nationalistic political parties, seem to prefer the democratic rules of the game as long as their political allies emerge victorious. At the same time, nearly all prefer the kind of political system that reduces the likelihood of demagogic reformist politics and encourages consistent management of cautious but deliberate development programs. They also want a game that gives them direct access to executive officials. More than anything else, businessmen, both large and small, want a government that acknowledges their role in the country's economic development and is open to their policy demands, regardless of whether it is authoritarian or democratic.

THE MILITARY

The active intervention of the military into politics is one of the most enduring features of Latin American political life. By the mid-1970s eight of the ten South American republics were governed directly by the military, as were five of the six Central American nations. When not ruling directly, the military has exerted its influence on the leaders of most Latin American countries, making demands that have affected the composition of governments, the treatment of opponents, and the content of public policy. We need not dwell on the fact of the military's involvement in Latin American politics, for it is obvious; instead, we should focus on why military officers feel compelled to insert themselves into their countries' politics. There is no single answer to this intriguing question, for military intervention, like other political phenomena, is the product of many different forces. Yet, by focusing on the conditions that appear to push and pull military men into the political process, we can identify some of the most prominent reasons for their involvement.

What is it about the military itself that drives or pushes it into the political arena? For the most part, the once traditional and poorly organized Latin American militaries have been transformed during the twentieth century into professional organizations led by well-trained officers and equipped with modern weapons. Today, nearly every country has an army, air force, and navy, with the army the largest of the three branches. The size of the military varies immensely throughout the region, ranging from 260,000 in Brazil to Costa Rica's 1,500-man national guard. The Brazilian army includes seven divisions; its navy has one aircraft carrier, eight submarines, and fourteen destroyers; and its air force has 160 combat aircraft. On the average, the Latin American militaries claim approximately 10 percent of their governments' budgets, somewhat less than their counterparts in Asia and Africa. Variations among countries are great, however; the Brazilian military, for example, received 11 percent of the country's budget in 1974, whereas Mexico's, which is among the smallest as a proportion of population, received only 2.2 percent. But size, even when measured in relative terms, does not appear to be a critical factor in accounting for military intervention. Large and small alike have intervened. Once the size gets beyond a minimal threshold that permits the creation of a professional officer corps and the acquisition of a handful of modern weapons, the military is capable of intervention. To explain why it meddles in politics, we must turn to other factors.

The military's disciplined, hierarchical organization is one such factor. Without it, most coups would be improbable undertakings. The techniques of implementing a military coup are well known. All that is required is agreement among the leaders of the different military branches and a few fundamental decisions about the deployment of troops. Although all the region's militaries are ostensibly organized for defense against external threats, the same weapons and tactics they would use to stop a foreign invader can be easily turned toward the removal of government officials and the suppression of civilian political groups. Yet, even though it is important, the military's organization is more a capability than a motive for intervention; it makes the coup possible, but does not necessarily cause it.

Another explanation of military intervention stresses the class background of officers. It has been argued that because most officers come from the *oligarquía,* they defend the wealthy from the masses. This was probably true before 1930, but as an explanation of contemporary coups it is quite inadequate. The class background of military officers has changed substantially during the last quarter century. Increasingly, officers have been recruited from the middle and lower middle classes. In place of the sons of the *latifundistas* one now finds the sons of small-town merchants, big-city industrialists, and former military officers. Though officers do not yet represent the urban and rural poor to any large degree, they are more diverse and less tied by blood to traditional elites than ever before. If they intervene in public affairs to protect the elite, it is less because of their class origins than because of other factors.

An understanding of military education may take us a little closer in our search for motives. Several features of military education merit attention. One is its isolation of military officers. The typical military career begins with a young man's admittance to a military secondary school at age thirteen or fourteen. After graduation come four years at a service academy, then advanced training in specialty schools, and, before promotion to the rank of general, additional training at a war college of some kind. The result is an educational and professional experience that occurs in relative isolation from civilian society and gives military officers a strong corporate identity that separates them psychologically and socially from civilian politicians. Equally important is the content of military education. Because he is taken from civilian life at a young age, the officer is heavily influenced by the content of his formal instruction as well as what he learns from his peers. Most military education is quite conventional, concentrating primarily on general strategy and tactics, military organization and administration, and technical training, especially in various types of engineering. Beyond rudimentary instruction in foreign languages, history, and economics, little attention is given to the social sciences in the officer's early training. These, however, become very important when the officer attends his nation's war college later in his career.

Since World War II war colleges have been established in most countries to provide advanced training in many nonmilitary as well as military subjects. The curriculum reflects the contemporary belief of officers that their country's defense depends on its social and economic development. At a war college officers are taught geopolitics, development economics, and advanced management techniques by civilian as well as military instructors. In some countries, such as Brazil, they are joined in the classroom by civilian students from government bureaucracies and private industry. What they learn about development varies from country to country. In Brazil, for example, capitalist economics and technological development have been stressed; in Peru, on the other hand, socialist points of view as well as capitalistic ones were taught during the 1960s. But regardless of the specific content of instruction, such advanced training cannot help but heighten the officer's concern for his country's economic development and increase his confidence in the military's ability to promote it.

Among the most important products of military education and experience are the attitudes of officers about politics, economic development, and the military's role in society. These attitudes give rise to the ideologies that guide military participation in public affairs. Unfortunately, the identification of military attitudes and ideologies is quite difficult; Latin American military officers do not welcome inquiries into their opinions. We are still dependent almost entirely on their public statements, writings in journals, and public behavior. From such sources we learn that the military is not always of one mind. Even though they may not be exposed to as diverse an assortment of ideas and development strategies as civilians, military officers nevertheless differ among themselves, especially on matters of economic policy and political philosophy. We can see these differences of opinion in the policies adopted by recent military governments – witness the conservative approach of the Brazilian military in 1964 in contrast to the more reformist line of the Peruvians in 1968 – as well as the disputes that arise within the military, such as those between officers who supported the Peronistas in Argentina and those who opposed them throughout the 1960s.

If military officers today share any attitude, it is their belief in the need to develop their countries economically. With few exceptions, they reject the traditional economic order in favor of a more modern one aimed at bolstering their nation's economic strength. One of the casualties of this drive toward development has sometimes been civilian politics. Many officers blame underdevelopment on the politicians who have governed their countries. Steady economic growth cannot, they argue, withstand the rancor, conflict, and uncertainty characteristic of civilian politics. Continual disputes over the rules of the political game, legislative indecision and delay, demagogic incitement of the masses, and the disruptive activities of urban and rural guerrillas all impede the kind of economic development envisioned by many officers. This intolerance for conventional civilian politics has led frequently to military intervention.

Having reviewed some of the traits that may push the military into politics, we can now turn to the conditions that pull it into the political process. The distinction between push and pull factors is somewhat arbitrary, as the two are closely related and interact continuously. By "pull factors" we mean conditions external to the military institution that provoke or heighten the desire to intervene. Obviously, military officers do not operate in a vacuum; their attitudes about politics and economic development are shaped as much by the society they observe around them as by the textbooks used in their classrooms. Their interventions are as much reactions to conditions within society as traits of the military itself. In recent years the officers have developed high expectations for their societies and have frequently judged civilian leaders harshly for not meeting them. Among the conditions that have drawn the military into politics, four stand out and deserve comment.

First, military officers abhor public disorder. They not only have a personal preference for order and hierarchy, but they also fear the consequences of internal disorder for national security and resent being called upon by civilian presidents to suppress domestic protests. They reason that the instruments of violence should be a monopoly of the state and not used freely in society by groups contending for political influence. They also prefer that civilian governments maintain order and judge them harshly for failing to do so. However, if they do fail, the military stands ready to step in and do the job, even if it means replacing civilian authorities. Some militaries have, in fact, assumed the role of guardians of the political order, driven by the belief that they are obliged to guarantee the maintenance of some kind of equilibrium among the country's contending political forces. In so doing, however, they are playing into the hands of those who use violence to upset the equilibrium and force the military to remove authorities whom they oppose.

Economic crises also promote military intervention. Since the 1930s military officers have taken a deep interest in their countries' economic progress, and regardless of the economic doctrine they prefer, none is very tolerant of governments that cannot keep their economic affairs in order. Unfortunately, economic instability has been the norm rather than the exception in many Latin American countries whose economies are extremely vulnerable to changes in conditions beyond the government's control (e.g., fluctuating world commodity prices, natural calamities, and imported inflation). Economic crises can lead to popular unrest and popular unrest can provoke disorder. The equation is simple, and the military is quick to make the connection. Consequently, civilian governments that find themselves besieged by inflation, foreign exchange crises, and mass discontent can also expect close scrutiny and intense pressures from the military guardians of public order. We should not, however, take this logic too far, for economic crises do not always provoke military coups. More than the crisis itself, it is the government's inability to cope with the crisis that appears to upset the military.

The performance of political institutions is a third factor that prompts military intervention. There are many ways in which governments can convince military leaders that political institutions have failed. If, for example, the government cannot maintain public order or deal with economic crises, one may conclude either that the individual public officials are incompetent or, more seriously, that existing institutions are incapable of promoting solutions to such problems. In the latter case, the military may feel compelled to remove public officials and reorganize the government. It is not only the extreme cases of political and economic disorder that prompt negative assessments of political institutions, but also the routine activities of slow and indecisive legislatures, timid presidents, and ineffective bureaucracies. In country after country officers have condemned constitutional governments because of their apparent failure to manage public affairs efficiently. This is a harsh judgment and one that is often motivated by a preference for authoritarian rule and a misunderstanding of democratic institutions, their costs and benefits. Nevertheless, it is a judgment that is made with increasing frequency throughout Latin America and shows no signs of abatement.

Fourth, we must acknowledge the influence of foreign governments on military intervention in Latin America. Some students of the region argue that one cannot understand military behavior without first analyzing how foreign governments and multinational corporations use local militaries to defend their interests when they come under attack. The range of techniques ascribed to such agents is quite wide, from the deliberate "destabilization" of the economy to the rewarding of military officers with bribes, military hardware, and economic assistance for post-coup military governments. Unfortunately, conspiracies involving foreign agents cannot be documented easily because they are organized covertly. Nevertheless, revelations like those that came from the United States Senate investigations of the Chilean coup of 1973 demonstrate how foreign agents can play an important role in provoking military intervention. As analysts we cannot dismiss such factors as the fantasies of involved partisans; instead, we must try to determine their effect on the conduct of the Latin American military.

One of the charges most frequently leveled against Latin American militaries is that they usually intervene in politics to protect the interests of society's most conservative forces. On balance, this bit of conventional wisdom appears true. However, the military has not always acted in defense of the *oligarguía*. Although it did try to protect the traditional order from the social unrest unleashed by the 1929 depression, the military has also brought down reactionary tyrants and helped create progressive populist and democratic regimes in several countries, especially during the 1940s and 1950s. Moreover, in the 1960s a new kind of military regime made its appearance on the Latin American scene. It was neither as traditional as the regimes of the 1930s nor as progressive as those created after World War II. What distinguished it from its predecessors was the determination of the military leaders to remain in office until they had completed the economic and political reconstruction of the country. This new military regime is autocratic, sometimes brutally so, and dedicated to the heavy-handed state supervision of the country's economic development. We will examine in Chapter 8 the political game it has created.

GOVERNMENT BUREAUCRATS

Why include government employees as players in the Latin American political game? Are they not just passive agents used by political leaders to accomplish their purposes rather than participants in the game itself? The answer is no, at least not any longer.

Bureaucrats play an important role in contemporary politics, one that endures while politicians come and go. During the twentieth century the state's responsibilities have grown immensely in capitalist as well as socialist societies. With the expansion of the state's authority has come the creation of a host of agencies that administer its many programs. And with these agencies there has arisen a new class of technicians and bureaucrats who administer them. They design development plans; manage state banks, utilities, and commercial enterprises; supervise educational systems; and supply social services. In theory, they are merely servants of political leaders and their constituents; in practice, they have developed resources and interests of their own that are distinct from those of the politicians they serve.

Even though the rapid growth of the public sector in Latin America is relatively recent, it has had an enormous effect on contemporary political life and economic development. During the past fifty years, the Latin American state has gone from regulating domestic and foreign trade to promoting industrialization and executing ambitious development programs. Governments that did little more than build roads and deliver the mail a half century ago now run oil companies, manage airlines, and produce a wide range of goods and services, from iron and steel to television programs. This sudden growth has not come without some difficulties. The Latin American state, despite its immense formal authority, is still quite weak in many areas, especially the enforcement of reform legislation, and is often hampered by a shortage of financial resources and managerial talent. This should not be surprising, for the Latin American state has come very far very fast; its bureaucracies have suddenly been given new responsibilities that require the skilled administration of very complex activities and an unprecedented degree of social engineering.

Frustration with unfulfilled development plans and inefficiently managed state enterprises has become common throughout the region, prompting a renewed interest in strengthening the state and its bureaucratic capabilities, especially on the part of the military officers and technocrats, who have seized control of many of the region's governments in recent years and tried to halt patronage, eliminate corruption, and promote efficiency. Most Latin American governments are still a long way from achieving these objectives. Patronage still influences many appointments, and bribery and other forms of corruption can be found almost everywhere. Yet, significant strides have been taken. The number of trained personnel in key agencies increases each year, and tasks that were left to foreign firms in the past are increasingly being taken over by the state and its newly nationalized enterprises.

It should now be clear why we must consider bureaucrats as players who have their own interests and resources as well as a distinct impact on development policy. Their particular interests vary from country to country depending on their historical experience and the prevailing ideology. Cuban bureaucrats, for example, are more influenced by a revolutionary ethic than Colombian officials, who continue to be bound by well-entrenched traditions. But regardless of their economic and political ideologies, the managers of the Latin American public sector share many things in common. First, they desire to preserve and expand their influence over public policy. Second, they seek to administer their programs with as little interference from political authorities as possible. And third, they want to dominate and control the clients who depend on their goodwill. What they enjoy most is the power they derive from the public's dependence on the goods and services they provide. To a large degree they have become the modern patrons of the industrialists, traders, farmers, laborers, and peasants who manage and labor in the private sector. To such clients government bureaucrats have become the critical suppliers of licenses, loans, roads, railroads, housing, and innumerable regulations and social services. In return they expect public recognition of their status, compliance with their decisions, and public support for their agencies.

The potential power of bureaucrats is evident when we recognize that no matter how noble a government's goals or how sophisticated its development plans, it accomplishes little without the support of administrators. Bureaucrats are supposed to be the servants of political officials, but political officials often find themselves the captives of their administrators. They rely on the administrators when they design policies as well as when they implement them. If bureaucrats disagree with official policy or find it threatening to their organizational interests, they have recourse to many weapons, which they can use to sabotage the government's effort. It is imperative, therefore, that political officials not sit back and assume that their programs will succeed simply because they are needed. If they do not closely supervise program implementation, making sure that policy goals are met and services delivered, their best efforts will likely come to naught.

The weakness of political analyses that focus primarily on "politics" rather than "government" is that they miss the impact of administrators on the country's public life and economic development. If we are to understand why some countries do well when they try to solve fundamental development problems and others do not, we cannot halt our analysis after examining elections, coups, legislatures, and presidents. Instead, we must go a step farther and ask what the state does with its authority and resources and what consequences, if any, this has on the welfare of its citizens.

FOREIGN INTERESTS

It is popular today to blame all Latin America's problems on foreign governments and multinational corporations. Foreigners have been deeply involved in the region's development since colonial times and still exercise great power over its domestic affairs. Some explain the impact of foreigners using the Marxist-Leninist theory of imperialism, which argues that industrial capitalism has survived by exploiting the less developed countries of Latin America, Asia, and Africa. Working through a system of neocolonialism that has placed the economies and governments of the peripheral regions under their control, foreign capitalists have, it is argued, reaped immense profits from the extraction of Latin America's minerals, the purchase of its agricultural commodities at low prices, and the sale of manufactured goods to the region's consumers. In return they have given Latin America poverty, economic stagnation, and authoritarian governments that brutally repress the masses. Others have stressed dependency rather than domination when describing the impact of foreigners on Latin American development. They acknowledge that the economic, social, and political transformations that have occurred in Latin America result primarily from the region's incorporation into the global capitalist system. But they also recognize that post-depression industrialization within the region has altered the structures of many Latin American economies and made them less dependent on the export of primary products. With industrialization has come a new form of dependence, however, for where in the past economic development was managed by a small elite of rural producers and foreign traders, it now relies heavily on the efforts of multinational mining, manufacturing, banking, and retail firms. Thus, even though the form has changed, the result is still the subordination of the region's economies to the dictates of foreigners.

You do not have to agree entirely with either of these popular explanations of Latin American underdevelopment to appreciate the degree to which foreign economic interests and governments influence the region's politics. The analysis of foreign players and their impact on domestic events requires that we focus on the structural linkages between local and foreign economies as well as on the behavior of foreigners within each country. We must also subject foreigners to the same questions about goals, resources, and rules that we applied to the other players.

What do we mean by foreign players? They are the citizens of other countries who seek to influence the selection of a Latin American country's officials or the choice and implementation of its public policies. Some are individuals who represent foreign governments and their many agencies. Each American embassy, for example, houses representatives from the State and Defense departments, and from the Treasury, Department of Agriculture, and Central Intelligence Agency, who pursue the interests of their government in the host country. Of course, the United States is not alone among the world's nations in its interest in Latin America and its propensity for meddling in the region's internal affairs. Representatives of other foreign governments and of international agencies, like the United Nations and the World Bank, are also active in Latin America, sometimes exerting influence over economic matters through their advice and financial assistance.

We also find many private citizens in Latin America, most of whom are employed by corporations active in the region. By the mid-1970s American firms alone had $16.5 billion (American billion) invested in Latin America, the largest share going to manufacturing, with petroleum close behind. Of this amount, $4.6 billion was invested in Brazil, $3.2 billion in Mexico, $2.1 billion in Venezuela, and $1.1 billion in Argentina. As elsewhere in the world the large multinational firms have led the way in the expansion of foreign investments in the region. They have absorbed domestic firms as well as launched operations where none previously existed, introduced new technologies and products, and frequently secured high returns on their investments. Yet, despite the multinational firms' contributions to national production and employment, they have become one of the most heavily criticized institutions in Latin America, accused of undermining native entrepreneurs, extracting excessive profits, bribing and manipulating governments, and dominating local economies. In recent years the multinationals' critics have succeeded in imposing more restrictive regulations on their ownership and conduct, ranging from requirements that a majority of the subsidiary's stock be sold to citizens of the country to outright nationalization. Although Latin Americans have stopped short of evicting all foreign firms, it is clear that the days of easy access to the region's resources and markets are over.

What do we need to know about foreign players in order to understand their impact on the Latin American game? At the outset we must recognize that not all foreign players have the same interests. The most notable difference is that between foreign governments and foreign firms. The two often work hand in hand, especially when a government decides to protect the investments of its citizens abroad, but for analytical purposes some important distinctions exist. Nor can we lump all foreign governments into a single category, for each has its own foreign policy objectives in Latin America. The interests of communist nations may at times differ sharply from those of capitalist ones, for example. Each government must be examined as a separate player if we are to understand its behavior. For illustrative purposes, let us look first at the United States government and ask about its interests, resources, and political preferences.

What does the United States government want in Latin America? Those who represent the United States abroad seldom give a clear answer to this question because their objectives are many and varied and, not infrequently, contradictory. Nevertheless, some general aims can be identified. They have sought the support of Latin American governments in their struggle with the communist nations. Few goals have been more important to American policy makers than the exclusion of communism from the hemisphere. In the economic realm the United States seeks to maintain a trading system that gives it access to Latin American resources, commodities, and markets. Although Latin America receives a smaller proportion of United States investments than does either Europe or Canada, it is an important supplier of raw materials and foodstuffs and a growing market for American goods. The United States prefers Latin American governments that respect its commercial involvement in the hemisphere and play by the prevailing rules of intraregional trade. American policy has also been characterized by an obsession with political stability because that facilitates trade, investment, and the pursuit of anticommunism. Some attention has been given from time to time to the promotion of democratic governments throughout the region, but when democracy has come into conflict with political order, the latter has usually prevailed.

What resources can the United States use to influence Latin American domestic affairs? At the diplomatic level there is always personal persuasion. American diplomats and technical advisors can persuade local officials to follow their advice using logical argument and expertise. But seldom does logical argument, by itself, succeed without the use of other modes of persuasion. And therein lies the strength of the United States in Latin America. It can use Latin America's dependence on American markets, investments, and assistance to good advantage, threatening to reduce or cut them off to punish nations that get out of line. It can also use its influence in international lending institutions to terminate or deny loans or to call in debts in order to bring pressure on uncooperative governments. The vulnerability of a government to such pressures depends on how dependent it is on foreign sources of financial support.

A second resource, and one that has received much attention of late, is direct intervention in local politics through various covert activities. To secure the kind of government or politics they want, agents of the United States government may enter directly into the political game by increasing the resources of players they favor, directing adverse propaganda against those they do not, bribing officials and party leaders, fomenting unrest, and encouraging military intervention. Even though such techniques frequently fail to achieve their objectives, their availability and the threat of their use may bring a government into line.

Finally, there is the threat of American military intervention. Popular at the turn of the century during the era of dollar diplomacy, American military intervention in Latin American countries occurs less frequently today. Nevertheless, the ability to intervene with troops, especially in the Caribbean as occurred in 1965, remains a weapon that can be employed to deter certain undesirable behaviors. More often than not, however, American policy makers are content to use their influence over Latin America's militaries to secure the results they desire.

In sum, what foreign governments such as the United States seem to want from Latin American politics is stability and cooperation – stability that will facilitate the pursuit of economic and political objectives in the region and cooperation in their achievement. At their disposal governments like the United States and the Soviet Union have immense resources that they can use to influence domestic politics throughout the region. The mere presence of such resources, of course, does not mean that they will always be used effectively. The Latin American political game is complex, and its outcomes are influenced by a multiplicity of factors, the activities of foreign governments being only one, though an important one. Moreover, resources have to be used with great skill in order to be effective, a requirement not always fulfilled by foreign governments. Thus, we must be careful in making inferences about the influence of foreigners without first examining their objectives and the instruments used to achieve them.

What about the multinational firms: How do their resources and objectives differ from those of foreign governments? They too are too diverse to be considered as a uniform group. They include manufacturers, mining companies, retailers, exporters, banks, transportation companies, and many others. Nevertheless, there are some methods and resources that such firms share in common. What they want from host governments is quite simple, at least on the surface. They desire a favorable investment climate that will generate a high rate of return for as long as possible. More specifically, they want easy access to resources and markets, a readily available but docile labor force, and the lowest possible costs of operations. They also demand low taxes, especially on their profit remittances, and a free hand to pursue their objectives. And like foreign governments, they prefer a stable political order that is predictable, especially in the management of economic affairs. They want to know what the economic rules of the game are and to be assured that they will remain the same in the future. What the multinational firm does not want is a government that is hostile to foreign investors and continually harasses them with unanticipated measures that constrain their operations and reduce their profits. Nor does it welcome the kind of economic uncertainty brought on by inflation and chronic balance-of-payments problems. Foreign firms, of course, seldom get everything they want. Nevertheless, they have survived quite well under less than optimal conditions, tolerating what they cannot change while exerting their influence on government policy makers to secure what advantages they can.

The multinational firm's major sources of influence are the resources and products it contributes to the host country. The more the local government wants what the firm offers, whether it be the extraction of petroleum or the production of toothpaste, the more vulnerable it is to the firm's demands. It is Latin America's misfortune (and conversely the multinationals' good fortune) that today the region finds itself in need of technology and capital, both of which are most readily supplied by the multinationals. Those who are in a hurry to increase the production of goods and services find the multinationals, with their transferable technologies, capital, and managerial skills, very attractive. But they are now also aware of the price they have to pay for foreign investment, most notably the absorption of domestic enterprises by the multinationals and increased foreign control over the economy. The challenge facing Latin America's leaders as well as foreign investors is to discover new arrangements that will contribute to national development without exacting such high costs.

Not to be overlooked are some of the less advertised ways in which multinational firms try to influence policy. Bribes are occasionally given to secure favorable government decisions. Low-paid Latin American public officials often encourage the payment of special fees to supplement their incomes. Some even argue that such payments can be justified as a kind of informal tax of the rich by the poor. A more indirect form of influence is the ability of multinational firms to block a country's participation in international markets. Boycotts of products, embargoes of exports in foreign ports, and the undermining of confidence in a country's creditworthiness are all techniques that have been used against Latin American nations in recent times.

Before concluding this introduction to the role of foreigners in the Latin American political game, some final observations are in order. The first is the need to recognize that we are dealing with something more complicated than a simple competition between foreign and domestic interests. There are many Latin Americans, including economists, consumers, and industrial managers, who believe that foreign firms can make important contributions to their economies. For them, it is not a question of nationals versus foreigners, but rather of how the country can make the best use of the resources available to it. It is not sufficient to label such people "lackeys of imperialism" or "tools of the multinationals" if we are to understand their behavior and its effects on national development. Instead, we must examine each of the issues raised by foreign involvement in Latin America, establish how they are resolved and to whose benefit in each case. Second, Latin America is changing rapidly, and nowhere is this more apparent than in its exertion of greater government control over multinational firms. As was stated earlier, the days of easy entrance into the Latin American economies are over. This is a challenging time for anyone concerned with innovations in the field of foreign investments. Throughout the region sophisticated technocrats are designing new approaches to the regulation of foreign firms. Joint ownership, mandatory domestic participation, foreign marketing arrangements are some of the measures now being used to cope with foreign investment. How well such innovations work and for whose benefit are questions yet to be answered.

FURTHER READING

Rural elites

Barraclough, Solon Lovett. *Agrarian Structures in Latin America: A Resume of the CIDA Land Tenure Studies of Argentina, Brazil, Chile, Colombia, Ecuador, Guatemala, Peru.* Lexington, Mass.: Lexington Books, 1972.

Dew, Edward. *Politics of the Altiplano: The Dynamics of Change in Rural Peru.* Austin: University of Texas Press, 1969.

Feder, Ernst. *The Rape of the Peasantry: Latin America's Landholding System.* Garden City, N.Y.: Doubleday (Anchor Books), 1971.

Hirschman, Albert O. *Journeys Toward Progress: Studies of Economic Policy-Making in Latin America.* New York: Norton, 1973.

Kaufman, Robert. *The Politics of Land Reform in Chile 1950–1970.* Cambridge, Mass.: Harvard University Press, 1972.

Keith, Robert, ed. *Haciendas and Plantations in Latin American History.* New York: Holmes & Meier, 1977.

Nichols, William Hord, and Ruy Miller Paiva. *Ninety-Nine Fazendas: The Structure and Productivity of Brazilian Agriculture, 1963.* Nashville: Graduate Center for Latin American Studies, Vanderbilt University, 1966.

Payne, James. "The Oligarchy Muddle." *World Politics* 20(3):439–53, April 1968.

Smith, Peter. *The Politics of Beef in Argentina.* New York: Columbia University Press, 1969.

Smith, T. Lynn. *The Process of Rural Development in Latin America.* Gainesville: University of Florida Press, 1967.

Business elites

Brandenburg, Frank. *The Development of Latin American Private Enterprise.* Washington, D.C.: National Planning Association, 1964.

Cardoso, Fernando Henrique. "The Industrial Elite," in Seymour Martin Lipset and Aldo Solari, eds., *Elites in Latin America.* New York: Oxford University Press, 1968, pp. 94–114.

Davis, Stanley M., and Louis Wolf Goodman, eds. *Workers and Managers in Latin America.* Lexington, Mass.: Heath, 1972.

Harbron, John W. "The Dilemma of an Elite Group: The Industrialist in Latin America." *Inter-American Economic Affairs, 19*(2):43–62, autumn 1965.

Imaz, José Luis. *Los Que Mandan* (Those Who Rule). Albany: State University of New York Press, 1970.

Kling, Merle. *A Mexican Interest Group in Action.* Englewood Cliffs, N.J.: Prentice-Hall, 1961.

Lauterbach, Albert. *Enterprise in Latin America: Business Attitudes in a Developing Economy.* Ithaca, N.Y.: Cornell University Press, 1966.

McMillan, Claude. "Industrial Leaders in Latin America," in William H. Form and Albert A. Blum, eds., *Industrial Relations and Social Change in Latin America.* Gainesville: University of Florida Press, 1965, pp. 24–46.

Purcell, John F. H., and Susan Kaufman Purcell. "Mexican Business and Public Policy," in James M. Malloy, ed. *Authoritarianism and Corporatism in Latin America.* Pittsburgh: University of Pittsburgh Press, 1977, pp. 191–226.

Strassman, Paul W. "The Industrialist," in John J. Johnson, ed., *Continuity and Change in Latin America.* Stanford: Stanford University Press, 1967, pp. 161–85.

Military

Barber, Willard R., and C. Neale Ronning. *Internal Security and Military Power: Counterinsurgency and Civic Action in Latin America.* Columbus: Ohio State University Press, 1966.

Einauldi, Luigi R., and Alfred C. Stepan. *Latin American Institutional Development: Changing Military Perspectives in Peru and Brazil.* Santa Monica, Calif.: Rand Corporation, 1971.

Huntington, Samuel. *Political Order in Changing Societies.* New Haven: Yale University Press, 1968, Chapter 4.

Jackman, Robert. "Politicians in Uniform: Military Government and Social Change in the Third World." *American Political Science Review* 70(4):1078–97, December 1976.

Janowitz, Morris. *The Military in the Political Development of New Nations: An Essay in Comparative Analysis.* Chicago: University of Chicago Press, 1964.

Johnson, John. *The Military and Society in Latin America.* Stanford: Stanford University Press, 1964.

Lieuwin, Edwin. *Arms and Politics in Latin America.* New York: Praeger, 1961.
    Generals vs. Presidents: Neo-Militarism in Latin America. New York: Praeger, 1964.

Lowenthal, Abraham F., ed. *Armies and Politics in Latin America.* New York: Holmes & Meier, 1976.

Needler, Martin. "Political Development and Military Intervention in Latin America." *American Political Science Review* 60(3):616–26, September 1966.

Nordlinger, Eric A. "Soldiers in Mufti: The Impact of Military Rule upon Economic and Social Change in the Non-Western States." *American Political Science Review* 64(4):1131–48, December 1970.

Nun, José. "A Latin American Phenomenon: The Middle Class Military Coup," in James Petras and Maurice Zeitlin, eds., *Latin America: Reform or Revolution?* Greenwich, Conn.: Fawcett, 1968, pp. 145–85.

O'Donnell, Guillermo A. *Modernization and Bureaucratic-Authoritarianism: Studies in South American Politics.* Berkeley: Institute of International Studies, University of California, 1973.

Putnam, Robert D. "Toward Explaining Military Intervention in Latin American Politics." *World Politics* 20(1):83–110, October 1967.

Stepan, Alfred C. *The Military in Politics: Changing Patterns in Brazil.* Princeton: Princeton University Press, 1971.

Government bureaucrats

Anderson, Charles W. *Politics and Economic Change in Latin America: The Governing of Restless Nations.* New York: Van Nostrand, 1967, Chapter 6.

Daland, Robert. *Brazilian Planning.* Chapel Hill: University of North Carolina Press, 1967.

Dietz, Henry A. "Bureaucratic Demand-Making and Clientelistic Participation in Peru," in James M. Malloy, ed., *Authoritarianism and Corporatism in Latin America.* Pittsburgh: University of Pittsburgh Press, 1977, pp. 413–58.

Graham, Lawrence S. *Civil Service Reform in Brazil: Principles versus Practice.* Austin: University of Texas Press, 1968.

Greenberg, Martin H. *Bureaucracy and Development: A Mexican Case Study.* Lexington, Mass.: Heath, 1970.

Grimes, C. E., and Charles Simmons. "Bureaucracy and Political Control in Mexico: Towards an Assessment." *Public Administration Review* 29:72–9, January–February 1969.

Grindle, Merilee S. *Bureaucrats, Politicians and Peasants in Mexico.* Berkeley: University of California Press, 1977.

Hopkins, Jack. "Contemporary Research on Public Administration and Bureaucracies in Latin America." *Latin American Research Review* 9:109–4, spring 1974.
La Palombara, Joseph, ed. *Bureaucracy and Political Development.* Princeton: Princeton University Press, 1963.
Weaver, Jerry L. "Value Patterns of a Latin American Bureaucracy." *Human Relations* 23:225–34, June 1970.
Wynia, Gary W. *Politics and Planners: Economic Development Policy in Central America.* Madison: University of Wisconsin Press, 1972.

Foreign interests: governments

Agee, Philip. *Inside the Company: CIA Diary.* New York: Stonehill, 1975.
Burr, Robert. *Our Troubled Hemisphere: Perspectives on U.S.–Latin American Relations.* Washington, D.C.: Brookings Institution, 1967.
Cotler, Julio, and Richard Fagen, eds. *Latin America and the United States.* Stanford: Stanford University Press, 1974.
Fann, K. T., and Donald Hodges, eds. *Readings in United States Imperialism.* Boston: Porter Sargent, 1971.
Hayter, Teresa. *Aid as Imperialism.* Baltimore: Penguin, 1971.
Levinson, Jerome, and Juan de Onis. *The Alliance that Lost Its Way.* New York: Quadrangle, 1970.
Linowitz, Sol, ed. *The Americas in a Changing World.* New York: Quadrangle, 1975.
Martin, John Bartlow. *Overtaken By Events: The Dominican Crisis from the Fall of Trujillo to the Civil War.* Garden City, N.Y.: Doubleday, 1966.
Needler, Martin. *The United States and the Latin American Revolution.* Boston: Allyn & Bacon, 1972.
Parkinson, F. *Latin America, the Cold War and the World Powers, 1945–1973.* Beverly Hills, Calif.: Sage, 1974.
Theberge, James D. *The Soviet Presence in Latin America.* New York: Crane, Russak, 1974.
Williamson, Robert, William Glade, and Karl Schmitt, eds. *Latin America–United States Economic Interactions: Conflict, Accommodation and Policies for the Future.* Washington, D.C.: American Enterprise Institute, 1974.

Foreign interests: multinational corporations

Baklanoff, Eric N. *Expropriation of U.S. Investments in Cuba, Mexico and Chile.* New York: Praeger, 1975.
Barnet, Richard, and Ronald Muller. *Global Reach: The Power of the Multinational Corporations.* New York: Simon & Schuster, 1974.
Gunneman, Jon, ed. *The Nation-State and Transnational Corporations in Conflict: With Special Reference to Latin America.* New York: Praeger, 1975.
Ingram, George M. *Expropriation of U.S. Property in South America: Nationalization of Oil and Copper Companies in Peru, Bolivia and Chile.* New York: Praeger, 1975.
Magdoff, Harry. *The Age of Imperialism.* New York: Monthly Review Press, 1969.

Moran, Theodore. *Multinational Corporations and the Politics of Dependence: Copper in Chile*. Princeton: Princeton University Press, 1974.

Petras, James, Morris Morley, and Steven Smith. *The Nationalization of Venezuelan Oil*. New York: Praeger, 1977.

Pinelo, Adalberto. *The Multinational Corporation as a Force in Latin American Politics: A Case Study of the International Petroleum Company in Peru*. New York: Praeger, 1973.

Sunkel, Osvaldo. "Big Business and 'Dependencia.'" *Foreign Affairs* 50(3):517–31, April 1972.

Tugwell, Franklin. *The Politics of Oil in Venezuela*. Stanford: Stanford University Press, 1975.

Vernon, Raymond. *Sovereignty at Bay*. New York: Basic Books, 1971.

4. Players – II

No introduction to the principal players in the Latin American political game would be complete without a discussion of the "middle sectors." One of the problems encountered in the identification of players, as we have already seen, is that many people do not fit into neat categories. Nor do they always act together in organized groups. This is especially true of those who constitute the middle sectors.

The term was popularized by historian John Johnson in his book, *Political Change in Latin America: The Emergence of the Middle Sectors.* In his study of politics in Argentina, Chile, Uruguay, Brazil, and Mexico during the first half of the twentieth century, Johnson concluded that the traditional view of Latin America as a society composed only of a rural oligarchy and peasant masses was inaccurate. Indeed, if we examined the histories of these countries closely, we would discover the gradual appearance of many individuals who did not belong to either social class. They were neither as poor and uneducated as the laboring masses nor as wealthy and powerful as the traditional elite. Yet they did form a distinct political force in several countries after the turn of the century and even won public office in a few. Labeled the middle sectors by Johnson, they included lawyers, small-business men, white-collar employees, teachers, and bureaucrats. What had changed was not their presence, for there had always been some people lodged between the elite and the masses, but their numbers, which were increased rapidly by immigration and export-induced economic expansion after 1900.

The principal goal of the middle sectors during the 1920s and 1930s was to gain admittance to the economic, social, and political mainstream of Latin American life. For some admittance came through sudden wealth and entrance into the economic elite, but for the majority it involved the acquisition of political power and the use of that power to make more of society's resources available to the middle sectors. The middle sectors sought to increase public services, especially education, secure state subsidization of private investment, and protect native entrepreneurs against competition from tradi-

Table 4-1. *Synthesis of dominant traits of players*

	Middle sectors	Organized labor	Campesinos
Composition	Middle-income professionals, teachers, small-business men, white-collar workers in public and private sectors	Labor union members in industry, commerce, transport, food processing, banking, and public sector	*Mestizo,* Indian, and Negro rural poor: *Colonos* Wage laborers Plantation workers Subsistence farmers
Political objectives	Government patronage State promotion of industrial growth Public services Protection of economic conquests	State support in collective bargaining High wages and fringe benefits State social services	Economic security Increased income Liberation from dependence on landowners Access to credit and technology
Political resources	Management of most urban economic institutions Skill as political organizers Numbers as voters, consumers, protesters	Influence over critical economic activities Numbers as voters and protesters Organizational capability	Numbers Capacity for violence at local level Potential for electoral support

tional elites, foreign investors, and militant workers. To secure their ends they drew on several resources. Although they were only a minority of the population, they were a large and growing minority that possessed the skills needed to manage businesses, public utilities, educational institutions, and government agencies. The more the elite came to rely on them for the maintenance of commerce and public services, the more they were able to demand and secure concessions to their demands. Their greatest resource, however, was their ability to organize large urban political parties that could force traditional elites to admit them to the political process. By adapting forms of political organization developed by the bourgeoisie in Europe to Latin American conditions, they changed the form, if not the essential structure, of politics in several countries. They gave elections new meaning, made widespread patronage a virtue, and made the state responsive to the demands of emerging urban elites. This was especially true in Argentina, Chile, Brazil, and Uruguay, where middle-sector parties occupied public office for extended periods after 1910.

Even though the importance of the middle sectors in Latin American politics is well recognized, they remain an illusive object of political analysis. There are several reasons why this is so, most of them having to do with the group's unusual and complex character. First, as Johnson pointed out, the middle sectors have not developed the kind of class consciousness that was found among the bourgeoisie in Europe and North America. They have remained a diverse aggregation of individuals who have joined together from time to time to support a particular political party, rather than a united force that has prevailed over its competitors. Second, they have not transformed their societies the way the middle class transformed Western Europe. Many have retained traditional social values and have sought to emulate the elite rather than destroy it. As a result, the elite has been allowed to survive in many countries by absorbing its middle-sector imitators. And third, the middle sectors have promoted an unconventional route to industrial development and in the process produced a political economy different from that which resulted from the European industrial revolution. In Europe the middle class gained influence over the economy and then captured political power. In Latin America, in contrast, the middle sectors, starting from a very weak industrial base, first gained public office and then used state authority to promote industrialization. The result has been the heavy involvement of the state in the subsidization of industrial enterprise and an entrepreneurial class that is very dependent on government support.

If we were to search today for the representatives of those whom Johnson called the middle sectors, we would find them in many different places. As society has grown more complex, the middle sectors have grown more diverse and less united by a common interest. Most of the reform parties of the 1960s that championed the cause of agrarian reform and long-range planning were led by individuals who came from middle-sector families. So did most of the military officers who now govern many Latin American countries. Other descendants of the middle sectors have joined the economic elite as commercial farmers, industrialists, merchants, and bankers. They also dominate the ranks of the technocrats, who now manage most Latin American government agencies. We would be hard-pressed to find a Latin American leader today whose parents were not members of the middle sectors.

Finally, there remains the question of whether the middle sectors are too diverse to be examined as a collectivity. If we are looking for a social class whose members work together for common objectives, we probably will be disappointed. Yet, we cannot ignore them simply because they are not readily classified and monitored. Their involvement in politics is too great and their impact on policy too critical to be dismissed. We must identify the mutiple roles played by middle-sector players as best we can and then assess their influence on the selection of rules, the behavior of other players, and the conduct of public officials.

THE MASSES

Before we introduce laborers and peasants, two problems that have hampered the analysis of the Latin American masses deserve mention. The first is the temptation to view the masses as a monolithic group whose members share the same economic and political interests. The mere fact that they are laborers in an economy dominated by owners and managers is thought to give them a common identity and similar political goals. To the outside observer this may indeed appear to be the case, for the majority of Latin Americans suffer from the burdens of poverty, political isolation, and exploitation by others. From the subjective point of view, however (i.e., in the perceptions of the masses themselves), their differences sometimes appear to be greater than what they share in common. Race, ethnicity, regional identities, economic activity, and levels of income traditionally have separated and isolated Latin America's poor from one another. Even today, the masses are seldom united to do battle with the rest of society. Instead, when they become involved at all it is usually through a variety of labor and peasant organizations that must compete with one another as well as with the elite for larger shares of the nation's scarce resources.

The second problem we face when analyzing the masses stems from the fact that few peasants and laborers belong to the organizations that claim to represent them in the political process. Less than one-third of Latin America's urban work force belongs to labor unions, and an even smaller proportion of rural workers is included in peasant organizations. We must, therefore, be cautious in attributing the views of union or peasant leaders to the entire sector they claim to represent. Although we have no choice but to regard such spokesmen as active players in the game, we must also try to establish how well they represent the political demands of their constituents.

Organized labor

Few players in the Latin American political game have become more conspicuous in recent years than organized labor. It was not always that way. The first unions were organized in Latin America in the late nineteenth century under the leadership of European immigrants inspired by the anarchist, socialist, and syndicalist ideologies they had brought with them from the Continent. The unions did not, however, meet with instant success. During their formative years they were torn by dissension from within and slowed by harassment from without. The first was caused by ideological disputes among competing factions within the movement itself; the latter was the work of antilabor entrepreneurs and governments. They were also hindered by the region's underdevelopment, most notably the lack of industry, which forced labor organizers to confine their efforts to the commercial and service sectors. But with the growth of industry after the 1929 depression the ranks of the urban work force swelled, giving labor organizers new opportunities to increase the size and influence of their movements. Yet, with only a few exceptions, labor leaders were unable to take full advantage of the new opportunities afforded them by industrialization. Instead, they were forced to fight to survive in the face of continual persecution by conservative political authorities who opposed mass organizations and their demands for social reform.

As long as labor fought on its own to secure a foothold within the national political arena, it met with only limited success. But once ambitious politicians discovered that the working class could propel them into public office, the labor movement suddenly found itself catapulted into the political mainstream. Politicians like Getulio Vargas in Brazil, Juan Perón in Argentina, and Lázaro Cárdenas in Mexico, and political parties like Acción Democrática in Venezuela, gave laborers the rights and privileges they coveted in exchange for their political support and personal devotion. In the process socialist and anarchist leaders often were forced to give way to union bosses, who tied their careers and movements to an ascending politician or party. Labor militancy did not cease, however, once these initial conquests were made. Ideological conflicts and leadership struggles within the movement have persisted, as have strikes and demonstrations aimed at embarrassing presidents, inducing favorable policies, and bringing down governments. As a result, some Latin American officials, especially in the military, still view labor as a hindrance to the maintenance of political order and the achievement of economic growth and have responded to working-class militancy increasingly by closing labor organizations and repressing the rank and file.

Once we recognize the role of the Latin American state as the patron of the labor movement, it is easier to understand why the region's laborers are among the world's most politicized. Detailed labor codes have given public officials abundant authority to regulate labor organizations, supervise collective bargaining, and set national wage and price policies. Before 1930 most governments employed their authority against organized labor, but with the rise of labor-supported regimes in the 1940s there came a new type of public official who sought to protect his supporters in the labor movement from economic hardship. As a result, a generation of labor leaders came to believe that only through their involvement in politics could they secure and retain their economic conquests.

The dependence of labor organizations on public authorities also accounts, in part, for the raucous character of labor relations in Latin America. Actually, most Latin American laborers do not strike any more often than their European or North American counterparts; nevertheless, Latin American governments seem constantly to be besieged by angry workers. Our impression of continuous labor-induced economic chaos results not so much from the frequency of strikes as from the manner in which they are carried out. In Latin America more than elsewhere unions direct their protests at public authorities who can set national wage rates, regulate collective bargaining, and give or take away labor's privileges. When quiet persuasion fails, unions are quick to resort to general strikes, demonstrations, and vocal protests aimed at securing policy concessions by disrupting vital economic activities and threatening public order. Such tactics, which are considered exceptional elsewhere, have become commonplace in Latin America because they have proved so successful in inducing governments to meet labor's demands.

Having reviewed the rise of organized labor and its dependence on the state for many of its economic conquests, we can now turn to its role in the contemporary political game. Is labor the vanguard of the proletariat, seeking to lead a revolution that will produce a more just society? Or is it content merely to increase the share of the economic pie going to the working class? Or have labor unions become corrupted by power, acquiescing to the dictates of political authorities who have bought off the movement's leadership in exchange for their keeping the rank and file in line? The answer is yes to all three questions, for Latin American labor movements have followed many different paths in their campaigns for influence. One finds Marxist unions that still hope to lead a proletarian revolution as well as unions that are content to set aside grandiose ideological objectives and work primarily for the immediate economic betterment of their members. There are also some that have become corrupt, autocratic organizations in which the workers' interests are sacrificed by self-serving leaders who use their control over the rank and file for personal political and financial gain.

To understand what it wants from politics, we must remember that organized labor represents the elite of the working-class movement. These are the working people who have to some extent "made it." Most laborers are not among this fortunate few, but are unorganized, protected by few laws, and without much clout when it comes to collective bargaining. Like most elites, organized labor has grown more concerned with its own conquests and their protection than with improvement of the welfare of those not within its organizations. Individual unions expend most of their energy on such bread-and-butter issues as wages, working conditions, and retirement benefits, while their national confederations concentrate on securing government policies favorable to them. Confederation leaders not only resort to strikes, demonstrations, and conventional lobbying, but also seek to secure a foothold within the government agencies that make labor policies.

Nearly all economic policy decisions affect labor in some way. Take antiinflation policies, for example. Rising prices reduce purchasing power and force unions to demand higher wages to compensate for their losses to inflation. Wage increases, however, may only provoke higher prices, touching off a wage-price spiral. One solution is to freeze wages temporarily, thereby asking labor to bear some of the burden of stopping inflation. But labor leaders seldom stand by idly while they are singled out to pay the price of fighting inflation. Instead, they use all means at their disposal to see that the costs are shifted to others. In this way they can at least protect themselves from harm in the short run even if they cannot secure the long-term benefits they desire.

Organized labor has many resources at its disposal that it can bring to bear in the political game. In a democratic system it offers votes to candidates who will further its interests. Despite the fact that organized workers are a minority of the work force, they can deliver large blocks of voters to their chosen candidates. They can also mobilize their supporters for rallies and demonstrations on a candidate's behalf. Neither of these facts was lost on the leaders who attracted working-class support in their rise to power in the 1940s and 1950s. They simply outflanked traditional elite parties by amassing a large bloc of labor voters and turning the often abused electoral process to their advantage.

But votes count only in elections; between elections organized labor must use other resources to get its way. One of the most important is its influence on the economy. More often than not the most unionized industries are also the most important to the economy. Workers in transportation, mining, petroleum, banking, and manufacturing have been organized for some time, and long ago they learned how to use their control over critical industries to good advantage. Through strikes, they can not only threaten owners and managers, but also undermine government economic programs in order to force the government to settle a strike in labor's favor or to adopt a particular policy demanded by the labor leadership.

Finally, as a resource of last resort there is the general strike or violent protest aimed at securing a desirable presidential response. Such extreme tactics are employed to undermine public order and force presidential concessions. They are especially effective in countries where weak presidents fear military intervention if order cannot be maintained. In such cases the president must decide whether to meet labor's demands and risk criticism from antilabor groups or to deny labor and risk continued disorder and possible military intervention. Of course, labor too runs some risks when it chooses such drastic tactics. A strong president may retaliate with force to break union protests, and should the military intervene, it too might exact a high price from the protesters by closing unions and jailing their leaders.

No matter how rich it is in resources, the labor movement cannot succeed without effective organization. It is not enough for a few leaders to claim to represent the rank and file; they must also enjoy their followers' loyal support. Unauthorized wildcat strikes or, conversely, an unwillingness to join in strikes can undermine labor leaders by destroying the unity they need to maximize their influence. Disunity and internal squabbling, in turn, encourage the divide-and-conquer tactics employed by businessmen and antilabor governments to break strikes and hold the working class in check. On the other hand, unity creates problems of its own. For example, once the labor movement is joined into a national confederation, it runs the risk of overcentralization and the kind of bureaucratization that makes labor leaders insensitive to the needs of the rank and file. The latter situation has led in some countries to the creation of rival union organizations that have sought, in most cases unsuccessfully, to break the monopoly of these unresponsive labor bureaucracies. One of the principal causes of the failure of such insurgents has been opposition to them by public officials, who over the years have worked out accommodations with labor leaders and are willing to defend them from their working-class critics.

The role of organized labor in Latin American development is still a matter of intense controversy. Some contemporary political leaders view labor's involvement in national affairs as essential to the mobilization of the nation's development resources and have included it in

ruling coalitions; others see its activism and economic demands as obstacles to capital accumulation and the maintenance of political order
and have repressed it brutally. There is also little agreement about the
contributions labor leaders have made to the welfare of the Latin
American masses. Have all workers gained from the conquests of
organized labor, or have such conquests been confined to a small
working-class elite? And what about rural workers? Can they share in
the gains of urban laborers or must they struggle alone? These questions will merit our attention when we examine several national experiences in Part II of this book.

Campesinos

The rural poor of Latin America are only beginning to be taken
seriously as participants in national politics. Most peasants are, in fact,
still excluded from the mainstream of national political life. They are
the neglected ones who have been ignored by politicians and bypassed
by the forces of economic modernization. Their world is confined to
the *latifundio* or commercial farm on which they work, the *minifundio,*
or subsistence farm, which they occupy, or the village in which they
reside. For them, effective political authority resides not in some distant capital but with landlords, village mayors, parish priests, and
local military commandants.

The Latin American peasant has not, however, always accepted his
subjugation by local elites passively. The region's history is filled with
peasant revolts, and violence is still common in the countryside. In
recent years dispersed protests have given way to organized campaigns to secure government intervention on the peasants' behalf.
Throughout the hemisphere governments have responded with diverse reforms aimed at redressing peasant grievances. Agrarian reforms have yielded impressive results in a few countries, most notably
Mexico, Cuba, Venezuela, Chile, and Peru. Nevertheless, most of the
rural poor survive at or just above the subsistence level because they
were either untouched by agrarian reform or given land but no capital to develop it. For many peasants agrarian reform has not lived up
to its promise; instead, it has become a false panacea used by urban
bureaucrats as an instrument for promoting large-scale commercial
farming rather than improving the welfare of the rural poor.

To understand why reform has benefited so few, we must look
more closely at the Latin American *campesino,* his political goals and
resources. By *campesinos* we mean the *mestizo,* Indian, and Negro subsistence farmers and laborers who populate rural Latin America.

Nearly all of them earn less than the average national per capita income and enjoy few opportunities for improving their condition. At the same time, they differ from each other in important ways. When grouped according to their means of employment, they fall into four distinct groups.

The first is the *colono,* who works as a laborer on the *latifundio* or as a sharecropper or tenant farmer. He has probably resided in the same region for generations and is bound to his employer by debts incurred over several years. Some *latifundistas* have taken their responsibilities as *patrones* seriously, protecting the *colono* and his family from catastrophe and providing him with a subsistence income in order to maintain the *latifundio* as an organic, self-sufficient community. Others have treated the *colono* harshly, ignoring his basic needs and abandoning him during hard times. As one might expect, *colonos* tend to be isolated from national politics by their physical separation from national capitals. When they vote in national elections, they usually are closely supervised by the *patrón.* As a group, they are hard to organize politically because of their dispersion throughout the countryside and their subordination to the *latifundista.* The latter can discourage *campesino* organizers by using the local police, his economic control over his workers, and his influence in local courts. It is not hard to understand why *campesino* movements have seldom survived without help from outside, for without public officials or party leaders to protect them from the reprisals of local elites, *campesino* organizers stand little chance of success.

A second type of *campesino* is the wage laborer. Many of the crops produced on Latin America's commercial farms are harvested by hand. This is true especially of cotton, coffee, sugarcane, fruits, and vegetables grown in areas with an abundance of labor. Many of those who work in the harvest are migrants who leave their villages and return at the end of the season. Some own their own land but must seek employment elsewhere because they cannot produce enough to meet the needs of their families. Others have become landless through population pressures or the loss of their land to creditors. They are the Mexican *braceros* who migrate legally and illegally to California and Texas, the coffee pickers who descend from highland villages in Guatemala or Colombia, or the cane cutters in northeast Brazil. Like migrants everywhere, they exist on the fringes of the political process and are seldom reached by government programs. They can ill-afford to become involved in political protests during the harvest season for fear of losing an entire year's livelihood. In the off-season they return to their villages and blend back into the local population out of reach of labor organizers.

The plantation worker is a third type of *campesino*. Like the *colono* he is bound to one place year-round, but like the migrant he works on commercial establishments rather than traditional estates. The plantation worker has more in common with the factory worker than he does with most of his fellow *campesinos,* for he works in a highly organized setting in which modern technology is applied to the production of commodities for export. In some instances, his employers are foreign corporations like the banana companies of Central America and Colombia, though he is just as likely to work for domestic firms or individual families. The relative ease of organizing plantation workers explains in part why the number of plantation unions has increased in recent times. Unlike most other *campesinos,* plantation laborers work in close proximity, communicate regularly, and develop skills that are needed by their employers. Thus, if the leadership is available, they are quite organizable, much like factory workers. To succeed, however, they must overcome the resistance of plantation owners, who are often backed by sympathetic government officials.

Not all *campesinos* work on *latifundios,* plantations, or commercial farms; many own land or occupy small plots to which they have no legal claim. The *campesino* farmer employs only the most primitive technologies and farms primarily for his own subsistence, selling a small surplus in local markets. He takes few risks with new seeds or fertilizers, most of which he cannot secure because of his poverty and lack of access to short-term credit. If he wants to ship his small surplus to distant markets, he must rely on private traders, who easily take advantage of his isolation and dependent status. The subsistence farmer confronts the agrarian reformer with one of his most difficult dilemmas. If he is given more land he may use it inefficiently because of his low level of technology; yet if agrarian reform is to lead to higher production, something must be done to increase the efficiency of such units. Usually the only alternatives considered are government financing of small farm modernization, which is quite costly, or farm reorganization into more efficient cooperative, communal, or state-run units to maximize the use of modern technology, a solution often resisted by the very independent *campesino.*

What do *campesinos* want from politics? Few questions are more difficult to answer because *campesinos* have seldom been asked what they want, and when the question has been raised, others, notably landed elites, reformers, and revolutionaries, have answered for them. Moreover, as we have seen, *campesinos* are a very diverse group, separated by economic interest, region, and ethnicity, and seldom speak with a single voice. Nevertheless, even though they are not united by a single set of policy demands, we can identify from recent historical experience the concerns their leaders have expressed in national political forums and the grievances that have often given rise to spontaneous protests by the *campesinos* themselves.

Campesinos want assistance in improving their life chances and the welfare of their families on their own terms. How that is to be done is not always clear. Some *campesinos* demand greater protection against exploitation by landlords and employers; some want land of their own; and still others ask only for easier access to credit, water, and markets. With only a few exceptions, their concerns are personal, local, and specific, rather than general and self-consciously ideological. *Campesinos* are not as opposed to innovation or the expansion of their production as is often assumed. If they appear to be risk-averting, it is because they can ill-afford to take chances when their annual crop is all that stands between their families and starvation. New technologies require expenditures they can seldom afford, especially if they lack access to credit. Only the state, through its supply of subsidized technology and redistribution of land, can break the vicious circle in which most *campesinos* find themselves. Thus, even though past experience has taught the rural poor that government is unwilling or ill-equipped to meet their needs, it remains the only source of their salvation. Understandably, however, they continue to be suspicious of grand promises, skeptical about the possibility of progress, and alert to the betrayal of their cause. But their apparent passivity should not be mistaken for apathy in the face of a desperate situation, for, like other players in the game, *campesinos* want a larger share of the nation's wealth. If they lack anything, it is confidence in their ability to secure that share.

The political strength of *campesinos* is yet to be tested in most Latin American countries. Their principal resource is their immense size as a social group, a resource they have seldom been permitted to use. Because they are a majority in most countries, *campesinos* would appear to have the most to gain from elections and democratic processes. Yet, although many of them dutifully march to the polls, their votes are usually the exclusive property of their employers or local elites. Only where modern political parties have recruited the peasantry into constituency organizations, as in Venezuela and Mexico, has their participation had a serious impact on electoral outcomes. Where electoral influence is denied them, *campesinos* can resort to violent attacks on their oppressors. But armed revolts are risky, especially against well-entrenched rural elites and their allies in local law-enforcement agencies. Nevertheless, occasionally rural revolts have been successful, as they were in Mexico in 1910 and Bolivia in 1952.

Given their limited influence in elections and the high risks of violent protests, how can *campesinos* influence national policy? To have any impact at all, they must overcome several obstacles. One is the obstacle of organization. It is not especially difficult to organize wealthy landowners, businessmen, or labor union members into effective political action groups. They are usually united by physical proximity, an agreement on basic issues, and their ability to support a permanent staff. *Campesinos,* in contrast, are separated physically, often do not perceive their common interests, and cannot finance their own organizations. Another is the communications obstacle. *Campesinos* are separated not only by physical distance but also by ethnicity and regionalism, especially in countries with large indigenous populations. As a result, issues and solutions that satisfy one group of *campesinos* may be inappropriate to the needs of others. The *campesino*'s organizational difficulties are aggravated by the fact that his enemies exploit his weaknesses in order to limit his success. It has been by taking advantage of the *campesino*'s isolation, fear, and inability to communicate over large distances that the landowner and his allies have until recently so successfully prevented the development of viable peasant organizations.

Obstacles to peasant organization and vulnerability to landowners' divide-and-conquer strategies have made the *campesino* more dependent on help from outside, especially from the state, than any of the other players in the Latin American game. As they did with the labor movement in the 1930s and 1940s, many ambitious aspirants for public office began reaching out to the *campesinos* during the postwar years, offering agrarian reforms and other measures in exchange for political support. Central to their political strategy was the mobilization of *campesinos* into constituent organizations that could deliver the peasant vote. Modeling their tactics after the highly successful organization of the Mexican peasantry by President Lázaro Cárdenas in the 1930s, reform parties throughout Latin America have tried to break the monopoly of local elites over peasant voters and use the latter to defeat their opponents at the polls. Peasants have been organized into local and regional groups much like urban labor unions and represented in national party councils and the legislature by leaders they have chosen at their national conventions. Their goals have been reformist rather than revolutionary, and in countries like Venezuela, Chile, and Mexico they have worked within the system rather than against it. In Venezuela, for example, thousands of peasants were organized by the Acción Democrática party in the early 1940s and were rewarded with an agrarian reform program after the party took office in 1948. After the military overthrew the Acción Democrática government, its peasant organizations survived clandestinely to re-emerge after the party was restored to power in 1959. The ability of Acción Democrática to win all but one presidential election during the following decade and a half is attributable in part to the peasant support it retained throughout the period.

Despite many successes, the kind of reformist agrarianism prac-ticed in Venezuela, Chile, and Mexico is not without serious problems from the *campesino*'s point of view. Democratic governments, which are vulnerable to countervailing pressures, have not always fulfilled their promises to their rural supporters. Government fears of retalia-tion by the rural elite or the military, as well as the desire to increase productivity by encouraging commercial rather than peasant farms, have seriously constrained the fulfillment of commitments to the rural poor. Another obstacle has been the frequent cooptation of *campesino* leaders by governments that exploit their desire for fame and fortune. In short, even though reformist agrarianism opens the policy-making process to *campesino* representatives and meets some of their demands for rural reform, it is vulnerable to countervailing pressures that often leave the peasants short.

Campesinos need not follow the peaceful path of reformist agrarian-ism. They can choose instead the more direct route of violent revolt, taking matters into their own hands and seizing land in order to force public authorities to meet their demands. The campaign of Emiliano Zapata during the Mexican Revolution is a classic example of such a strategy. Zapata was revolutionary only in the sense that he wanted to change the rural status quo. His was not a utopian vision of a new soci-ety, but a simple desire to regain for his village the land that it had held in the past and that had been taken away by local sugar barons with the government's encouragement. It was a struggle of armed peasants against tyrannical landlords who had destroyed their way of life. But Zapata's is not the only example of revolutionary agrarian-ism. In Cuba the rural cause was taken up by Fidel Castro's insurrec-tionists. Theirs was not a peasant revolt, but the campaign of urban-bred ideologues who acted in the name of the peasantry as well as other members of the masses. Once their revolt had succeeded, peas-ants were among the first beneficiaries of their revolutionary pro-gram.

Despite these successes – or perhaps because of them – the cause of rural revolution has been treated harshly by the region's governments and their military defenders in recent years. Nevertheless, radical peasant leaders continue to struggle. Those who have chosen guerrilla warfare as their mode of attack have been plagued by many problems, not the least of which is the reluctance of the suspicious *campesino* to support their cause, either directly by joining in the military struggle or indirectly by not betraying them to authorities. The challenge laid down by the guerrilla confronts the *campesino* with a more difficult choice than might first appear: If he does not support the revolutionary, his condition will not likely change, but if he does support him, he risks retaliation from landowners and local police and has no assurance that the results of the revolution, should it succeed, will be to his liking. This is why many revolutionaries have discovered to their disappointment that the exploited and potentially explosive peasant is often a reluctant participant in their struggle.

Finally, what about the peasants and the rules of the political game? As the least active and least encouraged participant in the conventional game, they have seldom been given the opportunity to shape the rules by which it is played. Moreover, regardless of the type of political system in which they live, they still find themselves on the receiving end of decisions made by others. In traditional autocracies, for example, they are dominated by local landlords and law-enforcement agents; in reformist democracies, a handful of peasant leaders and government bureaucrats usually manipulates them. And in revolutionary societies party leaders and government agents reorganize their lives for them. Their choice, it seems, is among being ignored, represented by a few well-intentioned reformers, or transformed by an elite that claims to act in accord with their objective interests.

The weakness of *campesinos* as players in the political game has forced them to deal with a difficult dilemma. Without strong allies among those in political authority, they have little chance of affecting the course of rural policy. Yet, if they do secure an alliance with other players, they risk being absorbed and used by their new allies. The fact that most leaders of peasant movements have been small-town professionals or urban functionaries with very weak loyalties to their rural constituents makes their cooptation even more likely. Moreover, internal conflicts are as common to peasant movements as they are to the interest groups of the rich, perhaps even more so, and without unity the peasant movement becomes even more vulnerable to its exploitation by ambitious politicians. Whichever path they choose, the *campesinos* will end up with less than optimal results.

The economic development of Latin America depends on the progress made in the rural sector in the years ahead. The region's rural poor are too numerous and too much of a drain on the economy to be ignored. Although most governments in Latin America recognize this fact, they are still plagued by conflicts over what should be done to bring the rural poor into the economic and political mainstream. Our analyses of Latin American politics and development policy in Part II will focus on these conflicts and the contributions of peasants and other players to their resolution.

POLITICAL PARTIES

At first glance political parties appear to be similar to other players, for they too have interests they seek to realize through the political process. On closer inspection, however, we discover some important differences. For one thing, political parties contest elections; most other players do not. They also act as aggregators of diverse interests who in exchange for votes or other expressions of support, use the resources of the state to reward or protect the interests they represent. Together these two attributes often place political parties at the center of the political game, where they act as brokers in the competition for influence over public policy.

When we study the politics of another country we usually begin with its political parties. Parties have come to be so closely associated with modern politics that we take them for granted. We expect to find them contesting elections, setting policy, or managing the affairs of state. However, if we carefully examine the world's nations, especially those outside Western Europe and Anglo-America, we discover that political parties are not always what we expect them to be and do not perform the functions we habitually assign them. For example, the first thing the student of Latin American parties learns is the uncertainty of elections throughout the region. Elections are sometimes rigged or otherwise controlled by elites or overturned by military coups and insurrections. Election is only one of many methods of gaining public office. Therefore, the winning of a national election does not guarantee that the victorious party will complete its term or even take office on schedule. To survive under such uncertain conditions, parties must not only contest elections but also expend much effort devising ways to resist assorted attempts to depose them.

The best insurance against the overthrow of a party government is the creation of a durable consensus in support of the electoral rules of the game. This, of course, is also very difficult to achieve. A second survival strategy, often employed when a consensus on democratic rules is unattainable, is to become a conspirator in the nonelectoral game, using the military and other means to intimidate and defeat opponents. A third possibility is the creation of a single-party regime that absorbs or destroys its opponents and uses elections only for ritualistic purposes. To carry out the first strategy, political parties must concentrate on making liberal democracy acceptable to all citizens, leading by example and educating the public to its benefits. Successes, however, have been few, limited primarily to Chile and Uruguay before 1973, and Costa Rica and Venezuela at the present time. The behavior of such parties is not unlike that observed in electoral democracies elsewhere. The behavior of parties that choose the second or third route to self-preservation is different and therefore merits closer examination.

First, the conspiratorial route. The goal of some political parties is winning and holding public office at any cost. They may be motivated by fear of being persecuted or destroyed by their opponents should the latter become the ruling party. Or they may only want to retain the spoils of politics for themselves. Whatever their motives, their conspiracies to retain control over the government weaken the democratic process by encouraging players to abuse democratic rules in order to dislodge the incumbent conspirators. To survive under such conditions a political party has to do more than carry out its normal electoral activities. In addition to the conventional tasks of recruitment, campaigning, and legislating, party leaders expend much of their effort conspiring with the military and important civilian groups against one another. Instead of concentrating on bargaining with their opponents over legislation, they devote their energies to undermining the opposition and reducing its ability to retaliate. Partisanship becomes intense and distrust common. As a result, political parties that under normal circumstances might have become the foundation for stable democracy transform themselves into the agents of conflict and dissension.

There remains the single-party route. Rather than live with the uncertainty that comes from constant conspiring to retain power, a party can try to institutionalize its rule. The creation of a one-party regime is no easy task, as many Latin American leaders who have tried and failed have discovered. Crucial to success, it seems, is the involvement of the military in the new ruling elite. In fact, one thing the contemporary one-party regimes of Mexico and Cuba have in common is their reliance on the military during their formation. In Mexico, the revolutionary generals who triumphed eventually created an official party and then gradually reduced the military's role in it; in Cuba, Castro replaced the traditional military with his own revolutionary armed forces and used them to govern until the Communist party could take over. In each case political parties did much more than act as electoral vehicles. In fact, their purpose has not been to contest elections, but rather to govern, using elections as one of many tools for legitimizing their mandate. Equally important to political parties organized to rule rather than contest elections is their control over political participation and their mobilization of resources to accomplish government objectives. Citizens are included in the party not as a means of gaining their votes but to secure their conformity with the decisions of party leaders. For them, the party is not an arena for debate but a means for eliminating conflicts through control over all social groups that might precipitate it.

The first lesson to be learned about Latin American parties, then, is that regardless of how familiar their labels or professed ideologies may be, we must not assume that they behave according to norms established in other societies. At the same time, however, we cannot write them off as abnormal entities that never fulfill the functions associated with parties elsewhere. As is true of the rules of the game themselves, we find the familiar coexisting with the unfamiliar, one set of norms in competition with others. Here too we must first examine each case in order to establish the role assumed by political parties and then compare different cases in search of dominant patterns of party conduct.

Having reviewed some of the different roles of parties, we can now turn to the structure of Latin American party systems. The term "party system" refers to the number of parties and the degree of competition among them. We usually speak of one-party systems, two-party systems, and multiparty systems composed of three or more parties. Within the last two categories different degrees of competition are present; in some countries several parties are close in their popular vote and exchange office frequently; in others, one or two parties dominate. Party systems in Latin America are especially fascinating because within the region one discovers examples of nearly every kind of party system. For instance, at various times during the postwar period, you could find two-party systems in Colombia, Uruguay, and Honduras; multiparty systems in Argentina, Chile, Costa Rica, Venezuela, Brazil, Panama, and Ecuador; and one-party systems in Mexico, Cuba, and El Salvador.

In many ways Latin America provides one of the largest laboratories in the world for the analysis and comparison of party systems. Nevertheless, those who have studied party behavior in the region have also had to face many difficulties. Latin American party systems may be varied, but with only a few exceptions, they have been of short duration. In contrast to the Anglo-American democracies or even the countries of Western Europe, many Latin American party systems have not survived for more than a decade or two. The principal exceptions are the one-party systems like Mexico's, where party competition is nonexistent, and democracies like Chile's and Uruguay's, whose impressive twentieth-century record of party government was abruptly halted by military coups in the early 1970s. Yet, despite the recent decline in competitive party systems, there is still much to be learned about the role of political parties in the recent political development of Latin America. Still to be satisfactorily explained, for example, is why the Chilean and Uruguayan party systems lasted as long as they did and why party competition survives today in Costa Rica and Venezuela but almost nowhere else in the region.

Before we can answer these questions, we must become better acquainted with the kinds of political parties that have played the Latin American political game in recent years. There are many ways of classifying and comparing political parties. One can focus on professed ideology, organization, leadership, bases of support, or election strategy, among other things. In studying Latin American parties it is also important to examine them within their historical contexts. Different kinds of parties have arisen in response to different societal needs and political opportunities: Some have come and gone; others have endured and still struggle to prevail. The story of the evolution of the region's political parties is also the story of the region's political development, for parties often arose at critical turning points in history, reshaping politics as they did.

The first organizations to call themselves political parties were little more than cliques drawn from the oligarchy, which contested public office during the last half of the nineteenth century. They differed not so much over who should rule – they all believed in elite rule – but over what policies the government should follow. Those who called themselves Conservatives were drawn primarily from the ranks of landowners and the clergy and wanted government to do little more than preserve the prevailing hierarchical social and economic structures. Their opponents, usually termed Liberals, were more ambitious, desiring to use government to promote commercial agriculture and commodity exports through the redistribution of Church and Indian lands to ambitious rural entrepreneurs. Election contests between Conservatives and Liberals were exclusive affairs, usually involving less than 10 percent of the adult population and frequently rigged by the party in power.

In a few countries, such as Colombia and Honduras, Liberal and Conservative parties forged deep and lasting loyalties that have assured their survival to this day, but in most of the region their monopoly was gradually broken by the rise of new parties at the turn of the century. As long as party politics was dominated by the elite, the new generation of immigrants, urban businessmen, professionals, and small commercial farmers that emerged in the larger Latin American countries between 1900 and 1920 had little hope of gaining a voice in domestic politics. No matter how hard they might try to affect government decisions, they were usually rebuffed by the leaders of traditional parties, who were unsympathetic to their pleas. Their only recourse was to create political parties of their own and use them to agitate for electoral reforms that would give them an opportunity to compete with the established parties. In several countries these middle-sector groups succeeded not only in securing the coveted reforms but also in gaining public office. Calling themselves Radicals in Chile and Argentina and by other names elsewhere, they used urban constituency organizations and the personal popularity of their leaders to evict traditional elite parties and fill the public payrolls with their supporters while implementing some modest educational and urban reforms.

The 1929 depression was a severe blow to the middle-sector parties, for it revealed their inability to solve the problems raised by world economic crises. They were attacked by conservatives and, in a few cases, evicted by the military. After World War II they were forced to compete for popular support with new political movements that had been unleashed by the depression and its aftermath. The most important of these were the Populist movements that suddenly appeared in Argentina and Brazil.

The Populists were ambitious and skillful civilian and military political opportunists who went a step further than the Radicals by mobilizing into political action the urban working class, which had suffered great deprivation during the depression. Most prominent among the populist leaders were Juan Perón in Argentina and Getulio Vargas in Brazil, two presidents whom we will examine and compare in some detail in Chapter 6.

The Populists took advantage of the rapid industrialization of their countries during the 1930s and 1940s and the rising aspirations of a growing urban proletariat as well as the latter's neglect and persecution by Radicals, Liberals, and Conservatives. Their party organizations were never very sophisticated; they relied more on the personal magnetism of leaders and the skills of a handful of organizers than on strong constituency units. Once in office, the Populists used their power not only to divide the spoils among their supporters but also to assist native entrepreneurs and promote industrialization.

The Populists were never accepted by most intellectuals and professionals, who resented their demagoguery and their use of strong-arm methods. Consequently, at the same time populism was on the rise, other anti–status quo politicians were busy creating the nucleus of mass-based democratic reform parties. Their goal was to make democracy work by combining the democratic ideals of the Radicals with the mass appeal of the Populists and the sophisticated party organization developed by Socialists and Social Democrats in Europe. They sought to involve not just the middle sectors, as did the Radicals, but also laborers and *campesinos*. The two essential ingredients in their campaign were a sophisticated national organization that penetrated to the grass-roots level and the mobilization of rural voters through the use of peasant organizations linked to their political party. They also offered their countrymen a commitment to the reform of traditional economic institutions and to development planning. Attempts to create democratic reform parties were made in most Latin American countries during the 1940s and 1950s, but they were successful in only a few – those like Chile, Venezuela, and Costa Rica where populism had never gained a foothold and where peasants were physically accessible to party organizers.

There are essentially two types of reform parties, one secular and the other theological. The origins of the first can be traced to the APRISTA party organized by Peruvian Raúl Haya de la Torre and dissident students in the 1930s, who were inspired by reformist Peruvian philosophers and modern socialism. The APRISTAs have been persecuted throughout most of their history and never allowed to rule Peru except in coalition with more conservative parties. The Acción Democrática party of Venezuela was more successful, however, governing briefly in the late 1940s and then for all but one presidential term since 1958. Similarly, the National Liberation party of Costa Rica has held the presidency on four occasions since its creation in 1948. The success of such parties in the late 1950s led many observers to conclude at the time that Latin Americans had finally found the vehicle needed to build democracy throughout the region. Their hopes proved unfounded, however, and democratic government did not spread beyond a handful of countries after 1960.

The second type of democratic reform party is labeled theological because of its identification with Christian democracy, a movement that began in Europe and later spread to other Catholic countries.

Inspired by the political thought of French philosopher Jacques Maritain, the Christian Democrats aspire to a democratic society that is neither socialist nor capitalist but that combines the former's belief in the common good and the latter's respect for the individual. Though not formally tied to the Roman Catholic Church, the party draws heavily on modern Catholic philosophy and the more progressive papal encyclicals for its ideology. Initially quite moderate in their goals and political techniques, the Christian Democrats gradually adopted many of the attributes of their competitors in the secular reform parties, expanding their organization to include laborers and peasants and preaching the doctrine of agrarian reform and state planning. Like the secular reformers, they created parties throughout Latin America; however, they have been successful only in Chile, where they governed in the mid-1960s, and Venezuela, where they held the presidency for one term in the early 1970s. They too were regarded as a major vehicle of democratic rule and reform policy, but with the exception of the two countries mentioned, they have not fulfilled their promise.

Last but not least are the revolutionary parties. Revolutionary movements have received much attention of late, but they are certainly not new to the region. There have been essentially two types of revolutionary parties in Latin America, one inspired by Marxist thought and the other non-Marxist. Among the first are several Socialist and all Communist parties. Socialists first organized parties in the late nineteenth century, primarily under the direction of European immigrants. After the Russian Revolution of 1917 Communist parties were also formed, some of them merging with the Socialists and others becoming rivals because of the Socialists' refusal to accept Soviet leadership of the international revolutionary movement. Thus, at the same time the Radicals were organizing the emerging urban sectors, small Socialist and Communist parties, led by intellectuals and labor leaders, were trying to build a following among the working class. Proletarian revolution and social justice were their causes; strikes, demonstrations, and the education of the masses their weapons. Seldom, however, did they speak with a single voice, for doctrinal disputes and personal rivalries bred divisive factionalism within their ranks. Throughout the 1930s and 1940s most remained marginal to their nations' politics, often being forced underground or into exile by hostile governments. Moreover, they had to compete with populists in the 1940s and democratic reformers in the 1950s and 1960s for the support of the proletariat and frequently fared poorly against both movements' more nativist appeal and ability to deliver on promises of social legislation. There have been exceptions, the most notable being Chile, where Marxist parties secured labor support in the 1920s, were admitted to Popular Front governments in the 1930s, and captured the presidency under Salvador Allende in 1970.

As analysts, we are fortunate that the Latin American laboratory of political experience offers two opportunities to examine the performance of Marxist parties in power. In Communist Cuba we have almost two decades of societal reconstruction and a notable example of how a Marxist society can be raised on a Latin American foundation. In Allende's ill-fated Popular Unity regime in Chile we have a much briefer example of Marxist rule, but one whose political strategy differs sharply from Castro's, providing an opportunity to study different routes to similar economic and social objectives. We will compare these two regimes in some detail in Chapters 9 and 10.

The principal non-Marxist revolutionary party is the Institutional Revolutionary party (PRI) of Mexico. Some might dispute the right of the ruling party of Mexico to the title "revolutionary." Critics claim it has been revolutionary in name only, interested more in maintaining political control over the Mexican electorate and in creating a mixed capitalist economy than in social and economic revolution. On the other hand, the party's defenders point out that during its first sixty years the revolutionary government has gone farther toward the elimination of the *latifundio,* the Church, and foreign investors than any other Latin American government prior to the Cuban Revolution. It also implemented significant agrarian reforms long before other governments began considering the issue. We cannot answer the question of how revolutionary the PRI is without examining its political and economic performance to date. By comparing its record with those of Allende's Chile and Castro's Cuba in Chapters 9 and 10, we shall learn not only about Mexico but also about the varieties of revolutionary experience in Latin America.

Finally, it is obvious that we have omitted some parties from this brief introduction. Recent Latin American history is littered, for example, with transitory, personalistic parties. Loyalty to a single leader rather than to a platform holds such parties together. Many rise and fall with a single election, beginning as splinter groups in existing parties or starting from scratch and then withering once their candidates are defeated. Of course, personalism is a factor in nearly all parties from the most conservative to the revolutionary, but some parties are organized to survive the loss of a leader, whereas those we have labeled personalist are not. During the nineteenth and early twentieth centuries one could also find regional parties in Latin America. Their purpose was not to capture the presidency, but to represent a regional point of view in legislatures and force conservative and liberal governments to accept their demands for local autonomy. There have also been Fascist parties of one kind or another. Modeled after the Fascist movements that arose after the depression in Italy, Spain, and Germany, they remained on the fringes of national politics in most countries, though they did attain some recognition in Brazil and Chile and influenced policies and attitudes in wartime Argentina.

The analysis of Latin American party systems would be much simpler if all countries conformed to the history of party development outlined above. But they do not. Instead, we find several different patterns throughout the region. Some approximate the course of gradual evolution described above; in others change has been more dramatic and results quite different, such as in the one-party systems of Mexico and Cuba. But regardless of the form each party system takes, we must still ask how a country's political parties affect the outcome of the political game. Parties too are players, whose influence on public officials varies with their political resources, skills, and determination. A party supports rules that help its cause and opposes those that do not. A party that enjoys widespread support obviously has more to gain from elections than does a less popular party. Conversely, a party that stands no chance of winning an election might gain more from a military coup or insurrection than from an election. But even a party that commands the support of a majority of the electorate may from time to time resort to nonelectoral means to remove a tyrannical government, to block threats from militant opponents, or to create some kind of populist autocracy.

The decade of the 1970s has become a critical time for political parties in Latin America. They are criticized by revolutionaries for being corrupt, conservative, and an obstacle to economic and social reform, and by conservatives as demagogic, narrow-minded, and incapable of creating orderly government and achieving steady economic progress. But are political parties really anachronisms, remnants of the liberal democratic state that is in retreat throughout the region? Only by examining their performance and the challenges they face can we begin to answer this important question.

OTHER PLAYERS

By now you should be familiar with the principal players in the Latin American political game. There are, to be sure, others we could have

included in this introductory survey. There is, for example, the
Roman Catholic Church, an institution that has played a prominent
role in the region's public life since colonial times. The economic and
political power of the Church has always been a subject of controversy
in Latin America. In the late nineteenth century the Church was
deprived of much of its wealth by political liberals who were determined to establish the supremacy of secular authority. As a result, its
political power has been on the decline throughout the twentieth century. Nevertheless, its influence on Latin American life remains significant, especially at the parish level, where the clergy affect popular
attitudes toward the family, the social order, and alien ideologies.
Despite the efforts of Church leaders to give the appearance of unity,
the Church ceased to be a monolith many years ago. The clergy
frequently disagree on social and economic issues as well as on theological matters. Priests today can be found among the supporters of a
wide variety of political ideologies; many, including the foreign
priests who form a large segment of the clergy, have dedicated themselves to the organization of the poor for economic action and the
promotion of radical social reform. Others hold fast to their conservative views of the social order. Ironically, at a time when the power of
the Church as an institution is in decline, the direct involvement of
the clergy in politics is increasing as individual priests become more
and more involved in ideological debates and social action.

Also deserving brief mention are university students. Throughout
the twentieth century, Latin American universities have been centers
of political activity, serving as testing grounds for political ideologies
and movements as well as schools where such political leaders as the
democratic reformers of Venezuela and Cuba's Fidel Castro were
trained in the art of political combat. But the university has been
more than a laboratory for political experimentation; students have
also been involved directly in the national political game, leading public protests against political authorities and mobilizing popular support for various causes. It is not uncommon to discover that the resignation or overthrow of a president was triggered by student protests,
which, after being violently suppressed by the government, touched
off a popular rebellion or provoked military intervention. In recent
times student involvement in national politics has been on the decline,
primarily because of the rise of military authoritarian governments
that have purged universities of politics and subjected students to
stern discipline. Nevertheless, one should not mistake temporary quiescence for the elimination of students from the game. They will undoubtedly remain critics of those who hold political power and pro-

moters of change even if they cannot confront authorities directly with their demands.

Intellectuals also deserve some comment. Although they seldom form a coherent group, they nevertheless influence the outcomes of the political game. They are the manipulators of symbols employed to undermine as well as bolster political authorities. Latin American intellectuals enjoy immense prestige in their societies and have been called upon repeatedly to serve as spokesmen for political causes. They have also influenced politics in more indirect ways, as publicists of political movements, adapters of imported ideologies, and creators of indigenous political philosophies. They have been the bane of presidents with their incessant criticism and questioning of government competence and legitimacy. Some presidents have tolerated their criticism, but many have not. As a result, intellectuals have been forced repeatedly to flee their countries to escape persecution by political authorities. In few eras has official antiintellectualism been greater than in the current one, when many political leaders have sacrificed the free expression of ideas in exchange for political order and intellectual orthodoxy.

Now that you have met many of the major and minor players in the Latin American game, you are ready to examine their varied behaviors in several different political settings. Before we turn to the analysis of political games in Part II, however, another component of the game must be introduced.

FURTHER READING

Middle sectors

Cardoso, Fernando Henrique. "The Industrial Elite," in Seymour Martin Lipset and Aldo Solari, eds., *Elites in Latin America*. New York: Oxford University Press, 1968, pp. 94–114.

Gillin, John P. "The Middle Segments and Their Values," in Lyman Bryson, ed., *Social Change in Latin America Today*. New York: Random House (Vintage Books), 1960, pp. 28–46.

Johnson, John. *Political Change in Latin America: The Emergence of the Middle Sectors*. Stanford: Stanford University Press, 1958.

Veliz, Claudio. "Introduction," in Claudio Veliz, ed., *Obstacles to Change in Latin America*. London: Oxford University Press, 1965, pp. 1–8.

Wagley, Charles. "The Dilemma of the Latin American Middle Class," in Charles Wagley, *The Latin American Tradition*. New York: Columbia University Press, 1968, pp. 194–212.

The masses: organized labor

Alba, Victor. *Politics and the Labor Movement in Latin America.* Stanford: Stanford University Press, 1968.

Alexander, Robert. *Labor Relations in Argentina, Brazil and Chile.* New York: McGraw-Hill, 1962.

Organized Labor in Latin America. New York: Free Press, 1965.

Baily, Samuel L. *Labor, Nationalism and Politics in Argentina.* New Brunswick, N.J.: Rutgers University Press, 1967.

Davis, Stanley M., and Louis Wolf Goodman, eds. *Workers and Managers in Latin America.* Lexington, Mass.: Heath, 1972.

Landsberger, Henry A. "The Labor Elite: Is It Revolutionary," in Seymour Martin Lipset and Aldo Solari, eds., *Elites in Latin America.* New York: Oxford University Press, 1966, pp. 256–300.

Payne, James L. *Labor and Politics in Peru: The System of Political Bargaining.* New Haven: Yale University Press, 1965.

Urrutia Montoya, Miguel. *The Development of the Colombian Labor Movement.* New Haven: Yale University Press, 1967.

Zeitlin, Maurice. *Revolutionary Politics and the Cuban Working Class.* Princeton: Princeton University Press, 1967.

The masses: peasants

Fals-Borda, Orlando. *Peasant Society in the Colombian Andes.* Gainesville: University of Florida Press, 1957.

Feder, Ernst. *The Rape of the Peasantry: Latin America's Landholding System.* Garden City, N.Y.: Doubleday, 1971.

Handelman, Howard. *Struggle in the Andes: Peasant Political Mobilization in Peru.* Austin: University of Texas Press, 1974.

Huizer, Gerrit. *The Revolutionary Potential of Peasants in Latin America.* Lexington, Mass.: Heath, 1972.

Landsberger, Henry A., ed. *Latin American Peasant Movements.* Ithaca, N.Y.: Cornell University Press, 1969.

Rural Protest: Peasant Movements and Social Change. New York: Macmillan, 1974.

Petras, James, and Robert LaPorte. *Cultivating Revolution: The United States and Agrarian Reform in Latin America.* New York: Random House, 1971.

Powell, John Duncan. *Political Mobilization of the Venezuelan Peasant.* Cambridge, Mass.: Harvard University Press, 1971.

Stavenhagen, Rodolfo, ed. *Agrarian Problems and Peasant Movements in Latin America.* Garden City, N.Y.: Doubleday, 1970.

Wolf, Eric R. *Sons of the Shaking Earth.* Chicago: University of Chicago Press, 1959.

Peasant Wars in the Twentieth Century. New York: Harper & Row, 1969.

Womack, John. *Zapata and the Mexican Revolution.* New York: Knopf, 1969.

Political parties

Bernard, Jean Pierre, Silas Cerqueira, Hugo Neira, Helene Graillot, Leslie F. Manigat, and Pierre Gilhodes. *Guide to the Political Parties of South America.* Baltimore: Penguin, 1973.

Gott, Richard. *Guerilla Movements in Latin America.* Garden City, N.Y.: Doubleday, 1971.

Kohl, James, and John Litt. *Urban Guerrilla Warfare in Latin America.* Cambridge, Mass.: MIT Press, 1974.

Martz, John. "Dilemmas in the Study of Latin American Political Parties." *Journal of Politics* 26(3):509–531, August 1964.

"Political Parties in Colombia and Venezuela: Contrasts in Substance and Style." *Western Political Quarterly* 18(2):318–33, June 1965.

Acción Democrática: Evolution of a Modern Political Party in Venezuela. Princeton: Princeton University Press, 1966.

McDonald, Ronald. *Party Systems and Elections in Latin America.* Chicago: Markham, 1971.

Poppino, Rollie. *International Communism in Latin America: A History of the Movement, 1917–1963.* New York: Free Press, 1964.

Ranis, Peter. "A Two-Dimensional Typology of Latin American Parties." *Journal of Politics* 30(2):798–832, August 1968.

Ratliff, William E. *Castroism and Communism in Latin America, 1959–1976: The Varieties of Marxist-Leninist Experience.* Washington, D.C.: American Enterprise Institute, 1976.

Scott, Robert. "Political Parties and Policy-Making in Latin America," in Joseph LaPalombara and Myron Weiner, eds. *Political Parties and Political Development.* Princeton: Princeton University Press, 1966, pp. 331–68.

Williams, Edward J. *Latin American Christian Democratic Parties.* Knoxville: University of Tennessee Press, 1976.

5. Economic strategy and development policy

Thus far we have focused primarily on politics as a process for gaining public office and influencing the decisions of public officials. But something more than the struggle for political power and influence is at stake in the political game. The game also involves the use of power to allocate society's scarce resources. Through such allocations by governments the game's winners and losers are determined. To understand the game in its entirety, we must examine what government does as well as who occupies public office and how they got there.

One of the principal goals of contemporary Latin American leaders is the promotion of economic growth and development. No longer is the question whether development is desired, but rather how it can be achieved. Decisions have to be made about how society's resources will be allocated and how the nation's economic product will be distributed among its citizens. Few issues have been more central to the playing of the political game than these. It is, therefore, appropriate that in our examination of the consequences of Latin America's political games we focus on economic development policies. We can begin our investigation with economic strategies and their use by players to guide the selection of government policies.

The pursuit of political power is seldom an end in itself. It is usually a means to an end. With the acquisition of public office comes the opportunity to shape a country's economic and social life. Governmental power can be used to maintain the status quo or to transform social relations. It may be applied with great skill or used as a blunt instrument. But it is used, one way or another, by political leaders who have sought public office not just for the prestige it gives them but also because they want to decide the fate of others. They make laws and select policies that distribute public resources and regulate private conduct. Of particular interest to the student of politics is how they choose among the many different ways of dealing with the problems they face.

Undoubtedly, their decisions are heavily influenced by the need to respond to the demands of constituents or the pressures exerted by powerful domestic and foreign players. But decisions are also shaped by ideas, such as the ideologies and economic theories that public officials and their advisors bring with them to their government posts. These are the filters authorities employ to help them assess the problems they face and choose among the many solutions available. These ideas may be drawn from general theory, the experiences of other countries, the advice of international agencies, or the previous training and experience of the officials themselves. When applied to a concrete situation, they yield a strategy of economic action that helps in the important task of allocating a society's scarce resources.

The idea of economic strategy and its use should be familiar to you, for it played an important role in the narrative of the fictional president described in Chapter 1. A review of that chapter reveals at least three distinct strategies that were followed in his country. One was employed between Independence and the 1929 depression, a second was tried after the depression, and a third was proposed by our fictional leader. During the late nineteenth century, it will be recalled, policy makers were guided by a belief that Latin American economic progress depended on the ability to export primary products like coffee, cotton, and minerals to the industrial countries. The private sector, both domestic and foreign, was responsible for the region's development; the state was confined to the promotion of foreign trade and the maintenance of economic and political order. The strategy yielded rich dividends for exporters, commercial farmers, and foreign investors, but it could not withstand the devastating effects of the 1929 world depression. In its place there arose the doctrine of industrialization, which sought to reduce the region's dependence on commodity exports. But instead of reorganizing the region's agricultural economies, the new strategy merely added industry to the traditional order, leaving many development problems unsolved. Finally, in the 1960s a group of democratic reformers, led by our fictional president, proposed a third strategy, which recommended fundamental reforms in the rural sector, state ownership of essential industries, and central development planning.

By now it should be apparent what we mean by "economic strategy." It is a set of ideas about economic and social development that guides the policy choices of public authorities. The word "guide" is used deliberately, for economic strategies do not determine policy choices, only guide them. The distinction is important. Economic strategies orient players and authorities in the pursuit of solutions to development problems. We do not study them to find out exactly what a government will do, for many other conditions, such as constituency pressures or unanticipated economic events, also influence policy decisions. Study of economic strategies helps us understand how political leaders assess the development problems they face and decide among competing solutions. It also enables us to compare the different ways separate countries deal with common problems because it directs our attention to the obvious similarities and differences in their approaches to economic development. Finally, economic strategies serve as standards against which we can compare a government's performance. If it promises to attain one set of objectives but actually achieves another, this is revealed through a comparison of its economic strategy with its policy achievements. In short, we can use the concept "economic strategy" just as we did the concept "rules of the game" to distinguish among the ways the game is played in different countries.

How do you recognize an economic strategy? It was not difficult to identify the three strategies contained in the tale in Chapter 1, but what about in the real world where political life is more complicated than in our example? Just as when we inquired into the process by which public office is won and lost, we need a guide to direct our search for economic strategies. It should tell us what to look for and how to distinguish among different strategies. Specifically, it should answer the "why," "what," "how," and "for whom" questions relevant to economic strategy. *Why* was the strategy created in the first place? *What* specifically does it plan to accomplish? *How* will it achieve its goals? And *for whom* are its benefits intended?

These four questions are translated into more useful terms in Table 5-1. Each term in turn is divided into its principal dimensions. We

Table 5-1. *The dimensions of economic strategy*

Why:	Causes of underdevelopment
What:	Policy objectives
	Production
	Distribution
	Foreign trade
How:	Policy instruments
	Public-private mix
	National-foreign mix
	Coercion-spontaneity mix
For whom:	Beneficiaries
	Immediate
	Long-range

begin with the "why" question: the *causes of underdevelopment*. Economic strategies contain a theory of the development process; they identify the sources of development and explain what causes it and what retards it. Sometimes the theory takes the form of a complex economic statement, but more often than not it is expressed as a kind of conventional wisdom that specifies the critical forces in the development process. The "what" question is answered by the *objectives* a government sets for itself. We have singled out three objectives that serve to distinguish one strategy from another. The first is *production:* the goods and services the government wants produced and the rates at which the production of each should be increased. The second objective is *distribution:* how goods and services will be divided among citizens. Few issues provoke more controversy or are more important to a country's development than the allocation of society's resources among different social classes. The third objective is *trade:* the kind of economic relationships officials want with other countries. Foreign trade has been an integral part of Latin American development and remains a major concern of policy makers. The latter have become especially preoccupied of late with the region's excessive dependence on the industrial nations for the purchase of their exports and the supply of capital and technology and have devoted increasing energy to the design of policies aimed at reducing this dependence.

The "how" question is answered by the means or instruments the government employs to achieve its objectives. Governments have at their disposal a wide range of powers that they use to influence economic behavior. They collect taxes and spend money, regulate the creation and circulation of money, set exchange rates, regulate imports and exports, operate industries, provide services, and on occasion, control prices, wages, interest rates, and other economic activities. We will focus on three dimensions that distinguish among different strategies. First is the mix of *public and private* economic activities. We want to know how much of the development burden the state takes upon itself and how much it leaves to the private sector. The second dimension is the mix of *foreign and national* participation in the economy. Latin Americans continue to disagree about the appropriate role of foreign capital in their development. They have, however, generated a host of innovative ways of dealing with foreign investors, many of which we will discuss in our examination of individual countries in Part II of this book. The third dimension is the mix of *control and spontaneity* permitted by the government. We want to know the extent to which the government tries to control private conduct in order to achieve its objectives instead of relying on unregulated economic behavior.

Finally, there is the "for whom" question: *Who benefits* from the strategy? Few development policies benefit all citizens equally; most greatly favor some players over others. It is important that we measure the results of development policy not only in terms of its effects on the size of the gross national product or per capita income but also in terms of its impact on the lives of the players we met in Chapters 3 and 4. Players usually try to secure the adoption of policies favorable to them. Conversely, when policies threaten them, they usually react, sometimes violently, against the officials responsible. Consequently, our interest in the beneficiaries of development policy is not limited to the policy's economic effects on them. We are equally concerned with the kinds of political behaviors such effects prompt and how such behaviors, in turn, affect the government's ability to achieve its objectives.

Before we examine the devlopment policies employed in particular countries, a brief introduction to the economic strategies that have influenced development policy in Latin America would be useful. Specifically, we need to know more about how Latin Americans have assessed their situation and responded to it. Of the many options available to Latin American leaders, four appear to have been followed most frequently. We have labeled them "traditionalism," "progressive modernization," "conservative modernization," and "revolutionism." A brief discussion of each strategy will acquaint you with some of the issues that are currently being debated in the region as well as the kinds of development policies they have yielded.

CONTEMPORARY ECONOMIC STRATEGIES

Traditionalism

The strategy we have labeled traditionalism prevailed throughout Latin America in the late nineteenth century, survived in some countries until World War II, and in a few is still followed today. Its traditionalist quality stems from the fact that it takes economic lessons learned a century ago and builds an economic strategy from them. Stressing the limits imposed on economic development by natural resources, it argues that a country must accept its natural limitations and work within them. Latin America is endowed with soils and climates that favor the production of many different agricultural commodities and the extraction of minerals coveted by the industrial nations of Europe and North America. Therefore, instead of trying to compete with the latter in the race to industrialize, say the traditionalists, Latin Americans should stick to what they are best equipped by nature to produce, even if it means risking the economic instability and dependence on foreign markets that usually accompany the primary product export economy. Latin Americans have no choice but to accept the existing division of labor in the world economy and the constraints imposed by their heritage, economic experience, and natural resources and do the best they can. Who are the advocates of the traditionalist strategy? Not surprisingly, they are found among the producers of primary products who dominated the region's economies during the nineteenth century and the foreign traders and bankers who have assisted them, all of whom have been waging a defensive struggle against the forces of industrialization and increasing state control over the economy in recent years.

The traditionalist strategy does not oppose all forms of economic change, as its name might imply. However, it usually confines its encouragement of change to the narrow realm of export production. The traditionalists want economic growth and modernization only as long as these do not threaten the prevailing system of mineral extraction and agricultural production. They are content to take a route to economic development that draws only on readily available foreign and domestic resources, convinced that through the gradual expansion of agricultural and mineral production they can improve their own lives as well as those of the merchants, bankers, and traders who support them.

Traditionalists are not especially preoccupied with the issue of distribution. They accept the notion that distribution will take care of itself as long as the market is working properly. In practical terms this means that the managers of the export economy – farmers, exporters, foreign investors, and bankers – will receive, as they believe they should, the lion's share of the nation's income. It also means that the idea of deliberately redistributing income from the richer to the poorer classes is unthinkable. Wages are to be kept as low as possible and the consumption of imported items confined primarily to the upper and middle classes. The only distribution issue that concerns traditionalists is the very narrow one of the distribution of wealth among the farmers, exporters, bankers, and foreign buyers who manage the economy. It is not uncommon for farmers to believe that exporters are getting richer at their expense or for both to be convinced they are being exploited by bankers. Nevertheless, their differences are minor compared with their support for the fundamental premises of the traditionalist strategy.

At the heart of the traditionalist strategy is its desire for strong ties to the economies of the industrial nations. It accepts an international division of labor that makes Latin America one of the principal suppliers of raw products to the industrial nations of Europe and North America. It also welcomes foreign investment, holding fast to the belief that raising capital in foreign markets is preferable to raising it domestically through higher taxes or forced saving. Economic dependence on foreigners is not viewed as an evil, but is accepted as a fact of life that cannot be changed. The idea that Latin America's excessive dependence on foreign capital may be one of the causes of its underdevelopment is alien to the traditionalists, who regard the involvement of foreigners in their economies as natural and, therefore, desirable.

The implementation of the traditionalist strategy is left primarily to the private sector. Unlike the more ambitious postwar development strategies described below, traditionalism has no use for government-coordinated attacks on development problems. It sees the state as a passive, rather than an active, agent, confined to the maintenance of public order and the promotion of entrepreneurial activity, especially in the export sector. Traditionlists use the doctrine of laissez-faire capitalism that became popular in some parts of Europe during the nineteenth century to justify the limited role of the state.

When under traditionalist control, especially at the end of the nineteenth century, the state confined itself to transferring land from the Church and the Indians to private entrepreneurs, promoting the production of commodity exports with its tax and monetary policies, and repressing political movements that challenged the status quo. Traditionalists assumed that public compliance with their programs could be secured through the use of traditional social and political institutions. Those who failed to conform to the existing order were dealt with through the stern measures of public authorities. If peasants or rural laborers tried to upset the status quo, for example, they were handled by local *caudillos* or rural police forces. When urban laborers tried to organize unions, they were harassed by strike-breaking government agents, and politicians who formed opposition parties were kept from public office by restrictive electoral laws and by fraud. It was not important whether the country was ruled by a military *caudillo* or an aristocratic civilian as long as he enforced the traditional way of life.

By now the principal beneficiaries of the traditionalist strategy should be obvious. Of the players we examined in Chapters 3 and 4, the producers of commodity exports, foreign investors, exporters, and bankers stand to gain the most. The distribution of income among them would vary depending on the structure of the economy and the relative economic and political strength of each player. In some countries well-organized and powerful producer groups might prevail; in others, exporters or foreign-owned mining firms might gain the upper hand from time to time. But whatever the case, the traditionalist strategy was designed first and foremost to benefit the minority that controls the means of export production. Secondarily, benefits would also reach the commercial and professional groups that share in the management of the system. Left off the list of beneficiaries are the peasants and laborers, who must sell their labor for low wages and depend on the goodwill of the economic elite for their livelihood.

But how long can a strategy that concentrates its rewards on a small minority survive, especially in societies where economic and political aspirations are rising? Undoubtedly, traditionalism invites opposition. Some potential opponents, such as the *campesinos,* may have insufficient power to alter their fate, but urban laborers, aspiring industrialists, and dissatisfied intellectuals and professionals are not so helpless. As the economy develops and becomes more dependent on middle-sector managers and laborers, the exporter elite becomes more vulnerable to their threats. It is one thing to maintain control over a traditional agrarian society and another to govern a modernizing urban one where systems of local social control are no longer capable of maintaining the existing order. And so it has been in many of the larger Latin American states where the traditionalist strategy has been challenged relentlessly since the 1930s.

Political opposition is not, of course, the only threat to traditionalism. Any economic strategy that depends on foreign trade for its success must live and die with the rise and fall of its commodity exports and the prices they bring. It continually courts disaster in the form of droughts, pests, a sudden fall in prices, and the loss of foreign markets owing to disasters elsewhere. Faced by these problems along with sustained political opposition, it is not surprising that traditionalists have been on the defensive since the 1930s and repeatedly forced to yield ground to their critics.

Progressive modernization

The strategy of progressive modernization began as a critique of traditionalism and the elitist political system that sustained it. Like the hypothetical president described in Chapter 1, its founders were frustrated by the economic dependency, poverty, and instability that had accompanied nearly a century of development under traditionalist policies. Their frustration was ignited by the 1929 depression and fueled by economic crises that arose during World War II. What began as little more than a depression-inspired desire for change gradually matured into a new and significant approach to the region's problems. It took its inspiration from many sources, including the Mexican Revolution, the American New Deal, and Catholic social philosophy, but none was more important than the doctrine of "structuralism" popularized by the United Nations Economic Commission for Latin America (ECLA), an organization created in 1949 to promote the region's development.

The structuralists, as their name implies, were concerned with the economic and social structures that impeded the region's development. Foremost in their thinking was the obvious vulnerability of Latin American countries to erratic prices for exports and their victimization by the adverse terms of trade between their primary product exports and the industrial goods they imported from abroad. The structuralists reasoned that Latin Americans had been unfairly treated in their trade relations with the industrial nations and would continue to suffer until their dependence on foreign trade was reduced. The structuralists were also disturbed by the maldistribution of income within Latin American societies and the adverse effects of this on domestic consumption. Surveying their economies in the 1940s and 1950s, they discovered a rural sector polarized between a minority of large holdings and millions of excessively small ones, an industrial sector composed of small, inefficient firms, and a working class that could not afford to consume the goods produced in national factories. The same economic structures the traditionalists had accepted as natural and inevitable the structuralists saw as obstacles to long-range development and social justice. The only way to progress, they concluded, was to dismantle the old structures and replace them with more productive and equitable ones.

Progressive modernization contains an important political dimension as well. Only the most naive could ignore the fact that any attempt to reform traditional institutions would be intensely resisted by the well-entrenched elite that had created and sustained them. Despite their technical sophistication, the proponents of progressive modernization were initially no match for the much more powerful elite. What they needed, they realized, was a larger following and the toleration of the military if they were to win their struggle against the defenders of the status quo. Eventually they turned for support to the only place they could – to laborers and peasants. The cooperation of the former was essential to the expansion of industrial production and urban consumption; the peasants were needed to reorganize the rural sector. Moreover, both groups were needed to defend the government against its opponents in the elite and the military.

In contrast to the traditionalists, who favored production over distribution objectives, those inspired by the structuralist critique of Latin American development were determined to achieve both types of objectives simultaneously. Not only were the two thought to be compatible, but they were absolutely essential to each other. The structuralists were convinced that the low rate of production that plagued their countries was attributable not just to a shortage of capital but also to the maldistribution of property and income that had led to inefficient enterprises and insufficient consumption. Therefore, to increase production over the long haul, economic resources had to be redistributed from less efficient to more efficient units and the size of the national market had to be expanded by including more citizens, both rural and urban, in the modern economy.

At the heart of the progressive modernizers' program is rural reform. The traditional system of land tenure is the primary cause of the region's underdevelopment. In the 1950s there still remained many large landholdings throughout the countryside, as well as millions of small farmers and landless peasants. Not only was rural output inadequate, but there remained intact a rural social structure that prevented the integration of the rural masses into the modern economy. It was imperative, therefore, that the government break up large estates, encourage more efficient land utilization, and bring the rural poor into the marketplace as producers and consumers. This could be done, it seemed clear, through a program of land reform that redistributed property from the larger *latifundios* to peasant farmers and then transformed the latter into efficient producers through education, technical assistance, and the introduction of modern farm practices. Land redistribution without the improvement of production techniques would obviously come to naught, for even though it might satisfy the immediate demands of land-hungry peasants, it would neither increase rural output nor bring peasants into the modern economy. Finally, there was a need to diversify commodity production if the region were to escape its dependence on only a few farm products. As long as it was bound to the fate of a few crops, stable economic growth would remain elusive; however, through a comprehensive diversification program, greater protection against shifting world prices could be secured and a steady flow of foreign exchange assured.

Rural reform is necessary to economic development, but is not by itself sufficient, according to the proponents of progressive modernization. Also needed is a comprehensive program of industrialization. Depression and war had taught a generation of Latin Americans that they could no longer rely primarily on the production of commodity exports for their livelihood. The lesson was clear: Instead of selling commodities in order to purchase consumer goods abroad, Latin Americans should manufacture their own goods. To some extent this occurred in many of the larger Latin American states after 1930 when, cut off from their foreign suppliers, governments tolerated spontaneous industrialization. But the industrialization of the 1930s and the war years was incomplete and costly because the region's industries still had to import their machinery and many of their raw materials from abroad, causing an immense drain on foreign exchange. What was needed, the progressive modernizers reasoned, was a more comprehensive effort that included the development of a capital goods industry.

The third objective of progressive modernization is the reduction of Latin America's dependence on the industrial nations. The region's disadvantageous relationship with its trading partners had originally provoked the structuralist critique of traditionalism. The proponents of progressive modernization do not want to separate themselves from the rest of the world, but only to strengthen their bargaining power and increase their margin of choice when setting their development course. They are nationalist, but not isolationist, determined to increase the region's control over its own destiny without denying it access to foreign capital and technology.

It is one thing to identify the causes of underdevelopment and set some reformist policy objectives, but quite another to execute them in the face of well-entrenched traditions and vested interests that staunchly defend the status quo. Exceptional skill, determination, and good timing, along with ample technical expertise, are required to make progressive modernization work. The reorganization of rural life, the modernization of farming, and the introduction of new crops cannot be achieved without abandoning habits that have been nurtured for decades. Nor can heavy industries be constructed without careful planning, substantial managerial talent, and the expenditure of large sums of money. But despite the enormous task they have set for themselves, the proponents of progressive modernization are convinced they can devise the instruments they need to get the job done. By adapting policies that have succeeded in the United States, Europe, Mexico, and elsewhere to their local situations, they believe they can generate a host of measures capable of solving the problems at hand.

The state has to be elevated to a position of strength in the management of the nation's economy in order for progressive modernization to work. No longer can public officials leave economic matters to the private sector alone. Structural change and technological innovation require bold leadership, and the state is the only institution powerful enough to assume that role. Government planners must design development programs and coordinate the activities of private industries through the use of incentives and regulations. To assist in the management of economic affairs, the government must also nationalize public utilities and strategic industries, like minerals, iron, and steel. And in those sectors where private enterprise is permitted the state should help finance development through low-interest loans and joint public-private ventures.

In the rural sector the state must redistribute property, but it should do so in an orderly way so as not to upset production. Land can be purchased with cash payments or government bonds at market prices or declared tax value, depending on what the government can afford. Land reform must be accompanied by easy credit and subsidized technology in order to increase production. Moreover, all government policies should be directed at the ultimate objective of redistributing income to the rural and urban poor. Agrarian reform and expanded industrial employment will go a long way toward this end, but the government, through its housing, educational, and health programs, must also do a great deal. A decent wage should be guaranteed all workers, and if necessary, food prices should be subsidized.

In the field of foreign economic relations two important policy innovations are encouraged. One is regional economic integration. It is obvious that national markets are too small in most countries to generate large-scale industries. Mass production is impossible as long as domestic markets include only 20 to 30 percent of the country's population and will increase very gradually even with agrarian reform. Through the missionary efforts of the economists at ECLA, who had closely studied the European common market in the 1950s, a way has been found to combine national markets into one large regional one that can support major industries. The advocates of progressive modernization propose regional economic integration through which each country agrees to specialize in certain products, reduce its tariffs on goods produced within the region, and coordinate its foreign exchange policies. The second innovation is the use of international commodity agreements to regulate the supply and price of raw product exports. The idea of commodity agreements among producer and consumer nations had circulated for a long time, but it was under the leadership of the proponents of progressive modernization that the idea became an integral part of a Latin American development strategy. Today, agreements apply to many commodities, the most successful being the OPEC (Organization of Petroleum Exporting Countries) agreement on petroleum, which was originally established in the 1960s under the leadership of a Venezuelan minister of mines.

The most perplexing issue facing the advocates of progressive modernization is their choice of the proper mix of control and spontaneity in the execution of their programs. As proponents of structural change and economic reform, they recognize they must assert their authority over those who would obstruct them. On the other hand, their preference for democratic politics and toleration of private enterprise makes them reluctant to use heavy-handed tactics against their enemies. A good example of their ambivalence is their implementation of agrarian reform. Clearly, in order to succeed land reform must confront and overcome the power exercised by the rural elite. The mere passage of legislation, assuming the government progresses that far, does not guarantee compliance with the new reforms. Landowners are skilled at forestalling government efforts to deprive them of their property. Consequently, agrarian reform can seldom be implemented without the use of some force by the state. Yet, extreme measures aimed at repressing reform's opponents risk undermining constitutional processes and provoking violent reactions leading to disorder. There is no easy escape from the coercion-spontaneity dilemma faced by progressive modernizers, for if they fail to use sufficient force, their programs may wither and die, but if they use too much, they may invite violent resistance and disappoint their more democratic followers. Failure to resolve the dilemma swiftly poses one of the biggest threats to the success of progressive modernization.

Who benefits from progressive modernization? In theory, the marginal rural producers and urban laborers stand to gain the most, for they will be freed from oppressive traditional economic institutions. But in practice their benefits will come slowly; agrarian reform, industrialization, and regional integration cannot be achieved overnight, but require sustained effort for several years to spread their benefits widely. During the strategy's initial phase, the state and its many agencies stand to gain most. Regulatory agencies will be increased, new state enterprises added, and planning operations expanded. Next in line come the industrialists who benefit from the state's promotion of their enterprises. Labor unions, especially when they are supported by the ruling party, will also gain in power and wealth.

So will the professionals in the middle sectors, who stand to profit from economic growth generally. Eventually peasants too will be incorporated into the mainstream of the nation's economic life, though much more slowly than any other group. Less noticed among the strategy's beneficiaries are the foreign investors who are encouraged under the new rules of the game. Though some will lose from nationalization, many others, especially in high-technology fields, stand to gain a great deal as the consumption of their products rises with economic growth. Technically trained military officers are also among the less obvious beneficiaries. They may create industries of their own in order to share in the bounties of industrialization or may be called upon to manage government enterprises, especially public utilities.

The last and most obvious question is: Why, if progressive modernization spreads its benefits so widely, has it not succeeded in transforming the entire region during the past three decades? We will explore this question in Chapter 7 when we assess the strategy's application in Chile and Venezuela during the 1960s. Yet, even before we look to the real world for answers, we can gain some insights into the question by critically examining the strategy's assumptions about economic development.

First, there is the question of whether a democratically inclined Latin American government has enough authority and popular support to implement the very substantial reforms proposed by the progressive modernization strategy. Undoubtedly it will encounter substantial resistance from those it deprives as well as from rival political parties threatened by its success. Whether it can overcome such opposition through peaceful bargaining without sacrificing the substance of its reforms is questionable. Second, progressive modernization carries a very high price tag, which Latin American governments may not be able to pay on their own. The wealth confiscated from the economic elite is seldom sufficient to cover the costs of the government's development projects. The government may borrow abroad, but that may only lead to a large foreign debt burden and the kind of financial dependence the government wants to escape. Last, there is the difficulty of fulfilling promises to workers and peasants without threatening the well-being of middle-sector supporters. If the government cannot satisfy both simultaneously, political conflicts may be provoked that will divide its coalition and undermine its authority. Clearly these problems must be faced directly by the advocates of progressive modernization even though there are no easy solutions for any of them.

Conservative modernization

Just as traditionalism generated its own critics, so has progressive modernization. Some fell back on old formulas to defend the status quo; others struck out in new directions. The most enduring contribution of the latter has been the strategy of conservative modernization. Unlike traditionalism, it shares the progressives' desire for industrialization and rural modernization; what it rejects is their reformist methods and redistribution objectives, preferring instead more conservative means for promoting economic growth. These differences of opinion stem in large part from disagreements over the causes of the region's underdevelopment.

Instead of placing the blame on natural resource constraints or growth-retarding economic structures, conservative modernizers stress the well-meaning but misguided policies of social reformers, which have stifled private investment and discouraged the efficient use of productive resources. Starting from the unquestioned premise that capitalist institutions offer the surest route to economic growth, they argue that the principal objective of government policy should be the encouragement of entrepreneurial activity in all sectors of the economy. They point out that entrepreneurs are unresponsive in an environment where political disorder and heavy-handed government regulation prevail, as is common throughout Latin America. What is needed, then, is orderly government that encourages private initiatives with its fiscal and monetary policies. Investors, industrialists, and commercial farmers must have confidence in economic authorities and their policies, and it is the duty of the government to provide that confidence. Demagogic politics, unattainable social programs, and the comings and goings of military and civilian governments must give way to strong and stable political rule dedicated first and foremost to the nation's economic growth.

The modernity of the strategy lies in its objectives. It has no interest in a retreat to the traditional export economy of the past, but wants to pursue rapid industrial growth and the expansion of agricultural exports through the use of large, modern farms. It rejects, however, the idea that the progressive redistribution of property and income is a necessary first step to economic growth. On the contrary, if economic growth is to be achieved, resources must be concentrated in the hands of investors who will put them to good use in building a modern economy. And if there is to be redistribution, it must be done primarily through the marketplace and not the deliberate efforts of government bureaucrats. The strategy is conservative in its rejection of social reform and acceptance of wide income disparities as a means for promoting economic growth. Accumulation, not redistribution, is its primary short-term objective because it believes the deliberate transfer of income to the poorer classes drains the economy of its vital resources and hinders productive investment. The benefits of growth will reach the poor, but only gradually, as new workers are absorbed into the expanding industrial economy.

To bolster their case, the advocates of conservative modernization point to the industrial revolutions of Europe and North America, arguing that several decades of sacrifice by the laboring masses were required to set the stage for the construction of mass consuming societies. In rebuttal, critics insist that it is difficult, if not impossible, to replicate the industrial revolution in contemporary Latin America given the tenacity of the region's traditional social structure and its surplus labor in an age of capital-intensive industrialization. They charge that conservative modernization's promise of employment and higher income for all citizens in the long run is hollow and is made only to rationalize a greater concentration of wealth in the hands of foreign and domestic entrepreneurs. Neither argument can be proved or disproved except by the test of experience. Each is based on assertions about an empirically inaccessible future and, therefore, can be assessed only indirectly through the use of historical example until the Latin American results are in.

Another difference between conservative and progressive modernization is in foreign trade objectives. Conservative modernizers stress the "interdependence" of industrial and nonindustrial nations rather than the excessive "dependence" of the latter on the former. They argue that the Latin American nations need the technology and investment capital held by the industrial nations and have no choice but to borrow them on available terms. One should not be ashamed of this relationship, they assert, for it is in the best long-term interests of both parties, providing profits for investors and gradual development for the borrowers. In the short run all that matters is the government's skillful channeling of foreign investment into the areas where it can do the most good.

In its choice of policy instruments conservative modernization stands midway between laissez-faire and state control. It assigns an important role to government technocrats, requiring that they orchestrate the nation's growth through their active manipulation of fiscal, monetary, exchange, and regulatory policies. Indicative economic planning can be used as long as it does not lose sight of its primary objective of promoting private investment. Nor does conservative modernization rule out state ownership of some enterprises, especially in those areas where private investment is not forthcoming. But again the purpose is to supplement the private sector rather than to replace it. The strategy encourages a kind of conspiracy between government technocrats and the managers of large domestic and multinational firms. There is something to be gained by both parties from the arrangement, for by working closely together government bureaucrats can secure the cooperation of private firms in the implementation of their growth objectives, and the latter can gain the order and encouragement they need to manage their long-term investments.

The foreign-national mix is not a pressing issue for conservative modernization. Foreigners are as welcome as nationals as long as their efforts contribute to growth objectives. Foreign trade must be encouraged and expanded through the diversification of agricultural exports and the addition of industrial ones. But instead of trying to promote higher rural production by redistributing unproductive land to *campesinos,* the government should turn to commercial farmers and help finance the expansion of their enterprises. Easier credit, high prices, better storage facilities, and easier marketing arrangements should be encouraged by government policy so that those who are already prepared to produce on a large scale can do so. If they succeed, the country will reap the foreign exchange it needs to finance its industrialization program without heavy borrowing abroad.

Underlying all conservative modernization's proposals is an important political commitment: The proposals cannot succeed without the imposition of a firm political order by a strong government. There is no doubt that these policies will exact high social costs and provoke some discontent. Labor unions, peasant organizations, and mass-based political parties will not stand by idly while the benefits of economic growth are monopolized by entrepreneurial and bureaucratic elites. The proponents of conservative modernization recognize this and are prepared to take harsh actions to deal with the problem. For them, politics is not an end in itself but only a means to fundamental economic ends. Therefore, the kind of politics used to maintain order and repress discontent is not as important as the ability to get the economic job done. In practice this may require the suspension of open, competitive politics in favor of harsh autocratic measures that keep social groups in line. In this game political protests are regarded as police problems and, like similar crimes, dealt with harshly. In most cases the result is a military government dedicated to implementing the strategy regardless of political costs.

The immediate beneficiary of conservative modernization is the investor, both foreign and national, in agriculture, commerce, or industry. Obviously the multinational corporation is the best prepared to take advantage of the strategy, though many national investors will gain as well. Less apparent among those it favors is the new generation of government technocrats, who will replace party politicians in designing and executing public policy. They will be accompanied by the professionals and white-collar workers who will staff the public and private enterprises used to implement the strategy. Left out in the short run are the *campesinos,* who will be confined to their small plots or continue to work as rural laborers on commercial farms, and urban laborers, who will be forced to forgo increased income in order to help finance capital investments.

Like all development strategies, conservative modernization raises many unanswered questions about its ability to achieve its objectives. Few would deny that capital must be accumulated in order to promote economic growth. Nor is there much doubt that a government can promote entrepreneurial investment by holding down wages and opening doors to multinational corporations. Less certain is how long it can deny well-organized urban laborers the gains they have come to expect in modernizing societies. Sooner or later the government will have to seek working-class acceptance if it is not to survive on repression alone. And when it does, it may have to pay a high price for its past neglect of the masses in the form of wage increases and social expenditures that may undermine the confidence of conservative entrepreneurs. Another question is: How long can the government tolerate increased dependence on foreigners? Even though the immediate economic benefits of foreign investment may be immense, the loss of national control over critical economic activities may prove costly, especially if it deprives national authorities of freedom to chart their own course. A third problem concerns the "trickle down" effect. Critics of conservative modernization argue that it leads to enclave capitalism rather than expanding affluence. With profits being repatriated abroad and social programs in suspension, the benefits of economic growth trickle down to the masses at an appallingly slow rate, if at all, thereby doing little to alleviate widespread poverty. Finally, there is the question of legitimizing a government that chooses conservative modernization. Undoubtedly, the strategy will generate strong support from the 10 to 30 percent of the population that profits immediately from it. But what about those who are initially left out? How long can the government survive in the face of their opposition? Force, intimidation, and public apathy will facilitate the government's task, but they will not eliminate the need to expend much energy and valuable resources on protecting the government from its subjects.

Revolutionism

What do the three strategies we have just examined have in common? According to their proponents, very little; they are three different ways of solving the development problem. There is, however, a fourth school of thought that says they are not really far apart.

Despite their disagreements over the choice of objectives and instruments, traditionalism and progressive and conservative modernization all strive to create a society in which public authorities and private entrepreneurs jointly manage the economy. They are in essence merely three different ways of organizing the capitalist economic system to meet the needs of Latin Americans. But what Latin America needs, say the proponents of this fourth view, is not capitalism but revolutionary socialism. Latin American underdevelopment, they argue, is not caused by a shortage of resources or by misguided policies, but by capitalism itself and the system of exploitation inherent in it. Neither progressive nor conservative modernization can overcome poverty and underdevelopment because neither is capable of displacing capitalism. Only through a revolutionary effort to seize public authority and reconstruct society can Latin America be saved from the dual evils of imperialism and capitalist exploitation. To that end the revolutionary strategy is dedicated.

What the revolutionist sees when he examines his society is not the progress evidenced by modern airports, high-rise office buildings, and cities congested with new automobiles, but the dehumanization and alienation of the Latin American masses. They are victims not only of traditional institutions like the *latifundio* but of the modern factory as well. Modernization, if allowed to take the capitalist form, will do little to alleviate this condition. Private property, competition, and the pursuit of narrow self-interests – the motivating forces of capitalism – cannot eliminate poverty and exploitation. Only through the reorganization of society around the principles of equality and community can underdevelopment be overcome. The revolutionist offers his countrymen the vision of a cathartic upheaval that destroys the squalid present and replaces it with a more just productive future. His appeal is to those who have rejected traditionalism, become disillusioned by reform, and been excluded by conservative modernization.

Unlike the proponents of capitalism, the revolutionist is not as concerned with production objectives as with the distribution of goods within his society. This does not mean he ignores production entirely, for only the most romantic revolutionist would delude himself that poverty and exploitation will cease once capitalist institutions have been destroyed. To meet the needs of all citizens production must be redirected toward the requirements of the common man and increased as rapidly as possible, often at some human cost. But the principal concern of the revolutionist is not what is produced, but how it is done and who gets it. His principal aim is the creation of an egalitarian society. Differences in personal wealth must be eliminated through the socialization of all property and the equalization of wages. Class distinctions must be ended once and for all. In their place must come a new sense of community in which laborers work for the common good rather than personal gain.

The foreign trade objectives of the revolutionist are explicit. He is convinced that exploitive capitalism is a mere extension of industrial capitalism in Europe and Anglo-America. Through a system of economic imperialism Latin America has been absorbed into these metropolitan economies, which have siphoned off its resources and abused its governments for generations. Most important, as long as the region's capitalist institutions are linked with the industrial nations through a network of foreign trade and investment, they cannot be easily dismantled. But if the external link is cut through revolutionary efforts, they will quickly collapse. Thus one of the revolutionist's first objectives is the eviction of the representatives of metropolitan capitalism from his country and the severing of trade relations with those who have exploited the nation in the past. Only after this objective has been achieved will he be free to create the socialist economy. Naturally there are costs to be paid for the sudden loss of one's trading partners, and the costs are especially high if in the past the country relied heavily on foreign trade and the importation of capital from abroad. But the revolutionist has little choice but to pay if he is to gain the power of self-determination he so desperately wants.

To create the socialist society, radical instruments are needed. First must come the transformation of the state from the regulator of private economic affairs to the owner of the means of production. Nearly all private property must be expropriated by the state and reallocated to cooperative or state-run production units. The rate of transfer will vary depending on how fast the state can assume its new responsibilities and overcome counterrevolutionary forces. Second, central planning must be instituted to manage the newly nationalized economy. The implementation of development plans is still a matter of some dispute among revolutionists. Some, especially those who emphasize distribution, favor decentralization and virtual autonomy for local production units; others, most often bureaucrats who place highest priority on the expansion of production, prefer firm central control over all economic processes. And third, during the initial phases of the revolution, a revolutionary elite must assume full control over the nation's economic and political reconstruction. Loyal to the masses they represent, they must make and enforce policies aimed at the fulfillment of revolutionary objectives. They must be guided by revolutionary ideology and their understanding of the needs of the masses rather than by their individual interests or the demands of citizen groups. Then, once the transformation has been completed, the revolutionary elite is no longer needed because true socialism will prevail.

There is no mystery about the means revolutionaries use to sever their ties to imperialism. Foreign properties are expropriated and all trade relations reorganized according to principles set down by the new authorities. Yet what appears so simple in ideological terms can prove very complicated when balanced against practical economic necessities. To desire economic autonomy is one thing; to achieve it is something else. Few nations possess all the raw materials or produce all the consumer goods they require. Sooner or later they must either trade with other nations in order to meet their needs or do without some basic materials. If the revolutionist chooses the latter, he initially must accept a lower standard of living and place severe constraints on national development; if he chooses the former, he must either select trading partners who share his ideology and views of equity or turn once again to the capitalist nations, though hopefully on more favorable terms than before. The same is true in his search for financial assistance and foreign technology. As much as possible he seeks out nations that support his revolution, reasoning that if he must be dependent on anyone, it should at least be an ally in the revolutionary cause rather than someone who desires the restoration of capitalism.

It might at first appear that the revolutionist handles the question of mixing control and spontaneity with ease. His goal is social reconstruction and he can leave nothing to chance, so wherever necessary he resorts to controls without hesitation. Attitudes, institutions, and work habits must be changed; political loyalties must be transformed; and a new order must be quickly imposed. Counterrevolutionaries have to be deterred and made to respect the strength of the new regime. None of these objectives can be accomplished without the use of force. But what about after the transition is well under way? After all, is it not the revolutionary's objective to create an egalitarian society where the control of one person by another is unnecessary?

The revolutionist cannot escape the dilemma created by his need to use force in order to create a new society of free people. His way out is not to choose between control and spontaneity, but to combine them in a special way. The key is the ideological reeducation of the masses. If they can be taught to follow the community ethic of socialism, control will eventually become unnecessary. Individuals will conform not to government power but to their belief in a shared ideology. Spontaneity will be redefined to include all behavior consistent with the ideology. Of course, reeducation of the population, so compelling in theory, is extremely difficult to achieve. Values and habits built up and reinforced during centuries of Iberian rule and decades under capitalism do not yield quickly to a new ethic that is centrally imposed. Resistance and counterrevolutionary acts may persist for some time, requiring the constant use of force by central authorities. The greatest danger is that in his determination to transform society the revolutionist will lose sight of his ultimate objectives and never relinquish central control for fear of losing control altogether.

Who benefits from revolutionism? Ideally, the peasants and laborers who were exploited under capitalism have the most to gain. The elimination of the *latifundista,* commercial farmer, and factory owner should benefit the masses. So too should their admission to schools and hospitals that previously excluded them. But how rapidly will the condition of the poor be improved under socialism? The rate of redistribution depends primarily on how much of its resources the government allocates to capital accumulation and how much it reserves for social welfare. If it chooses to emphasize capital accumulation, as it has in some socialist nations such as the Soviet Union, the masses will have to wait until substantial economic development has been achieved before they will see their condition improve significantly. On the other hand, an emphasis on social services may immediately improve their welfare, but at the expense of rapid economic growth. In either case, however, it is the new revolutionary elite that profits the most at the outset of the socialist revolution. Its members gain status, power, and personal comfort from their positions of leadership. Only gradually, as the economy develops and the supply of goods increases, will others begin to rise to the leaders' level of well-being.

The losers under revolutionism are apparent. Landowners, industrialists, merchants, bankers, foreign investors – all members of the capitalist elite – are deprived of their property and power. Some will survive longer than others depending on how much the revolution temporarily requires their services, but eventually nearly all will go. There is no way their continued existence can be tolerated in a society dedicated to egalitarianism and central control. Survival of a large private sector means the revolution has failed, so only by eliminating that group can the revolutionist demonstrate that he has achieved his objectives.

Despite its obvious appeal to anyone frustrated by the failures of other strategies to cure Latin America's ills, revolutionism is no easier to implement than other strategies. In fact, because it is more ambitious it faces more obstacles and opposition. First, the eviction of foreign and domestic investors exacts a high price in the loss of liquid capital and managerial talent. When the revolutionary regime deprives entrepreneurs of their property, it alienates many of the professionals and technicians who depend on the entrepreneurs for their livelihood; although some may join the new regime, many flee in search of better opportunities elsewhere, depriving the new government of their talents. Second, in executing radical social change, the revolutionist risks making very large mistakes. The sudden transformation of the rural sector, for example, may lead to a breakdown in agricultural production, and new industrial organizations may prove inefficient on a large scale. The revolutionist must take chances if he is to achieve his objectives, but when he errs, he often does so on a grand scale, and entire programs may have to be abandoned, setting back the revolution by months or years.

It is also apparent that the creation of a revolutionary regime does not by itself guarantee that the new programs will be implemented. To succeed, the revolution must penetrate deeply into society and transform the attitudes and values of citizens. An elaborate and well-organized bureaucracy must impose its will on areas of life that were previously ignored by public authorities. In the larger Latin American states an immense effort would be needed to reach remote areas and bring their isolated populations under the central government's control. And finally, the revolutionist must continually grapple with the growth-equity dilemma. On the one hand, he wishes to spread wealth throughout society in order to increase equality. On the other, he recognizes that he has to concentrate his resources in order to build solid foundations for sustainable economic growth. The problem is especially difficult for the revolutionist because, unlike the conservative modernizer, he is committed, in theory at least, to equality. Seldom, however, can he sacrifice his economic growth objectives to achieve it.

ECONOMIC STRATEGIES COMPARED

You are now familiar with four of the economic strategies that have inspired the policy choices of many Latin American leaders in recent years. You have seen how we can distinguish among different strategies by asking about each a common set of questions concerning the causes of underdevelopment, the strategy's objectives and instruments, and who gains or loses through its application. Two additional questions are in order. First, by comparing the four strategies, what can we learn about their likely effects on Latin American societies? Second, if Latin American politics is surrounded by uncertainty over the rules of the game, as described in Chapter 2, what are the chances that any of these strategies will be implemented?

What can be learned from comparisons? Clearly, differences among the four strategies stem in large part from their contrasting views about the causes of the region's underdevelopment. Traditionalism stresses natural obstacles to development and argues that nations must live within the constraints these obstacles impose; progressive modernization and revolutionism, in contrast, claim that man-made economic and social structures are responsible for underdevelopment and urge reform or transformation of these structures in order to promote economic growth and social justice. Conservative modernization takes a narrower view, blaming ill-conceived social and economic polities for underdevelopment and calling for the efficient application of foreign and domestic capital to the task of industrial and agricultural modernization.

When we turn to their objectives we discover that the four strategies differ in fundamental ways on the issues of production and distribution. The issue of growth versus equity has haunted economic policy makers throughout Latin America since the 1930s and remains the central issue in current policy debates. Traditionalist and conservative modernizers believe that substantial economic growth must precede attempts to deal with equity issues, pointing to the experiences of the industrialized nations and the logic of capitalist economics to demonstrate that capital formation must precede the satisfaction of mass demands. The revolutionist disagrees. For him nothing is more important than equity, regardless of cost, for without equality economic growth will not serve the needs of the people. However, even the revolutionist has been forced to admit that some temporary sacrifice of absolute equality may be required in order to meet production objectives in the short run. That leaves the progressive modernizer. To a certain extent he is the most ambitious of the four, for he wants both

Table 5-2. *Economic strategies compared*

Strategy	Causes of underdevelopment	Objectives	Instruments	Beneficiaries
Traditionalism	Scarce resources Insufficient talent	Production of export commodities Trade with capitalist nations Preservation of social institutions	Encouragement of rural entrepreneurs Welcome of foreign investment Firm social control using traditional institutions	Commercial farmers Traders and exporters Foreign investors and consumers
Progressive modernization	Concentration of rural land Insufficient industrialization Exclusion of masses from modern economy	Increased rural and industrial production Progressive income redistribution Integration of masses into modern economy Greater economic autonomy	Land reform Industrialization Nationalization of critical enterprises Balance between state power and liberty	State bureaucracy Urban middle sectors Industrialists Organized labor Peasants
Conservative modernization	Misguided nationalism Progressive income-redistribution policies Excessive regulation of private entrepreneurs	Increased rural and industrial production Closer ties to international economy	Assistance for commercial farmers Promotion of large industries Welcome of foreign investors and traders Imposition of firm political order	Foreign investors Industrialists Commercial farmers Exporters Urban middle sectors
Revolutionism	Capitalism Imperialism	Redistribution of political power Redistribution of property and income Increased production	Nationalization of private property Equalization of income Severance of trade with capitalist nations Mass ideology and organizations	Revolutionary elite Urban labor Peasants

growth and equity simultaneously. He strives to generate rapid growth while at the same time increasing the economic opportunities of the underprivileged. But the greater one's ambition, the greater the obstacles he faces. Progressive modernizers must overcome not only the opposition of elites to their redistribution of income but also the practical difficulty of reconciling welfare objectives with the promotion of rapid industrial growth.

Many questions remain about the ability of each of these four strategies to achieve its objectives. For example, can the proponents of progressive modernization carry out all their projects simultaneously, or will some programs have to be sacrificed in order to realize others? Can the revolutionist achieve equality without impoverishing his countrymen? And can he reorganize an entire society without a system of tight regimentation? Finally, can the conservative modernizer do all that he wants to stimulate investors without inducing the working class to rebel? And will he too have to repress his fellow citizens in order to achieve his objectives?

To these questions another must be added: Why does each strategy have so little to say about the critical issue of population growth in Latin America and its effects on economic development. Rapid population growth places an immense burden on efforts to accelerate economic development and improve social welfare. Impressive gross national product growth rates of 5 or 6 percent are cut in half on a per capita basis by population growth rates of 2.5 or 3 percent. Moreover, high population growth rates contribute to the acceleration of migration from the countryside to the cities, where social services are already woefully inadequate. And as more and more people compete for scarce and maldistributed resources, the gulf between the rich and the poor widens.

Currently there are many obstacles to the execution of programs aimed at reducing birth rates in the region. The best known is the opposition of the leadership of the Roman Catholic Church to contraception. The influence of Church doctrine is widespread, yet it is not an absolute impediment to birth control. It has not, for example, stopped an increasing number of middle-sector couples from limiting the size of their families in order to improve their economic security. Nor has it prevented affluent, urbanized countries, like Argentina and Uruguay from keeping their population growth rates quite low. Clearly, other forces, such as education and economic affluence, are at work in such cases.

Another source of opposition is the nationalist political leaders, who view the insistence of international lending agencies on the adoption of family-planning programs as illegitimate intervention in their internal affairs. Some go so far as to argue that the affluent industrial nations want to limit Latin America's population growth in order to reduce the region's claim on the resources now consumed by the industrial nations. Others see the demand for birth control as part of a conspiracy by foreign and domestic elites to hold down the size of the masses in order to reduce the likelihood of revolutionary upheavals. Rebuttals that point to the drain on a nation's development caused by population growth are dismissed by such spokesmen as mere rationalizations for the political and economic status quo.

Even if religious and political opposition to birth control were overcome, economic obstacles would remain. The greatest impediment of all is poverty. In contrast to middle-sector couples, who can gain economically by limiting the size of their families, many of the poor believe they gain economically from large families. Working children bring desperately needed income into the family; moreover, once they are adults, they can care for their parents when the latters' working years have ended. It is also among the poor that Roman Catholic doctrine is more influential because it helps justify what many must do of necessity. Clearly, if family-planning programs are to have any effect in the less affluent Latin American countries, they must transform the attitudes and institutions that have perpetuated poverty and this survival-through-numbers ethic.

In sum, the population issue is a very complex but important one that is often neglected by economic strategies because of the many obstacles to its resolution. Yet, the success of any economic strategy will be determined in part by the way this problem is solved. In assessing the economic performance of Latin American governments, we must examine the ways officials have dealt with it and determine the consequences of their actions for the welfare of the people they govern.

Finally, can any economic strategy be effective within the context of the unsettled Latin American political game? We have learned that disagreements about the rules of the game have led to the frequent overthrow of governments in some countries, a condition that is hardly conducive to the implementation of development policies. Ideally, one wants a predictable political environment, legitimate authority, and a capable bureaucracy in order to make and execute policy. Failing that, one would hope for enough authority to secure the conformity of citizens with government policies and enough stability to carry programs through to their conclusion. This ideal political world is seldom found in Latin America. Consequently, at the same time they are implementing controversial development programs public officials must also cope with the uncertainty and political conflict that traditionally haunt the Latin American political game. To make matters worse, they themselves contribute to the uncertainty with policies that threaten particular groups and prompt them to take matters into their own hands rather than respect the government's authority. How then does the government survive?

The best it can do is employ the political instruments at its disposal to deter its opponents, while mobilizing its supporters in the hope that the latter will be strong enough to sustain its rule. Although none of the strategies says a great deal about the problem of political uncertainty, it is not hard to see how the kinds of political processes employed by proponents of particular strategies in the past have conditioned policy execution. Some progressive modernizers, for example, have relied on political parties and parliamentary and bureaucratic authority to achieve their reformist objectives. Conservative modernizers, in contrast, have usually ignored the demands of the masses, preferring instead some kind of military autocracy that can impose order on society. Revolutionaries also require much authority to govern and frequently combine mass organizations with a powerful, centralized state bureaucracy.

The likelihood that democratically inclined progressive modernizers will succeed depends in part on their ability to use the rules of the constitutional game against their conservative and radical opponents. A weakness in the democratic approach to reform is the ease with which its procedures can be abused by those who are determined to obstruct change. The military autocrats who try to implement a policy of conservative modernization must, in contrast, create a system of control that protects them from the inevitable protests of the many citizens who suffer under their rule. Their biggest political problem is the development of popular acceptance of the autocratic regime. The revolutionary relies primarily on the use of a mass-based political party to mobilize the needy into an assault on traditional and capitalist institutions. His success depends on how well his system of control can transform cultural values and existing institutions without alienating the masses he claims to serve.

The only way to discover how different economic strategies have fared under Latin American conditions is to examine the experiences of governments as they have struggled with development problems. That will be one of our objectives in Part II. Not all the strategies we have just reviewed were followed in each country we will examine; nor did actual policies adhere to our four strategies in all details. Nevertheless, they are similar enough to supply us with insights into how these different strategies have influenced the outcomes of the Latin American political games. In our examination of the populist regimes of Juan Perón and Getulio Vargas in Chapter 6, we will discover how an economic strategy that was the precursor of progressive modernization led the first major attack on the prevailing doctrine of traditionalism. The democratic reformist governments of Chile and Venezuela, discussed in Chapter 7, offer examples of two different versions of the progressive modernization strategy in action. The military authoritarian regimes created in Brazil and Argentina in the 1960s, examined in Chapter 8, demonstrate what happens when the conservative modernization strategy is applied to the region's economic problems. And finally, through a comparison of the revolutionary regimes of Mexico, Cuba, and Allende's Chile, discussed in Chapters 9 and 10, we will assess the effects of three different modes of revolutionary development.

FURTHER READING

Anderson, Charles W. *Politics and Economic Change in Latin America: The Governing of Restless Nations.* New York: Van Nostrand, 1967.

Baran, Paul. *The Political Economy of Growth.* New York: Monthly Review Press, 1957.

Berger, Peter. *Pyramids of Sacrifice: Political Ethics and Social Change.* New York: Basic Books, 1974.

Campos, Roberto de Oliveira. *Reflections on Latin American Development.* Austin: University of Texas Press, 1967.

Farley, Rawle. *The Economics of Latin America: Development Problems in Perspective.* New York: Harper & Row, 1972.

Frank, Andre Gunder. *Latin America: Underdevelopment or Revolution.* New York: Monthly Review Press, 1969.

Furtado, Celso. *Economic Development of Latin America.* Cambridge: Cambridge University Press, 1970.

  Obstacles to Development in Latin America. Garden City, N.Y.: Doubleday, 1970.

Glade, William P. *The Latin American Economies.* New York: Van Nostrand Reinhold, 1969.

Gordon, Wendell. *The Political Economy of Latin America.* New York: Columbia University Press, 1965.

Hirschman, Albert O. *Latin American Issues: Essays and Comments.* New York: Twentieth Century Fund, 1961.

  A Bias for Hope. New Haven: Yale University Press, 1974.

McCoy, Terry L., ed. *The Dynamics of Population Policy in Latin America.* Cambridge, Mass.: Ballinger, 1975.

Mesa-Lago, Carmelo, and Carl Beck, eds. *Comparative Socialist Systems.* Pittsburgh: University of Pittsburgh Press, 1975.

Powelson, John. *Latin America: Today's Economic and Social Revolution.* New York: McGraw-Hill, 1964.

Prebisch, Raúl. *The Economic Development of Latin America and Its Principal Problems*. New York: United Nations, 1950.
   Change and Development: Latin America's Great Task. Washington, D.C.: Inter-American Development Bank, 1970.
Tancer, Shoshana Baron. *Economic Nationalism in Latin America: The Quest for Economic Independence*. New York: Praeger, 1976.
United Nations. *The Economic Development of Latin America in the Post-War Period*. New York, 1964.
   The Process of Industrialization in Latin America. New York, 1966.
Wilczynski, J. *Socialist Development and Reforms*. New York: Praeger, 1972.

Part II

The political games of Latin America

In Part I you learned how to study Latin American politics by focusing on political rules, players, and economic strategies. We saw, for example, how the rules of the game affect the organization of governments, the conduct of public officials, and the relative influence of different players in the development-policy-making process. We also met several players, identified their primary political interests and resources, and discussed the ways they play the game. Although their general characteristics were easily identified, it was also apparent that their actual behaviors vary from country to country depending on the opportunities available to them, the rules that regulate the political game, and their ability to form effective coalitions. Our interest in players is not confined, however, to their competition for public office. We are also concerned with their participation in the government itself as policy makers or representatives of various constituencies who seek to influence policy choice and execution. Finally, we learned that players and public authorities rely on economic strategies to guide their choices of development policies. These strategies can be classified according to their principal dimensions and used to describe and assess the performance of Latin American governments. Economic strategies have both technical and political dimensions. Therefore, they must be evaluated not only according to their efficiency in achieving a particular set of economic objectives but also for their effect in distributing resources and power among different players.

You are now ready to discover how the political game is played in several Latin American countries. To assist you, Part II is devoted to the analysis of some recent political experiences. But rather than devote a separate chapter to each Latin American country, we will focus instead on the four types of political games that have dominated Latin American politics during the postwar period. They are the populist, democratic reformist, military authoritarian, and revolutionary games. Each will be illustrated by the political experiences of at least

131

two countries. In this way, at the same time you are learning about the varieties of Latin American political experience, you will also discover how you can classify and compare different kinds of politics and assess their contrasting effects on economic development and public welfare.

No effort is made in the chapters that follow to provide a comprehensive introduction to the politics of each Latin American country. Instead, we will concentrate only on those aspects of the political game that are relevant to answering the questions asked in Part I. Once you conclude Part II, you should be prepared to study on your own the politics of each country examined in this text as well as those not discussed. To assist you in that effort a list of English language books from which much of the material in each chapter was taken is provided at the end of each chapter.

6. The populist game

Many different political movements have tried to alter the status quo in Latin America, but few have created more confusion about their character, purpose, and accomplishments than those led by the Populists. Making their first appearance at the end of World War II, Populist movements had a lasting impact in several countries, most notably Brazil beginning with the second presidency of Getulio Vargas in 1951 and Argentina under Juan Domingo Perón from 1946 until his death in 1974.

The Latin American Populists are a diverse group and defy simple characterization. The populist label itself contributes to some of the confusion that surrounds them. For those familiar with North American politics, the term "populist" describes an American political party formed to represent agrarian interests in the presidential election of 1892, which advocated public ownership of railroads, the free coinage of gold and silver, and a graduated federal income tax. The use of the same term to identify Latin American political movements that arose a quarter century later and had little to do with agrarian interests appears to obscure more than it illuminates. However, what makes the term appropriate in Latin America is its utility in distinguishing a new mass-based political movement from the traditional elitist political groups that had dominated most of the region's politics before 1930.

A second cause of the confusion that surrounds the term is the variety of populist regimes that have arisen in Latin America. As we shall see in our comparison of Brazil and Argentina, Populist movements differed in the manner of their conquest of power as well as their conduct in office. Consequently, when we speak of the Latin American populist game, we are really referring to a general type of which there are many variations.

Third, the term is troublesome because of the historical association of Latin American populism with European fascism. Populists did adopt some of the political symbols and rhetoric used by the Fascists during the 1930s. What they created, however, were not carbon copies of European models but hybrid regimes that integrated imported doctrines with many indigenous traditions and institutions.

Latin American Populist movements were led by opportunistic poli-

133

ticians with anti–status quo programs who drew their support primarily from an urban working class that had arisen with postdepression industrialization. They were loosely organized, lacked coherent
ideologies, and relied primarily on the political skills of their leaders
and the enthusiasm of the urban masses they mobilized. Their goal
was to capture public office so that they could employ the power of
the state to promote industrialization and distribute its rewards to native entrepreneurs and laborers. Equally important was their desire to
prevent the radicalization of the urban masses so that they could gain
their conformity with the requirements of capitalist industrial development. They ruled in only a few countries, but by challenging political and economic privilege they stimulated reassessments of the
export-oriented development tradition throughout the region.

ARGENTINA'S PERÓN AND BRAZIL'S VARGAS

Few twentieth-century leaders have dominated their countries' politics to the extent of Juan Domingo Perón in Argentina and Getulio
Vargas in Brazil. They altered the rules and scope of the traditional
elitist political game and led their people into new eras of postwar industrialization by transforming the state and increasing its economic
responsibilities. Many of the economic and social gains of their countries during the past forty years, as well as many of their contemporary political difficulties, can be traced to the regimes of these two
populist leaders.

Juan Perón governed Argentina between 1946 and 1955 and
again briefly from October 1973 until his death in July 1974. His two
administrations were separated by eighteen years of exile and the efforts of his working-class followers to restore their control over
Argentine politics by returning Perón to the presidency. He began his
public career as a military officer, rising to the rank of colonel during
World War II. In 1943 he participated in a military coup that deposed
the conservative regime that had governed the country since 1930.
Working within the new military government from his posts in the
Ministry of War and the Secretariat of Labor and Welfare, he adroitly
secured a working-class and military following that carried him to victory in the presidential election of 1946. Once inaugurated, he immediately set out to create a modern industrialized Argentine welfare
state. For nine years Perón dominated the Argentine political process
through the use of his working-class-supported Peronista party, the
demagogic appeal and political skill of his wife Evita, the physical and

Table 6-1. *The Argentina of Juan Perón: historical background*

1816	Independence from Spain declared
1835	Autocrat Juan Manuel Rosas imposes order on strife-ridden country
1852	Rosas overthrown in revolt led by rivals in economic elite
1853	Republican government created under new constitution, and Argentina governed by succession of conservative leaders, who promote immigration from Europe and development of agricultural export economy
1916	Middle-sector-led Radical party wins first election under Hipólito Irigoyen; Radical party again wins presidential elections in 1922 and 1928
1929	World economic depression strikes Argentine economy
1930	Conservative-supported military coup deposes Radical party administration and secures election of conservative presidents in 1932 and 1938
1943	Military takes control of government to prevent election of pro-British conservative president
1944	Colonel Juan Domingo Perón is made vice-president under military President Farrell
1945	After being forced to resign vice-presidency and sent to jail by military colleagues, Perón is released and becomes presidential candidate of Laborista party
1946	Perón elected president for first term
1949	Constituent Assembly promulgates new Peronista Constitution
1951	Perón elected president for second term
1952	Perón's wife, Evita, dies
1955	Military insurrection forces Perón to flee into exile
1973	Juan Perón, at age seventy-eight, returns to Argentina and is elected president
1974	President Perón dies of natural causes and is succeeded by his wife and vice-president, Isabel Martínez de Perón, whose administration is overthrown by Argentine military in early 1976

psychological intimidation of his opponents, and the tacit support of the military.

Perón had many enemies, of course. Foremost among them was the farmer-exporter elite, whose power he threatened with his industrial and welfare policies. This group was joined by the foreign investors, whose properties Perón expropriated, and eventually also by the Roman Catholic hierarchy, whom his legalization of divorce and prostitution angered, and by many dissidents in the military, who came to resent his personalistic and increasingly autocratic rule. After several unsuccessful attempts, Perón's opponents finally overthrew him in September 1955. But his removal proved much easier than the destruction of his movement, and after eighteen years of bitter political struggle, the Peronistas regained the presidency and a congressional majority in 1973. But this time Perón's tenure was brief, for he died at the age of seventy-nine, just before completing his first year in office. In the midst of the political and economic chaos that followed his death, the military intervened once again, overthrowing the Peronistas for a second time in March 1976.

The first Peronista regime is a prototype of Latin American populism. Nevertheless, the regime is not easily described, for it combined many diverse and seemingly contrasting characteristics. For example, it enjoyed substantial electoral support and used that support to defeat formidable opposition in honest elections in 1946, yet Perón often governed as an autocrat determined to impose his will on Argentina by force. Moreover, though the Peronista movement was primarily built on the support of the urban working class, it was not exclusively a labor movement, but also included many members of the urban middle sectors and rural working class. The complexity of Peronism as a political phenomenon is attributable in large part to the unusual condition of Argentina at the end of a decade of economic depression and war and the limited options available to anyone who sought to challenge the rule of the traditional elite. There were little time and few opportunities to create a political movement according to a premeditated strategy; instead, leaders such as Perón had to seize their opportunities where they could, often combining unlikely elements in their campaign against the defenders of the status quo.

We have only to move from Perón's Argentina to the Brazil of Getulio Vargas to discover how varied the populist experience has been. In contrast to Perón, who erected a populist regime in only three years, Vargas had ruled Brazil for thirteen years – from 1930 to 1943 – before he began to create his Populist movement. A lawyer from the southern Brazilian state of Rio Grande do Sul and the member of an upper-class ranching family, he began his political career as a federal deputy in 1924, served as finance minister in 1926, and returned to his home state as governor in 1928. After losing the 1930 presidential election – an election rigged by his opponents – Vargas led a heterogeneous coalition of disgruntled civilian politicians and young military officers in an insurrection that deposed the incumbent president. For fifteen years thereafter he personally dominated Brazilian politics as the country's president. But his strength as a political leader came not from a political ideology or the size of his following, but from this mastery of the rules and norms of Brazilian politics and his ability to guide the country through the difficult days of the postdepression era.

Table 6-2. *The Brazil of Getulio Vargas: historical background*

1822	Independence declared by Portuguese Prince Dom Pedro, who is crowned Emperor Pedro I of Brazil
1840	Dom Pedro II, aged fourteen, is declared second emperor of Brazil
1889	Army overthrows emperor and two years later promulgates first constitution of the Republic of the United States of Brazil
1917	Brazil enters World War I on side of allies
1929	World economic depression strikes Brazilian economy
1930	Military-civilian insurrection led by defeated presidential candidate Getulio Vargas ends republic created in 1891
1932	Provisional government of Getulio Vargas puts down constitutionalist revolt in São Paulo
1934	Second republican constitution is adopted, and Congress elects Getulio Vargas president
1937	Just before election of his successor, Vargas leads coup and creates Estado Novo, appointing himself president with indefinite tenure
1942	Brazil enters World War II on side of allies
1945	Vargas is forced to resign by military after creating Populist movement drawing heavily on support of organized labor
1950	Vargas wins legitimate presidential election with support of Social Democratic party and Brazilian Labor party, receiving 49 percent of popular vote
1954	President Vargas commits suicide at age seventy-two

Vargas used nearly every means but direct election to sustain his rule during the 1930s. For four years he played off different influential groups against one another. Then in 1934 he was confirmed as president by a popularly elected constituent assembly. However, when his term expired in 1938, he drew on the services of the military once again to reconfirm himself as president before new elections could be held. This time he created a new political regime, the Estado Novo (New State), which he modeled loosely after the fascist regimes of Italy and Germany. But the new constitution was little more than window dressing for Vargas's strong but manipulative presidency and his expansion of state power in order to regulate more closely the new economic forces that were emerging in the 1930s. Although he never seriously challenged the power of the traditional agrarian elite, he did lead his country into the industrial era by promoting the interests of industrial entrepreneurs and paternalistically securing the cooperation of urban workers in the new economic system.

Vargas was also quick to adapt to the changing political realities of wartime Brazil. Like Perón, he recognized the emergence of the urban masses as a potent political force in the late 1930s. At about the same time his ambitious neighbor was organizing a mass movement to support his assault on public office in 1946, Vargas set out to integrate urban laborers into the national political game before they forced their way in by promulgating progressive labor laws. Yet, before he could make use of his new working-class following, he was forced by the military to vacate the presidency in 1945, just before new elections were held. Undaunted, he returned five years later to campaign on a populist platform and, with the support of organized labor and most of his old political following, he regained the presidency with 49 percent of the popular vote in 1950. This time, however, the pressures exerted by increasingly vocal opposition groups were greater than even the skilled Getulio Vargas could handle. In the midst of rising domestic conflict and a well-orchestrated campaign against him, Vargas ended his incredible political career by committing suicide in his presidential office in 1954.

THE RULES OF THE POPULIST GAME

Before we can understand the Populists' use of political rules, a brief look at the traditional order they fought against is necessary. Populist movements arose in countries whose politics were still dominated by rules employed by political elites to block the access of the masses to power. Lip service was given to democratic procedures; when elections were held, only members of a small elite were allowed to compete for public office or vote. Landowners, bankers, traders, foreign investors, and regional political bosses who tightly controlled their emerging middle-sector constituents ruled without mass-based political parties or any concern for mass opinion. For them, democratic rules were merely convenient devices that could be manipulated for personal advantage.

Around the turn of the century the rules of the traditional game were challenged by some of those they had effectively disenfranchised. In some countries the expanding middle sectors were the first to assail them, using newly created political parties to campaign for electoral reforms that would open the political process to urban professionals, small-business men, and the urban labor elite. Simultaneously, insurgent Socialist and Anarchist parties also attacked the traditional system, demanding economic as well as political change. The last two were seldom successful, but in a few cases, notably Chile, Argentina, and Uruguay, the middle-sector parties were. Electoral reforms were adopted, and new parties captured public office, though after doing so they were quick to accommodate their programs to interests of traditional elites.

Given the elite's ability to abuse or ignore democratic processes and survive electoral reform, it is not suprising that populist leaders had little faith in democratic rules of the game. They recognized that military-supported conservative parties could annul their election, subvert their governments, or completely remove them from office with relative ease. Thus, when they plotted their ascent, Populists were more concerned about securing irreversible victories than about the purity of the means they employed to capture and hold public office. Political power was what they wanted, and they were prepared to use almost any means to acquire and retain it.

Capturing public office

What is notable about the Populists' rise to power is not only the variety of means they used but also their ability to exploit the political opportunities open to them. Both Juan Perón and Getulio Vargas, for example, began their national political careers by seizing opportunities made available by military coups. Perón participated as a junior officer in a coup in June 1943 that overthrew a conservative government that had demonstrated its inability to cope with the complex issues opened by the outbreak of World War II. From within the new military government he cultivated the support of junior officers who shared his vision of an industrialized Argentina and mobilized the country's urban workers in support of his presidential candidacy. Getulio Vargas played a prominent role in the coup that overthrew the Old Republic in 1930 after its leaders had violated norms that had regulated the presidential selection process. Once in office, he skillfully consolidated his position by playing off different interests against one another and organizing a firm base of support among patronage-seeking urban middle sectors, aspiring industrialists, and junior military officers. The rise of these two populists testifies to the political dexterity required to succeed in the rapidly changing societies of Brazil and Argentina in the 1930s and 1940s and merits closer examination.

We begin with Perón and a problem in political strategy. How does a young military officer who wants to be president of his country plot a course that will take him from relative obscurity to the presidency in only three years? Moreover, how does he do it in a country ruled by a conservative political and economic elite that has no intention of sharing public office with any competitors? These were the questions that faced Juan Perón at the time of the military coup of June 1943. His answers emerged in a series of decisions that catapulted him to the Argentine presidency less than three years later.

Perón's sudden rise to power is an example of political opportunism at its best. What catapulted him to the presidency was his exceptional skill in taking advantage of conditions created by the Conservatives who governed Argentina during the 1930s (see Table 6–3). The monopoly of the agro-exporter elite over public office had been broken temporarily by the middle-sector Radical party in 1916. The Radicals opened the political process to their supporters, but they did little with their new power to alter the structure of the Argentine economy or reduce the influence of the elite that managed it. The 1929 depression and declining confidence in the ability of the Radicals to protect the traditional economic order against the social protests it unleashed prompted intervention by the conservative-backed military in 1930. Two years later, a conservative regime was restored and harsh austerity imposed on the depression-ravaged Argentine economy.

In rescuing the Argentine economy from the depression, the Conservatives antagonized Argentine nationalists, who resented the country's heavy dependence on foreign investors and traders. Nationalists condemned conservative officials for the price they paid to restore trade with Great Britain, the principal buyer of Argentine beef. Through the Roca-Runciman pact, the Argentine government agreed to guarantee a market for Engalnd's manufactured goods in exchange for the latter's purchase of beef, claiming it had no choice but to accept the British terms because there were few other available markets for Argentine commodities. But for a vocal and expanding collection of nationalists within the opposition Radical party and the lower ranks of the military the treaty was a distasteful reminder of Argentina's subservience to its trading partners. Their desire for a reversal of this relationship became a resource Perón later exploited.

The Conservatives also alienated the country's growing working class. Until the 1930s Argentina's organized laborers had been few in number but militant in spirit under the leadership of Socialists and Anarchists. After the 1930 coup working-class militancy was met with harsh repression by a government determined to preserve the old order, and within a few years the labor movement was left impotent by the combined pressures of unemployment and government oppression. Nevertheless, the size of the working class grew rapidly as a result of internal migration from the countryside to the cities, which

Table 6-3. *Perón's rise to power*

Existing socioeconomic conditions (1930s) →	The opportunity →	Sources of authority for mobilizing support →	Precipitating event →	The seizure of power
Postdepression national humiliation Working-class alienation Elite decay	Military coup of 1943	Under secretary of war (June 1943); minister of war (February 1944) Secretary of labor and social welfare (October 1943) Vice-president (July 1944)	October 17, 1945, demonstration by labor supporters forcing military to tolerate Perón's candidacy	Presidential election of February 1946 56% of popular vote Two-thirds of seats in Chamber of Deputies All but two seats in Senate

accompanied the spontaneous industrialization prompted by the shortage of imported consumer goods during the early years of the depression. Consequently, by the early 1940s Argentina had an enlarged industrial work force whose attempts to organize and assert itself were continually frustrated by a hostile government. Here was another opportunity Perón would exploit by using his authority as a member of the military government that overthrew the Conservatives in 1943.

Perón's campaign was also bolstered by the declining competence of conservative officials. Prior to 1916, the agro-exporter elite had easily dominated Argentine politics through its control over the country's economy. That feat could not be replicated after 1930 in a polity that had changed significantly during the 1920s. Over 1 million immigrants had entered the country in the interim, bringing its population to nearly 6 million. The middle sectors had asserted themselves and could be excluded from the government only through physical force and electoral fraud. And constant vigilance and repression were needed to contain the aspirations of a growing working class. Nevertheless, the country's conservative rulers held fast to the traditional practices that had served them so well before 1916. But by so doing they not only discredited party politics and constitutional government in the eyes of most Argentines, they also gradually undermined the confidence of the military in their ability to create a stable and durable political order. When President Ramón Castillo tried to secure military support for the reactionary *latifundista* he had nominated as his successor in 1943, the military resisted. And then when pro-Axis and pro-Allies officers became dissatisfied with Castillo's vacillating war policies, they joined together long enough to depose him in June 1943.

Colonel Juan Domingo Perón did not lead the coup, but he was an active participant in it as a member of a nationalist, pro-Axis faction of young officers. He was rewarded first with the under secretaryship of war and a few months later added the post of secretary of labor and social welfare. In February 1944 he became secretary of war and in July of the same year was named vice-president.

Perón used his authority as labor minister and war minister to build his Populist movement. Within the War Ministry he secured the support of young officers whose careers he advanced in exchange for their political support. From the Labor Secretariat he organized thousands of workers and built a loyal following by rewarding unions that supported him with favorable collective bargaining settlements and social security laws and punishing those who refused to accept his leadership. For Argentine laborers the advantages of the alliance were obvious. After years of being ignored or harassed by a succession of governments and poorly served by socialist and anarchist leaders who could not secure the wages and social services demanded by the rank and file, here at last was a leader who could deliver the goods almost overnight. By the middle of 1945 Perón had converted the General Labor Confederation, the nation's largest labor organization, into one of the strongest political forces in the country.

The last obstacle to Perón's ascendancy was overcome on October 17, 1945. A military faction opposed to him, in a desperate move to block his path to the presidency, persuaded President Farrell to arrest and jail him until after the elections were held. His incarceration came to an abrupt end, however, when his working-class followers, mobilized by Evita and loyal labor leaders, marched on the presidential palace and remained there until Perón was released on October 17. Four months later the Peronistas were swept into power in one of Argentina's most honest elections.

Getulio Vargas took a more direct route to the presidency but a much longer and more circuitous one to the inauguration of his populist regime. Vargas's first thirteen years as president were noted not for populism but for his very personal style of authoritarianism, which he used to regulate old and new political forces while managing Brazil's recovery from the 1929 depression. Populism requires the support of urban masses, and not until the late 1930s, at the end of the first decade of Vargas's presidency, did the opportunity for mass mobilization created by postdepression industrialization and urbanization materialize in Brazil. To understand the populist Vargas of the 1943–54 period we must first comprehend the authoritarian Vargas and the game he played between 1930 and 1943.

From 1889 to 1930 Brazil had been governed under the rules of the Old Republic, a constitutional regime created after the overthrow of the monarchy of Dom Pedro II. Despite its republican form, it was in reality a government run through the collusion of the leaders of the state political machines that dominated politics at the local level. By agreement, the presidency was alternated between the two most powerful states, São Paulo and Minas Gerais. In 1930, however, the retiring president, Washington Luis of São Paulo, broke the agreement by selecting another Paulista to replace him instead of accepting Getulio Vargas, the nominee of the Minas Gerais and Rio Grande do Sul political machines. Soon thereafter Vargas led the military-backed opposition in an insurrection that brought the Old Republic to an end.

Washington Luis's violation of the electoral agreement was the

Table 6-4. *The rise of the authoritarian Vargas*

Precipitating conditions	Opportunity	Bases of support
1929 depression Corruption of leaders of Old Republic Military demand for strong leadership	Coup of 1930	Development-minded military Commercial farmers Patronage-seeking middle sectors Emerging industrialists

principal cause of the 1930 insurrection, but it was not the only one. The 1929 depression and the failure of the Luis government to act decisively to relieve the crisis it caused had undermined the confidence of coffee growers, bankers, and traders in his administration. Moreover, the military had grown weary of the old regime and was disturbed by its failure to accelerate the country's economic development. Increasing professionalization, foreign travel, and greater awareness of Brazil's untouched economic potential had heightened the concern of younger officers about the way the country was governed. From one-time supporters of the republican regime they were gradually transformed into its strongest critics, convinced that only a new generation of bold leaders could impose on Brazil the kind of moral order needed to realize the country's full potential.

Finally, there was the skilled leadership of Vargas himself. What the opposition needed most in 1930 was a leader who could join together politicians, ambitious young military officers, professionals, and businessmen to overthrow the old regime and create a new one. Vargas became that leader. What he organized was not a populist coalition – that did not come until the early 1940s – but a loose coalition of disparate forces that he alone held together. He was a supreme political negotiator who understood the diverse forces involved in the Brazilian political game and knew how to appear to be all things to all

Table 6-5. *The rise of the populist Vargas*

Precipitating conditions	Opportunity	Bases of support
Industrialization and urbanization Mobilization of urban masses Loyalty to Vargas of rural and industrial elites, middle sectors, and bureaucrats	Election of 1950	Old Vargas political network of local political bosses Organized labor Nationalistic enterpreneurs Middle sectors, especially public employees

factions. For some, he seemed to be the long-awaited leader of a march toward true political democracy. For others, he offered the hope of a new nationalism that could generate accelerated industrial development. For still others, he became a leader who appeared stronger and more dedicated to imposing order on the country's warring political machines than any of his predecessors. It was, of course, impossible to please all these factions simultaneously, but by playing them off against one another and constantly mediating their disputes through the institutions of an increasingly powerful state, Vargas consolidated his hold on the presidency and retained his control over it until forced to step down by the military fifteen years later.

To establish authoritarian rule, Vargas had to subvert a campaign to restore constitutional government begun by middle-sector groups after the 1930 coup, a task he accomplished with amazing skill and political dexterity. He began by suppressing a revolt of constitutionalists in the state of São Paulo in July 1932. The leaders of the revolt had accused Vargas of postponing a return to constitutional government so that he could increase the power of the federal government at the expense of states like São Paulo. But in waging and losing a brief war with the central government, the insurrectionists only enhanced Vargas's stature as the guarantor of public order, a role he coveted and used skillfully to augment his authority. In 1933 Vargas consented to the election of a constituent assembly. Less than a year later the assembly drafted a new constitution, converted itself into a chamber of deputies, and elected Vargas to a four-year term as president.

But instead of working to strengthen the democratic process, Vargas dedicated himself to undermining it. To draw attention to the vulnerabilities of democratic government, he encouraged the activities of political extremists – Communists as well as Fascists – playing each off against the other in order to convince all other participants in the Brazilian game that a more autocratic government was needed to protect them from radical groups that would destroy Brazilian institutions. He finally succeeded in 1938 when, just before an election to replace him, he persuaded the military to overthrow the constitutional regime and appoint him president with indefinite tenure. This remarkable feat succeeded not because of Vargas's personal popularity but because of his ability to manipulate the players in the political game, using their fears of a challenge to the status quo to justify his expansion of authority over the game itself.

Immediately after the 1937 coup Vargas consolidated his gains through the creation of the Estado Novo, an elaborate authoritarian regime inspired by notions taken from the ideology of European corporatism then popular among fascist regimes. Yet, despite the complexity of its design, the Estado Novo was little more than window dressing to clothe Vargas's expansion of state control over Brazilian life. He drew his authority primarily from his ability to join two nineteenth-century Brazilian traditions and adapt them to postdepression conditions. One was the tradition of paternalistic central authority, which was developed through the imperial rule of Emperor Dom Pedro II between 1841 and 1889; the other was the dependence of private economic groups on the Brazilian state. The state political machines that had governed Brazil between 1889 and 1930 had weakened central authority but had not destroyed the habits that had supported strong government in the past. Vargas drew on the need and desire for firm central authority and transformed the presidency and the national bureaucracy into powerful promoters of the nation's economic development. He also encouraged the development of private interest groups, especially among industrialists and urban laborers, but did so on his own terms, making clear that all such groups were dependent on the state for their existence and survival. Once these two powerful traditions were merged and adjusted to the needs of an industrializing society, Vargas's reconstruction of the Brazilian political game was complete. Or so it appeared in 1938.

The Estado Novo survived only a few years. Even before its life was abruptly terminated by a military coup in 1945, Vargas was well on his way to becoming a Populist. The reasons for this transformation were many, but none was more important than the threat posed to the traditional order by a growing urban working class and the opportunity it gave a skilled leader like Vargas to retain his control over the Brazilian state.

No single date marks the beginning of populism in Brazil, but its origins can be traced to the last years of the Estado Novo. Vargas recognized the possibility that the existing order might be undermined by the rise of a militant working class. As early as 1937 he began a campaign to avert such a fate by bringing organized labor under the protection of the state through inclusion in the 1937 Constitution of provisions for minimum wages, paid vacations, an eight-hour day, and social security. Repeatedly, he reminded Brazilian workers that these were gifts from their benevolent leader rather than conquests they had won on their own. In return, their allegiance to Vargas and through him to the state was expected. He did not begin to organize labor for political participation until 1943, however, when it became apparent that he would need electoral support to extend the life of his regime. After being forced by middle-sector opponents and military officers to call elections in 1945, he decided to broaden his coalition by adding organized labor to the local politicians, bureaucrats, industrialists, and landowners who were already part of his nationwide political network. He did not, however, get a chance to test the strength of his new coalition, for military officers, fearful he would subvert the restoration of constitutional rule as he had done in 1937, forced Vargas to retire quietly to his ranch in Rio Grande do Sul and watch the 1945 elections from the sidelines.

The rise of populism was slowed, but not stopped, by Vargas's temporary retirement. Other ambitious politicians, such as São Paulo's governor Adhemar de Barros, used populist appeals to the urban masses with great success in 1947, igniting a stampede by politicians in pursuit of the urban voter. But again it was Getulio Vargas who took full advantage of the new politics. With the support of his Brazilian Labor party and a Social Democratic party created from the remnants of his old political following, Vargas won the presidency in 1950 with 49 percent of the popular vote.

Populists in power

The Populists used many of the same resources and rules to retain public office that they had employed to gain it. They mobilized working-class and middle-sector voters to win elections, called for mass demonstrations against their opponents, and on occasion, especially in the case of Perón, jailed or exiled their most vocal critics. They used patronage extensively to reward their supporters and put the resources of the state to use promoting economic development and regulating entrepreneurs and laborers. It is the diversity of their methods that makes the description of the Populists so difficult and creates such confusion about their intentions and achievements.

The regimes created by Perón in 1946 and Vargas in 1951 had several things in common. As we have seen, both drew on a variety of political rules, some quite conventional and others of their own making. Elections were useful because Populists controlled the votes of the urban masses. Perón won the 1946 election with 56 percent of the popular vote, defeating a coalition of Conservatives and Radicals in an honest election. He drew his support not only from urban workers but also from the rural lower class and from many in the lower middle class. Similarly, Vargas won an honest election in 1950, supported by workers, industrialists, rural elites, and many in the middle sectors. Moreover, in addition to serving the needs of populist leaders, elec-

Table 6-6. *The structure of populist regimes*

Dominant components	Vargas (1951–4)	Perón (1946–55)
Origins of leader	Rural upper class Professional politician Authoritarian president, 1930–45	Small-town middle sectors Professional soldier Instructor in military history, military attaché in Western Europe, participant in 1943 coup
Means of securing office	Election	Election
Role of political party	Supported by Social Democratic party and Brazilian Labor party, loose federations of local patronage machines, and organized labor	Supported by Peronista party created in 1945 on labor base and dominated by Perón
Role of ideology	Limited to nationalist and populist symbols with little substantive content Almost no impact on policy	Very simple principles, emphasizing ties of leader to masses, nationalism, industrial welfare state Influenced policy only during initial phase of regime
Treatment of opposition	Cooptation Manipulation through use of, access to patronage and public purse	Verbal and physical harassment Economic discrimination Occasional jail or exile

tions also fulfilled the aspirations of the urban masses for participation in the political process.

Populists also drew on their personal popularity to augment their power. This was even more true of the Peróns than of Getulio Vargas. Using virulent attacks on the agro-exporter elite and foreign imperialists as well as the vocal defense of working-class interests, Juan and Evita Perón achieved unprecedented popularity among the Argentine masses. Evita was especially effective as a leader of the country's *descamisados* (shirtless ones). An ex-radio actress of lower-middle-class origins, she was, like her husband, a skilled orator who could evoke deep emotional responses from those who had been previously ignored by the country's leaders. From her social welfare foundation she distributed money, food, and clothing to thousands of Argentines to reinforce their identification with the first lady and the president.

Undoubtedly, her untimely death in 1952 took some of the luster from the Peronista regime and weakened the government's hold on the masses.

A third characteristic of populist rule was the harsh treatment of political opponents. Here again Perón was the more extreme of the two. According to the Peronista demonology, the landed oligarchy, foreign imperialists, and bankers and traders were responsible for the country's underdevelopment and social injustice and, therefore, had to pay the price for alleviating such conditions. Nevertheless, despite his tough rhetoric, Perón stopped short of eliminating the agro-exporter elite from the game. He could evict its members from office and confiscate their profits, but he could not do without their valuable meat and grain exports, which earned the foreign exchange he needed to finance industrialization. As a result, the agro-exporter elite survived and remained influential, causing Perón to fear constantly that they were conspiring to overthrow him, either by using the conservative press to mobilize public opinion against him or by promoting a coup by conservative officers. He was driven by such fears to punish critics harshly before they could mount an attack. Anti-Peronistas in the Roman Catholic Church, the universities, Conservative and middle-sector parties, and even the labor movement were driven to silence or exile in the early 1950s. Only after several unsuccessful tries did they mobilize enough popular support and military force to overthrow the Peronistas in September 1955.

Getulio Vargas tried to avoid direct confrontations with his opponents, preferring instead to coopt them or, if they refused, to punish them with the denial of critical state resources, as he had done so successfully during the 1930s. But Brazil had changed a great deal since his first presidency; the class structure was more differentiated, foreign investors more involved in the country, industrialists and labor unions more assertive, and economic policy issues more complex and difficult to resolve to everyone's satisfaction. The techniques that had worked a decade earlier were no longer adequate for controlling the opposition. The National Democratic Union, the principal opposition party, repeatedly refused Vargas's invitations to join his government. Its campaign to undermine him picked up support within the middle sectors as inflation worsened in 1953. The opposition was also joined by junior military officers who had become critical of patronage and corruption and by foreign investors who were disturbed by Vargas's increasingly strident nationalism. As the attacks of the opposition gained momentum in 1954, it became increasingly difficult for Vargas to deter them. The end finally came when the assassination of an anti-Vargas military officer stirred demands for the resignation of the seventy-two-year-old president. Vargas responded by shooting himself on August 24, 1954.

There is also the matter of the corporatist inclinations of the Populists. A "corporatist regime" is one in which private interests are represented in politics entirely through organizations which are ordered hierarchically and controlled by the state. This is quite different from pluralist democracy, where private interests are usually represented by voluntary and nonhierarchically ordered organizations that compete for influence in the political process. The exact institutional form of a corporatist regime may vary from one country to another, but common to all is the practice of governing through the state control of private groups.

Clearly Perón and Vargas admired the corporatist regimes created by Mussolini, Franco, and, to a lesser extent, Hitler. And they did make extensive use of corporatist rhetoric when it served their needs, emphasizing the importance of the strong leader, the organic society, and the need for the commitment of all private groups to common goals. Nevertheless, this should not obscure the fact that their regimes were sustained as much through the use of loosely organized, personalistic networks of political control, as through formal corporatist organizations.

Neither Perón in 1946 nor Vargas in 1951 created a full-scale corporatist regime that converted all private economic groups into instruments of an authoritarian state. Vargas had come close to doing so in 1938 when he launched the Estado Novo and increased the dependence of private groups on the legal and financial support of the state. Yet, even though many economic groups remained heavily dependent on the state after the demise of the Estado Novo, Vargas did not complete the construction of the corporate state when he returned in 1951. Instead, he was forced by the new rules of the game to rely primarily on well-established but informal links with economic and political groups. Unlike Vargas, Perón did not inherit a legacy of interest group dependence on the state when he launched his populist regime in 1946. Industrial and agricultural groups had opposed his election and remained bitter antagonists afterward. They were accustomed to getting their way in the traditional game and resented being ordered about by inexperienced Peronista officials. Perón tried to control industrialists and farmers by forcing them to join a government-subsidized national association, which, along with labor, was to assist in the administration of government policy. What he gained, however, was not control over the private sector but increased hostility and a quiet but sustained effort to secure his overthrow.

Finally, what about the role of political parties in the populist game? Here the differences between Argentina and Brazil become most apparent. Modern political parties were not created in Brazil until 1945; in Argentina, in contrast, they had played an important role since 1916, when the political monopoly of the agro-exporter elite was broken by the Radical party, a middle-sector-led organization that drew its support from small-business men, professionals, and some blue-collar workers, many of them immigrants who had entered Argentina at the turn of the century. At about the same time Socialist and other minor parties also joined the Argentine game. Radical party government lasted only until 1930, when the military, acting on behalf of the agro-exporter elite, overthrew the government of Hipólito Irigoyen. When Perón began his quest for the presidency thirteen years later, he sought the support of the Radicals as well as several minor parties, only to be turned away by party leaders who saw little to gain from sharing their voters with an ambitious military officer. It was then that he created his own party, using the General Confederation of Labor and hastily created constituency organizations to mobilize voters and defeat a coalition of Conservatives, Radicals, and Socialists. Thereafter, the Peronista party remained a personal vehicle employed by Perón to control Congress and win reelection in 1951. After his exile in 1955 the party was continually persecuted by the military; nevertheless, Perón held it together from abroad by promising to return and lead it back into power, which he did in 1973. Throughout his presidency and eighteen-year exile the party remained his personal instrument. This fact was never more apparent than in the year after his death in 1974 when, without Perón to hold it together, the party was torn apart by a power struggle among his would-be successors.

Modern political parties came late to Brazil and their life was very short. During the Old Republic, Brazilian parties were little more than loose aggregations of state political cliques with no ideological content or formal organization. After 1930, Getulio Vargas ruled through his own authoritarian system, using patronage and public spending to satisfy his followers. When new parties were created in 1945 to contest national elections, they were tailored to the needs of the political networks already in existence rather than organized according to the principles employed by mass parties elsewhere. Three parties dominated the election scene in Brazil from the restoration of constitutional government in 1945 until its demise two decades later. They were the Brazilian Labor party, which had been created by Vargas as an instrument for controlling urban workers; the Social Democratic party, composed of the local political machines Vargas had relied on during the 1930s; and the National Democratic Union, a loose aggregation of middle-sector politicians who sought the defeat of Vargas and his followers. Party strength at the polls was determined not by the appeal of party platforms but by the popularity of individual candidates. Moreover, as long as elections could be won through populistic appeals to the urban masses, there was little incentive to create sophisticated mass organizations or write detailed platforms.

Institutionalization of the populist game

The populist game had many weaknesses, but none were greater than the informal nature of its rules and the failure of its founders to create a more durable system of government. The loose organization of the Populist movements and the informal relationship created between leaders and followers continued after the Populists were in power. They used elections when appropriate, resorted to force on occasion, bargained when necessary, and appealed to nationalist sentiments and high principles when it proved useful, but they never gave their rules and practices the institutional coherence needed to sustain them.

There was a striking contrast between form and practice in the populist game. Populists claimed to be creating elaborate new structures to regulate political conduct. Few of their schemes ever left the drawing board, however, and those that did soon fell into disuse. Instead, political conduct was determined by each president's use of his personal political resources to regulate the behavior of all other players. Political survival depended not on the government's program or the protection provided by the rules but on the ability of populist leaders to keep other players dependent on them through the manipulation of multiple rules and resources.

The price paid for the informal and personalistic character of the populist game was the vulnerability of its leaders to their opponents. Had the populist leaders consolidated their authority by securing widespread acceptance of a single set of rules, they would have made opposition attempts to undermine them more difficult. But by relying heavily on conspiratorial politics and the use of force, they encouraged their opponents to do likewise. Consequently, they had to spend much time worrying about the conspiracies of the military, the antigovernment campaigns of political parties, and the economic blackmail of domestic producers and foreign investors. Of course, it might be argued that the Populists had little choice but to rule as they did. Their opponents were many and powerful and were determined to undermine them regardless of the form their regimes took. But even if that were so, the Populists played into their opponents' hands by legitimizing all means of political combat by the example they set. The only way the Populists could have withstood the attacks of opponents over the long haul was through the development of rules and processes whose regularity made players dependent on them rather than on the leaders who manipulated them.

What has been the impact of the Populists on the rules of the Latin American game? Clearly, theirs were the most transitory of the regimes we will examine in this book. Their importance rests not on what they created but on their impact on what they tried to destroy. They broke the rural Conservatives' monopoly on public office and forced their countrymen to reassess the structure and practices of the traditional political game. They also initiated a debate that still rages about the role of the Latin American state in the region's development. Many of the development strategies that gained currency in Latin America during the postwar period began in response to the challenge the Populists had laid down. Finally, they opened the political process to many who had been disenfranchised in the past. The fact that they paternalistically dominated those whom they admitted to the political process does not detract from the effect the admission of the urban masses had on the future politics of their countries.

THE POPULIST COALITION

Populism was supported primarily by a heterogeneous coalition of urban have-nots who sought to break the political monopoly of the agro-exporter elite. Many were also reacting against the early pains of industrialization and rapid urbanization by seeking state protection against the adverse consequences of these occurrences. Their goal was not the complete destruction of the traditional political and economic systems but the attainment of larger shares of the bounty. Populist leaders came from no single social class or political group. Perón, for example, was a military officer from a small-town middle-sector family; Vargas was an experienced politician from the rural upper class. Both were joined in the populist leadership by countrymen from the urban middle and upper classes who shared their desire to promote industrial development through the subsidization of domestic investment and the carefully controlled integration of the urban working class into the national political game.

Perón and Vargas brought the urban working class into their coalitions by exploiting the frustrations and disorientation of thousands of workers who had migrated to cities like Buenos Aires, São Paulo, and Rio de Janeiro looking for a better life during the 1940s. For many migrants the transition from rural to urban life was a shattering experience. Consequently, when a new class of paternalistic political leaders appeared with promises of economic security, they responded enthusiastically. Few among the rank and file objected as Perón and Vargas took over the labor movement by expelling its more radical leaders and replacing them with functionaries personally loyal to the two men. In exchange for their political support of populist leaders workers were given state assistance in their collective bargaining, the enforcement of progressive labor laws, and a host of new fringe benefits.

Had the Populists depended only on organized labor to sustain their movements, they would not have survived as long as they did. They also needed the cooperation of the entrepreneurs who managed their nations' financial, commercial, and industrial enterprises. The collaboration of such groups did not come easily, however, especially in Argentina, given the Populists' demagoguery and cultivation of working-class support. Nevertheless, the Populists gained the support of many entrepreneurs, at least temporarily, by promoting the kind of economic development that fostered the growth of their enterprises while protecting them against working-class radicalization.

Not to be overlooked as part of the populist coalition were the bureaucrats whose jobs were created by populist policies. Until Perón and Vargas, the Brazilian and Argentine bureaucracies had been relatively small by world standards and, like those of most Latin American governments in the early twentieth century, were confined primarily to such rudimentary activities as the maintenance of public order, the provision of roads and postal services, and the management of conservative fiscal and monetary policies. Under the Radicals and the Old Republic, both governments grew as new services were incorporated into the public sector. Their growth accelerated during the administrations of Perón and Vargas. Both leaders were motivated by two considerations: a desire to increase state involvement in the promotion of economic growth and the provision of social services and a need to provide patronage for their followers. But in transforming the state into a powerful economic force and public employer, they also added an important new player to the political game in the form of thousands of public employees who would use their bureaucratic power to protect themselves and their agencies against political leaders and movements that threatened them. Thereafter, government policy would be influenced as much by the people who administered it as by the interest groups and public officials who formulated it.

Last there was the military. Like civilians, military officers were divided in their assessments of the Populists. Yet, without their collaboration Perón never could have taken office in 1946 and dominated Argentine government for ten years, nor could Vargas have returned in 1951. Initially the young and more nationalistic officers were among the most enthusiastic supporters of the Populists. For some, it was a matter of personal and institutional pride to support anti–status quo movements that promised to increase the nation's economic strength; others welcomed populism because it opened new opportunities for a more direct military involvement in the direction of state enterprises. The support of the military proved a mixed blessing, however. Direct military involvement in the populist game helped protect the government from its opponents; yet, by exposing their administrations to military scrutiny, the Populists could not conceal the excesses and incompetence that often plagued their personalistic rule. Military officers who took pride in the economic achievements of populism were quick to assail the economic crises it provoked and the inefficiencies it encouraged. Moreover, the participation of the officers in the populist game also increased the military's politicization, touching off factionalism and bitter rivalries between officers favored by the president and those not so favored. Eventually, Argentine and Brazilian officers concluded that their countries could no longer afford the demagoguery and waste of populism and took action to bring populist rule to an end.

One player was conspicuously missing from the populist game. The *campesinos* were among neither its loyal supporters nor its active opponents. Although Perón received many votes from Argentina's poor farmers and rural laborers, he never brought them into his ruling coalition or tried to change their condition through agrarian reform. Vargas ignored the plight of the rural poor even more than Perón did. In fact, he actively cultivated the support of the landed elite by refraining from threatening the rural power structure. The populists looked to the urban centers for the salvation of their countries and saw little to be gained, in the short run at least, from meddling with the economic and social structure of the countryside. It was left to their reformist successors to demonstrate that industrialization could not succeed without the modernization of the rural sector as well.

A difference between the populist coalitions formed in Argentina and Brazil was the greater fluidity and diversity of the latter. Few political coalitions have been broader than the one created by Getulio Vargas in the late 1930s and expanded upon his return to office in 1951. It was not really a coalition in any formal sense, but a loose collection of economic groups whose leaders believed there was more to gain by cooperating with Vargas and his bureaucrats than by opposing them. Instead of relying on any single group, Vargas tried to appeal to nearly all, using his authority to reward them for cooperative behavior or deprive them if they opposed him. The more he showered them with favors and regulations, the more dependent each became on the Brazilian state. And the more dependent they were, the easier it was for Vargas to secure their collaboration.

The death of Vargas in 1954 opened the door to other populist leaders who adapted his coalition to their particular needs. For example, his successor, Juscelino Kubitschek, sought to win greater support from industrialists and foreign investors while retaining a working-class following. Jânio Quadros used appeals to citizens from all classes who had become disillusioned with the old-style machine politics to win the presidential election of 1960. João Goulart tried to broaden the populist coalition by moving it to the left in an unsuccessful attempt to hold on to the presidency in 1964. What did not change after 1954 was the appeal of Brazil's political leaders to the urban masses for their support.

Perón's coalition was narrower than Vargas's and his political style more combative. Where Vargas managed to integrate rural and urban, upper- and lower-class players into his coalition, Perón attacked the agro-exporter elite and limited admission into his movement to organized labor and a new class of small-business men and industrialists. These differences were due in large part to the two men's contrasting development strategies. Perón was convinced that he had to deprive Argentine cattlemen and farmers of their profits in order to finance industrialization. Vargas believed that industrialization could be encouraged without doing harm to the traditional landowning elite or the producers of coffee and other cash crops.

POPULIST DEVELOPMENT POLICY

Populists were not noted for their contributions to economic theory. They were policy practitioners, not sophisticated strategists. They followed their instincts, taking ideas where they could find them and putting the ideas to work in the pursuit of short-term objectives. What drove them was a desire to adapt their nations' economies to the post-depression era. The 1929 depression had taught them how vulnerable their primary product export economies were to forces beyond their control, and the reaction of conservative leaders to the depression made it clear that their countries would remain subservient to the industrialized nations until their own economic structures were changed.

The Populists needed a development strategy that would promote industrial development and social welfare simultaneously. As there was none readily available, they made do with programs aimed at increasing urban consumption and financing the development of domestic industries to meet increased consumer demard. They relied heavily on the use of conventional policy instruments, including liberal monetary policies, public investments in roads, ports, airports, and public utilities, and high tariffs. But they did more than just adapt to their needs some of the policy instruments used by Conservatives. They also nationalized a few strategic industries, created new ones and put them under state management, mandated higher wages for workers, and executed a host of new regulations designed to give them more control over the economy.

To its detractors and proponents alike populism represented a radical break with the past. In retrospect, however, the transition was less dramatic than it appeared at the time. Although the Populists did expand the economic role of the state, increase its size, and promulgate substantial social legislation, they managed to leave most traditional

Table 6-7. *Initial populist economic programs*

	Vargas (1951–2)	Perón (1946–8)
Objectives	Industrialization Elimination of trade deficits Moderate improvement of welfare of urban workers	Industrialization National economic autonomy Major improvement of welfare of urban worker
Instruments	High level of investment, especially in public enterprises Currency devaluations and import controls Increased wages Mild economic nationalism	State control of banking State control of foreign trade and redistribution of rural profiits to public and industrial sectors Nationalization of foreign-owned utilities and payment of foreign debt Increased wages and income transfers to urban workers High level of public investment in infrastructure

economic institutions intact. That is, they transferred income from some players to others, but they left fundamental property relations very much as they were.

Populist policies do not fit neatly into any of the four development strategies we examined in Chapter 5. Instead, they fall somewhere between traditionalism and progressive modernization, representing a first step in the transition from the export to the industrial economy. The Populists deserve credit not for their economic achievements – which were few – but for their spirited attack on traditional ideas and practices. Their failure to solve most of the development problems they took on is attributable primarily to the simplicity of their assault and their obsession with quick solutions to very difficult problems. But, of course, the Populists were leaders in a hurry, fighting to gain a foothold in conservative countries against formidable opposition – hardly conditions conducive to patience, reflection, and long-range problem solving.

Peronista development policy

At the outset Perón dedicated himself to increasing Argentina's economic independence and improving the welfare of the urban poor through a deliberate program of industrialization and social reform. Economic independence required the eviction of the foreign investors who had financed the development of Argentina's export economy. The reduction of foreign control could be managed, the Peronistas believed, through the nationalization of the Central Bank, the paying of the country's foreign debt, and the purchase of the British-owned railways and the communications company owned by International Telephone and Telegraph (ITT). The Central Bank, which had been managed by a consortium of national and foreign banks, was nationalized at the insistence of President-Elect Perón just before he took office. Simultaneously, all private bank deposits were placed under the control of the state to enable government officials to supervise all investment decisions more closely. Perón next drew on the immense gold reserves that had been accumulated during the war to pay off the country's foreign debt and to purchase, at prices favorable to their foreign owners, the railways and communications facilities. By 1949 he had nearly exhausted the country's gold reserves, but he could point with pride to his liberation of Argentina from the most onerous symbols of foreign control.

To promote industrialization, the Peronistas relied heavily on high tariffs to protect Argentine manufacturers from foreign competitors and an overvalued exchange rate that encouraged the importation of capital goods. The government also inaugurated the country's first development plan, a loose collection of projects aimed at improving economic infrastructure. The most important – and most controversial – instrument of industrialization, however, was the creation of a government monopoly over all agricultural commodity trading, permitting Perón to take the profits from commodity sales abroad and transfer them to industrial and public-sector investors. The monopoly was managed by the Argentine Trade Promotion Institute (IAPI), an organization created in 1946 to purchase beef, mutton, and grain from farmers at low official prices; sell them abroad at high postwar prices; and retain the profit to finance government programs. Few things Perón did were more resented by farmers, large and small alike, than his creation of the IAPI. Yet, though the farmers campaigned vigorously throughout Perón's tenure for a return to the free market, they could not weaken his commitment to the scheme.

The Peronistas also worked hard to redistribute income from the propertied classes to urban workers. By using government authority to force wage settlements favorable to loyal unions, they increased real wages by almost 50 percent between 1946 and 1948. Perón also elevated the working class by increasing the number of jobs available in the public as well as the private sector, staffing the newly nationalized enterprises like the railways with thousands of laborers, many of them recent migrants to the cities.

Missing from the Peronista program was any commitment to agrarian reform. Perón's goal was the redistribution of rural profits, not rural property. He encouraged the purchase of land by tenant farmers by freezing rents, but he was content to leave cattlemen and farmers, large and small alike, alone as long as they supplied the beef, mutton, and grain that would bring high postwar prices in foreign markets and finance the government's development programs. He left the rural power structure intact because he needed its produce to pay for industrialization. Ironically, at the same time the Peronistas were trying to reduce their economy's dependence on the rural sector, they found themselves highly dependent on it.

Perón wanted to launch Argentina on a course that would quickly place it among the elite of the world's industrial nations. Its dependence on foreigners was to give way to a new sense of national autonomy as the agrarian export economy was transformed into an industrially self-sufficient one. And workers who in the past had been exploited by an insensitive economic elite were to be given the kind of social justice they deserved. But prosperity, national autonomy, and social justice eluded the Peronistas, and by 1955 Argentina, the country they had tried to launch into a new era, had become a sorry paradox, divided politically and demoralized economically. Between 1945 and 1950 the per capita gross national product had increased at an annual average rate of 2.8 percent and real income at an impressive rate of 3.7 percent. But during the next five years, the per capita product declined at an annual rate of 0.2 percent and real income by 0.5 percent. The quality of the country's economic infrastructure deteriorated, and rural and industrial entrepreneurs lost confidence in the country's public authorities. Perón had tried to build a new Argentina, but had only created a more desperate and discouraged one.

There are many explanations for the failure of Peronista policy. Peronistas blame their problems on several enemies, both domestic and foreign, whom they accuse of subverting their programs. Their critics point to economic mismanagement, governmental corruption, and Perón's failure to heed the warnings of his critics in the private sector. The truth, as usual, lies somewhere in between.

Several unanticipated external conditions did hurt the Peronista program. Perón, for example, had counted on the continuation of high commodity prices in European markets to finance investment, but with the creation of the Marshall Plan and the delivery of millions of tons of American grain to Europe, Argentine trade prospects declined. To make matters worse, two of the country's worst droughts came in 1950 and 1951, further limiting its production. But the Peronistas must share some of the blame. They could have used their gold supply more cautiously to protect themselves against a sudden decline in exports. They also underestimated the high cost of industrialization, especially in imported fuels and raw materials. And they contributed to the decapitalization of the private sector with their financial policies and mismanaged public enterprises, like the nationalized railways, which became a source of featherbedding and a cause of huge fiscal deficits.

Finally, and most important, through his combative, autocratic style and often arbitrary policy decisions, Perón helped demoralize his country's rural and industrial entrepreneurs at the very time he needed their cooperation to execute his programs. Although he made a valiant effort to reverse many of his policies in 1952 and 1953 in order to hold labor in check and encourage higher commodity production, the attempt was too little and came too late to satisfy his growing opposition.

Perón, like Vargas, was given a second try at leading Argentina. After eighteen years in exile, during which time Argentina was plagued by seemingly irresolvable conflicts between Peronistas and anti-Peronistas, Juan Perón, at age seventy-eight, was invited home to restore order to the country he had helped divide. It was a more cautious Perón who offered to heal the country's economic divisions through the use of an innovative "social contract" in 1973. The idea was not especially new: By securing the agreement of the representatives of industry, commerce, agriculture, and labor to a common set of price, wage, and tax policies in advance of their implementation, he hoped to induce these groups to cooperate with the state's campaign to solve fundamental inflation, growth, and production problems. This creative approach to Argentina's problems was never given a full opportunity to prove its worth, however. After a relatively successful first year, Perón died in July 1974, touching off a bitter power struggle among his successors. The result was the collapse of the social contract, which provoked one of the country's most severe economic crises and the intervention of the military once again in late March 1976.

Populist policy in Brazil

Brazilian economic policy was dedicated to the achievement of two objectives during the 1950s: industrial development and the distribution of its benefits to the players responsible for it. The first reflected the government's determination to accelerate a process that was well under way by the time Vargas returned to the presidency in 1951; the second was part of a calculated political campaign to integrate industrialists, foreign investors, and labor leaders into the ruling coalition. To be understood, Brazilian policy and the economic development it fostered must be examined against the background of the 1930s and 1940s and the rise of industrialization in Brazil. We can begin with the 1929 depression and the Brazilian response to it.

After his inauguration as president in 1930, Getulio Vargas turned immediately to the problem of protecting Brazil's export economy from the ravages of the world depression he inherited. He began by purchasing coffee and withholding it from the market in an attempt to propel prices upward. What he managed, however, was not higher prices – the efforts of Brazil acting alone could not lift prices significantly – but the prevention of a collapse in domestic demand within Brazil. It was this maintenance of the level of Brazilian consumption coupled with a decline in imports and repeated currency devaluations that ignited the development of a consumer goods industry within Brazil during the 1930s.

The government's reliance on the stimulation of market forces gave way to more direct state intervention in the economy after the creation of the Estado Novo in 1938. At the urging of his nationalist military advisors, Vargas accelerated the process of industrialization prompted by the depression using investment-promoting taxes, exchange and credit controls, import quotas, and the development of state-owned petroleum and steel enterprises. An added boost to state intervention came with the outbreak of World War II in 1940, which prompted Vargas to initiate full economic mobilization under the direction of the Brazilian state and its rapidly multiplying public enterprises. It was this process that made Brazilian industrialization so different from that of early industrializers like Great Britain and the United States. Where industrial growth was promoted and managed largely by entrepreneurs in the latter, much greater state intervention and direction were necessary to accelerate it in a late industrializing nation like Brazil.

In addition to the protection of coffee producers and the promotion of industrial growth, Vargas introduced a host of social reforms in the late 1930s aimed at consolidating his control over the urban working class. He sought to make the state the patron of organized labor and labor the loyal servant of the state by creating an elaborate welfare system, increasing basic education, improving health care, and supporting unions in their collective bargaining. Such measures, though beneficial to the elite of organized workers, did not apply to the majority of unorganized Brazilian workers who labored in the countryside or in small towns. Yet, by bringing urban workers under the care of the state, Vargas weakened the power of the political Left and gained the control over labor he needed to manage the country's peaceful industrialization.

When Vargas returned to the presidency in 1951, the process of import substitution industrialization prompted two decades earlier by the depression had gathered momentum, but was still far from complete. His initial goal was the acceleration of industrial growth and the diversification of Brazilian production. His economic advisors recognized that Brazil still suffered from structural bottlenecks and a low capacity to import because of insufficient returns on its primary product exports. What was needed, they concluded, was the increased domestic production of consumer goods for local markets. Like most Populists, Vargas cloaked his program in strong nationalist rhetoric, promising to liberate the country from the tyranny of world markets and economic control by foreigners. But his words could not hide the fact that what he prescribed was actually a balanced effort to stimulate economic growth by combining rather orthodox international trade policies with state promotion of industrialization using heavy investments in economic infrastructure, the liberal financing of private entrepreneurs, and the expansion of state enterprises involved in the production of iron, steel, petroleum, and other basic materials.

The skills Vargas had used to dominate the Brazilian polity and stimulate its economic growth after the depression were no match for the task of managing a more complex economy and satisfying the more diverse economic interests that had arisen by the 1950s. For example, when the rate of inflation accelerated and the balance-of-payments deficit reached record levels in 1953, Vargas could devise no solution that pleased all the dominant economic forces. Instead, much like Perón in 1952, he chose to bow to economic realities and adopt a conventional economic stabilization program that cut public spending, limited imports, and tightened credit – to the displeasure of industrialists, merchants, and union leaders. To make matters worse, stabilization did not immediately rescue the economy or save Vargas from his critics. As conditions worsened, so did his control over his office, until in a moment of desperation he took his own life.

Vargas's elected successor, Juscelino Kubitschek, proved more adept at using economic policy to placate the members of the populist coalition while at the same time promoting rapid economic growth. A product of the Vargas school of politics, he recognized that without the deliberate acceleration of economic growth there was little chance of satisfying industrialists, organized labor, and other economic groups simultaneously. So instead of stressing redistribution, he encouraged investment and industrial expansion by promoting the efforts of domestic and foreign entrepreneurs and supporting them with increased public investments in infrastructure and government enterprises. And to demonstrate that he was a modern leader who would launch Brazil into a new age, Kubitschek also promoted the construction of an ultramodern new capital, Brasília, in the country's interior.

Bolstered by improving external conditions, Kubitschek achieved impressive results with his program: Industrial production rose 80 percent and the gross national product increased at an annual average rate of 6.1 percent between 1955 and 1961, one of the highest rates in the hemisphere. Equally impressive was Kubitschek's ability to use his policies to satisfy the demands of competing economic groups. He supplied easy credit and tariff protection to industrialists, price supports to farmers, favorable terms to foreign investors, new jobs and rising wages to labor, and pay raises to the military. Only the peasantry and the urban poor – albeit 50 percent of the population – were excluded from the new bounty, but as nonparticipants in the Brazilian game, they could be ignored without serious political repercussions.

The rapid acceleration of economic growth and the simultaneous satisfaction of diverse groups had its costs. For Kubitschek the cost took the form of record budget deficits, which boosted inflation and contributed to balance-of-payments difficulties. But unlike Vargas, who had earlier responded to similar conditions by imposing unpopular stabilization measures, Kubitschek ignored the pleas of foreign creditors and International Monetary Fund advisors, who insisted on cooling off the overheated Brazilian economy. His defiance won him immense popularity within the country, but it only postponed several tough economic policy decisions, many of which were not made until the military seized control and executed a stabilization program with brutal efficiency in the mid-1960s.

Before concluding this review of populist economic policy in Argentina and Brazil, a brief comparison of the two efforts is in order. As we can see from Table 6-6, there were many differences between the programs of Perón and of Vargas, the latter's being the more moderate and less ambitious of the two. But what about their similarities? What stands out most is their ad hoc character. Populists wanted immediate payoffs rather than gradual development and employed a host of short-term measures to secure them. There was, however, a price to be paid for their rush to prosperity; neither Perón nor Vargas escaped accelerated inflation and balance-of-payments difficulties, which limited the achievement of their original objectives. The failure to promote structural change is the second common feature of populist development policy. Populists wanted to increase the wealth of certain groups without redistributing resources in any significant way. And they did, at least temporarily, increase the income of industrialists and laborers as well as the economic power of the state. But they also left intact a rural economic structure that, especially in Brazil, kept millions of people outside the modern production process and retarded the achievement of balanced economic growth. A third trait of populist policy is its often chaotic administration. This was especially the case in Argentina. The Populists' patronage-ridden bureaucracies seldom met the challenge laid down by policy makers who sought to impose greater financial control and economic regulation on the economy. Corruption, incompetence, and duplication of effort haunted the execution of populist policy and contributed to the reputation of Populists as promoters of financial and administrative disorder, a reputation that fueled the opposition fires and hastened military disillusionment with populist government.

The Populists arose in response to the social changes that accompanied industrialization and urbanization. They were imaginative and opportunistic leaders who skillfully mixed the new idea of mass electoral politics with such old Latin American practices as personalism and authoritarianism. In so doing they transformed political participation from a privilege exclusively of the elite and the middle sectors to a process that for the first time involved the urban masses as voters and emotionally committed followers of the country's political leadership. The fact that urban workers were led into the political process by paternalistic leaders rather than through their own efforts has had a lasting impact on the region's politics. Most notable has been the workers' continued heavy dependence on the state. At times this has placed immense burdens on the state by forcing authorities to cope with expectations they have not always been able to satisfy with their limited resources.

Populist rhetoric raised hopes that populist economic policies seldom fulfilled. The Populists secured short-term prosperity and some redistribution of income, but they did not sustain either for long. They demonstrated how the state could raise the living standard of the organized worker when it committed itself to his betterment. Through industrial, infrastructure, and wage and social policies, they gave the illusion of powerful governments capable of creating mass consuming societies almost overnight. Actually, their efforts were aimed only at promoting the welfare of those most easily reached by government programs: industrialists and urban workers. Landowners and *campesinos* were not so accessible, however. Populists, therefore, had little interest in them or in transforming the economic structures that governed power relationships in the countryside. Nor, despite their nationalism, did they do much to reduce dependence on foreign investors and trading partners. It was the survival of these conditions along with the Populists' tendency to mismanage their economic programs that made it impossible for them to sustain the economic expansion they had so easily ignited at the initiation of their administrations.

The Populists also demonstrated the limitations of personalized autocratic rule as a durable form of government. Their sudden rise to and equally abrupt fall from power demonstrate that something more than clever opportunism and the mobilization of the urban masses is needed to create a stable political order. Greater consensus on the formal and informal rules and more consistency in their application are essential if a government is to escape the kind of insecurity that plagued populist regimes.

The populist experience also contains a message for would-be reformers. It demonstrates that industrialization will not endure long or penetrate deeply into society unless it is accompanied by profound structural changes, especially in the rural sector whose population lives outside the modern economy. Populist programs were halfway measures that increased domestic consumption in urban areas and promoted the growth of light industrialization. But they ignored nearly half the population. By the mid-1950s it became apparent that if economic development was to be accelerated and its benefits distributed widely, this neglected half of the population would have to be included in the development process. And that could be done, the Populists' successors concluded, only through drastic reform of the Latin American political game and the economic structures that sustained it.

FURTHER READING

General

Di Tella, Torcuarto. "Populism and Reform in Latin America," in Claudio Veliz, ed., *Obstacles to Change in Latin America*. London: Oxford University Press, 1965, pp. 47–74.

Lipset, Seymour Martin. "Fascism: Left, Right and Center," in Seymour M. Lipset, *Political Man: The Social Bases of Politics*. Garden City, N.Y.: Doubleday (Anchor Books), 1963, pp. 127–82.

van Niekerk, A. E. *Populism and Political Development in Latin America*. Rotterdam: Rotterdam University Press, 1974.

Argentina

Alexander, Robert. *The Perón Era*. New York: Columbia University Press, 1971.

Baily, Samuel. *Labor, Nationalism and Politics in Argentina*. New Brunswick, N.J.: Rutgers University Press, 1967.

Blanksten, George. *Perón's Argentina*. Chicago: University of Chicago Press, 1953.

Díaz Alejandro, Carlos F. *Essays on the Economic History of the Argentine Republic*. New Haven: Yale University Press, 1970.

Di Tella, Torcuarto. "Stalemate or Coexistence in Argentina," in James Petras and Maurice Zeitlin, eds., *Latin America: Reform or Revolution*. Greenwich, Conn.: Fawcett, 1968, pp. 249–63.

Falcoff, Mark, and Ronald Dokart, eds., *Prelude to Perón*. Berkeley: University of California Press, 1975.

Potash, Robert A. *The Army and Politics in Argentina, 1928–1945: Irigoyen to Perón*. Stanford: Stanford University Press, 1970.

Silvert, Kalman H. "The Costs of Anti-Nationalism: Argentina," in K. H. Silvert, ed., *Expectant Peoples: Nationalism and Development*. New York: Random House (Vintage Books), 1963, pp. 347–72.

Smith, Peter. *Argentina and the Failure of Democracy: Conflict Among Political Elites, 1904–1955*. Madison: University of Wisconsin, 1974.

Snow, Peter. *Political Forces in Argentina*. Boston: Allyn & Bacon, 1971.

Brazil

Bello, José Maria. *A History of Modern Brazil 1889–1964*. Stanford: Stanford University Press, 1966.

Dulles, John W. F. *Vargas of Brazil: A Political Biography*. Austin: University of Texas Press, 1967.

Furtado, Celso. *The Economic Growth of Brazil*. Berkeley: University of California Press, 1963.

Ianni, Octavio. *Crisis in Brazil*. New York: Columbia University Press, 1968.

Jaguaribe, Helio. *Economic and Political Development: A Theoretical Approach and a Brazilian Case Study*. Cambridge, Mass.: Harvard University Press, 1968.

Leff, Nathaniel H. *Economic Policy-Making and Development in Brazil 1947–1964*. New York: Wiley, 1968.

Roett, Riordan. *Brazil: Politics in a Patrimonial Society*. Boston: Allyn & Bacon, 1972.

Schmitter, Philippe C. *Interest Conflict and Political Change in Brazil*. Stanford: Stanford University Press, 1971.

Skidmore, Thomas E. *Politics in Brazil: 1930–1964*. New York: Oxford University Press, 1967.

Stepan, Alfred. *The Military in Politics: Changing Patterns in Brazil*. Princeton: Princeton University Press, 1971.

Weffort, Francisco C. "State and Mass in Brazil," *Studies in Comparative International Development* 2 (12):187–96, 1966.

Wirth, John D. *The Politics of Brazilian Development: 1930–1954*. Stanford: Stanford University Press, 1970.

Young, Jordon M. *The Brazilian Revolution of 1930 and the Aftermath*. New Brunswick, N.J.: Rutgers University Press, 1967.

7. The democratic reform game

Latin America's democratic reformers were more ambitious, better organized, and more concerned with long-term political and economic change than their populist predecessors. But being more ambitious, they also faced greater obstacles, not the least of which were those placed in their paths by players who did not welcome their efforts to transform the traditional political game. The reformers rose to prominence during the 1950s and 1960s in several Latin American countries; yet by the 1970s they were on the retreat throughout most of the region, forced from office by military leaders and economic elites who had lost confidence in their ability to maintain political order and achieve rapid but stable economic growth.

An inquiry into the performance of the democratic reform game must focus not only on its political dynamics and its development policy achievements, but also on its failure to survive in more than a few Latin American countries. Is its apparent decline attributable to the weakness of its leaders, the political power and skill of its opponents, misguided development policies, or other, less obvious, conditions? And does the displacement of democratic reformism by military authoritarianism in many countries represent only a pause in the march toward economic and political reform or is it evidence of reformism's demise? To answer these questions we must examine the democratic reform experience, focusing on its goals, its impact on the traditional political game, and its policy achievements in the face of concerted opposition.

At the outset it should be recognized that democratic reformism, like populism, encompasses several Latin American governments that differed from one another in many details of political organization and economic policy. They were not created through a single, centrally directed campaign. Democratic reformers took their ideas from foreign as well as indigenous theories, including traditional liberal philosophy, European social democratic and Christian democratic ideology, the American New Deal, the Mexican Revolution (especially during its Cárdenas phase of the 1930s), and the populist and structuralist critiques of Latin America's export-induced development. But they did more than adapt the doctrines of others to their needs. They

168

were also astute political strategists who put their democratic ideals to work in societies where such ideals were given little chance of success. They tempered their idealism with a heavy dose of political pragmatism aimed at reorganizing the Latin American political game and the economic structures that sustained it.

Although the origins of democratic reformist regimes are diverse and their histories dissimilar, the regimes do share several traits. Foremost is a commitment to the pursuit of structural economic reform and the creation of mass-based, representative government. Their desire for structural reform was prompted by a recognition of Latin America's excessive dependence on the foreign consumers of its mineral and agricultural commodities and the foreign suppliers of its development capital. They recognized, however, that something more than the stimulation of domestic consumption and light industrialization – the instruments used by the Populists – was required to reduce their economic dependence. They had learned a great deal from the mistakes of the Populists as well as from the sophisticated analyses of the region's underdevelopment prepared by the United Nations Economic Commission for Latin America, which argued that fundamental changes in the region's agricultural as well as urban industrial economies were needed to create modern mass consuming societies.

The most important policy innovation proposed by the democratic reformers was agrarian reform. They were convinced that without the liberation of the rural poor from the bondage of the *latifundio* and the subsistence farm, the formation of a national market capable of sustaining large-scale industry was impossible. Consequently, they set out to integrate all citizens into an enlarged capitalistic economy that could generate its own growth without heavy reliance on foreigners. Of the four development strategies we examined in Chapter 5, the democratic reformers came closest to the one we called progressive modernization. They rejected the export dependence and elitism of traditionalism, the regressive character of conservative modernization, and the high-risk, disruptive methods of revolutionism, and insisted instead on the gradual modernization of economic institutions and the progressive redistribution of income.

The democratic reformers' economic objectives were complemented by their political strategies. They began with the notion that the masses should be integrated into the modern polity as well as the market economy. But instead of mobilizing the masses in some authoritarian manner, they chose to encourage participation in representative institutions using political parties that could develop mass followings and capture public office. Their preference for democratic institutions was strategic as well as philosophical, for democratic rules gave an advantage to those who could organize the masses and control their votes rather than to the economically powerful minority that had traditionally dominated the political game.

Any political movement that seeks to use mass support to acquire political power and then use the power to implement structural reforms must be prepared to meet many obstacles along the way. Two kinds of problems, one technical and the other political, are inevitable.

The technical problems are immense. For example, how do you organize rural and urban masses under the watchful eye of a traditional political elite that opposes your cause? Unprecedented organizational effort and skill are required to penetrate local political arenas and win the allegiance of distrusting *campesinos* and laborers. Similarly, great managerial skill is required to formulate and execute development programs that satisfy all members of the democratic reform coalition while promoting structural reform and economic growth. On the political front you must devise some means for overcoming resistance to your programs. Democratic processes afford opportunities to cultivate widespread public support, but they also give opponents great latitude for obstruction. Reformers can be blocked by parliamentary maneuvers and forced to accommodate the demands of their opponents. Bureaucrats can be bribed or otherwise influenced to sabotage programs, and economic leverage can be applied by landowners, foreign investors, or businessmen to undermine government programs. The courts can also be used by opponents to slow policy execution. In short, there are many ways in which democratic rules can be employed to good advantage by the opponents of reform who are determined to make the democratic reformer a prisoner of his own game.

Gaining the acceptance of the democratic rules of the game by the other players in the game is the reformer's primary long-term political problem. Election victories and legislative success are necessary to the development of democratic rule, but they are not sufficient. The reformer must also build consensual support for democratic processes. That might be done by convincing those initially opposed to democracy that in the long run they will be better served by a process that invites bargaining, compromise, and competitive elections than by any alternative. In practice this involves convincing conservatives that democratic reform is the surest means to prevent radical change and persuading political radicals that democratic reform offers the only way to secure economic and social change without provoking a conservative reaction and military authoritarian rule – difficult tasks at best.

In addition to securing the toleration of his opponents, the democratic reformer must also deliver on his promises to peasants and laborers if he is to retain their support. Given the region's limited resources, it is much easier to raise aspirations than to fulfill them. Moreover, reform takes time: New roads cannot be built, land redistributed, factories put into operation, and jobs increased immediately; such projects require months or even years to complete. And the longer it takes to fulfill promises, the harder it is to hold the reform coalition together.

Last, there is the political problem created by foreign involvement in Latin America's democratic reform movements. The rise of the democratic reformers in the 1950s coincided with the increasing involvement of the United State government, international agencies, and multinational firms in the region. Consequently, at the same time he was trying to reduce his country's dependence on foreigners, the democratic reformer was confronted with an abundance of offers of investments and technical and financial assistance. As a result, no matter how hard he tried to assert his independence, the need for funds to finance his ambitious programs necessitated his heavy reliance on foreigners and his involvement in the ideological struggles of the Cold War era.

Democratic reform movements gained prominence throughout Latin America during the 1950s and 1960s. Their leaders became presidents of several countries, including Guatemala, Costa Rica, Venezuela, Ecuador, Honduras, the Dominican Republic, Peru, Chile, and Bolivia. Two of the most significant experiments in democratic reformism were those of the Christian Democrats in Chile and the Acción Democrática party in Venezuela. Using them as examples, we can identify the dominant features of the democratic reform game and assess its achievements and failures.

DEMOCRATIC REFORM IN CHILE AND VENEZUELA

In Chile and Venezuela we find two contrasting approaches to the creation of the democratic reform game. Although the reformers pursued similar goals, they confronted different political traditions and structures and were forced to adapt their strategies and tactics to these dissimilar conditions.

Table 7-1. *Chile: historical background*

1817	Independence from Spain
1830	Autocratic republic created under President Diego Portales
1871	Liberal republic created through efforts of Liberal, Radical, and National parties
1891	Parliamentary republic organized to reduce power of strong executive and give supremacy to Congress
1921	Liberal reformer, Arturo Alessandri, elected president
1924	Military closes Congress and then installs Alessandri as president with decree. powers to implement constitutional reforms, including proportional representation and strengthening of executive
1927	Colonel Carlos Ibáñez seizes power and creates personal dictatorship
1931	Colonel Marmaduke Grove creates "socialist republic," which lasts six months
1932	Republican government restored and Arturo Alessandri elected president
1938	Popular Front government of Radicals, Democrats, Communists, and Socialists elected
1952	Carlos Ibáñez elected president on populist-type platform
1957	Christian Democratic party created from Falange Nacional (organized in late 1930s) and Social Christian wing of Conservative party
	Communist and Socialist parties form coalition called Frente de Acción Popular (FRAP)
1958	Conservative-Liberal candidate Jorge Alessandri elected president
1964	Christian Democratic leader Eduardo Frei elected president
1965	Christian Democrats win majority in Chamber of Deputies
1970	Socialist leader of Unidad Popular coalition, Salvador Allende, elected president
1973	Unidad Popular government overthrown by military, ending forty-one years of uninterrupted constitutional government

Chile escaped the *caudillo* wars that plagued most Latin American countries after Independence because of the unusual unity of its small political elite and the loyalty of the military to it. The strong executive-dominated governments that ruled Chile throughout most of the nineteenth century were replaced in 1891 after a brief civil war by a "parliamentary" regime dominated by an elite-controlled national congress. The latter, torn from the outset by interparty conflict that manifested itself in continual cabinet instability, collapsed in 1924, and after a succession of brief military governments was replaced in 1931 by a constitutional regime that governed Chile without interruption until 1973. Not only did the Chileans enjoy greater political stability than most Latin American countries after 1931, but they did so using an unusually mature multiparty system and a stubborn commitment to competitive electoral politics. It was a system, however, that was controlled effectively by upper-class and middle-sector parties, which tolerated working-class parties only as long as their interests were not threatened. When working-class parties got out of line, they were outlawed, as was the Communist party between 1947 and 1958.

It was into this unusually sophisticated but as yet moderate political game that the Christian Democratic party (PDC) came in the 1940s. It did not have to fight for admission against authoritarian leaders, as did its counterparts in Venezuela and elsewhere. Liberal democratic rules were already accepted and the PDC had only to turn them to its advantage. Consequently, what the PDC needed at the outset was not a plan of political reconstruction but an election strategy that could generate a large enough following to defeat its conservative, moderate, and radical rivals. Two decades after they commenced their uphill struggle, the Christian Democrats finally succeeded. Under the leadership of Eduardo Frei, they won the presidency with Conservative party support in 1964 and spent the next six years implementing their program of economic and social reform.

The creators of Venezuela's Acción Democrática party (AD) were not as fortunate as their Chilean colleagues. Until 1935 the Venezuelan political game was a dictatorial one. After the death of strongman Juan Vicente Gómez in 1935, the government remained in the hands of the small agricultural and commercial elite that had supported the Gómez regime. It was against this elite monopoly of political power that the campaign of Acción Democrática was launched. The party's origins can be traced to a student protest against the Gómez dictatorship in 1928. Not long thereafter the protesters formed their own political party and set out to evict the elite from power. Lacking the economic power or social prestige needed to play the elitist political game, the party's leaders turned to the rural and urban masses in hopes of gaining through force of numbers what others had secured through wealth or military might. They took advantage of the growth of the urban working class and the discontent of the peasantry, promising both political rights and economic rewards in exchange for vocal support. Their road was longer and their struggle more difficult than those of the Chilean Christian Democrats, yet once they gained public office they held it much longer than the Chileans. In fact, with the overthrow of the Chilean democracy in 1973 Venezuela became one of the few remaining islands of political democracy in a sea of military dictatorships.

Table 7-2. *Venezuela: historical background*

1821	Independence from Spain
1859	Federal (civil) War lasting four years, killing 40,000, and leaving country in economic ruin
1870	Eighteen-year dictatorship of Liberal Antonio Guzmán Blanco begins
1908	Dictatorship of Juan Vicente Gómez begins
1921	Export of petroleum commences
1935	Juan Vicente Gómez dies
	Generation of 1928 student leaders, led by Rómulo Betancourt, create Movimiento de Organización Venezolana (ORVE, later renamed Partido Demócrata Nacional), predecessor of Acción Democrática party (AD)
1945	Unión Patriótica Militar, organized by young officers and supported by Acción Democrática, overthrows conservative government of General Isaías Medina Angarita
1947	Under new constitution Acción Democrática wins presidential election and congressional majority
1948	Acción Democrática government overthrown by military, which creates ten-year dictatorship of General Marcos Pérez Jiménez
1958	Military overthrows Pérez Jiménez government
	Rómulo Betancourt, leader of Acción Democrática, elected president
1963	Raúl Leoni, of Acción Democrática, elected president
1968	Rafael Caldera, of Christian Democratic party (COPEI), elected president
1973	Acción Democrática regains presidency with election of Carlos Andrés Pérez
1976	All foreign petroleum and iron-mining firms nationalized

THE RULES OF THE DEMOCRATIC GAME

The electoral route to power

How do reformist leaders who begin their campaigns with little public support capture public office for themselves? The answer depends on the conditions they face. Specifically, their strategy is shaped by the political rules under which they must operate and the strength of their opponents. If elections are already in use, they must mobilize new voters or win over those who have supported other parties in the past. If elections are not held, they must try to secure their adoption and then use elections to defeat their opponents. But if public office can be gained only through the force of arms, they may have to rely on the military to place them in power, no matter how much it violates their principles.

Although the Chileans and Venezuelans shared a preference for the electoral route to power, they differed in the ways they pursued it. Their different strategies were attributable, in large part, to the contrasting rules under which they were compelled to operate. Chile's Christian Democrats arose in a society where regularly scheduled elections were the norm rather than the exception. By the time they were ready to enter the political process, the country had already experienced two decades of constitutional rule and multiparty parliamentary politics. Their task was not the creation of rules they could use to capture public office but the more conventional one of defeating well-established political parties by winning a plurality of the vote. To succeed, they had to outorganize their rivals and take voters away from them. In contrast, the Venezuelans had no electoral tradition on which to draw. Although there had been some opening of the political process after the dictator Gómez died in 1935, the likelihood of free elections was still remote when Acción Democrática leaders began their campaign in earnest in the early 1940s. Consequently, the Venezuelan reformers had to be prepared to evict political incumbents through other means if the electoral route was denied them.

The rise of Chile's Christian Democrats from a small faction within the Conservative party in the late 1930s to the presidency in 1964 is an impressive, though unspectacular, story. The origins of what became the Christian Democratic party in 1957 can be traced back to a group of law students at the Catholic University of Chile in the late 1920s. Sons of conservative Catholic families, Eduardo Frei, Radomiro Tomic, Bernardo Leighton, and Rafael Agustín Gumucio took their inspiration from Catholic philosophers who sought to revitalize Roman Catholicism as an agent of social change. Frei and his associates had become disillusioned with the status-quo-oriented Conservatives; yet they wanted no part of the Marxist or anticlerical Liberal parties then active in Chile. For them social catholicism offered an alternative to the excessive individualism and economic exploitation fostered by nineteenth-century liberalism and the atheism and collectivism of communism. There was, however, no Chilean party ready to embrace their new ideology during the 1930s. The Conservative and Liberal parties sought only to preserve the power and privileges of urban and rural elites and foreign investors, the middle-sector Radicals were anticlerical and little concerned with social justice in the countryside, and the Socialists and Communists rejected Christian theology. The only option, it became clear in 1937, was to organize a party of their own that could challenge the others.

The transformation of a small, obscure political party into an organization that attracted a majority of the Chilean electorate in the presidential elections of 1964 involved a long and patient struggle that did not generate concrete results until the mid-1950s. The young Falangists, as they were called at the outset, played the game according to the conventional rules of Chilean politics, winning an occasional seat in the legislature and from time to time accepting a cabinet post in a coalition government. The party's breakthrough began in 1957, when Eduardo Frei, its recognized leader, was elected a senator from Santiago, the capital. Still, in the presidential elections of 1958 Frei and his party – now renamed the Christian Democratic party to associate it with similar parties in Germany and Italy – managed only 21 percent of the popular vote. Nevertheless, the Christian Democrats emerged from the election with an appetite for the presidency and a strategy for capturing it.

In the past they had relied on local constituency organizations built around particular candidates, but after 1958 they accelerated efforts to build mass organizations. Central to their strategy was the mobilization of the so-called marginals – urban slum dwellers, peasants, and the unemployed, who had been ignored by the political process in the past. By capturing them and denying their support to Communist and Socialist parties, the Christian Democrats hoped to reduce the latter to permanent minority status. Accordingly, they created neighborhood associations in the slums of major cities, organized women's associations, and energetically recruited supporters among the urban unemployed, using thousands of students to organize these new voters. Along the way they were given a boost by the Roman Catholic Church, whose leaders encouraged their parishioners to support the party. The leadership of the party, however, remained in the hands of politicians and progressive businessmen.

Most important to the Christian Democrats' success in 1964 was their ability to devise a campaign strategy that exploited recent changes in the Chilean electorate. Electoral democracy had been acceptable to Chilean Conservatives because of restrictions placed on mass participation that confined the enfranchised electorate primarily to elite and middle-sector men, thereby preventing true mass involvement in Chilean politics. In 1949 the franchise was extended to women. Still, administrative roadblocks to voter registration continued to limit turnout. Finally, in 1962 these hurdles were removed with the adoption of a system of permanent registration. Immediately, the proportion of the population that was registered to vote increased from one-eighth to one-third. The organization of these new voters before the 1964 election became the primary objective of the Christian Democrats.

The support of new voters was, by itself, not enough to catapult the Christian Democrats to victory. They also needed the votes of thousands of citizens who had opposed them in 1958. As we can see from Table 7-3, only 21 percent of the electorate had voted for the Christian Democrats in 1958, whereas almost 30 percent had supported the Socialist-Communist coalition, FRAP, led by Socialist Senator Salvador Allende. The likelihood of the Christian Democrats' taking votes from the Left was remote, for the Marxist parties had, since the 1920s, developed a hard core of supporters, especially in the labor movement. The only viable option was to pursue voters who had supported the Conservatives, Liberals, and Radicals in 1958.

But how does a political party that campaigns on a platform of social and economic reform attract conservative and middle-sector voters? It does so, the Christian Democrats decided, by convincing Conservatives that the Christian Democratic party was the most appropriate vehicle for preventing a dreaded Marxist victory in the 1964 elections. The logic of their argument was simple. In 1964 Chileans were locked in a three-way electoral battle involving parties of the Left, Center, and Right, with each standing a chance of victory. Thus, if the Conservative, Liberal, Radical, and Christian Democratic parties divided slightly less than two-thirds of the electorate equally among them, they could give the election to the Marxist coalition on the Left. Because a Marxist victory was the least desirable option from the Conservatives' point of view, the Conservatives might be persuaded to pool their resources with the Christian Democrats to forestall a FRAP victory.

If the Christian Democrats needed some assistance in persuading

Table 7-3. *Chilean presidential elections, 1958 and 1964 (percent)*

Party	1958	Party	1964
Conservative-Liberal parties		Democratic Front	
Jorge Alessandri	31.6	Julio Duran	5.0
Christian Democratic party		Christian Democratic party	
(PDC)		(PDC)	
Eduardo Frei	20.7	Eduardo Frei	56.1
Popular Action Front (FRAP)		Popular Action Front (FRAP)	
Salvador Allende	28.9	Salvador Allende	38.9
Others	18.8		

Conservatives to support their candidates, they received it in March 1964, six months before the presidential election, when a Conservative was upset by the FRAP candidate in a special congressional election for a minor rural seat. The threat of a Marxist victory was suddenly very real and, exploiting it to the fullest, Christian Democratic candidate Eduardo Frei secured enough Conservative and Liberal party support at the last minute to block Salvador Allende's path to the presidency. With the assistance of his allies on the right, Frei, who had received only 21 percent in 1958, polled an amazing 56 percent of the popular vote in the September 1964 election. Thus, playing by the Chilean rules and turning them to his personal advantage, Eduardo Frei ended a thirty-five-year uphill struggle with one of Chile's most impressive presidential victories.

Venezuela's Acción Democrática party also had to wage a long and difficult campaign to gain public office. In fact, in order to secure its hold on the government it had to go through two successive campaigns against heavy opposition, for after winning office the first time in the mid-1940s, it suffered the humiliation of a military coup that forced it into exile until it was given a second try in 1958.

The movement that became the Acción Democrática party in 1941 was, like the Chilean Christian Democratic party, created by university students in the late 1920s. Led by Rómulo Betancourt, Raúl Leoni, Jovito Villalba, and other students who opposed the dictatorship of Juan Vicente Gómez, the Generation of 1928, as they were known, did not cease their activities once Gómez had died in 1935, but continued to campaign for the democratization of the Venezuelan political process. Posed against them were the combined forces of a well-entrenched political elite that drew its support from the country's larger landowners and businessmen, the military, and the foreign-owned petroleum industry, which, after entering Venezuela in 1915, accounted for 90 percent of the country's export earnings by 1930. Venezuela's post-Gómez political leaders were determined to build a modern urban economy by using oil revenues to construct a sound economic infrastructure and to finance industrialization. At the same time, they wanted nothing to do with the kind of open, competitive democratic politics that threatened their political control. For those who objected to their rule, as did Betancourt and his colleagues, they offered either jail or exile.

Despite continual harassment by the government, the Generation of 1928 managed to lay the foundations for a formidable political party by 1945. They did so by introducing the idea of mass political organization to Venezuela. Inspired by the success of Mexico's revolutionary party, the peasant- and labor-based APRISTA party of Peru, as well as developments among mass parties in Europe between the wars, they traveled to every corner of the country to secure recruits and create constituency organizations. They reasoned that their only hope of taking power rested in the kind of popular support that would force the conservative regime to open up the political process and respect the results of free elections. Because the vast majority of rural and urban workers still remained outside of the political process, it would be through their mobilization that democracy would be created in Venezuela.

But it was not a free election that brought down the Venezuelan regime in 1945. Instead, a military coup, led by young officers and encouraged by Acción Democrática, deposed the government. Their support of the military coup of 1945 proved an embarrassment to Acción Democrática leaders because it so clearly violated their democratic principles, opening them to accusations of crude opportunism and raising questions about their commitment to the creation of democratic processes. In their defense, Betancourt and his colleagues argued that they had no other option. Despite the elite's promise of democratization, the government had moved very slowly, limiting the franchise to the upper and middle classes and the electoral process to indirect voting for public officials. Under such conditions the coup was not the act of desperate self-serving political opportunists, but the logical response of a democratic party determined to make a clean break with the authoritarian past.

True to their promises, Acción Democrática leaders persuaded the military to permit the free election of a constituent assembly, which wrote a new constitution in 1947. To no one's surprise, AD polled 78.8 percent of the Assembly vote, and then went on to win the presidency with 74.4 percent and capture two-thirds of the seats in Congress. The magnitude of its victory bore witness to the success of the mass organization strategy, which by 1948 had brought 300,000 urban workers into the AD-controlled Venezuelan Workers Confederation (CTV) and 43,000 peasants into its Venezuelan Peasant Federation (FCV).

Venezuela's new democracy was short-lived, however. In 1948 the opposition struck back with a military coup that overthrew the new government, sent most AD leaders into exile, and disbanded all labor and peasant organizations. Massive electoral victories and a new constitution had not been enough to ensure that all players would conform to the new rules of the Venezuelan game. Acción Democrática's success had been too swift and its break with the past too sharp for

Venezuelan Conservatives. When the AD government tried to use its mandate to execute a sweeping agrarian reform and revise the petroleum law, Conservatives responded with the coup. The democratic reformers spent the next ten years in exile reassessing their past campaigns and planning future ones. They came away from their deliberations convinced that more caution was required in their relations with Venezuela's agricultural and commercial elite and more attention had to be given to creating a new role for the military in the democratic game. Despite the immense popularity of democratic government, it was still vulnerable to the economic power and military strength of its opponents. If reform measures were to succeed, they would have to be implemented slowly and carefully, avoiding direct attacks on those who were capable of striking back. Thus, instead of concluding that reform required the immediate destruction of the conservative elite, AD strategists, like other Latin American reformers during the 1950s, decided they would have to meet the elite half way, accommodating themselves to its needs while subtly but steadily reforming the structures that sustained it.

The new strategy was put to the test after the military overthrew dictator Marcos Pérez Jiménez in 1958. During the election campaign that followed the coup, Acción Democrática candidates assured their opponents that they planned to implement a reformist program without depriving the Church, the business community, the military, or farmers of their wealth. They would instead concentrate on transferring public and unexploited private lands to peasant farmers, raising taxes on petroleum exports, and financing a long-range program of industrialization. They were opposed in the 1958 election by several new parties, many of which sought to emulate their example and success. As in Chile, a Christian Democratic party (COPEI) arose to represent moderate Conservatives and Catholic reformers. The addition of the Republican Democratic Union (URD), a party dedicated primarily to the candidacy of Jovito Villalba, a member of the Generation of 1928 who had abandoned his colleagues several years before, made it a three-way contest. The rise of opposition parties was a mixed blessing, for although they posed a threat to AD's electoral dominance, they also reinforced the drive for democracy by bringing other constituencies into the democratic game.

The opposition cut deeply into Acción Democrática's support, but it did not prevent the election of Rómulo Betancourt to the presidency with 49.2 percent of the popular vote. He was followed by URD's Jovito Villalba with 34.6 percent, and COPEI's Rafael Caldera with 16.2 percent. Although it received only 13 percent of the vote in metropolitan Caracas, Acción Democrática had polled 57 percent in small towns and 66 percent in rural areas, where its peasant support was still strong.

Taking different routes to power, democratic reform parties came to govern Chile and Venezuela in the 1960s. Skilled leadership, sophisticated organization, and tenacity in the face of tough opposition had served them well. In Chile the Christian Democrats broadened the democratic process and put to the test the idea that social and economic reform could be realized through democratic means. The Venezuelan reformers, in contrast, had created new democratic institutions and opened them to the masses. The real challenge to democratic rule, however, was not its creation, but its ability to survive and fulfill its promises to the underprivileged.

Managing the democratic reform game

The democratic reformer's problems only begin once he has taken office. He must not only use the electoral process to defeat his opponents but must also adhere to the rules of the democratic game while executing his reform program, tolerating the efforts of his opponents to obstruct him at every turn. Success is determined not by the amount of force he can bring to bear against the opposition but by his legislative skill and the persistence and creativity of his bureaucracy.

The democratic policy maker requires skills seldom needed by the authoritarian leader. His world is one of campaigns and elections, interest groups and political parties, legislatures, coalitions, and constant bargaining. To survive in such a world he cannot rely on his power to command, but must become a mobilizer of public opinion, a negotiator with opponents and allies alike, and a survivor of occasional defeats. His high ideals must be matched by a commitment to political practicality. He must be able to assess his own political strength as well as that of his opponents and move quickly to take advantage of the latters' weaknesses. He is a leader who is as concerned about means as about ends. The tools of his trade are negotiation and compromise. He will not win on every issue or achieve all his objectives; nevertheless, if he makes the best of the opportunities open to him as well as the skills he has developed, he should win often enough to satisfy his desire for political and economic reform. Or so it is hoped.

Although one is initially impressed by the obstacles that confront the democratic reformer, further examination reveals some of his strengths as well. Competitive politics can be an effective means for generating a wide range of policy alternatives, making the policy maker better informed about the options available to him. The representation of diverse interests also forces decision makers to take private wants and needs into account. Moreover, an open policy-making process encourages the kind of feedback that policy makers need to correct their errors and avoid wasteful mistakes. Finally, and perhaps most important, democratic processes help generate popular support for, and public cooperation with, the government's programs. Unlike authoritarians, who often must impose their policies on a reluctant society, the democratic reformer can, through the use of coalitions, bargains, and propaganda, secure voluntary compliance with official policy.

The performance of the democratic reformer depends, of course, not only on his political skills or the policy-making properties of the democratic process, but also on the conduct of the other players in the game. If players refuse to bargain with the government or are determined to block it at every turn, democratic processes are greatly impaired. Moreover, if, as is common in Latin American democracies, some players are determined to secure the government's violent overthrow, the regime itself is in constant danger. Consequently, the task of the democratic reformer, which is formidable under the best of conditions, becomes exceptionally difficult under the conditions often found in the Latin American political game.

Neither Chile's Christian Democrats nor Venezuela's Acción Democrática was spared the kinds of obstacles that have plagued democratic rule throughout the hemisphere. Both had enemies within the system and outside it and both had to bargain with obstinate opponents. Nevertheless, they worked hard at making democracy work, taking up the challenges laid down by opposition parties and interest groups. Their ability to operate under the democratic rules of the game is revealed most clearly in the ways they managed three problems: increasing their political strength through legislative coalitions and other means, holding their parties together, and retaining public office in the face of stiff electoral opposition.

First, the problem of legislative coalition building. Eduardo Frei won the 1964 election by attracting conservative voters to his party. But once the Conservatives had accomplished their objective of denying Socialist Salvador Allende the presidency, the coalition dissolved. To make matters worse, the Christian Democrats were still a minority party in Congress. Congressional elections, which in Chile do not coincide with presidential elections, would not be held until March 1965. In the meantime the PDC held only 23 of 147 House seats and 4 of 45 Senate seats, hardly enough to secure the passage of its reform legislation against the combined opposition of Communist, Socialist, Radical, Conservative, and Liberal party legislators. But, instead of seeking a coalition with one of these parties, the Christian Democrats put all their effort into the 1965 elections, asking Chileans to sustain the mandate they had given in September 1964. The strategy was in large part successful, for the PDC increased its hold on the House by taking 81 seats; however, it gained only 13 seats in a Senate election in which only half the seats were contested. Consequently, throughout the remainder of his term President Eduardo Frei had to work with a divided Congress in which the parties of the Left and the Right could unite to block PDC measures in the Chilean Senate.

Acción Democrática President Rómulo Betancourt was initially more successful in his coalition-building efforts. As the leader of a party that did not receive a majority of the popular vote or legislative seats in the 1958 election, he had little choice but to seek the support of other political parties. He began with a three-party coalition composed of the Christian Democrats and the URD as well as his own AD. Actually, an agreement among the three parties had been signed before the election guaranteeing the formation of a national unity government under the direction of the victorious party. This was AD's way of assuring its opponents of its commitment to a collaborative rather than a combative strategy during its second try for public office. Although the coalition proved useful in securing the adoption of much of AD's legislative program, its duration was cut short by the withdrawal of the URD in 1960. COPEI, however, remained until the 1963 elections, gaining the exposure and experience it needed to bolster its own campaign for the presidency. With the election of AD candidate Raúl Leoni in 1963 to replace Betancourt, the formation of a coalition was again necessary. This time the URD rejoined the government, but COPEI withdrew, hoping to strike out on its own in preparation for the 1968 elections. Like legislative coalitions elsewhere, those formed by Acción Democrática lacked permanence and stability. Nevertheless, they served the government well during the first eight years of Venezuela's restored democracy. Not only did they assist in the passage of most of the government's reform program, but they also helped fortify an ethic of cooperation and peaceful competition among the country's leading parties. Without such beliefs, the democratic experiment would not have succeeded.

Not only are democratic reform parties often forced to take on coalition partners, they must also work hard to prevent division within their own ranks. One might think they would be spared internal dissension given their strong party organizations and dedication to principle over personality. But parties that try to attract so many different supporters and bridge the wide gap between the radical Left and conservative Right, as do democratic reformers, cannot escape doctrinal disputes, serious disagreements over public policy, and even occasional conflicts of personality.

Neither Chile's Christian Democrats nor Venezuela's Acción Democrática escaped such problems. The Christian Democrats had brought together middle-sector moderates once supportive of the Conservative, Liberal, and Radical parties with students and young professionals who believed in a program of economic and social reform. Throughout Frei's presidency the PDC was divided into three factions: one that supported Frei's moderate course, a second that demanded a more socialistic program, and a third that sought a middle position. Disputes over the government's development program were common during the Frei administration, but serious conflicts were initially avoided through the distribution of cabinet posts among members of all three factions. Gradually, however, frustration with the slow rate of reform increased, and conflicts among the three wings of the party became more intense, especially during the 1967 party conference. Just as Frei was preparing to introduce austerity measures to deal with rising inflation, he was met with demands for the acceleration of reform through the adoption of the Plan Chonchol, a proposal prepared by agrarian reform minister Jacques Chonchol advocating greater state control over the economy and more rapid land expropriation. The battle was eventually won by Frei and his supporters in the moderate faction, but their victory came at the expense of the loss of Chonchol and his followers, who left the PDC in 1969 to form their own party, the United Popular Action Movement (MAPU), which allied itself with the Marxist coalition that supported the candidacy of Salvador Allende in the 1970 election.

Factionalism was an even greater problem for Acción Democrática and eventually cost it the election of 1968. From the outset, the more radical members of the party opposed its conciliatory approach to post-1958 politics. In April 1960 a pro–Fidel Castro faction left the party. A second split occurred in early 1962 when a group of middle-level party leaders broke with the old guard led by Betancourt and Leoni. In 1967 AD split once again, this time over the selection of the party's presidential candidate. Although it survived the first two splits with most of the party intact, the third split contributed to AD's loss of the presidency. Led by party president, Luis Beltran Prieto Figueroa, whom a group of dissidents supported for president in 1968, the rebels formed their own party when the dominant faction, guided by Betancourt and Leoni, insisted on the nomination of Interior Minister Gonzalo Barrios. The result, as we can see in Table 7-4, was the unexpected victory of Christian Democrat Rafael Caldera in 1968.

This brings us to the third condition that affected the survival of democratic reform parties: their ability to defeat their opponents in elections. As we can see from Table 7-4, despite its inability to secure a majority of the vote, Acción Democrática won reelection in 1963, but went down to defeat in 1968. The COPEI victory in 1968 was not, however, as great a threat to AD and its reform program as first appeared. By the time of its election, COPEI had already adopted much of AD's platform and during its campaign had promised to retain most of the reforms already implemented. Nor did COPEI offer much of a future electoral challenge, with its 29.1 percent of the popular vote in 1968. To have blocked the inauguration of the COPEI government by conspiring with the Venezuelan military was clearly not in AD's self-interest, for in the long run it would suffer even more than its competitors from violation of the democratic rules of the game. The rules were still in AD's favor, as became clear in 1973, when the party, more united than it had been in a decade behind the candidacy of Carlos Andrés Pérez, regained the presidency with 44.3 percent of the popular vote.

The Chilean story is a much more tragic one. After a stunning congressional victory in 1965, the Christian Democrats' electoral support began to decline as Conservatives returned to their own party and the Marxist Left continued to build toward the 1970 elections. Although we will examine the 1970 Chilean presidential election in detail in Chapter 10, when we discuss the rise and fall of Chilean Socialist Salvador Allende, it merits a brief comment here as well, for with it came the beginning of the end of Chile's Christian Democratic experiment and the Chilean democratic game.

The 1970 election was once again a three-way contest involving a

Table 7-4. *Venezuelan presidential elections (percent)*

Party	1958	1963	1968	1973
Acción Democrática (AD)	49.2	32.7	28.3	44.3
Christian Democrats (COPEI)	16.2	20.2	29.1	30.3
Republican Democratic Union (URD)	34.6	17.5	12.0	3.2
Peoples' Electoral Movement (MEP)	—	—	19.3	5.1
Others	—	29.6	22.3	18.1

choice among the National party (formed by the merger of the Conservative and Liberal parties in 1966), which nominated elder statesman Jorge Alessandri, president between 1958 and 1964; the Christian Democrats led by Radomiro Tomic, one of the party's founders and a close associate of Eduardo Frei; and a coalition on the Left, led again by Salvador Allende but this time called Popular Unity (UP). Alessandri promised a retreat from the reformism begun by the PDC, Tomic a more radical reformist program than Frei's, and Allende a peaceful socialist revolution. The Conservatives once again held the trump card, for if they supported the PDC, it would undoubtedly win, but if they supported Alessandri, the election would be close with any one of the three the possible winner.

This time both the National party and the Christian Democrats chose to gamble for victory by going it alone. National party leaders were convinced they stood to gain little from the accelerated reformism of another PDC administration. Bolstered by preelection polls that predicted Alessandri's victory, they fully expected to win a three-way race. Tomic believed that another alliance with the Conservatives would retard reform and make a mockery of his promise of radical change. Yet, because the leadership of the PDC refused to allow him to pursue a coalition with the Marxist parties, as he desired, Tomic was forced to adopt an electoral strategy that sought to undercut Allende's support by appealing again to the urban and rural poor as well as the middle sectors.

When the ballots were counted, Salvador Allende the Socialist, not Tomic or Alessandri, had won. In the weeks that followed the National and Christian Democratic parties had to make some of the most difficult strategic decisions ever to face Chilean party leaders. This period was also the severest test of Chilean democracy in its forty-two-year history. Because Salvador Allende had received less than a majority of the popular vote (36.5 percent), he could not be inaugurated until he was confirmed by a vote of the majority of the National Congress. And for that he needed the support of parties outside his coalition because they still controlled a majority of the seats.

Few decisions could have been more difficult for a democratic reform party than the one taken by the Christian Democrats in December 1970. If they confirmed Allende's election, they were gambling that he would respect the country's democratic traditions long enough to allow the PDC to regain the presidency in the 1976 elections. If they voted against confirmation, they would break the rules and invite others to do likewise, eventually perhaps undermining the whole system. In the face of clandestine efforts by the United States government and Chilean Conservatives to secure Christian Democratic support for a plot to block Allende's confirmation, the PDC made its choice: It confirmed Salvador Allende after requiring that he sign a statute of guarantees, which committed him to respecting the constitution as well as the independence of the press, trade unions, and the educational system.

The story does not end there, as we shall see in Chapter 10. In September 1973 Allende's government was overthrown by the Chilean military. Some time later the Christian Democratic party, along with most others, was outlawed and many of its leaders forced into exile. Thus, one of Latin America's most durable constitutional democracies came to its end.

THE GRAND COALITION OF DEMOCRATIC REFORMISM

Democratic reformers are coalition builders. They have to be, for operating alone, the intellectuals and professionals who lead democratic reform movements would stand little chance of success against entrenched domestic and foreign elites. They draw their political strength primarily from their ability to join diverse players into a common front to do battle with Conservatives on the Right and Marxists on the Left. But large and diverse coalitions also have their costs, as democratic reformers have discovered repeatedly.

When the diversity of interests included within a reformist coalition increases, so does the likelihood of conflict among its members over policy matters. Sooner or later the gains of some coalition members may have to come at the expense of others, making it difficult to hold the coalition together. There is also a high probability of conflict between the democratic reformer's ambitious and wide-ranging policy objectives and the interests of some members of his coalition. His reforms may threaten political moderates or critical players such as foreign investors or the military. When they do, he will have to decide whether to abandon the offensive policies in order to retain the support of a valued ally or to pursue them and risk creating a new opponent. In most instances, democratic reformers drift back and forth between these two tactics, trying to preserve as much of their programs as they can without irreparably damaging their base of support. One of the consequences of such behavior is the appearance of indecisiveness and lack of purpose. This has provoked revolutionaries to denounce democratic reformers as vacillators incapable of imposing their will on a reluctant society and military leaders to criticize them for not showing the determination needed to execute the harsh measures frequently required to promote stability and growth. Such criticism has led to revolutionary campaigns to undermine democratic reformism and military decisions to overthrow those rsponsible for it.

To appreciate the dilemmas faced by the creators of democratic reform coalitions, we have only to look again at Chile and Venezuela. Their goals were quite similar: They sought to avoid revolutionary change by integrating the rural and urban poor into mass organizations controlled by leaders drawn from the middle sectors. Unlike the Populists who limited their efforts primarily to the urban working class, the democratic reformers also sought the support of the peasantry. In so doing they undertook the biggest challenge of all, that of bridging the gap between the forces of urban modernization and those of rural tradition and isolation.

When the Chilean Christian Democrats set out to create a mass organization in the early 1960s, the country's urban middle sectors and industrial proletariat were already well organized and deeply involved in politics. The former had governed the country through the Radical party during the 1940s, using their power to promote industrialization and the expansion of the public sector; organized labor participated primarily through the Socialist and Communist parties. Only the peasants and the unorganized urban poor were unrepresented in the political process; the latter seldom voted, and peasants, when they did vote, conformed to the dictates of the landowners who controlled them.

Christian Democratic leaders recognized that they could not succeed by relying only on progressive middle-sector groups or on temporary alliances with Conservatives opposed to their platform. With most of organized labor already loyal to Marxist parties, they had to turn for support to unorganized urban laborers, white-collar workers, and the peasantry. They built their coalition from the top down, starting with professionals, intellectuals, and idealistic students, and then adding thousands of the urban poor who were organized into neighborhood associations (juntas de vecinos), lower- and working-class women through the use of mothers' clubs, and rural workers and small farmers whom they organized into peasant associations. They even promoted the formation of new unions among workers not already controlled by the Marxists. Together, these newly organized groups formed the foundation of the Christian Democrats' "national community" uniting Chileans of different social strata and economic sectors behind the one party dedicated to bringing the rewards of capitalist development to all citizens.

When Acción Democrática began its quest, very few Venezuelans participated in the political process. It was to the unorganized, excluded masses that the ad leaders turned for support. They began in the early 1940s with the labor movement. By promoting unionization and then securing the victories of their own candidates in union elections, they were able to establish control over organized labor. At about the same time they began the more arduous task of organizing peasants through a campaign that resulted in AD command of the peasant vote in most regions. They also received some support from the middle sectors, although these groups remained small and divided their loyalties between AD and various conservative groups. Through this broad, multisector, multiclass coalition, Acción Democrática overwhelmed its opponents when an honest election was finally held in 1946.

Conspicuously missing from the democratic reform coalition, yet essential to its survival, was the military. Unless the military was neutralized or won over to the government's cause, it posed a serious threat to the government's survival, as the Venezuelan military demonstrated when it overthrew the AD government in 1948. When the constitutional regime was restored to Venezuela in 1958, AD leaders were careful to cultivate military support by lavishly financing military programs, encouraging the suppression of rural guerrillas, and refraining from direct confrontations with the military's allies within the economic elite. In return, the Venezuelan military respected the norms of democratic politics. Chilean democratic reformers were more fortunate. Since its last coup in the late 1920s, the Chilean military had left politics to civilians. As long as the Christian Democrats maintained public order, respected the military's institutional integrity, and did not permit the radicalization of Chilean politics, they were not challenged by military leaders.

Not to be overlooked was the United States government, which became an informal ally of democratic reform governments throughout the hemisphere during the 1960s. The democratic reformers rose to prominence at the time of Fidel Castro's triumph in Cuba. The administration of President John F. Kennedy reacted to Castroism by offering to help democratic reformers defeat revolutionary movements wherever they threatened. Through the Alliance for Progress, economic and military assistance was supplied to most Latin American governments. United States officials also meddled frequently in the internal affairs of several countries, helping players whom they favored and undermining those, especially on the Left, whom they opposed. One of its most notable efforts came during the 1964 Chilean elections when American funds paid for much of the Christian Democratic campaign. Undoubtedly, democratic reformers could have operated without foreign assistance. The aid did, however, facilitate their efforts by increasing the resources they had to keep their coalitions together.

What about the opponents of democratic reformism? Among them are, potentially, most *latifundistas,* many conservative businessmen, the foreign investors who faced the threat of nationalization, and political parties on the Left and Right who did not welcome competition from a new mass-based party. In the short run these opponents had little choice but to accommodate themselves to reform. Of course, it helped that democratic reformers were usually willing to make concessions to their opponents, especially in the economic elite. In Chile, Eduardo Frei, for example, agreed to limit his expropriation of *latifundios* to one-third of those available; the Venezuelans relied heavily on the redistribution of public land and the generous purchase of private properties. Moreover, businessmen and foreign investors often benefited more from the government's development programs than did the masses. Mutual accommodation was the order of the day, and those willing to adapt to the new economic rules seldom suffered from reformist policies.

The democratic reform coalition was never as strong or as secure as its creators intended. Disputes over the substance and pace of reform haunted it and led to frequent defections, especially by interest groups and party factions who thought presidents were too willing to compromise with their conservative opponents. Reformers were also plagued by the immense difficulty of holding together a coalition that sought to unite peasants with urban workers and both of them with the middle sectors. As long as resources are plentiful there is a chance that such a coalition can be held together, but when the competition for scarce resources intensifies, as it does frequently in Latin American countries, each coalition member tends to go its own way in the struggle for survival.

REFORMIST DEVELOPMENT POLICY

Like revolutionaries, Latin America's democratic reformers aspire to a more equitable and just society, but unlike revolutionaries, they are not willing to destroy all traditional institutions and practices in order to achieve their objectives. Instead, they want to change the existing order by modifying it, preserving those parts that have served society well and discarding those that have not.

The idea of reform is not new to Latin America. The Liberals of the late nineteenth century were reformers in their day, determined to reduce the power of the Church, improve the condition of commercial farmers, and develop the export economy. The middle-sector political parties of the 1920s were also reformers, devoted to opening the political process. What made the mid-twentieth-century democratic reformers different was their desire for structural change and mass participation. Where their predecessors had been limited by a very narrow view of economic development, they took a wider perspective, convinced development could be achieved only through a well-planned attack on a host of interrelated problems. Driven by a fear of Marxist revolution and a desire for economic development and social justice, they offered programs aimed at escaping from the grip of tradition without abandoning all traditional values and capitalist institutions.

The Chilean and Venezuelan development programs were among the most complex of those adopted by democratic reformers during the 1960s. Both followed the outlines of the progressive modernization strategy. Taking their ideas from the United Nations Economic Commission for Latin America's structuralist critique of Latin American development, they identified antiquated and inequitable agrarian structures, retarded industrialization, exclusion of the masses from the market economy, and excessive dependence on mineral exports as the causes of underdevelopment, and they set rural modernization, progressive income redistribution, diversification of production, and integration of the masses into the modern economy as their objectives. The true test of the reformist approach to development, however, is found not in its objectives but in its selection and application of instruments that can attain those objectives in the face of well-entrenched traditions and determined political opposition.

The Chilean and Venezuelan reformers offered their countrymen structural reforms along with a host of short-term remedial measures. Among the former were the redistribution of land from *latifundistas* to *campesinos,* state promotion of heavy industry and industrial diversification, and an increase in national control over critical mining and utility enterprises previously owned by foreigners. Their short-term economic policies included progressive tax reform and increased expenditures for economic infrastructure and social services, especially education, health care, and housing, and the elevation of working-class income. These were ambitious undertakings. Not only did the reformers invite opposition from several players, but they also faced many technical problems that came with the reorganization of the rural economy, the bureaucratic management of development plans, and the inflationary consequences of increased public expenditures and higher wages. To determine how well the Chileans and Venezuelans dealt with these and other problems, a brief assessment of their performance during the 1960s is in order.

Agrarian reform

Little insight is needed to appreciate the traditional failings of Chilean and Venezuelan agriculture. Both countries are blessed with fertile regions, yet throughout the 1950s both had to import large quantities of food. Moreover, each suffered from a constant exodus of the rural poor to already overcrowded cities because of the impossibility of economic survival on the land. The causes of low production and rural-to-urban migration were the same – the maldistribution of property and its inefficient use by landowners. By the time the reformers had come to power, their countries' rural economies had been extensively analyzed by domestic and foreign experts. The problems were well known; the only question that remained was whether the government could do anything about them. Drawing on the advice of a host of experts as well as many foreign examples, each adopted an agrarian reform program aimed at increasing productivity and redistributing property to the landless.

Eduardo Frei was not the first Chilean president to sign an agrarian reform bill, but he was the first to implement one. In 1962, under the pressure of his coalition partners in the Radical party, Conservative President Jorge Alessandri secured the passage of Chile's first agrarian reform bill. But like so many other agrarian measures adopted throughout the hemisphere at the time, it had very limited application, having defined eligible property as only that which had been abandoned or was used inefficiently. It is no wonder, then, that Eduardo Frei made agrarian reform a campaign issue in 1964 and a central part of his legislative program in 1965. Nevertheless, despite its compelling nature, Frei's bill did not become law until 1967 because of the opposition of conservative and Marxist legislators, the former because they stood to lose property and power under the law and the latter because they did not want the Christian Democrats to be credited with alleviating the land tenure problem through the use of its modest reforms.

The new law contained several innovative measures. First, size rather than use would determine expropriation. Large estates, regardless of how they were farmed, would be broken up. Second, the land would be purchased by the government at its declared tax value rather than its current market value. Because Chilean landowners habitually underdeclared their land value at tax time, this approach would penalize them for such practices as well as save government funds by lowering the cost of expropriation. Third, the landowner would be paid only 10 percent of the price in cash with the other 90 percent in twenty-five-year bonds. Finally, the expropriated estate would be turned over to the peasants who had worked it or lived in the immediate area and then organized into an *asentamiento* under the direction of an elected peasant committee and experts from CORA, the government agrarian reform agency. The actual administration varied from one *asentamiento* to another, with some dividing property into private plots, others formed into cooperatives, and a few farmed collectively. Frei's rural reforms were not, however, limited to the reallocation of property. He also encouraged the organization of farm workers' unions and their use to raise rural wages. At the same time, new incentives were given to farmers to raise production, and self-help projects were encouraged in rural villages to build schools, roads, and health care facilities.

Throughout his campaign and during his first year as president Frei had promised to transfer land to 100,000 of the country's approximately 200,000 landless peasant families. It was a promise he could not complete. In fact, only 21,000 peasant families had received land by the time Frei left office in 1970. Legislative opposition, bureaucratic delays, technical problems, and obstruction by landowners turned a noble promise into a bitter disappointment and gave Marxist opponents a campaign issue they could use to attract peasant support in 1970. The Frei government did raise the income of rural workers by an estimated 70 percent and increase rural production by an average of 3.8 percent a year, but it became clear in 1970 that despite their bold initiatives, the Christian Democrats had not solved their country's rural problems. They had made a beginning, but in the process had raised hopes they could not fulfill and alienated a conservative elite that was prepared to risk defeat by the Marxists rather than lend further support to the Christian Democrats in 1970.

The Venezuelan agrarian reform came soon after the inauguration of the Acción Democrática government in 1959. In contrast to the Chilean legislation, which was tied up in the Senate for two years by its opponents, the Venezuelan law was an exercise in interparty cooperation, having been designed by a coalition of parties that included the Christian Democrats and Communists as well as AD. The law was a moderate one that stressed production and distribution objectives and the purchase of expropriated lands at market value, a luxury the oil-rich Venezuelans, unlike most Latin American governments, could afford. Although the Agrarian Reform Law of April 19, 1960, authorized the expropriation of unproductive lands, farms worked by tenants and sharecroppers, and lands used for large-scale cattle raising, most of the land that was redistributed was government-owned rather than privately owned. Of the estimated 300,000 families who needed land, approximately 100,000 received it between 1960 and 1970, a major accomplishment in comparison with the performance of most agrarian reform programs in Latin America, though nevertheless one that fell short of government objectives.

The purpose of the new law, however, was not only to improve the condition of *campesinos*. It was also used by the AD government to promote the more productive use of privately owned land. And here it was even more successful. Under threat of expropriation, farm production increased dramatically after 1960, rising in value by 58 percent in ten years and making Venezuela self-sufficient in most commodities. Nevertheless, in the mid-1970s the agrarian reform program was still a matter of controversy in Venezuela, though in contrast to the early years, the criticism came increasingly from the Left rather than the Right, with the former claiming that agrarian reform had done more for the large commercial farmer than for the rural poor, for it had left the country with a rural proletariat that was migrating to the cities in greater numbers than ever before.

Industrialization

In the area of industrialization we find the most marked contrast between policies in Chile and Venezuela. The difference is due not so much to their development strategies as to their different starting points and the resources available to them. Chilean industrialization had been underway for several decades when the Christian Democrats won the 1964 election, but Venezuelan industrialization was just beginning in earnest at the initiation of the second Acción Democrática administration in 1959. Both governments wanted to reduce their dependence on industrial imports, especially consumer durables, but Venezuela, with its high income from petroleum exports, could finance new industrial projects more easily than could Chile, with its lower per capita return from copper exports. Thus, whereas manufacturing increased by an annual average of 6.6 percent during the first ten years of AD rule, it grew by only 1.5 percent annually during the Frei administration.

At its inception the Betancourt administration dedicated itself to a program of centrally planned development that included the creation of a large and diverse industrial sector to reduce the country's dependence on petroleum exports. The situation was especially acute in the early 1960s because oil prices had declined by 8 percent between 1958 and 1961. Venezuela's industrial development objectives have been set in successive five-year economic plans drawn up by CORDIPLAN, the national planning agency, and executed by the Ministry of Development and the autonomous Venezuelan Development Corporation. Although the public and private sectors have worked closely together to implement the plans, the most spectacular achievements have been those of public enterprises like the Venezuelan Guayana Corporation, an organization created to supervise one of the most ambitious regional development projects in Latin America. Located in the basin of the Orinoco River, the project includes hydroelectric facilities, iron ore mines, steel and aluminum industries, and several petrochemical enterprises. The Venezuelan Development Corporation has also financed may other public and private ventures, using revenues from petroleum taxes. After specializing in import substitution industries for six years, it switched to intermediate and capital goods enterprises in 1966. Largely because of these efforts Venezuelan industrial production was 75 percent greater in 1970 than it had been ten years before. Though the economy is still heavily dependent on its petroleum industry, Venezuela is well on the way toward the construction of an industrial base that could sustain the economy once petroleum resources are exhausted.

Nationalization

Few countries have been more dependent on the export of a single commodity than Chile is on copper and Venezuela on petroleum. The development programs of both countries have benefited from the revenues yielded by these valuable commodities, yet both have also been the prisoner of them. When commodity prices fluctuate, so does the performance of highly dependent economies. To make matters worse, the exploitation of copper and petroleum has traditionally been under the control of large multinational corporations, a circumstance that even further reduces the country's control over investment and export decisions critical to its development. The reformer's response to the foreign exploitation of minerals is a cautious one that tries to balance the need for capital and technology with a desire for greater national control over strategic resources. Neither the Chileans nor the Venezuelans found the situations they inherited acceptable. But instead of evicting the foreigners immediately after taking office, they sought more moderate solutions aimed at securing higher returns in the short run and greater control over the long haul.

Frei called his solution to the copper problem "Chileanization" rather than nationalization because it was a halfway solution that increased Chilean participation in the industry without evicting the three multinational firms – Braden, Anaconda, and Kennicott – that owned Chile's copper mines. The Chileanization Law, which was passed with some Conservative party support in 1965, provided for the Chilean government's purchase of 51 percent of the shares in the largest mine (owned by the Braden Company) and the smelting of copper ore within Chile. However, to finance the purchase of the stock, the Braden Company lent the Chilean government the funds in exchange for a 35 percent reduction in the taxes the company paid to the government. The deal, which was supported by moderates within the PDC and tolerated by foreign investors, was severely criticized by Socialists and Communists, who called for outright nationalization. Frei nevertheless held firm to his compromise and applied similar policies to the Chilean purchase of American-owned utilities. His goal was not to drive foreign investors from the country, as he feared the Marxist proposals would do, but to join them in a partnership beneficial to Chile. The issue became one of the most controversial the Christian Democrats faced during Frei's tenure because it forced them to confront directly the costs of compromising with the foreigners whose control over the Chilean economy they were trying to reduce. It divided the party during the 1970 presidential campaign and gave the Marxists another popular issue to use against the PDC.

Petroleum has transformed Venezuela from one of the poorest countries in Latin America to one of the wealthiest on a per capita basis. Since the early 1920s petroleum has dominated the Venezuelan economy. In 1960 it accounted for 96 percent of the country's export earnings, 69 percent of all government tax revenues, and 30 percent of the gross national product. The constant flow of oil revenues, even in times of price decline, has given Venezuela a resource denied most Latin American countries. The question facing the Venezuelans since the early 1920s has been not where to find financial resources but how to put them to good use. The dictator Juan Vicente Gómez squandered oil revenues; his immediate successors channeled them primarily into the business sector, and Marcos Pérez Jiménez used them primarily to construct expensive infrastructure projects.

The Acción Democrática strategy was different. AD leaders first increased Venezuela's share of oil profits, raising it to 60 percent in

1959 and 70 percent a few years later. At the same time, however, they quietly began negotiations with other oil-producing countries aimed at the formation of a common marketing strategy. Under the leadership of Venezuelan minister of petroleum and mines, Juan Pablo Pérez Alonso, the Organization of Petroleum Exporting Counties (OPEC) was formed in 1960. Not until the early 1970s, however, after the world demand for petroleum had increased dramatically, were the OPEC nations able to take advantage of their strategic position. Prices were raised from $1.90 a barrel in 1972 to $9.80 two years later, bringing immense returns to producer nations like Venezuela. The economic impact was enormous: From 30 percent of the gross national product petroleum rose to 47 percent in 1974, and the Venezuela balance-of-payments surplus, which was a respectable $372 million in 1972, rose to $4.3 billion (American billion) in 1974. The OPEC feat, despite the damage it did to the sixteen oil-importing nations in Latin America, gained Venezuela new respect throughout the hemisphere.

Venezuela's petroleum reforms were not completed until one final step was taken on January 1, 1976, by the Acción Democrática government of Carlos Andrés Pérez. Pérez had campaigned on a platform calling for the complete nationalization of the petroleum industry. With near unanimous congressional support he secured passage of the necessary legislation in 1975. The move had actually been planned well in advance, and by the time it was completed thousands of Venezuelan technicians had been trained to manage the new government petroleum company, PETROVEN. To placate the nationalized firms the Venezuelan government compensated them handsomely, retained the services of several company technicians, and agreed to market Venezuelan petroleum through the networks of several multinational companies.

Venezuelan petroleum policy, with its gradual but deliberate assertion of national control, is regarded by many as one of the highest achievements of reformism in contemporary Latin America. Certainly it is an impressive feat. However, it should be recalled that the Venezuelans enjoyed several advantages not held by their neighbors. Their commodity is desperately needed by the industrial nations and therefore brings a high price. Moreover, because petroleum has risen to the center of international economic policy and public attention, retaliatory actions by either foreign governments or multinational firms are less likely than ever before. The Venezuelans have exploited these advantages wisely, to be sure, but they are among the fortunate few who have them to exploit.

Managing economic growth

Deliberate structural change is the most dramatic aspect of reformism. Because it attracts so much attention, we often ignore the more mundane short-term economic policy making. However, it is in the day-to-day management of the economy and its inflationary, growth, and balance-of-payments problems that the reformer encounters some of his most frustrating problems.

Reformist economic policy confronts a government with several difficult assignments. Not only does it ask public officials to coordinate a well-planned program of public investments, but it also requires the promotion of rapid economic growth through the use of tax, price, and wage policies that can lead to inflation and heavy indebtedness to foreigners. Success is handicapped because several years of structural change may be required to eliminate the principal causes of inflation, capital will have to be imported in large quantities to finance ambitious development plans, and in the short run raw products and capital goods must be imported in order to build and operate new industries. Consequently, even more than the populist, whose economic objectives are less ambitious, the reformer must be a consummate manager of economic policy, able to weave together long-term and short-term objectives and instruments, constantly adjusting his measures to avoid excessive foreign debts and uncontrollable inflation.

As one might suspect, the short-term economic policies of Chile and Venezuela during the 1960s were heavily influenced by the status of copper and petroleum in the international marketplace. Eduardo Frei was fortunate that his term as president coincided with a gradual rise in world copper prices, a condition that helped finance his initial public investments and build up an impressive foreign exchange reserve. Venezuela's Rómulo Betancourt, in contrast, saw petroleum prices decline by 8 percent between 1958 and 1961 while the prices of imported goods were rising. To guide an economic recovery from a growth rate of only 1.3 percent in 1958, Betancourt adopted conservative fiscal and monetary policies while at the same time encouraging long-term investments in the public and private sectors that would contribute to future economic growth. Frei, in contrast, used his foreign exchange resources to promote industrial growth and the rapid expansion of social programs.

The results of the two policies are also dissimilar. Betancourt's moderate policies slowed the progress of social reform, but they contributed to higher investments, relative price stability, and the gradual improvement in the country's balance of payments. He was aided throughout by a steady flow of petroleum revenues, which, though slightly diminished, were still substantial. Frei, on the other hand, after an impressive performance in his first two years, was forced to retreat from his expansionary policies thereafter. He had hoped to combat inflation by increasing the supply of consumer goods and agricultural commodities, making his large government bureaucracy more efficient, and improving the performance of the commercial and service sectors using selective controls and regulations. He also wanted to transfer resources to poorer Chileans through progressive tax reform and higher wages while at the same time reducing inflation from its 46 percent rate in 1964 to near zero by 1967. Frei did bring inflation down to 18 percent by 1967, but in 1968 it began to rise again, reaching 33 percent in 1970. By 1967 tax increases had reached their limit, foreign credits began to decline, and unions became more militant in their wage demands – all conditions that slowed the fight against inflation and reduced the rate of economic growth to 2 percent in 1967 and 3 percent in 1968. Frei sought relief through an austerity program that required worker and manager matching contributions to an investment fund, a measure aimed at reducing demand and increasing investment. But opposition from legislators on the Left and Right blocked passage of the bill, leaving Frei to struggle to the end of his term with inflation and growth problems (see Table 7-5).

Frei's economic performance was an especially bitter pill for the Christian Democrats to swallow, not only because it threatened their chances in the 1970 election, but also because it demonstrated that Chile's reformers had not begun to overcome the country's produc-

Table 7-5. *Average annual real growth rates of Chile and Venezuela*

	Chile		Venezuela
	1965–70 (Frei administration)	1960–73	1960–73
Gross national product	3.6	4.0	5.7
Total imports	8.7	5.7	6.4
Total exports	4.0	4.2	6.7
Gross domestic investment	4.1	3.6	4.7
Retail price index	27.2	34.2	1.6

Source: World Bank. *World Tables 1976.* Washington, D.C., 1976, pp. 74–5, 242–3.

tion and price stability difficulties. They had, of course, not been given enough time to deal adequately with the causes of Chile's endemic inflation. Moreover, Frei's congressional opponents must share some of the responsibility for these shortcomings. Nevertheless, his performance raised many questions about the ability of reformers to solve fundamental development problems. By 1970 it was apparent that the structural changes the Christian Democrats had attempted were taking much longer than anticipated, that parliamentary delays had taken a high toll, that the bureaucracy was less responsive to new programs than expected, and that internal disputes within the Christian Democratic party and the party's failure to motivate and mobilize the masses to the degree hoped for had cost its programs dearly.

Do these contrasting results indicate that Betancourt and his successors were superior economic managers or that their programs were better conceived than Frei's? Not necessarily. The most one can conclude is that it is easier to attain relative economic growth and stability if one enjoys the support of opposition parties in Congress, is blessed by the steady flow of revenues from valuable commodity exports, and can postpone costly social policies temporarily. It also demonstrates

Table 7-6. *Reformist development programs*

	Venezuela (1959–76)	Chile (1964–70)
Agrarian reform	Conservative approach stressing use of public lands and compensation for private land at market value	Moderate approach stressing expropriation of large estates and compensation at declared tax value
Industrialization	Public financing of private investment and creation of public enterprises in basic industries	Financial and tax incentives to domestic and foreign investors
Nationalization	Gradual expansion of state control ending in nationalization with compensation of petroleum and iron ore industries	Purchase by state of 51 percent of foreign-owned copper mines
Short-term growth	Initial conservative monetary and fiscal policies accompanied by infrastructure investments and delay in delivery of social programs until mid-1960s	Expansionary monetary and fiscal policies aimed at expanding production and social programs until 1967, followed by antiinflation measures

the advantage of an adequately financed late start for industrial development. Where Chileans had lived through three decades of deliberate government attempts to promote economic development and had developed a wide variety of competing vested interests in the public and private sectors, Venezuela was still relatively new at the development game, and its leaders were therefore freer to innovate. Chile's three principal political parties disagreed on the fundamentals of economic development and its management, but Venezuela's leading parties were in almost complete agreement on all but the details. Consequently, Frei had to struggle against powerful opponents, whereas Betancourt and his successors could rely on a much higher degree of consensus. These political conditions as well as more fundamental economic ones seem to account for their dissimilar performances.

Finally, a word about the consequences of reformist policy in Chile and Venezuela. Undoubtedly, the reformers changed their societies in important ways by introducing new economic strategies and executing innovative development policies. Some of the players who had enjoyed great privileges in the past were disadvantaged by reformism, and many who had been previously ignored benefited from it. But how deep and extensive were these changes and who actually benefited from them?

There is no clear answer to this critical question. Nevertheless, some general observations can be made. First, the reformers accelerated the expansion of state power and economic control. Those who managed state enterprises became a new technocratic elite with lasting influence in politics. Whereas the traditional elite relied primarily on its economic and social power, the reformist technocrats drew strength from their bureaucratic power and expertise. Second, many peasants and laborers did gain access to the political process and did use it to improve their economic condition. For most the improvement was marginal, but for a few it was great.

It is equally apparent that most foreign and domestic economic elites have survived and, in many cases, even prospered under democratic reformism. To be sure, they have been forced to make many concessions: Private property has been expropriated and foreign enterprises nationalized. For some, these losses were severe. Yet, on the whole the elites have adapted very well, learning how to tolerate reform without giving up a great deal to it. The traditional elite's world is no longer one of quiet isolation where its members are the complete masters of their own enterprises; it is a world filled with bureaucratic regulation, government economic planning, and a constant flow of communications between the managers of public and private enterprises. It is also a world where progressive labor legislation and nationalistic regulations have to be accepted and visibly enforced. Yet, like their counterparts in the more industrialized capitalist systems of the world, the entrepreneurs who have survived reformism have learned to profit from economic modernization. As a result wealth remains highly concentrated in both Chile and Venezuela, despite reformist policies, as we can see from Table 7-7. In Venezuela the concentration has increased substantially under the development programs of reformist governments, which clearly have benefited entrepreneurs, politicians, and foreign investors more than the masses.

THE LIMITS OF DEMOCRATIC REFORMISM

It should be evident by now that the democratic reformer has one of the most difficult jobs in the Latin American political game. Unlike the conservative, who can cling to the status quo, or the revolutionary, who can physically eliminate his adversaries, the democratic reformer must operate within the traditional order while trying to change it. It is his commitment to the middle road and to compromise that makes his task so frustrating. Because he cannot change power relationships fast enough to reduce the strength of his conservative opponents, he is forced to do battle with them, often on their terms. At the same time, his commitment to the democratic rules of the game leaves him vulnerable to the efforts of revolutionaries who do not respect such rules. His only hope is to create a coalition powerful enough to overcome his enemies on the Right and deter those on the Left.

Before concluding our assessment of democratic reformism, we must try to identify the conditions that appear to contribute to its success or failure in Latin America. Clearly, there is no simple mix of necessary or sufficient conditions that guarantee reformist success. Nevertheless, certain political, social, and economic conditions do appear to contribute to the fate of democratic reformers and merit comment.

First, the political conditions. A large multiplayer coalition that integrates peasants and laborers with elements of the middle sectors, progressive industrialists, and bureaucrats appears to be needed to sustain the democratic reform regime. The support of the masses is necessary to secure electoral victories and effect structural change in the countryside and in the factories. And because entrepreneurs and

Table 7-7. *Income distribution, 1960 and 1970*

	Chile		Venezuela		Argentina		Brazil[a]		Peru[a]		Mexico[a]	
	1960	1970	1960	1970	1960	1970	1960	1970	1960	1970	1960	1970
Percent of national income received by poorest 20% of population	N.A.	5.0	3.0	2.0	7.0	5.0	5.0	5.0	3.0	2.0	4.0	4.0
Percent of national income received by wealthiest 5% of population	N.A.	30.0	27.0	40.0	29.0	21.0	23.0	27.0	50.0	34.0	29.0	36.0

[a] The significance of the data on Argentina, Brazil, Peru, and Mexico will be discussed in later chapters.
Source: World Bank. *World Tables 1976.* Washington, D.C., 1976, p. 517.

bureaucrats control the allocation of most of society's resources, they too must participate in the ruling coalition. Critical to holding the coalition together is the availability of sufficient resources to allow the democratic reformer to satisfy peasants and laborers without having to deprive entrepreneurs and professionals. He must be able to take enough from the rural elite and external sources to fulfill his promises without having to demand sacrifices from his middle-sector supporters. Seldom, however, are ample resources available, and sooner or later one member of the coalition is asked to sacrifice for others. When that occurs, the unity of the coalition is threatened. It can be held together in the short run if trust in democratic reform leaders is high or if the deprived player can be convinced that his sacrifice is only temporary. Unfortunately, trust is in short supply in the Latin American political game, and few players believe they will be compensated tomorrow for what they sacrifice today.

Second, there are several social conditions that appear to facilitate the democratic reformer's task and increase the probability of his success. He can, for example, more easily organize and communicate with a small, homogeneous population than with a large diverse one. The fewer the number of people he must deal with and the greater their unity as a nation, the easier it is to secure their acceptance of the democratic rules of the game, other things being equal. Conversely, the deeper and more widespread the class and ethnic cleavages he faces, the more difficult it is to build a coalition large enough to sustain the democratic reform game. The absence of such cleavages during most of the postwar era undoubtedly facilitated the operation of democratic processes in small countries like Costa Rica, Venezuela, Chile, and Uruguay. Large, diverse populations divided by cultural and social cleavages are not insurmountable obstacles to democratic reform, but they do make its adoption and maintenance very difficult, as we have seen repeatedly during the past few decades.

The democratic reformer must also be a skillful economic manager. He not only has to execute complex economic reforms but also must do so without alienating the foreign and domestic entrepreneurs on whom he depends for the production of agricultural and industrial goods. He is faced by the constant dangers of inflation and foreign exchange shortages and is under the watchful eye of Conservatives, multinational firms, and international agencies who judge unorthodox economic policies and poor performance harshly. Should they decide to oppose the reformer, they can make the implementation of his program very costly by placing many financial obstacles in his path. To complicate matters, the reformer must operate with a bureaucracy that is usually unprepared for the burdens thrust upon it. Some agencies can be easily captured and controlled by Conservatives opposed to reform; others lack the resources and dedication needed to enforce complex reformist measures.

The reformer's failure to avoid economic crises has fueled opposition fires and encouraged the military to intervene repeatedly. Even when the economic crises are caused by conditions beyond the president's control, they still provide the excuse needed by his opponents to declare his experiment a failure and bring it to an abrupt halt. In the early years of democratic reformism, the removal of one administration often led to the election of another after the supporters of the reformist coalition forced the military to give them another chance. But since the mid-1960s Latin America's militaries have dealt harshly with democratic reformers, not only removing them from office but closing down the democratic game as well in Brazil, Peru, Ecuador, Bolivia, Chile, Argentina, and Uruguay. What the military officers who deposed reformers during the 1960s and 1970s did after they seized power will be the subject of Chapter 8.

FURTHER READING

General

Anderson, Charles W. *Politics and Economic Change in Latin America: The Governing of Restless Nations.* New York: Van Nostrand, 1967.
Hirschman, Albert O., ed. *Latin American Issues: Essays and Comments.* New York: Twentieth Century Fund, 1961.
    Journeys Toward Progress. New York: Twentieth Century Fund, 1963.
Prebisch, Raúl. *The Economic Development of Latin America and Its Principal Problems.* New York: United Nations, 1950.

Chile

Edwards, Thomas. *Economic Development and Reform in Chile: Progress Under Frei 1964–1970.* East Lansing: Michigan State University, Latin American Studies Center, 1972.
Gil, Federico. *The Political System of Chile.* Boston: Houghton-Mifflin, 1966.
Gross, Leonard. *The Last Best Hope: Eduardo Frei and Chilean Democracy.* New York: Random House, 1967.
Kaufman, Robert. *The Politics of Land Reform in Chile 1950–1970: Public Policy, Political Institutions, and Social Change.* Cambridge, Mass.: Harvard University Press, 1972.
Operations and Policy Research, Inc. *The Chilean Presidential Election of September 4, 1964.* Washington, D.C., 1965.
Petras, James. *Politics and Social Forces in Chilean Development.* Berkeley: University of California Press, 1969.

Williams, Edward J. *Latin American Christian Democratic Parties*. Knoxville: University of Tennessee Press, 1967.

Zeitlin, Maurice. "The Social Determinants of Political Democracy in Chile," in James Petras and Maurice Zeitlin, eds., *Latin America: Reform or Revolution*. Greenwich, Conn.: Fawcett, 1968, pp. 220–34.

Venezuela

Alexander, Robert J. *The Venezuelan Democratic Revolution: A Profile of the Regime of Romulo Betancourt*. New Brunswick, N.J.: Rutgers University Press, 1964.

Blank, David Eugene. *Politics in Venezuela*. Boston: Little, Brown, 1973.

Bonilla, Frank, and José Silva Michelena, eds. *The Politics of Change in Venezuela*, Vol. I. Cambridge, Mass.: MIT Press, 1967.

Farley, Rawle. "The Economics of Realism: A Case Study of Economic Change in Venezuela," in Rawle Farley, *The Economics of Latin America*. New York: Harper & Row, 1972, pp. 279–303.

Freidmann, John. *Venezuela: From Doctrine to Dialogue*. Syracuse: Syracuse University Press, 1965.

Martz, John. *Acción Democrática: Evolution of a Modern Political Party in Venezuela*. Princeton: Princeton University Press, 1965.

Martz, John, and David Myers, eds. *Venezuela: The Democratic Experience*. New York: Praeger, 1977.

Petras, James F., Morris Morley, and Steven Smith. *The Nationalization of Venezuelan Oil*. New York: Praeger, 1977.

Powell, John Duncan. *Political Mobilization of the Venezuelan Peasant*. Cambridge, Mass.: Harvard University Press, 1971.

Tugwell, Franklin. *The Politics of Oil in Venezuela*. Stanford: Stanford University Press, 1973.

8. The military authoritarian game

The dominant force in Latin American politics during the past decade has not been democratic reformism or revolutionism, but militarism. Repeatedly the generals have seized control of their unruly nations, convinced they are uniquely qualified to deal with the many development problems that have frustrated civilian officials. As a result, it is the military regime, not the democratic or revolutionary one, that now dominates the Latin American scene.

Governments whose officials are not selected by the people they claim to serve are not new to Latin America. Throughout the nineteenth century most Latin American nations were governed by autocrats who relied primarily on the force of arms to stay in office. They ruled in a personalistic, but conservative, manner, acting like stern fathers intent on keeping their children in line. Under their firm leadership, landowners and exporters prospered while the masses languished. By the turn of the century, however, the small armies that had sustained these traditional autocrats had begun to change, gradually transforming themselves into professional organizations with the assistance of European advisors. Occasionally they were called upon to do combat with neighboring countries or to fight in foreign wars, but more often they turned their attention inward, devoting themselves to the preservation of the existing institutional order against the threats posed by potential enemies of the ruling class.

In Chapter 6 we saw how the Brazilian and Argentine militaries intervened in national politics frequently after 1929 – the Brazilians playing the role of arbitrator in domestic conflicts in 1930, 1937, and 1945; the Argentines overthrowing the Radicals in 1930, the Conservatives in 1943, and Perón in 1955. Military intervention was also common in the rest of the region, especially after 1930. Immediately after the depression, military officers intervened to protect or restore conservative leaders who were determined to preserve the traditional order by dealing harshly with depression-induced economic crises and social conflicts. In later years they also stepped in occasionally to bring down dictatorial presidents and help launch democratic governments, as occurred in Venezuela in 1945 and 1958. Military intrusions persisted in the 1960s and 1970s, but the succession of coups that began with Brazil in 1964 was markedly different from the interventions that had come before. Between 1930 and 1964 Latin America's armies had used their weapons primarily to replace one group of civilian leaders with another more to their liking. With only a few exceptions, military rule was temporary, serving as a bridge between nonmilitary governments. The generals who took over after 1964, in contrast, came to stay.

The military officers who have organized authoritarian regimes throughout Latin America during the past decade and a half were driven by more than their traditional fear of Marxist revolution. They were also prompted by increasing disillusionment with liberal democratic politics. What disturbed them were not the rules of the democratic game per se, but the rules' effects on national development. Too frequently, constitutional governments, though well-intentioned, had been associated with political disorder and economic stagnation. Instead of ruling with a firm hand, civilians had, in the view of development-minded officers, tolerated, and in some instances even encouraged, intense social and political conflict; moreover, they also frequently pursued demagogic objectives that led them to appease consumers rather than to promote the kind of capital accumulation needed to achieve sustained growth. Undoubtedly, these perceptions were badly distorted by the military's narrow view of political order and economic development. Nevertheless, accurate or not, such perceptions led it to seize power and organize authoritarian regimes in most of the hemisphere after 1964.

Foremost among the military's objectives has been the creation of a more orderly political process, free of the uncertainty and conflict that traditionally accompanied disputes over political rules. Of course, the military too had contributed to political instability with periodic coups in support of one player or another. But this time the officers were determined to break with the past and create an entirely new political game. Where conservatives, populists, and democratic reformers had failed, they expected to succeed by forcing all citizens to conform to a single set of political rules of the military's own design.

A second goal of the military was to lay the foundation for stable economic growth. Postwar economic development had been managed primarily through a process of import substitution industrialization that had been ignited by the 1929 depression. Although impressive growth rates had been achieved in some instances, the creation of consumer goods industries did not bring self-sustaining economic expansion to the region. Nor did it halt the political unrest caused in part by the unfulfilled promises of populists and democratic reformers. Instead, many countries continued to suffer from periodic inflation, foreign exchange shortages, and increasing conflict between the haves and the have-nots. Two of the most frustrated observers of these shortcomings were ambitious, development-oriented military officers and civilian technocrats who were anxious to use the authority of the state to put an end to political dissension and construct a new economic order. Together they launched their new version of the military authoritarian regime.

BRAZIL, ARGENTINA, AND PERU

In April 1964 Brazilian military leaders created a government that set an example since emulated by the militaries of several other Latin American countries. Not long after overthrowing the government of President João Goulart, they suspended the constitution, closed all political parties, and canceled the political rights of many prominent elected officials. A succession of Institutional Acts was promulgated over the next decade that defined the scope and power of the new government, giving it almost complete authority over Brazilian politi-

Table 8-1. *Postwar Brazil: historical background*

1950 Getulio Vargas elected president with support of Social Democratic party and Brazilian Labor party, receiving 49 percent of popular vote
1954 President Vargas commits suicide at age seventy-two
1955 Juscelino Kubitschek, candidate of Social Democratic party and Brazilian Labor party, elected president with 36 percent of popular vote
1960 Jânio Quadros, candidate of National Democratic Union party, elected president with 48 percent of popular vote
1961 President Quadros resigns and is succeeded by Vice-President João Goulart; military allows Goulart to become president after imposing parliamentary system to reduce his powers
1963 Presidential system restored by national plebiscite
1964 On March 31 military overthrows Goulart and creates authoritarian regime under Marshal Humberto Castelo Branco, who is elected president by Congress
1967 Marshal Artur Costa e Silva selected as president
1969 President Costa e Silva forced to resign because of ill health and replaced by General Emílio Garrastazú Médici
1974 General Ernesto Geisel selected as president

cal life. The economy was placed under the direction of civilian and military technocrats, who were assigned the task of coordinating the contributions of state agencies, foreign investors, and Brazilian entrepreneurs to the country's development. During its first phase (1964–7) the new government concentrated on combating astronomical inflation, restoring investor confidence, and discouraging working-class unrest. Then, after its harsh stabilization measures had taken effect, it promoted economic growth, achieving record levels of industrial expansion between 1968 and 1973. On the political front, it cautiously organized a government-controlled two-party system, but blocked all attempts to restore effective democracy to the country.

Unlike the Brazilian military regime, which has survived into the late 1970s, the one directed by General Juan Carlos Onganía in Argentina lasted only four years, from 1966 to 1970. In 1966 Onganía had other plans, however. Like the Brazilians, he announced his intention to stay in office until steady economic growth had been achieved and a new system of government put into effect. He too suspended the constitution, closed down political parties, and imposed

Table 8-2. *Postwar Argentina: historical background*

1955 In September President Juan Perón is overthrown by military insurrection known as Revolución Libertadora. After brief interlude under General Eduardo Lonardi, General Pedro Aramburu becomes president

1958 Constitution of 1852 restored, and Arturo Frondizi, candidate of Intransigent Radical party (UCRI), elected president

1962 Frondizi overthrown by military after Peronista candidates in March 1962 gubernatorial and congressional elections are victorious in several provinces

1963 Arturo Illía, candidate of Peoples' Radical party (UCRP), elected president with 26 percent of popular vote

1965 Peronistas win plurality in March congressional elections

1966 In June military overthrows Illía government and creates new regime under General Juan Carlos Onganía

1970 In June military commanders replace President Onganía with General Roberto Levingston

1971 In March Levingston is replaced by General Alejandro Lanusse

1973 Peronista candidate, Héctor Cámpora, wins presidential election in March, and Peronistas win majority of seats in Congress

Cámpora resigns and Juan Domingo Perón is elected president in September

1974 Perón dies and is replaced by his wife, Vice-President Isabel Martínez de Perón

1976 Military overthrows Peronista government in March and creates new military regime under General Jorge Videla

presidential control over all public affairs. To a greater degree than the regime the Brazilians had created, that of Juan Carlos Onganía was a one-man affair. The Brazilian high command had retained effective control over the officer it chose to serve as president; the Argentine officers who had selected Onganía encouraged him to operate on his own.

Onganía turned over economic policy to civilian technocrats with instructions to end the boom-bust cycles that had plagued the Argentine economy since 1946. In only two years they brought the economy under control, restoring investor confidence through what appeared to be a successful replication of the Brazilian experience. Almost overnight, the country in which foreign investors had given up hope was transformed into a land of great opportunity and high promise. Onganía's victory was, however, short-lived. In May 1969 student and worker riots against the government shook the new authoritarian order to its foundations. One year later Onganía was deposed by military colleagues who three years later restored constitutional government to Argentina once again.

Peru stands in marked contrast to Brazil and Argentina. The officers who placed General Juan Velasco Alvarado in the presidency in 1968 rejected at the outset the conservative modernization development strategy followed by the Brazilians and Argentines. In 1968 Peru was still a very underdeveloped country that had not gone through a long process of industrialization, as had Brazil and Argen-

Table 8-3. *Postwar Peru: historical background*

1945 José Bustamante, conservative diplomat, elected president

1948 Military overthrows Bustamante government and governs through presidency of conservative General Manuel Odría for eight years

1956 Manuel Prado, president between 1939 and 1945, again elected president

1962 None of three major candidates – Haya de la Torre of APRISTA party, Fernando Belaúnde Terry of Popular Action party, or Manuel Odría of National Union party – receives required one-third of popular vote, nor can Congress agree on one of three. Military then annuls election

1963 New election won narrowly by Fernando Belaúnde Terry

1968 In October Belaúnde government overthrown by military; General Juan Velasco Alvarado is named president and in 1969 announces sweeping agrarian reform program

1975 In August General Velasco is replaced by General Francisco Morales Bermúdez, who shifts policy in more moderate direction and purges most reformist officers from government

tina. Half its population was Indian and more than half were rural dwellers who lived at or just above the subsistence level. It was not until the 1960s that Peru began to undergo the kind of social change the region's more industrialized countries had begun to experience thirty years before.

The Peruvian military had in the past defended the rural and commercial elite from its enemies by blocking the access of reformist and revolutionary parties to power. But in 1963 the military stood by while an elected reformist party took office and watched closely as it tried to manage the forces of change in the face of increasing peasant and worker activism. A new generation of officers, more rural and lower middle sector in origin than their predecessors, judged the weak performance of the reformers harshly and, in 1968, decided to take matters into their own hands by overthrowing the government of President Fernando Belaúnde Terry and creating an authoritarian reformist regime of their own.

With the assistance of civilian technocrats, the military, under the leadership of General Juan Velasco Alvarado, transformed the Peruvian state into an instrument of agrarian and industrial reform. Its goal was the integration of all Peruvians, Indian as well as *mest*[...] officers, a cohesive, productive society. The government closed [...] 1968 its parties and replaced most labor, peasant, and industrial [...] me[...] groups with a hierarchy of government-sponsored mass organizations, which were to act as mobilizers of popular support and executors of economic and social reforms. By the early 1970s nearly all large land holdings in the country had been redistributed to peasant farmers; many private enterprises, including some foreign ones, had been expropriated; and several industries had been placed under joint worker-owner management. Political reconstruction did not come so easily, however, especially as many Peruvians of all social classes were reluctant to be controlled by the regime through its new mass organizations, and military leaders were not anxious to share their power with the leaders of groups representing the masses. The Velasco government was still in the midst of its campaign to organize the Peruvian masses in August 1975, when conservative officers, disturbed by mounting fiscal and foreign exchange problems – brought on in part by the high cost of the government's programs – and growing opposition in many quarters to Velasco's increasingly personalistic rule, suddenly deposed the president in a quiet palace revolt and began dismantling the reformist programs he had initiated seven years before and cautiously preparing the way for a return to constitutional rule.

The Peruvian experience, with its emphasis on structural reform and the mobilization of the masses rather than on industrial growth and the containment of popular aspirations, as was the case in Brazil and Argentina, offers us the opportunity to examine contrasting uses of military authoritarianism. By comparing these three versions of the military authoritarian game, we can assess the contributions of this increasingly common form of politics to the solution of the region's development problems.

THE RULES OF THE MILITARY AUTHORITARIAN GAME

The seizure of power

The techniques of the military coup are well known. The coup is one of the oldest and most common practices in the Latin American political game. To succeed, a coup needs a leader, the support of the commanders of the major military units, good timing, and the efficient execution of steps that remove the officials of the old regime and install a new government. Seldom, however, does the military act without some encouragement from other players, though their support is seldom essential for the execution of the coup itself. Popular resistance may, of course, slow the coup or prompt some officers to withdraw their support; but more often than not, when the leaders of the three branches of the military decide to evict a president from office, there is little civilian players can do to stop them.

At first glance the coups that brought the military to power in Brazil, Argentina, and Peru during the 1960s appear to have been conventional affairs. Military intervention was no stranger to these countries, and officers had been deeply involved in the domestic politics of all three since the 1930s. Moreover, each coup appeared to involve the conventional pattern of the long-anticipated removal of a president whose political competence and policy choices had been questioned by high-ranking military officers. The Brazilian military, for example, doubted President João Goulart's ability to cope with a severe economic crisis and was disturbed by his attempts to mobilize supporters among the urban and rural poor and from within the ranks of enlisted military personnel. Onganía and his colleagues were preoccupied with the resurgence of Peronism after the Peronista party won a plurality in the 1965 congressional elections. Similarly, the Peruvian military was displeased by the Belaúnde government's failure to secure a more nationalistic solution to the country's dispute

with the International Petroleum Company and was concerned about
the possible election of APRISTA Victor Raúl Haya de la Torre, its
principal civilian antagonist, in the 1969 elections.

But initial appearances are deceiving, and nowhere is this more apparent than in the aftermath of these three coups. Despite their use of
familiar techniques, these were not conventional takeovers. Their
perpetrators wanted more than the removal of a few civilian politicians. They also sought to destroy the political processes by which the
deposed leaders had been selected and to substitute an entirely new
set of authoritarian rules.

The 1964 Brazilian coup. Traditionally the Brazilian military had acted
as a moderating force in national politics, intervening from time to
time to restore an equilibrium among the country's contending political forces. Since the fall of the emperor and the creation of the republic in 1889, the Brazilian political game had been characterized by its
reliance on a balance of power among the most influential players.
Before 1930 regional political machines held the game together by
regularly exchanging public offices and policy favors. After 1930,
Getulio Vargas expanded the power of the state at the expense of the
state machines. Under Vargas, moreover, new players were admitted
into the game as long as they did not seriously threaten those already
involved. Thanks to his efforts, industrialists, urban professionals and
bureaucrats, foreign investors, and organized labor were added to the
political process, and a new equilibrium was created and maintained
by the powerful Brazilian state. With the inauguration of a constitutional regime in 1945 came the addition of political parties. But they
too took on uniquely Brazilian characteristics, eschewing ideology and
mass mobilization in favor of regional electoral organizations dedicated primarily to capturing the presidency and seats in the legislature.

Essential to the governance of Brazil between 1945 and 1964 was
the maintenance of a balance among its dominant players through the
state's promotion of a growing industrial economy. This required the
execution of policies that satisfied some of the demands of each player
without seriously offending anyone who mattered. As we saw in
Chapter 6, few Brazilian presidents directed this system more skillfully than Juscelino Kubitschek did between 1955 and 1960. His successors, however, proved less adept at making the system work.

The first was Jânio Quadros, a man who had promised to purge the
Brazilian game of patronage, corruption, and political balancing
acts – all legacies of the Vargas years that had been perpetuated by

Kubitschek. What made Quadros unusual was his determination to operate independently of the ruling coalition that had been held together and expanded by presidents since 1930. Instead of acquiring power by becoming an indispensable mediator among coalition members, he sought to secure it through the mobilization of popular support for his political purification campaign. It was an experiment that failed, however. In less than a year Quadros had alienated the party politicians, who had thrived on patronage, and the bureaucrats, who had lived on corruption; antagonized industrialists with an antiinflationary tight credit policy; prompted labor opposition with wage controls; and upset the military with a neutralist foreign policy. When Quadros suddenly resigned in August 1961 in an attempt to generate an outpouring of popular support that he could use against his opponents, few Brazilians responded, and his leave of absence became permanent.

Vice-President João Goulart, who succeeded Quadros, also upset the traditional equilibrium. Goulart, a former protégé of Getulio Vargas and labor minister in his last administration, initially tried to replicate the development program employed by Kubitschek. He was haunted, however, by his reputation as an opportunistic and unreliable labor operative deeply distrusted by the military. Convinced that he could not retain conservative and middle-sector support under such conditions, Goulart struck out in a new direction in early 1964 by appealing for the support of the Brazilian masses in the hope of gaining enough popular support to sustain his rule. He announced an agrarian reform program, nationalized private oil refineries, asked Congress to increase presidential authority and give the vote to illiterates, and, most disturbing to the military and conservative players in the game, called on the masses to demonstrate their support for the government and encouraged enlisted men to assert themselves against their officers. In so doing, however, Goulart broke two of the fundamental rules of the Brazilian game: one that prohibited the mobilization of the masses against other players and another that prohibited the deliberate redistribution of property from one player to another. With encouragement from the United States government, foreign investors, and most of Brazil's industrial and commercial elite, who were distressed by record inflation as well as the president's demagoguery, the military swiftly ended the Goulart government at the end of March 1964.

The Argentine coup of 1966. The pre-1966 Argentine political process was in many ways just the opposite of the Brazilian. Where the Brazilians had stressed balance under the tutelage of the state, the Argentines had, since the rise of Perón in 1945, been immersed in continual political conflict between players loyal to Perón and those who opposed him. The state was not the arbiter in these battles, but the prize which, when taken by one side, was used against the other. On the Peronista side were the remnants of the political party created by Perón in the 1940s; the majority of the labor unions belonging to the General Labor Confederation; nationalists from the middle sectors, especially the managers of small businesses and industries; and many students. In the opposition were most other political parties, especially the Radicals; large and medium-sized farmers, who produced the country's meat and grain exports; and most industrialists, bankers, exporters, and foreign investors. The military became the moderator in the conflict, though more often than not it sided with the anti-Peronistas.

From Perón's overthrow in 1955 until Onganía's coup in 1966, Argentine politics was a constant struggle between Peronistas and anti-Peronistas. The latter sought to eliminate the Peronistas from the political process; the Peronistas, relying primarily on militant working-class organizations, struggled not only to survive constant persecution but also to undermine insecure non-Peronista governments and thereby promote their own return to power. During this period two presidents, both from the Radical party, were elected: Arturo Frondizi in 1958 and Arturo Illía in 1963. The victories of both were tarnished, however, by the fact that the military had excluded the Peronista party from electoral participation in 1958 and 1963. The military officers, who supervised both elections, were confronted by a dilemma not uncommon in societies where political divisions run deep. They had to decide whether to (1) exclude the Peronistas, whom they believed to be a threat to democratic institutions, from elections in the hope of forcing the working-class rank and file to support other parties; (2) encourage competition between Radicals and Peronistas in the hope of defeating the latter at the polls; or (3) eliminate party politics entirely. If they chose the first option, they risked alienating the nearly 50 percent of the electorate that remained committed to Peronism and undermining public support for any government elected under rules that excluded popular Peronista candidates. If they chose the second, they risked defeat by the Peronistas, especially if non-Peronista parties divided the other 50 percent of the vote. And if they chose the third option, they would have to assume the immense burden of running the country themselves in the face of opposition from Peronistas and non-Peronistas alike.

In 1958 and 1963 the military, after bitter internal disputes, chose the first option and, not unexpectedly, created weak Radical party governments that, in an attempt to increase their popular legitimacy, challenged the Peronistas in midterm elections. But in both cases the Peronistas, not the Radicals, were victorious. After the Peronistas won the 1965 congressional elections and were on the verge of doing the same in 1966 gubernatorial elections, the military, under the leadership of General Juan Carlos Onganía, finally chose the third option, giving up on electoral democracy with the expectation that it could create a more effective alternative.

The Peruvian coup of 1968. The motives behind the Peruvian coup were more complex than those that prompted coups in Brazil and Argentina. To be sure, the Peruvian military had frequently intervened in presidential politics to protect conservative interests. It had also developed a strong antipathy toward APRISTA, the country's primary reform party from the 1940s to the early 1960s, because of APRISTA's strident antimilitarism. But the military coup of 1968 represented more than a predictable reaction to the possibility of an APRISTA victory in the 1969 presidential elections. It was also an unusual military response to significant social and economic changes in Peruvian society.

During the first half of the twentieth century Peru's conservative leaders had successfully absorbed the country's small but growing middle sectors by giving them a role in the management of the export economy and the state bureaucracy. At the same time, the leaders ignored the plight of the peasantry and dealt harshly with the labor movement and the political parties that encouraged it. But Peruvian society continued to change, nevertheless, promoted by the expansion of copper mining, the growth of local industry and commerce, and accelerating urbanization in the 1950s and 1960s. The Conservatives' failure to adapt their policies to these changes yielded land invasions by disgruntled peasants, student protests, illegal strikes, strident nationalism, and the formation of a small but potentially disruptive guerrilla movement in the countryside during the 1960s. The election of reformer Fernando Belaúnde Terry in 1964 represented the first effort to adapt public policy to these new conditions. Belaúnde modeled his Popular Action party (AP) after the democratic reform movements already active in the hemisphere and campaigned on a platform of Agrarian reform and economic modernization. His ability to deliver on these promises after his election was slowed, however, by the opposition of APRISTAs and Conservatives in Congress. As a result, instead of sweeping reforms, Belaúnde added to the frustrations of those who desired immediate solutions to the country's increasing social problems.

The military's reaction to Belaúnde's travail was hard to predict at the time. In the past it might have welcomed his failures as evidence of the strength of the old order. But the military had changed during the 1960s, and many of its younger officers, fresh from battles with guerrillas in the countryside which had awakened them to the increasing political costs of defending traditional social institutions, saw Belaúnde's failures as heightening the possibility of radical upheaval. No longer, it appeared, could Peru afford the kind of reformist political game that became immobilized by interparty squabbles. The only solution, the officers concluded, was the suspension of democratic politics in order to permit a more direct assault on the country's development problems by a military-led state bureaucracy.

To explain these three military coups as the reponses of professional soldiers to civilian governments they found deficient in some way neither justifies the soldiers' actions nor excuses the brutality that has characterized their authoritarian rule. Military coups are not inevitable. They have many causes and the perceptions of military officers are only one of those causes. Nevertheless, by stressing the political and social conflicts that persuaded them of democracy's failure, we can better understand the course they took once in power.

THE MILITARY RECONSTRUCTION OF THE POLITICAL GAME

Military officers may be competent managers of their own organizations and harsh critics of civilian political behavior, but they possess no unique knowledge about the reconstruction of political systems. Seldom do they have a comprehensive plan to guide them, and quite often they begin their rule without even a clear idea of the kinds of institutions needed to deal with their society's problems. Their choice of political rules and processes is influenced by many things, including their own prejudices, advice solicited from civilians, and examples taken from the experience of countries they admire. As a result, if anything characterizes the political innovations of the military authoritarians, it is a process of trial and error involving a search for ways to construct a durable political game.

The principal problem facing military leaders is not how to eliminate democratic institutions or prevent the creation of communist ones, but how to create completely new political processes. Almost overnight they must become social engineers capable of designing solutions to such old problems as the organization of political authority and the regulation of political participation. They must establish the new rules under which the national political game can be played. In theory, their options are many. But in practice they are limited by their own imaginations and skills and the conditions that prevail in their countries. And there is no reason to believe that Latin America's military officers are any more creative or adept at political engineering than their civilian counterparts, as the recent experiences of military regimes in Brazil, Argentina, and Peru clearly demonstrate.

Two issues dominated the selection of new political rules in Brazil, Argentina, and Peru: One was the question of how to establish government control over increasingly combative societies; the other was the identification of the appropriate mode of public involvement in the governing process. The control problem confronts the military with the need to develop an appropriate mix of physical force and voluntary compliance in the enforcement of the new rules. This may involve decisions regarding the use of political ideology and mass organizations as well as the role of state security agencies. Inevitably, military leaders have to decide whether it is enough to rely on force alone to sustain their authority or whether some appeal for popular support is required for the new order to survive. The political participation issue is even more troublesome for military governments. Whether they like it or not, they have to deal with players who demand to be included in the policy-making process, especially when government decisions affect their welfare. The leaders cannot ignore such demands entirely because they need the cooperation of several players in order to accelerate the nation's development. If they want to implement an agrarian reform program, for example, they must mobilize the peasants and channel them into new activities using bureaucratic agencies, government-sponsored mass organizations, or other means. Similarly, if they seek to promote industrialization, they have to gain the cooperation of investors, bankers, and laborers, either by offering them inducements or by threatening them with deprivations. In sum, even though military leaders may not want to restore traditional forms of mass political participation, they have to devise some means for involving relevant players in the execution of their development programs. Few problems have frustrated the military rulers of Brazil, Argentina, and Peru more than this one.

Military authoritarians in Brazil

The foundation of Brazil's military regime was laid over five years. Military leaders began immediately after the coup by securing congressional confirmation of Marshal Humberto Castelo Branco as president and then authorizing him to jail several thousand political activists, civil servants, and military officers believed to have supported the Goulart administration, and to deprive 400 elected officials of their political rights for ten years. Not long thereafter, political parties were closed down, leftist political organizations and most student groups persecuted, and an elaborate state security network created to enforce the ban on political activity and protect the regime from its opponents. Repeatedly, after 1964, the government has used its security apparatus to terrorize citizens it considers a potential threat to its political control.

The formal rules of the new game were announced through a series of seventeen Institutional Acts and seventy-seven complementary acts between 1964 and 1969. The Institutional Acts created a hierarchical political structure that was not entirely unfamiliar to Brazilians, who recalled monarchical rule during the nineteenth century and the authoritarianism of the 1930s. At the apex of the system was the presidency, where ultimate political authority resided and where nearly all important political and economic decisions were made in consultation with military leaders and civilian advisors. Below it was a reconstituted national legislature and state and local governments, all of which were controlled by the president through a government-sponsored two-party system. The military created its own political party, called the National Renovating Alliance (ARENA), and staffed it with politicians from the banned National Democratic Union and Social Democratic parties. In order to maintain the pretense of a two-party system, an official opposition party, the Brazilian Democratic Movement (MDB), was also created and filled initially by politicians from the Social Democratic and Brazilian Labor parties. To assure that the party system remained a docile instrument of authoritarian rule, the president was given the authority to veto candidates from both parties, annul elections, and deprive uncooperative elected officials of their political rights. In practice this meant the control of the legislature by ARENA, whose candidates won all elections until 1974. In October of that year the MDB received a majority of the vote – though not of the congressional seats – for the first time. The president responded, however, by reaffirming that the MDB would not be allowed majority control of Congress if it won future elections. To

Table 8-4. *The political structure of military authoritarianism*

	Brazil (1964–76)	Argentina (1966–9)	Peru (1968–75)
Composition of government elite	Military officers Civilian technocrats	Military officers Civilian technocrats	Military officers Civilian technocrats
Political organizations	Official party (ARENA) Opposition party (MDB) Congress, state, and local governments controlled through official parties and presidential interventions	None outside executive Provincial governments placed under military commanders	Military-led mass organization (SINAMOS) and constituency groups of peasants and laborers
Structure of interest group participation	Traditional dependence on state with authoritarian government acting as coordinator of private group participation	Government isolation from contesting groups modified by selective, informal contacts	Abortive corporatist system in which government controlled functional groups through bureaucracy and mass organization
Treatment of political opposition	Physical repression Expulsion from politics	Physical repression Isolation from policymaking process	Mild repression Cooptation of rank and file through mass organizations

emphasize his point he has repeatedly suspended Congress whenever the MDB minority succeeded in blocking legislation requiring the approval of two-thirds of the members. In short, the Brazilian Congress has been allowed to survive only as long as it does not challenge the president or threaten military rule.

The selection of the president is the most critical decision taken in the military authoritarian game. In Brazil it is entirely an internal military affair, involving negotiations among ranking officers carried out in secrecy. The fact that the decision is confined to the military does not, however, mean that it involves no risks. No matter how well the decision-making process is organized, it invites divisions within the high command because more than one high-ranking officer covets the job and seeks the support of his colleagues. Yet, despite these dangers, the Brazilians to date have managed the task without adverse effects on government unity. Castelo Branco was succeeded by Marshal Artur Costa e Silva in 1967, and General Emílio Garrastazú Médici became president in 1969 after Costa e Silva became incapacitated. He, in turn, was replaced by General Ernesto Geisel in 1974.

Why, if the military intended to rule autocratically, has it bothered to create two parties and carry out its election ritual? The answer is not obvious, perhaps even to the military itself. There are, however, some plausible explanations. First, there have always been differences of opinion within the military over the institutional form the regime should take. Some officers support a gradual return to a competitive political process under the leadership of a strong presidency. Others fear the return of disruptive political conflict and the rise of political extremism if political competition is restored. The first group has managed to secure some of the symbols of competitive politics, but the hard-liners have successfully blocked all attempts to open the political process. Another explanation of the electoral façade is that it provides an outlet for opposition politics that can be controlled by the regime. Instead of forcing its opponents to operate clandestinely, the military encourages them to participate openly where they can be watched closely. However, if this is the military strategy, it has not been entirely successful, for the regime's opponents have frequently boycotted elections in large numbers.

The operation of the military regime relies heavily on traditional authoritarian processes that matured under Emperor Dom Pedro II during the nineteenth century and were modernized by Getulio Vargas, who significantly increased the economic power of the Brazilian state in the 1930s. To manage the economy, the military has closely supervised the activities of commercial, financial, agricultural, and labor interests. But instead of creating an elaborate corporatist system through which authorities could control the nation's entrepreneurs and laborers, the military has strengthened existing ties between the state and the private interests who already rely heavily on it for financing, regulation, and subsidization. It has also added a sophisticated internal security network to deal with dissidents and a more complex policy-making apparatus through which skilled technocrats can coordinate fiscal, monetary, credit, exchange, price, and wage policies. This has enabled the execution of finely tuned economic programs, which have induced rapid economic growth. It has also brought the government the support of many Brazilian and foreign entrepreneurs, who are delighted to have a government that can enforce the economic rules of the game and assure some policy continuity.

The power of the Brazilian president is immense, but it is not unlimited. In addition to the constraints imposed by the need to maintain the support of the ranking military commanders, he is limited in his decisions by the dictates of the Brazilian economy and his commitment to the kind of economic growth that simultaneously satisfies entrepreneurs and middle-sector consumers. Many Brazilian institutions, both public and private, rely for their survival on his promotion of steady economic expansion. If he does not meet their expectations, his job of maintaining control over the country becomes much more difficult. He may not need votes to retain his office, but he does require the cooperation of those who produce the nation's goods and services if the military authoritarian regime is to achieve its development objectives. To secure cooperation, he must act as a kind of superadministrator who has been given great authority by military and entrepreneurial elites. It is his responsibility to keep the complex Brazilian enterprise operating smoothly so that those who benefit from it can prosper. Should he fail, much more force would be required to sustain military rule, and it is doubtful that military authoritarianism would survive for long on the use of force alone.

Argentina's military autocracy

The government created by General Juan Carlos Onganía in Argentina lacked the complexity of the Brazilian military regime. Onganía did not organize an official party or use corporatist organizations to control the private sector. Rather, he created a very simple authoritarian regime through which he and his civilian advisors could repress the political conflicts that had plagued the country since the 1940s and could implement economic policies aimed at attracting foreign investors to Argentina to help complete its industrialization.

At the outset Onganía gave little indication of the course his new regime would follow. He closed Congress and all political parties and in a series of Revolutionary Acts proclaimed he would assume all the authority that had previously resided in the Congress and use it to promote spiritual unity, political order, social discipline, and economic stability. Later he announced a three-stage program to guide the country's reconstruction. It began with an economic phase during which, like the Brazilians in 1964, he would attack inflation and stagnation and restore foreign and domestic confidence in the government's management of the economy. Once economic stability had been attained, a social phase would follow in which most of the conflicts that had undermined national unity in the past would be eliminated. Finally, the country would enter a political phase in which a new governmental system would be constructed.

But Onganía never progressed beyond the first stage of this ambitious proposal. After reorganizing the executive branch to give immense power to his minister of economy, the civilian technocrat Adalbert Krieger Vasena, he devoted himself entirely to curing the country's economic ills. His principal use of state authority was against the militant labor movement, whose subjugation to government control was necessary to attract investors to the country and restore the confidence of Argentine entrepreneurs. Once labor had been subdued, however, he did little to restructure participation in the political process. Instead, he created a simple political game in which one player, the president, dominated all others.

Under Onganía, Argentina's public affairs were divided into two arenas, one political and the other economic. The political arena was controlled tightly by the president, who relied primarily on the use of force to subdue his opponents. Neither political parties nor economic interest groups were welcome in the presidentially directed policy-making process. Within the economic arena, however, competition was encouraged. Once the government had set the rules of the economic game – which included labor quiescence – entrepreneurs, both domestic and foreign, were free to pursue their self-interests. The result was a government-manipulated market economy in which multinational firms financed much of the country's development.

The Onganía regime represented the temporary displacement of the politician by the technician, of bargaining and compromise by coercion, and of stopgap policy making by long-term problem solving. The military officers and civilian technocrats who created this new game believed that the causes of the country's economic problems were essentially political and that by eliminating politics they could solve the problems. Their political rules were negative rather than positive, aimed at repressing conflict rather than creating new procedures for resolving it. But Argentines were accustomed to intense political competition, and although they could be temporarily suppressed, they could not be conquered easily, even by Onganía's tough autocracy. The leaders of the disbanded political parties and the persecuted labor movement continued to demand greater participation in the game, and economic interest groups insisted on more influence over government policy. Onganía responded by ignoring their pleas and postponing any resolution of the political participation issue.

The beginning of the end of the Onganía regime came in late May 1969 when several days of working-class riots in the interior industrial city of Córdoba required the intervention of the regular army to restore order. Although the formal control of the government over the country was not seriously threatened by the protests, the disorders did damage Onganía's authority by demonstrating that after three years of his special brand of autocratic rule, he had not subdued the popular forces as he had claimed. Equally important, the Córdoba riots brought to center stage again the issue that had plagued and divided the military since 1955: how to deal with a militant Peronista labor movement that accepted the authority of no one but Perón himself. One faction of the military had favored the hard-line approach of Onganía, aimed at forcing the labor movement to respect government authority through sustained harsh treatment. Another preferred a softer stand, stressing the need to accept the fact that the Peronistas were too strong to be subjugated and therefore belonged within any government that ruled Argentina. In the middle was a majority of the officer corps, who opposed the physical repression of millions of Argentine workers, yet did not want to turn the government over to the Peronistas. Thus, in contrast to the Brazilians, who faced a less well organized and less militant labor movement and who were more united in their determination to suppress it, the Argentine military was divided over how high a price it was willing to pay to break the back of working-class resistance. This division led to the indecisiveness that forced the military to retreat after the Córdoba riots of 1969 and eventually to remove Onganía in June 1970 in order to restore constitutional government through elections won by the Peronistas in March 1973.

At the root of the demise of the Onganía regime was his failure to solve the problem of political participation. Like most of Argentina's postwar military rulers, he had assumed that, in the short run at least, the Argentine masses could be controlled through physical force alone. But once again this assumption proved faulty, as Argentina's most militant unions refused to accept total exclusion from the national political arena.

Peru's reformist military autocracy

Peru's military leaders did not share Onganía's reluctance to confront the issue of political reconstruction. The officers who led the Peruvian coup were more audacious than either the Brazilians or the Argentines. They believed they not only could assert their control over the nation's politics but could reconstruct the political game on a mass-based foundation as well. In the end, however, their ambitions far exceeded their capacity for political innovation. Nevertheless, their hastily contrived experiments in mass organization and reformist policy were notable for their boldness; they also put to rest much conventional wisdom about the impossibility of experiments in radical reform under military leadership.

Like the Brazilians and the Argentines, the Peruvians immediately disbanded all political parties and suppressed dissent. But unlike them, the Peruvians also launched a campaign aimed at creating mass organizations that could be used to mobilize support for a centrally coordinated attack on traditional economic and social structures. The interest groups that had represented the economic elite in the past were closed or severely restricted, labor unions were weakened, newspapers seized, peasant associations closed, and universities deprived of their autonomy. Only the Church and the military were left alone, the former because it posed no threat to the new regime and the latter because its support was essential to the reconstruction of the political game.

The new political order was corporatist in concept, organized hierarchically and by economic sector, starting with government-sponsored local economic organizations, which were joined into sectoral organizations and finally into a national body called the National System for the Support of Social Mobilization (SINAMOS), created in June 1971. Within each economic sector new production organizations were to be created. Under the 1969 Agrarian Reform Law, for example, most private holdings were reorganized into collective enterprises known as Agrarian Production Cooperatives (CAPs) and Agricultural Societies of Social Interest (SAISs). And in 1970 firms involved in manufacturing, mining, telecommunications, and fishing were forced by the new Industrial Law to admit worker participation in their ownership and management. The objectives of such measures were the involvement of the masses in the economic decisions that affect them most directly and the reconciliation of conflicting class interests. Building on these reforms, SINAMOS was to integrate the masses into the new political system and regulate their involvement in the making and implementation of government policy. In practice, however, SINAMOS became little more than a means of control used by the new government to impose its will throughout Peruvian society. Instead of becoming a mass-based political party capable of organizing a new political order, it remained an instrument that segregated the masses into functional economic sectors and coordinated their involvement in the administration, but not the formulation, of government policy.

At the top of the hierarchy was the president – until mid-1975 General Juan Velasco Alvarado – and the Presidential Advisory Committee (COAP), an all-military body charged with designing legislation and coordinating its implementation. They were advised by a host of civilian technocrats, but they did not consult directly with the leaders of peasant, labor, or other mass organizations when designing their policies. They were, however, occasionally forced to revise their programs when they met resistance from such groups.

The Peruvian military leaders created their own version of an authoritarian, corporatist regime, whose principal purpose was the economic elevation of the masses and the reconciliation of class interests at the expense of the traditional elite. They did not follow a preconceived plan, but instead merely replaced traditional political organizations with new ones through a process of trial and error. Undoubtedly, they went farther than any other contemporary Latin American military regime toward the creation of a mass-based political structure. However, despite their impressive initiatives, the Peruvians did not achieve their original goal of mass participation and national integration. They were plagued throughout their experiment by a persistent gap between policy innovation and policy execution. Repeatedly, ambitious proposals for the creation of new organizations and enterprises foundered on the shoals of citizen resistance and the inability of bureaucratic agencies to deal with local conditions. Control, not participation, became the military's goal, leading it to place damaging constraints on SINAMOS and other mass organizations in order to prevent their capture by groups not completely loyal to military leaders.

Whether the Velasco administration would have adapted itself to the requirements of mass participation in due time will never be known, for in August 1975, officers who did not share Velasco's faith in economic and social reforms and who had become disturbed by the deterioration of the Peruvian economy in 1973 and 1974 deposed the president in a swift and bloodless coup. Soon thereafter they shifted course, expelling reformers from the government, repressing groups that claimed to represent the interests of the masses, adopting conventional stabilization measures aimed at rescuing the Peruvian economy from its fiscal and foreign exchange crises, and promising future elections. Thus, after seven years the Peruvian experiment in reformist military authoritarianism was brought to a sudden and unexpected halt.

The creators of military authoritarian regimes do not look with favor on the coalition politics practiced by populists and democratic reformers. They are disturbed by its inherent instability and its reliance on deals struck between partisans who are motivated primarily by narrow self-interests. For them, coalition politics is just another manifestation of political processes that are dominated by continuous squabbling and that undermine political order and economic development. At the same time, however, the military authoritarian recognizes that even he cannot avoid making alliances with other players in the game. The coalitions he creates are different from the conventional civilian variety, but they are coalitions nevertheless. He already possesses powerful political resources and, therefore, is not as dependent on the resources of others to sustain his control. Moreover, he does not need the kinds of allies who will secure the legislative ratification of government policy because he already controls the legislature, if one exists. What he needs is not political party allies, but the collaboration of those economic groups that are critical to the execution of his policies. Force alone is not sufficient to administer complex economic programs in a capitalistic economy. The government must also secure the cooperation of investors, traders, and laborers, and one of the most effective ways of doing so is by including them in the ruling elite.

The military authoritarian coalition is directed by military officers, assisted by civilian technocrats. Military leaders, as we saw in Brazil, Argentina, and Peru, usually designate one of their number to serve as president while reserving some influence over him. In matters of economic and social policy, they rely heavily on civilian advisors, most of whom have been recruited from the bureaucracy, private business, and the professions. They are also very dependent on government bureaucracies for the implementation of their programs, for even though they can place officers in command of public enterprises and line agencies, they can accomplish little without the support of civil servants at the national and local levels. The second rank in the military coalition is filled by the players who help finance and manage the country's economic development. The membership of this constituency varies according to the course followed by government policy. As one might suspect, the composition of the Brazilian and Argentine coalitions differed from the one created in Peru.

In Brazil and Argentina the military drew its collaborators from the ranks of foreign investors and international financial agencies, who welcomed harsh stabilization programs and firm political order; commercial farmers, who desired economic stability; the domestic industrial, commercial, and financial elites, who supported the suppression of popular movements; and even some in the middle sectors, who had become disillusioned with competitive politics and frustrated by high inflation and economic instability. Conspicuously missing were representatives of organized labor and peasant farmers and laborers, all of whom were subordinated to the military's will to maintain political order while concentrating resources in the hands of investors. Brazilian and Argentine military leaders and their civilian advisors blamed inflation and economic disorder on the demagogic wage and welfare policies of civilian politicians. Economic growth could be achieved, they reasoned, only by suspending such policies until after each country's productive capacity had been increased substantially. And that required the repression of all groups who expressed the demands of the masses for a larger share of the national wealth.

Because it had different development policy objectives and operated in a less industrialized society, the Peruvian military created a coalition unlike those found in Brazil and Argentina. In 1968 the Peruvian economy was still controlled by commercial and agricultural elites and foreign investors. Instead of defending such groups, as his predecessors had done, General Velasco demanded they share their power and wealth with the masses. When he began his reform program, he had few collaborators. Rural and industrial elites were disturbed by his proposals for industrial and agrarian reform, foreign investors were displeased by the nationalization of the International Petroleum Company, students were upset by the reorganization of the universities, urban and rural laborers resented government intervention in their organizations, and political party leaders were bitter about the closure of all parties. The new government, therefore, began with a very narrow coalition that included only the military, some technocrats, and the bureaucracy. Gradually, however, it tried to increase its base of support by mobilizing laborers and *campesinos* using SINAMOS and its constituency organizations. Its goal was not the polarization of Peruvian society by pitting the masses against the economic elite, but the reconciliation of all players in the Peruvian game through the elevation of the powerless and the reduction of the resources of the powerful. The creation of this new consensus was not completed, however, as we have seen. In fact, General Velasco's inability to expand and consolidate his base of support greatly facilitated the task of those who deposed him in mid-1975.

The military leaders of Brazil, Argentina, and Peru tried to establish new political rules that would help them secure public conformity to their wishes without becoming captives of their constituents. Some players have benefited immensely from the military authoritarian game; others have suffered a great deal. The travail of the latter has led to a continuous, if muted, struggle to end military rule. Political party leaders have persisted with their campaigns for the restoration of constitutional rule, and spokesmen for the masses have urged their constituents to rise up against their autocratic rulers. Both have discovered that the military authoritarians are not as invulnerable as they claimed. As we have seen, in 1969 worker riots in Argentina undermined confidence in the Onganía regime and led to the restoration of constitutional government in 1973; the opposition of foreign investors and Peruvian entrepreneurs along with adverse economic conditions helped launch a coup by conservative officers that brought down the Velasco government in 1975.

THE MILITARY MANAGEMENT OF
ECONOMIC DEVELOPMENT

Despite differences in economic purpose and political methods, the military authoritarian regimes of Latin America have one thing in common. Whether they favor market capitalism or social reformism, they share a faith in the ability of the state to plan and direct their nations' development. In this they are similar to the democratic reformers whom they replaced. Both accept the notion that the state should determine the rules of the economic game and use its power to manipulate them in pursuit of long-term development objectives. They differ in that the military believes it is the only group capable of managing this feat. The officers have not reached this conclusion suddenly. Only after several decades of experience in the management of public enterprises, advanced studies in various war colleges, and observation of civilian regimes did they conclude that they alone could do the job.

The first thing one discovers when comparing the Peruvian, Brazilian, and Argentine economic programs is the difference between the first and the other two. (see Table 8-5). The Peruvians designed their own version of what we have termed the progressive modernization strategy in an effort to redistribute power and wealth from the rich to the poor through the agency of the state; the Brazilian and Argentine officers chose the conservative modernization strategy with its empha-

Table 8-5. *The initial economic programs of the military authoritarians*

	Castelo Branco (1964–7)	Onganía (1966–9)	Velasco (1968–72)
Objectives	Price stability Balance-of-payments equilibrium Acceleration of economic growth Increased private investment Alleviation of sectoral and regional economic disparities Expansion of exports	Price stability Industrial growth Attraction of foreign investment Increased efficiency of public and private sectors	Reduction of public debt burden Integration of peasantry into market economy Sharing of industrial wealth with workers Reduction of dependence on foreign investors
Instruments	Fiscal restraint Wage controls Unification and freeing of exchange market Tax incentives to encourage private domestic and foreign investment Increased efficiency of tax collection	Wage freeze Devaluation of currency Tariff reductions Removal of restrictions on foreign investors Tax increases	Credit restraint Devaluation of currency Tax increases Redistribution of rural property Nationalization of selected foreign and domestic enterprises Worker participation in ownership of private firms

sis on capital accumulation and heavy industrialization. A brief review of the performance of each, taken in chronological order, will illustrate their achievements and failures.

The Brazilian "miracle"

The Brazilian military boasts of having worked a miracle by taking the country from the depths of economic chaos to record growth in only five years. There is some evidence to support the claim, as we can see from Table 8-6. After three years of economic stabilization, the Brazilian economy suddenly accelerated, growing at a record pace between 1968 and 1973. At the same time, inflation, which reached nearly 100 percent in 1963, was reduced to an annual average of 23 percent after 1965, and entrepreneurial confidence was restored. Nevertheless, claims of a miracle are exaggerated. The military did

Table 8-6. *Brazilian economic performance, 1950–73 (average annual real growth rates)*

	1950–60	1960–5	1965–73
Gross domestic product per capita	3.1	1.2	6.0
Agricultural product per capita	1.5	1.5	1.6
Industrial product per capita	6.0	0.8	8.1
Retail price index	—	54.0	23.3

Source: World Bank. *World Tables 1976.* Washington, D.C., 1976, p. 396.

not break with the past as much as it claims. Rather, it skillfully consolidated and expanded upon a process of industrial development that had begun in the late 1940s but had become stalled in the early 1960s because of erratic government policies.

The Brazilian economy grew steadily after World War II largely because of a policy of import substitution encouraged by high tariffs and favorable exchange rates. But unlike Peronist Argentina, where foreign investment was discouraged until the early 1960s, the Brazilians welcomed capital-intensive foreign enterprises, especially between 1955 and 1960. With the help of foreign investment and imported management techniques, the production of consumer durables, machinery, and transportation equipment increased by approximately 50 percent between 1949 and 1964. By 1964, approximately one-third of Brazil's manufacturing industries was owned by foreigners. At the same time, however, because Brazilian entrepreneurs often proved unable to compete with foreign enterprises, the state also increased its production of goods and services by expanding the operations of public enterprises in banking, transportation, petroleum and petrochemicals, steel, and public utilities. It was primarily the combination of foreign and state investment, supplemented by domestic private efforts in agriculture and commerce, that launched Brazil along the path of rapid economic growth. Problems developed in the early 1960s, however, as rapidly rising public expenditures and wages contributed to an annual average inflation rate of 52 percent between 1959 and 1963. With confidence in the Brazilian economy declining and the per capita growth rate falling to less than 0.5 percent in 1962 and 1963, the military intervened, blaming the country's plight on the populist demagoguery and managerial incompetence of President João Goulart.

The new government's solution to the country's economic malaise involved the immediate reduction of inflation through a harsh austerity program backed by authoritarian rule. With the assistance of civilian economist Roberto Campos, President Castelo Branco executed a program that combined several conventional austerity measures with an innovative system of monetary correction involving the indexation of wages, savings, and exchange rates to prices. Indexation did not prevent, however, some regressive income redistribution as real wages fell and wealth became even more concentrated in the hands of entrepreneurs. Nevertheless, popular protests were muted by the heavy hand of the authoritarian state.

To the government's relief, the program bore significant results after 1968. The flow of foreign investment accelerated rapidly, the Brazilian stock market, with the encouragement of government tax incentives, boomed, and the per capita gross national product increased by an impressive annual average of 7.0 percent betwen 1968 and 1973. Moreover, because it could produce goods at competitive prices, Brazil increased its exports of manufactured goods and diversified its trade.

The principal beneficiaries of the military's development program are not hard to identify. Most of them are concentrated in the southern third of the country where most industry and commercial agriculture are located. Multinational corporations from Japan, Western Europe, and the United States have taken full advantage of the new opportunities opened to them in Brazil, as have domestic industrialists, bankers, and retailers. Commercial farmers who have shifted from traditional to new export crops (e.g., from black beans to soybeans), as well as the producers of coffee, grain, and other commodities, have also done well under the new regime. Even the landed elites of the Northeast have survived with most of their economic resources undiminished. Urban professionals, bureaucrats, white-collar workers, and others associated with public and private enterprises have also profited from the new prosperity. Less fortunate are the factory workers and unskilled laborers, who saw their real wages decline until the early 1970s, when the government began compensating them for past losses. But their condition is still better than the estimated 50 percent of the population that survives on the fringes of the modern economy. The plight of the peasant is as ignored by the military regime as it was by previous Brazilian governments. And though significant strides have been made in literacy and basic education, most of the country's increased wealth has yet to trickle down to the masses. As a result, income disparities between the middle sectors and the masses have increased during the past decade.

Not surprisingly, Brazil is now held up as an example of what the conservative modernization strategy can do in Latin America. Using authoritarian methods to impose harsh austerity and then encourage domestic and foreign investments in industry and commercial agriculture, the Brazilians have indeed achieved one of the highest rates of economic growth in the hemisphere. At the same time, Brazil has also been used by the strategy's critics to draw attention to the costs of conservative modernization. By worshipping at the altar of growth the Brazilians have postponed efforts to solve the critical social problems that still plague the country. While they were expanding the modern sector for one-half the population, the other half languished at or just above the subsistence level. In 1970 the poorest 20 percent of the population still received only 5 percent of the national income, whereas the wealthiest 5 percent received 27 percent (see Table 7-7).

Before we conclude our assessment of Brazil's economic performance, four considerations are in order. First, what the military regime has demonstrated is not the unqualified success of the conservative modernization strategy, but only its ability to promote rapid industrial growth in a country that already enjoys an established foreign and state-financed industrial base. Post-1964 governments did not start from scratch, but only reinforced, albeit quite skillfully, a growth process well underway.

Second, Brazil's recent performance is attributable not to free market capitalism but to the heavy involvement of the state and large multinational enterprises. Of Brazil's twenty largest firms in 1970, sixteen were owned by the state. Moreover, 60 percent of the investment undertaken during the boom years 1967–73 came from the state as budgetary expenditures, as a percentage of gross national product, rose from 19.4 percent in 1949 to 27.7 percent in 1973, exclusive of what was spent for the state's industrial enterprises.

Third, Brazil's economic boom began to cool off in 1974. Although it recovered from recessions in 1974 and 1975 with an increase of 5.9 percent in per capita gross national product in 1976, growth came at the expense of a 46 percent rate of inflation. Moreover, the country's foreign debt, affected in part by the rise in the cost of imported petroleum from $276 million in 1972 to $3 billion (American billion) in 1975, rose to $29 billion in 1976, the highest of the Third-World countries. Such an astronomical debt burden could not help but increase Brazil's vulnerability to the predatory operations of the multinational firms and financial institutions that covet its raw materials.

Finally, immense structural problems remain unsolved. Though the government began to allocate more resources to social welfare items in the early 1970s, it has only scratched the surface of the poverty problem. Despite the immense success of commercial agriculture, rural poverty persists, especially in northeastern Brazil, where conditions have improved little in the past two decades. Until the conservative modernization strategy is modified to deal with these conditions, the bounty of the Brazilian miracle will be confined to the already affluent middle- and upper-class minority.

Argentina's new economic order

The achievements of Argentina's Juan Carlos Onganía were neither as impressive nor as durable as those of the Brazilians. However, judged by the standards of postwar Argentine experience, they were, at least until mid-1969, considerable. In only three years Onganía and his advisors transformed a country torn by general strikes and civil disorder and plagued by chronic inflation into a nation where labor unions became quiescent, inflation was reduced to its lowest rate in two decades, and foreign confidence ascended to unprecedented heights. But these achievements, like so much else in Argentine public life, were short-lived, and by 1971 Argentina was once again struggling to overcome the effects of political conflict and economic crisis. In Onganía's rise and fall some of the weaknesses of military authoritarian government are clearly revealed.

With the assistance of Argentine economist Adalbert Krieger Vasena, Onganía launched a comprehensive program in March 1967 aimed at stabilizing prices and expanding investment. Krieger Vasena and his associates were convinced that Argentina's economic instability stemmed from slow and irregular growth in real production, high inflation caused by wage-price spirals and occasional shortages of foodstuffs, and a recurring fiscal deficit attributable to bloated public enterprises and bureaucracies. The fundamental problem was gross inefficiency in both the public and private sectors caused by high tariffs, disincentives to rural production, undisciplined workers, overambitious welfare policies, and a political elite too dependent on patronage. What the country required, they concluded, was a global attack on waste and inefficiency under the supervision of a strong government guided by considerations of technical necessity rather than political expediency. The program included a 40 percent deval-

uation of the peso intended to cheapen Argentine goods and stimulate an influx of foreign capital, tax incentives for industrial investors,
and lower tariffs to encourage competition with cheaper foreign
goods. The key to Onganía's program, however, was not its fiscal,
exchange, and monetary measures, but the government's approach to
labor relations. No attack on inflation would succeed, Onganía's advisors were convinced, unless the labor movement was repressed
much as it had been in Brazil a couple of years before. Accordingly,
Onganía used all the state's power to break union resistance and then
impose a wage freeze until inflation had been reduced significantly.

Among the immediate beneficiaries of the new economic order
were the many foreign investors and bankers who entered Argentina
to buy out vulnerable Argentine firms or build new ones, as well as the
larger domestic firms that could withstand foreign competition.
Argentina's cattlemen and grain farmers were not singled out for
special favors, but they did gain through the government's efforts to
promote commodity exports. The smaller Argentine industrial firms,
which were vulnerable to foreign competition, and the urban working
class, which was forced to forgo wage increases in order to fight inflation, suffered most under the program. Although the latter's real income losses were less than those suffered by Brazilian workers under
similar measures, they were sufficient to promote worker discontent
and sustain the working-class struggle against the military regime.

By early 1969 it appeared that Onganía had unlocked the door to
Argentine economic growth. The per capita gross national product
rose steadily after 1966, reaching a rate of 6 percent in 1969 alone.
Inflation, which had risen to nearly 40 percent in 1966, was cut to 7.6
percent in 1969, and in 1968 Argentina attracted more foreign investment than it had in any year since 1960. Then, suddenly, the bubble
burst. The culprit, not unexpectedly, was the Argentine working
class.

Unlike the Brazilian workers, who were highly dependent on the
state and who lacked strong organizations, the Argentine working
class had been well organized and extremely militant since its mobilization by Perón in the 1940s. In 1966 and 1967 it was subdued, but
not conquered, by Onganía, and in mid-1969 its frustrations ex-
ploded into several days of rioting in the interior industrial city of
Córdoba, forcing Onganía to dismiss his economic advisors and moderate his course. His rigid autocratic regime, though capable of imposing tough economic measures on a resistant population, could not
hold off its opponents long enough to see the program through to its

conclusion. Argentina was not Brazil, and the strategy and tactics that worked in one could not succeed in the other. In Brazil the military could draw on the resources of the well-established traditions of authoritarianism and state paternalism. In Argentina, by contrast, labor was determined to secure the return of Perón to power, the state was distrusted by most entrepreneurs, and the population was still divided by intense conflict between Peronistas and anti-Peronistas. Bringing political order and economic growth to Argentina was much more difficult than it had been in Brazil, and Onganía's military authoritarian regime proved incapable of manging the feat.

Peru's reformist reconstruction

The economic development strategy followed by the Peruvian military was, as we have seen, strikingly different from the conservative modernization approach taken in Brazil and Argentina. Though the Peruvians called their program revolutionary, it actually was closer to the progressive modernization strategy discussed in Chapter 5. Its goal was the integration of all Peruvians into the modern economy through a series of structural reforms that broke the elite's domination over rural and industrial life.

The new government began with initiatives in three areas. First came the nationalization of several foreign and domestic enterprises. The petroleum and fish-meal industries, most banks and insurance companies, the import and export trade, and most utilities were placed under state control. These measures appeared quite radical within the context of Peru, but they actually did little more than raise the level of state ownership to one commensurate with that already achieved in the more industrialized Latin American countries. Second came agrarian reform. A modest program had already been begun by democratic reform President Fernando Belaúnde Terry before the military overthrew him in 1968. But in three years Belaúnde had managed to expropriate only 795 estates, covering 1.5 million hectares valued at 834 million soles. In a similar amount of time military President Velasco expropriated 1,939 units, covering 3.2 million hectares valued at 8.6 billion (American billion) soles, including the valuable foreign-owned sugar estates along Peru's Pacific coast. As a result, only 20,000 peasant families gained land under Belaúnde, whereas approximately 87,000 received it from Velasco. The third component of Velasco's program was industrial reform. This included a scheme for joint ownership by workers and entrepreneurs.

In practice this meant the government would require the country's larger firms to implement profit- and stock-sharing plans that would gradually turn over a large share of the firm to its employees.

The military's program of structural reform was, of necessity, accompanied by economic stabilization measures not unlike those initially adopted in Brazil and Argentina. Stabilization was dictated by the fiscal and balance-of-payments crisis the military inherited upon taking office. Between 1964 and 1968 the production of exportable commodities had declined, while imports continued to increase. In addition, the Belaúnde government's ambitious public expenditures in health, education, transportation, and agriculture were not accompanied by concomitant increases in revenues owing to the obstruction of the government's tax reform proposals by a coalition of Conservatives and APRISTAs in Congress. The result was heavy borrowing abroad and an excessive debt burden that created a financial crisis in 1968. The logical response was a 45 percent devaluation of the currency, a tightening of credit, and emergency tax measures, all of which brought economic growth to a standstill in 1968 and throughout much of 1969.

Economic growth was ignited again in 1970 owing to the positive effects of stabilization and high world prices for fish meal, Peru's principal export. But after 1970 it was the Peruvian state rather than the private sector that accounted for most of the investment in the country. Between 1968 and 1975 government investment grew at an annual average rate of 23 percent, increasing the state's share of the gross product from 4.1 percent in 1968 to 9.4 percent in 1975. This proved costly, however, because Velasco, like Belaúnde before him, failed to expand the government's fiscal base through a program of tax reform aimed at capturing a greater share of the available economic surplus. In the absence of new sources of revenue, he was forced to borrow heavily abroad, thereby increasing the government's dependence on the foreign creditors it had hoped to escape.

In the short run, the principal beneficiaries of the new reforms were the bureaucrats and military officers who manned state agencies. In a matter of two years the Peruvian state had taken control of several economic activities, a feat that gave immense power to the managers of new public enterprises and regulatory agencies. Many in this technocratic elite were military officers, though a substantial number were civilians from middle-sector and upper-class families who were committed to reform. Those peasants who were fortunate enough to receive land under the agrarian reform also profited from the government's programs. But a majority of the rural work force, both hired laborers and subsistence farmers, were bypassed by the reforms, which were restricted primarily to the transfer of the ownership of the largest *latifundios* to the *campesinos* who worked on them. A minority of industrial workers who were affected by the profit-sharing legislation also gained from reform.

The Peruvian experience not only teaches us something about what the military can achieve if it chooses a progressive path, but it also holds some cruel lessons about the limitations of military or any other kind of reformism. First, there are natural limitations not of the military's making. Take the rural sector, for example. It might appear that the Peruvians have solved their rural development program by redistributing land to peasants and organizing the land into various types of cooperatives. But not all peasants have benefited from agrarian reform. In fact, after the completion of land redistribution, 300,000 rural families remained landless because there was not enough land to go around. Only 2 percent of Peru's total area – the lowest proportion in Latin America – is under cultivation. More land could be made available, but only at a very high cost because the project would require the irrigation of desert regions or the clearing of tropical lowlands.

Nor has the military government escaped the kinds of externally induced balance-of-payments difficulties and foreign debt burdens that plagued previous Peruvian governments. In June 1976 it faced a crisis similar to that which it had inherited in 1967. The problem was largely one of resources. The government, encouraged by foreign bankers who foresaw an oil boom for Peru in the mid-1970s, borrowed heavily abroad to finance the most ambitious development program in the country's history. In a period of four years Peru took on a host of new creditors, raising its foreign debt fivefold to $5 billion (American billion) and its annual debt servicing to 43 percent of its total export income in 1976. But when the expected flow of oil turned out to be only a trickle and the prices of copper, fish meal, and sugar exports declined, the military officers who had removed General Velasco in mid-1975 were forced to impose tough austerity measures once again on their overextended, debt-ridden economy, including a 44 percent devaluation of the currency in mid-1977. To make matters worse, in order to secure financing from a consortium of American banks, Peru was forced to pay a very high price not just in the rate of interest, but also in the adoption of more conservative policies, including selling half the national fishing fleet back to private interests and reopening Amazonian and continental shelf areas to foreign petroleum companies, measures that had been opposed by the Velasco administration but were reluctantly accepted by his successors.

The second limitation is political. The Peruvian regime, though reformist in its initial phase, has remained elitist and autocratic. Disputes over policy and decisions about its administration have been confined to a small circle of officials within the executive. Criticism of the government is repressed or ignored, and organized opposition is not tolerated. Moreover, despite its avowedly corporatist intentions, the regime's mass organizations have been weak and ineffective. In short, the military has yet to prove itself capable of creating the mass base and political institutions needed to sustain its rule without the continual use of force.

Finally, there is the lingering issue of population growth. The military leaders of Peru and Brazil have disagreed on many policy issues, but they appear to share an opposition to policies aimed at controlling the expansion of their populations. Peru's civilian reformers, like those elsewhere, had cautiously promoted family planning and the sale of contraceptives by the private sector; General Velasco gradually curtailed the government's family-planning activities, however. Like Brazil's military leaders, he rejected the argument of those who blamed population growth for underdevelopment. Undoubtedly, national pride, resentment of foreign pressures to control population growth, and a naive faith in their ability to expand their economies to meet the needs of their populations have also influenced the military leaders' views on the population issue. Only after the 1975 coup removed President Velasco did the Peruvian government cautiously renew its family-planning programs. It did so, however, on a scale that was hardly sufficient to dent the country's 2.9 percent population growth rate.

THE CONSEQUENCES OF MILITARY AUTHORITARIANISM

Before concluding our analysis of the military authoritarian game, an assessment of its strengths and weaknesses as revealed by the Brazilian, Argentine, and Peruvian experiences is in order. Many of its strengths are obvious. Principal among them is the ability to impose temporary order on conflict-ridden societies. The methods of military authoritarianism are harsh and the punishment it deals out to recalcitrant players often severe. Nevertheless, its proponents believe that such oppression is justified by the development objectives they seek to achieve. Another strength, and one that makes military authoritarianism appealing to foreign investors, international lending agencies, and domestic economic elites, is its ability to execute unpopular economic policies over the objections of the masses. Military authoritarians do not suffer from the same political constraints as elected regimes, which rely on popular support or the voluntary compliance of influential players with their policies. Increasingly, economists who are committed to the capitalist form of development have accepted the necessity of authoritarian rule to achieve their ends. In Brazil, Argentina, and Peru austerity measures were successfully carried out by using physical force to secure the compliance of laborers and consumers, giving further support to those who defend the utility of military authoritarianism in such circumstances.

But are these achievements enough to sustain a new political order? Most of them are primarily short-term in nature and, as we saw in both the Argentine and Peruvian cases, do not produce durable solutions to political and economic problems. And therein rests the principal weakness of the military authoritarian game. It can destroy institutions and alter political behavior by physical force, but its capacity to destroy old political institutions is not necessarily matched by an ability to create new ones. Military authoritarian regimes have yet to create enduring solutions to the problems of political participation, communication between the government and its citizens, and political succession. Of the three regimes we examined, the Brazilian has come closest to the achievement of a durable political game, but even it is still plagued by the uncertainties associated with its experiments in manipulated electoral politics and by a large opposition that seeks its demise.

One of the obstacles to the military's reconstruction of the political game is its failure to develop a political theory to guide the design of new political institutions and processes. The leaders have a clearer idea of the kind of polity they oppose than of what they hope to organize in its place. They lack a theory that specifies the rules and institutions best suited for the achievement of their long-term political objectives. They may have some notion of the ultimate form the game should take, but they seldom have a strategy that sets out the steps that must be taken to achieve their ultimate goals. They lack knowledge of the mechanisms needed to implement the transition from simple autocratic rule to a more complex participatory system. To be sure, their task is not easy: Great feats of political engineering are necessary to rebuild the political game. Moreover, some trial and error is unavoidable during the process of political reconstruction, no matter how sophisticated the plan followed. Nevertheless, once these constraints are acknowledged, the performance of military authoritarianism is still disappointing.

Nor have military authoritarian regimes proved any more adept than civilian ones at solving fundamental economic development problems. They can execute short-term measures aimed at restoring entrepreneurial confidence in their economies, and if they are so inclined, they can also reform traditional institutions more quickly than can populists or democratic reformers. They can even sustain a process of economic growth for several years, as they have done in Brazil. Yet, they are just as constrained by resource limitations, rapidly expanding populations, and bureaucratic incompetence as populists and democratic reformers. Moreover, the Brazilian, Argentine, and Peruvian economies are just as dependent – if not more so – on foreign sources of capital and just as reliant on their commodity exports after several years of military rule as they were before.

Military authoritarianism appears to suffer from an illusion that stems from the belief that politics as practiced by populists and democratic reformers is the principal obstacle to economic development in Latin America. The belief is drawn from observations of the often unsuccessful struggle of elected governments to execute consistent development policies in the face of intense opposition and constant political conflict. It is reinforced by an image of Latin American countries as nations plagued by intense, destructive competition between haves and have-nots over scarce national resources. To promote economic development, then, politics must be eliminated and a nonpolitical approach to growth problems undertaken.

Such a deduction, it would seem, mistakes symptoms for causes of Latin America's development problems. Combative politics is caused not just by self-interested politicians but also by scarce resources and by political rules and economic structures that breed widespread distrust of powerful minorities. By disbanding political parties and ruling through harsh autocratic measures, military authoritarians do not eliminate these problems. More often than not, because they concentrate resources in entrepreneurial or state hands, they only reinforce hostilities and the kind of conflictual behavior they provoke. Thus, it is not enough for the military president to promise that all citizens will be better off once his program of national development yields enough growth to meet all social needs. Promises of future gain that appear to be contradicted by regressive measures that accelerate the concentration of resources and widen disparities between rural and urban life only perpetuate the kinds of social conflicts the military abhors.

FURTHER READING

General

Huntington, Samuel. *Political Order in Changing Societies*. New Haven: Yale University Press, 1968.

Johnson, John. *The Military and Society in Latin America*. Stanford: Stanford University Press, 1964.

Malloy, James M., ed. *Authoritarianism and Corporatism in Latin America*. Pittsburgh: University of Pittsburgh Press, 1977.

Needler, Martin. *Political Development in Latin America: Instability, Violence and Evolutionary Change*. New York: Random House, 1968.

Argentina

Mallon, R. D., and J. V. Sourrouille. *Economic Policymaking in a Conflict Society: The Argentine Case*. Cambridge, Mass.: Harvard University Press, 1975.

O'Donnell, Guillermo. *Modernization and Bureaucratic-Authoritarianism in South American Politics*. Berkeley: University of California Institute of International Studies, Politics of Modernization Series, No. 9, 1973.

Snow, Peter. *Political Forces in Argentina*. Boston: Allyn & Bacon, 1971.

Wynia, Gary W. *Argentina in the Postwar Era*. Albuquerque: University of New Mexico Press, 1978.

Brazil

Ellis, Howard, ed. *The Economy of Brazil*. Berkeley: University of California Press, 1969.

Roett, Riordan. *Brazil: Politics in a Patrimonial Society*. Boston: Allyn & Bacon, 1972.

Brazil in the 1960's. Nashville: Vanderbilt University Press, 1972.

Schneider, Ronald M. *The Political System of Brazil: Emergence of a "Modernizing" Authoritarian Regime 1964–1970*. New York: Columbia University Press, 1971.

Stepan, Alfred. *The Military in Politics: Changing Patterns in Brazil*. Princeton: Princeton University Press, 1971.

Authoritarian Brazil: Origins, Policies and Future. New Haven: Yale University Press, 1973.

Syvrud, Donald. *Foundations of Brazilian Economic Growth*. Stanford: Hoover Institution, 1974.

Peru

Astiz, Carlos. *Pressure Groups and Power Elites in Peruvian Politics*. Ithaca, N.Y.: Cornell University Press, 1969.

Bourricand, Francois. *Power and Society in Contemporary Peru*. New York: Praeger, 1967.

Dew, Edward. *Politics of the Altiplano: The Dynamics of Change in Rural Peru*. Austin: University of Texas Press, 1976.

Einauldi, Luigi R. *The Peruvian Military: A Summary Political Analysis.* Santa Monica, Calif.: Rand Corporation, 1969.
  Revolution from Within? Military Rule in Peru Since 1968. Santa Monica, Calif.: Rand Corporation, 1971.
Fitzgerald, E. V. K. *The State and Economic Development: Peru Since 1968.* Cambridge: Cambridge University Press, 1976.
International Bank for Reconstruction and Development. *The Current Economic Position and Prospects of Peru.* Washington, D.C., 1976.
Lowenthal, Abraham, ed. *The Peruvian Experiment.* Princeton: Princeton University Press, 1976.

9. The revolutionary game: origins and rules

Many Latin American governments have claimed to be revolutionary. Few, however, have deserved that label. A revolution requires more than a military coup or a simple change in leadership. It also involves rapid and fundamental changes in the rules of the political game and the transformation of political institutions, social values, and economic organizations. Since they achieved their independence very few Latin American countries have experienced that kind of change.

The life of a revolution can be divided into three essential parts. It begins with the defeat of the incumbent administration and its replacement by the revolutionary party or insurrectionary clique. Next comes the transformation of the political game through the consolidation of power, a process involving the elimination of some players from the game and the reorganization of the state. The third part involves the transformation of social and economic institutions. Of course, these three processes seldom occur in neat succession. Some social transformation may occur during the struggle to seize power, as happened in China when the Maoist revolutionaries reorganized rural life in the process of defeating the Nationalists. Similarly, the consolidation of power and the reconstruction of economic institutions are sometimes accomplished simultaneously, especially when revolutionary governments redistribute property in order to bring down the elite and promote a new form of economic development. But whatever their order, all three parts are essential to the completion of the revolution.

The seizure of power may involve anything from a quick assault on the government to a protracted and costly struggle. The path taken by the revolutionaries is dictated by the political and military opportunities open to them and the means available to take advantage of the opportunities. When they design their strategies, most aspiring revolutionaries recognize that as long as they threaten the existing power structure with their proposals for radical change, all normal channels of political influence will be denied them. A notable exception to this rule was Salvador Allende in Chile, who was able to exploit the democratic rules of the game to secure the presidency, only to be overthrown by antirevolutionary opponents. In most cases, however,

245

revolutionaries wage their struggle from outside the conventional political process, trying to inflict a defeat on the government that will result in its collapse. Some form of physical combat is often used: a mass insurrection by laborers or peasants, a focused military campaign by a small band of guerrillas aimed at demoralizing government troops, or merely the promotion of the kind of general disorder that makes it impossible for the government to rule. In each case the risks are high because revolutionary forces usually face a larger and better equipped, though perhaps not as highly motivated, enemy. The fact that most would-be revolutionaries in Latin America have been stopped before they could seize power testifies to the difficulty of their task.

The revolutionaries' problems do not end once they have evicted the incumbent administration. To begin with they must establish their control over the state and society in the face of opposition from within and outside the country. Whereas some of their opponents will flee, many will not. Highest on the list of players who threaten the survival of the revolution is the defeated military, which must be demobilized and replaced by the new revolutionary army. Other players, especially those seeking to weaken the new leadership and alter the course of the revolution for their private gain, must be separated from their political resources and made to conform to the new rules. Landowners must be deprived of their property, entrepreneurs of their firms, and foreigners of their investments in order to eliminate the threat they pose to the new regime. Equally important are the creation and staffing of new government organizations that can not only penetrate all areas of society and impose the government's control on them but also implement revolutionary programs. Finally, some effort must be made to build support among the potential beneficiaries of revolutionary change. Ideological education, charismatic leadership where it is available, and mass organizations must be used to generate support for the revolution.

The ultimate purpose of the revolution is, in theory at least, not merely the acquisition of power by a new elite, but the creation of a new society. It is their vision of a better life that drives the revolutionaries and their supporters. The translation of this vision into reality is the most difficult part of the revolutionaries' job. To succeed they have to overcome not only opponents but also many well-entrenched traditions and the ever-present temptation to sacrifice revolutionary objectives to the dictates of economic expediency or personal ambition. They need wisdom, skill, and the efficient use of state power to reach their goals. In the end they are judged not on how they

Table 9-2. *Cuba: historical background*

1898	Cuba achieves independence from Spain at end of Spanish-American War
	Cuba occupied by American troops until 1902
1901	Platt Amendment to new Cuban Constitution gives United States right to intervene in Cuba to "maintain government adequate for the protection of life, property and individual liberty"
1906	American governor appointed to replace Cuban president
1909	José Miguel Gómez elected president
1913	Mario García Menocal elected president; United States continues to intervene frequently with troops and advisors
1921	Alfredo Zayas elected president and advised by American General Enoch Crowder
1925	Gerardo Machado becomes president and rules in dictatorial manner
1933	Machado overthrown by popular revolt
1934	American President Franklin Roosevelt abrogates Platt Amendment
	Provisional government overthrown by "sergeants' revolt" led by Fulgencio Batista
1940	Batista elected president under new constitution
1944	Opposition candidate, Grau San Martín, elected president
1948	Carlos Prío Socarrás elected president
1952	Fulgencio Batista seizes power through coup
1953	Rebel attack on Moncada barracks fails, and revolt leader, Fidel Castro, is jailed
1955	Fidel Castro flees to Mexico after general amnesty
1956	In July Castro-led rebels sail to Cuba and twelve survivors of government attacks on landing party flee to Sierra Maestra to organize guerrilla campaign
1958	In December urban and guerrilla insurrections force Batista to flee island
1959	Fidel Castro creates coalition government in January
	In June moderates in cabinet resign, leaving control to Castro and 26th of July movement
1961	In January United States breaks relations with Cuba and imposes trade embargo
	Bay of Pigs invasion of island by Cuban exiles supported by United States government fails
1962	Cuban missile crisis in October in which President John F. Kennedy forces Russians to withdraw offensive missiles from Cuba in exchange for American promise not to intervene militarily in Cuba in future
1965	Cuban Communist party created
1975	In December first Communist party congress held
1976	New system of local, provincial, and national assemblies created and representatives to each elected

position both within Cuba and from abroad. With the assistance of an urban resistance movement committed to the overthrow of the dictatorial government of Fulgencio Batista, Fidel Castro and his small 26th of July movement of no more than 3,000 armed guerrillas defeated the Cuban army, sent Batista into exile, and began transforming Cuba into a socialist society. Castro's success inspired the use of similar guerrilla tactics throughout Latin America during the 1960s in the hope of bringing revolutionary change to other nations. But as the ill-fated campaigns of Che Guevara – who was captured and killed in Bolivia in 1968 – and of many other guerrilla leaders have painfully demonstrated, the emulation of the Cuban example elsewhere has not been easy.

After a short-lived experiment with Popular Front government in 1959, Fidel Castro and his 26th of July loyalists consolidated their control over Cuba. They have used their authority to expropriate all industries and commercial establishments and to transform the rural sector through the conversion of large plantations and ranches into state farms and cooperatives. Significant progress has also been made in the fields of education, public health, and nutrition. Yet, by the mid-1970s Cuba's economic development was still hindered by many problems, not the least of which is its continued dependence on one crop – sugar – a condition socialism has yet to overcome.

The brief rule of Marxist Salvador Allende in Chile between 1970 and 1973 is a major anomaly of postwar Latin American politics. Some might even question the inclusion of the Allende administration in a discussion of Latin American revolutions. Allende did not seize power through a violent insurrection, as did the Mexicans, or through a guerrilla struggle, as did the Cubans, but through the regular electoral process of one of Latin America's most stable constitutional democracies. Nor, once in the presidency, did he dismantle democratic institutions or eliminate his most prominent opponents in order to consolidate his control. Instead, he dedicated himself to accomplishing the unusual feat of implementing a social and economic revolution within the confines of the liberal democratic political game. In so doing he challenged the contention of revolutionary strategists throughout the hemisphere that a socialist revolution is incompatible with democratic politics. Undaunted, Allende and his Popular Unity coalition secured the nationalization of foreign-owned copper companies and many other private enterprises, including all banks and heavy industries, and implemented a massive agrarian reform program in only two years. But before he could consolidate his gains, Allende's experiment was brought to an abrupt and brutal halt by the Chilean military and its conservative supporters, making the Chilean revolutionary experiment one of the briefest and most tragic in the region's history.

THE REVOLUTIONARY CONQUEST OF POWER

The Latin American revolutionary experience demonstrates once again that there is no single route to power and no single set of tactics that will defeat ruling elites. Strategy and tactics vary with the resources and skills of the revolutionaries and the opportunities open to them. Moreover, social, economic, and political conditions not only differ from country to country, but also change over time. Tactics that might have worked against the narrowly based traditional dictatorships of the 1930s are no longer appropriate in industrialized states, whose militaries have been trained in counterinsurgency techniques. The revolutionary, like the army general, is always in danger of trying to fight the last war or insurrection again, using tactics no longer appropriate in the society he seeks to conquer.

The diversity of strategies employed in Latin America has also helped sustain debates among aspiring revolutionaries over the most appropriate route to follow. Rural guerrilla strategies that mobilize the peasantry, as was done in Asia, were advocated during the 1950s and 1960s, as were those that stressed a focused insurrection like that used by the Cubans in 1958. When the rural guerrilla struggle suffered repeated defeats in the 1960s, urban strategies were tried. In addition, some still advocate the more orthodox proletarian revolution using a revolt by industrial workers. And finally, there are a few, like the late Salvador Allende, who believe one can gain power and use it to execute revolutionary programs by playing according to the rules of democratic politics.

The Mexican upheaval

Regardless of the route taken, the principal short-term objective of the revolutionary is to seize the government from the players who dominate the national political game. In Mexico this required a lengthy and destructive civil war involving diverse forces who initially shared little more than their antipathy toward the existing regime. The revolution began in 1910 with popular opposition to the reelection of Porfirio Díaz, the dictatorial ruler of Mexico since 1877, and ended seven years later with the adoption of the Constitution of 1917 and the establishment of the new revolutionary regime. The struggle was led by men as diverse as Emiliano Zapata, a peasant leader; Francisco "Pancho" Villa, a rural outlaw; Venustiano Carranza, a landowner politician; Alvaro Obregón, a small farmer; and Francisco Madero, a cultured gentleman from an upper-class family. It took an immense toll in Mexican lives, not just among the masses who fought it but also among its leaders as they tried to consolidate power after 1917. By 1928 Zapata, Villa, Carranza, Obregón, and Madero had all met violent deaths.

Principal among the long-term causes of the Mexican Revolution was opposition among the emerging middle sectors, labor unions, and *campesinos* to the repressive elitist rule of Porfirio Díaz. Díaz, an inheritor of the liberal regime created by reformer Benito Juárez in 1857, was dedicated to the economic development of Mexico through the exploitation of its resources by foreign investors and domestic capitalists supported by a strong government that could impose its will on the peasants who resisted the transfer of their communal lands to commercial farmers and laborers who protested harsh conditions and depressed wages in the mines and factories. Through the use of a system of loyal regional political bosses backed by the federal army and rural police, Díaz secured the political order and rapid economic development that strife-torn Mexico had lacked before 1880. Yet, by monopolizing the fruits of economic growth for distribution among a small elite, he added to the frustration of those in the middle sectors, peasantry, and working class, whom he denied a share of his political power or the country's increasing economic bounty.

When Díaz announced in 1908 that he would not seek reelection and then backed away from his pledge, he provoked a violent reaction by his frustrated opponents. The opposition, inspired by the radical writings and agitation of intellectuals like Ricardo Flores Magón, turned to the more moderate Francisco Madero for leadership. Madero, the son of a wealthy northern Mexican family, was dedicated to the restoration of constitutional government rather than radical economic or social change. As the candidate of the Anti-Reelectionist party, he campaigned vigorously against Díaz before the 1910 election, only to be arrested and jailed for his efforts. After his release Madero reluctantly took to arms, joining an uprising already in progress in several parts of the country. One year and several minor battles later, Madero's forces captured the border city of Juárez, embarrassed Díaz's army, and forced the seventy-eight-year-old patriarch to abandon the presidency and flee into exile in Europe, where he spent the last four years of his life. What followed, however, was not a simple transition that added a few new players to the game, but a decade of turmoil and civil war that changed many aspects of Mexican life.

The first phase (1911–13) was dominated by the figure of Francisco Madero, elected president after Díaz's departure. Madero's goal was not the economic transformation of Mexico, but the creation of a political democracy whose procedures individual Mexicans could use to improve their condition. He was a constitutional democrat concerned more with political means than socioeconomic ends. Instead of eliminating the traditional elite and Díaz's army and bureaucracy, he invited them to accept a place in the new constitutional order. And instead of responding to the demands of Emiliano Zapata and other peasant leaders for the return of the village land sugar planters had taken, he asked them to wait until their claims were duly processed and evaluated by the government. Nevertheless, it was not Zapata or Madero's other disappointed supporters who did him in: Victoriano Huerta, an army general backed by antidemocrats in the elite, and arch-conservative American Ambassador Henry Lane Wilson, who sought the restoration of a government more sympathetic to foreign investors, deposed and killed Madero on February 22, 1913.

Huerta's coup, which represented a last-ditch attempt by the followers of Porfirio Díaz to reestablish their political control, touched off the second and most violent phase of the Mexican Revolution (1913–16). Those who had seen their reformist aspirations frustrated by the proceduralism of Madero and ignored altogether by Huerta's vengeful autocracy turned to the battlefield to accomplish what they could not secure through the political process. Northerners Carranza and Obregón wanted to create a constitutional democracy and promote Mexican nationalism; peasant leaders like Zapata wanted their land returned; labor leaders wanted their rights protected by the state; and an assortment of urban intellectuals aspired to lead Mexico down a path of liberty and social reform. Between 1913 and 1916 they waged war, first against Huerta, who was forced to resign in 1914, and then against one another for the right to create a new government. In late 1914 Villa and Zapata took control of Mexico City, and then in 1915 both were evicted by Obregón and Carranza. For nearly three years Mexico was engulfed in one of the most violent struggles in Latin American history. The revolution was, in the words of revolutionary novelist Mariano Azuela, "like a hurricane, and the man who enters it is no longer a man, but merely a miserable dry leaf beaten by the wind."

Exhaustion and the military superiority of the forces led by Carranza and Obregón finally brought peace in 1916. Soon thereafter the revolutionary generals met in Querétaro to settle their differences and write a new constitution. Conspicuously missing from the convention were the *latifundistas,* clergy, bureaucrats, and army officers who had been the mainstay of the old Díaz regime. Instead, it was the opposition middle sectors from northern Mexico, labor leaders, intellectuals, and peasant leaders who met in Querétaro. Though most of the document was inspired by the same kind of liberalism that had influenced the 1857 Constitution, written a half century before under the leadership of Benito Juárez, the proponents of social reform did secure the inclusion of significant new powers that would later enable the implementation of drastic social and economic reform. Article 3 limited the power of the Church by prohibiting religious instruction in Mexican schools. In Article 27 the traditional right of the Spanish Crown to all land and water within its domain was allocated to the Mexican state, as was the right to expropriate land and pay for it at declared tax value using twenty-year bonds that carried a 5 percent rate of interest. And laborers were guaranteed an eight-hour day and given the right to strike in Article 123.

Through the inclusion of these statutes the door was finally opened to social and economic reform in Mexico. Or so it appeared in 1917. Still to be settled were equally important issues of how the new Mexican political game would be organized, who would dominate it, and how dedicated revolutionary leaders would be to fulfilling the promises contained in the Constitution of 1917.

The Cuban insurrection

Where the Mexican Revolution was a long, protracted struggle, the Cuban Revolution was relatively short and concentrated; and where the Mexican upheaval involved nearly all members of Mexican society at one time or another, the victory of the 26th of July movement brought only a minority of the Cuban people into combat. Both, however, were driven by a determination to defeat brutal dictatorships and liberate their economies from foreign domination.

Despite the fact that they were widely observed both within Cuba and from abroad, the defeat of Fulgencio Batista and the means by which it was accomplished are still subjects of intense dispute. Memories are short and the pull of ideological causes strong. As a result, the history of the Cuban struggle has been rewritten frequently to fit the preconceptions of competing revolutionary theorists. Some claim the struggle was primarily a guerrilla-led peasant war, fought and won in the countryside. Others, especially those who were involved in the urban resistance campaign against Batista, claim their efforts and not those of Castro's guerrillas brought down the Batista regime. Still others, such as French Marxist Regis Debray in his provocative book, *Revolution in the Revolution,* argue that Castro won because he adapted guerrilla tactics to Cuban conditions, placing emphasis on the military *foco* rather than the mass insurrection. The issue would be of interest only to historians were it not for the fact that so many Latin American strategists have tried to extract from the Cuban experience lessons that would aid them in their own guerrilla campaigns.

In many ways Cuba did not appear to be the prime candidate for Marxist revolution in the late 1950s. It was neither the poorest nor the most industrialized of the Latin American countries. In per capita income it ranked third, behind Argentina and Venezuela. It ranked fifth in industrialization, and 57 percent of its population was urban. At the same time, Cubans suffered from many frustrations. Their fate was tied to sugar and, as in any monoculture economy, economic growth fluctuated with the performance of the primary export crop. The Cuban class structure was also conditioned by the sugar economy, most notably in the creation of a rural proletariat of seasonal laborers who divided their time between six months in the sugar harvest and six months of unemployment. And sugar also tied the Cuban economy and polity to the United States, its principal trading partner. American businessmen dominated the Cubans' economy, American tourists occupied their capital, and the American underworld managed the country's flourishing gambling and prostitution industries. The political control of Cuba by Americans after its independence in 1898 and its economic domination thereafter bred an intense nationalism that was used as an effective instrument of the Cuban revolutionaries.

If there was a catalyst to the Cuban revolution, it was the increasingly brutal dictatorship of Fulgencio Batista. Batista had long been active in Cuban politics, beginning with his leadership of a "sergeants' revolt" in 1934 and then his legitimate election in 1940 under a democratic constitution he helped create. More opportunistic than ideological, Batista sought to please both the United States and the Cuban nationalists. He retained close ties with the American economy, while at the same time defusing his nationalist critics by securing the abrogation of the Platt Amendment, which since 1901 had permitted American intervention in internal Cuban affairs. He also promoted the country's economic growth through the Sugar Act and Reciprocal Trade Agreements of 1934, which guaranteed Cuban access to American markets. And Batista even stepped aside when a successor from the opposition was elected president in 1944. After two well-meaning but corrupt and patronage-ridden reformist administrations proved themselves incapable of providing Cuba with a progressive, well-managed government, Batista intervened once again in 1952. Backed by foreign investors, the United States government, and the sugar industry, he rejected political democracy this time in favor of a corrupt and harsh dictatorship. By so doing he left his opponents only one option: To change his policies they would have to bring down his government, and the only way to accomplish that was through a violent struggle.

The war against Batista was waged on several fronts after 1952, the two most prominent being the urban resistance and the guerrilla campaign of the 26th of July movement. Both were led by the idealistic generation of 1953 who, as university students and young professionals, had opposed Batista's return to power and his perpetuation of a corrupt, elite-dominated regime subservient to the Americans. Because it was more diffuse and produced no leaders to match the charisma of Fidel Castro, the urban resistance has received less credit than it deserves for the overthrow of Batista. While Castro was trying to consolidate his position in the Sierra Maestra in 1957 in preparation for his attack on the Cuban army, many Cubans were already at work in the cities, bombing government installations, assassinating government leaders, and undermining public confidence in the Batista regime. Several thousand of them were killed and many jailed and tortured by government police forces between 1953 and 1959.

The other front belonged to Fidel Castro and his guerrilla army. His campaign began with an ill-fated attack on the Moncada military barracks in Oriente province on July 26, 1953, which led to his capture and imprisonment. Before his conviction, however, he delivered his famous "History Will Absolve Me" speech announcing his commitment to the overthrow of Batista and the creation of a nationalistic, reform-oriented social democracy to replace the dictatorial regime. A general amnesty in mid-1955 allowed Castro to flee to exile in Mexico, where he met Argentine Marxist Ernesto "Che" Guevara and prepared for his return to Cuba and the guerrilla struggle that followed. After a near disastrous landing on the Cuban shore on December 2, 1956, from which only twelve of Castro's eighty-two-man force escaped capture and fled to the Sierra Maestra, the guerrilla struggle was launched.

Most remarkable about the 26th of July movement was the speed of its military success. It did not begin its attacks on government outposts in earnest until early 1958. Yet, less than a year later Batista had fled the country and Castro was welcomed as a national hero in Havana. Several factors accounted for Castro's unexpectedly brief campaign, including an American embargo on arms sales to Batista, a decision that hurt the government's morale more than its military strength; the persistent agitation of the urban resistance; and middle-sector disaffection with the repressive Batista regime. The most critical factors, however, were the incompetence and corruption of Batista's army and the ability of the 26th of July movement to exploit this weakness through the use of guerrilla tactics that harassed and demoralized poorly led government troops.

The beginning of the government's collapse came in May 1958, when it overextended itself in an all-out offensive against the guerrillas, who were still lodged in the Sierra Maestra. Fidel Castro and his army absorbed the offensive with only moderate losses and counterattacked with great skill, gradually transforming the offensive into an embarrassing retreat that led to the rapid demoralization of Batista's troops. Despite its larger size and heavier armament, the army was no match for the dedicated guerrilla fighters within the confines of the Sierra Maestra, where the latter enjoyed superior intelligence, better knowledge of the terrain, and greater mobility. In August two columns led by Che Guevara and Camilo Cienfuegos moved from the mountains into Las Villas province to cut communications in the middle of the island. Then in December the guerrillas launched their own offensive, which hastened the collapse of Batista's defenses. On December 31, much sooner than Castro and Guevara had anticipated, Batista gave up the fight and fled to the Dominican Republic, leaving his army to surrender to the guerrillas the next day. The final victory came so swiftly, in fact, that several days were required for Fidel Castro to organize his triumphal march across the island to Havana to join Guevara and the victorious troops.

What then was the Cuban insurrection? We can begin by establishing what it was not. It was not a mass-based revolutionary war like the struggle of the Communist Chinese against Chiang Kai-shek and his Nationalists. Although several thousand people were involved in the fight against Batista, the striking force was more concentrated and much smaller than that of the Chinese. Nor was it a peasant uprising like those led by Zapata in Mexico or Ho Chi Minh in Viet Nam. To be sure, Castro could count several peasants among his guerrilla army, and some peasants did assist the guerrillas with food and communications. However, it was not the Cuban peasantry that Castro led, but a small group of students, professionals, and workers drawn

from the lower-middle sectors. Had the struggle lasted longer a peasant army might have been created, but victory came so swiftly that a
peasant army was unnecessary. And finally, the Cuban insurrection
was not an urban proletarian revolution. Organized labor, which was
largely controlled by the Communist party, sought to discourage the
guerrilla struggle until near its conclusion, when labor leaders belat-
edly lent their support to Castro. When we strip away the rhetoric and
revolutionary mythology, we are left with a focused armed insurrection by a small band of dedicated revolutionaries supported by elements of the urban middle sectors and rural poor who sought the
defeat of a corrupt tyrant. That the revolution would turn into something more ambitious than the middle-sector opponents of Batista
had expected did not become clear until after Castro had consolidated his power and begun his program of radical reconstruction.

The Chilean election of 1970

Against a background of civil war in Mexico and armed insurrection
in Cuba, Salvador Allende's choice of the electoral route to power in
Chile seems most bizarre. There was no precedent for implementing
a Marxist revolution within the framework of a constitutional democracy. Revolutionary change, it had long been argued, requires the
concentration of power in the hands of political authorities, a condition that is seldom achieved under the rules of the liberal democratic
game. Nevertheless, Allende defied such warnings. He did so, however, not from an ignorance of revolutionary history but from his
long experience as a participant in the Chilean political game, which
had convinced him that he stood a better chance of achieving his objectives by obeying and manipulating its rules than by defying them.

Unlike Mexico and Cuba, Chile was spared the kind of dictatorial
rule practiced by Díaz and Batista. As we saw in our study of the
Christian Democrats in Chapter 7, Chile earned the distinction of
being one of the most stable and democratic republics in Latin
America after 1932. Elections were held on schedule; parties on the
Left, Right, and Center competed vigorously for public office; and
the military gave its blessing to the entire process. Although public office was a near monopoly of moderate and conservative parties, the
nation's Marxist parties, both Socialist and Communist, were allowed
representation in the Congress and an occasional minor post in pre-
World War II Popular Front governments. On the surface, Chilean
politics appeared to have more in common with that of postwar
France and Italy than with conditions in prerevolutionary Mexico or
Cuba.

Had the Marxist parties seriously threatened elite and middle-sector control over the Chilean political process, they undoubtedly would not have been given as much freedom as they were. But in the beginning they posed no threat at all. The Chilean Socialist and Communist parties were small organizations that competed with each other for the support of organized labor and together claimed less than 20 percent of the popular vote during the 1930s and 1940s. Moreover, the leaders of both parties believed they would survive longer by playing the liberal democratic game and winning a few legislative seats instead of attacking it and inviting persecution. As a result, where other Latin American governments were constantly on the defensive against the Marxists, the Chilean leaders took pride in having established a relationship between Marxist parties and political authorities that allowed the former to speak for the masses in public forums while the latter dominated the decision-making process.

The game changed in 1958 when the election of a Marxist government suddenly became a possibility. In preparation for the election the Chilean Socialist and Communist parties formed a coalition, the Popular Action Front (FRAP), and nominated Socialist Senator Salvador Allende as their presidential candidate. It quickly became apparent that the divide-and-conquer strategy which had worked so well against the quarreling Marxist parties in the past was no longer operative. Instead, the parties of the Center and the Right found themselves competing against a Marxist coalition that could control up to one-third of the popular vote. A hard-fought campaign did bring victory to Conservative-Radical-Liberal party coalition candidate Jorge Alessandri, who secured 47 percent of the vote in the 1958 presidential election. Allende, however, polled an impressive 28.9 percent to capture second place, ahead of Christian Democrat Eduardo Frei.

As we have seen in Chapter 7, the 1964 presidential election was not a repeat of the 1958 contest. Instead, the enterprising Christian Democrats, using the threat of a Marxist victory to induce Conservatives to support Eduardo Frei and generously funded by the United States government, won the election with 56.1 percent of the popular vote. But in the same election, Salvador Allende received 38.9 percent, an increase of 10 percent over 1958.

Like the 1964 election, the one held in 1970 was a three-way race that confronted Conservatives and Christian Democrats with some difficult and critical choices. Allende was again the Marxist coalition candidate, the National party nominated ex-president Jorge Alessandri, and the Christian Democrats chose Radomiro Tomic. If the National party joined with the Christian Democrats to form a common anti-Marxist front, as had been done in 1964, they would defeat

Allende with ease once again. However, Chilean Conservatives were displeased with the reforms executed by Eduardo Frei and fearful their pace would accelerate under Tomic. Thus, when their own polls showed Alessandri to be the likely winner, the Conservatives decided to bypass the coalition strategy for a direct assault on the presidency. In taking this route they chose the strategy that promised the greatest reward if they won, but also the maximum loss if they were defeated by the Marxists. It was at the time a risk they believed worth taking. Their decision left the Christian Democrats in the middle and dictated that Tomic try to take votes away from both Right and Left in the hope of securing a plurality of moderate anti-Marxist, reform-oriented voters.

The Marxists too were faced with some difficult campaign strategy decisions. First, they had to determine the size and breadth of their coalition; this involved a decision about how much they could afford to admit nonrevolutionary parties to their coalition without sacrificing their radical economic and social objectives. In the end a six-party coalition was created, with cabinet posts to be divided proportionately among them if they won. Equal shares would go to the Socialists, Communists, and recently converted Radicals, and smaller shares to the United Popular Action Movement (MAPU), the Social Democratic party, and the Independent Popular Action party. The second decision involved the choice of a presidential candidate. Despite his three previous campaigns for the presidency, Salvador Allende's nomination was not automatic. In fact, his candidacy ignited a bitter struggle within the frequently divided Socialist party. Allende won endorsement only after thirteen of the twenty-five members of the party's central committee abstained from voting as a protest against Socialist participation in the 1970 election. Divisions like these, as well as differences among the parties that made up the Popular Unity coalition, were to plague Allende continuously. Most of the disputes centered on the issue of how fast to proceed with the government's promised social and economic revolution. Throughout his presidency, Allende held fast to a course of gradual socialization, though many in his coalition demanded immediate revolution even if it meant violating democratic rules and procedures.

To the surprise of Conservatives, Christian Democrats, and Marxists alike, Allende narrowly won the 1970 presidential election, even though he received a smaller share of the popular vote than he had in 1964 (Table 9-3). As we saw in Chapter 7, Chilean law required that Congress ratify the election of a president who did not receive a majority of the popular vote. Despite the plots of Chilean Conservatives,

Table 9-3. *Chilean presidential election, 1970*

Party	Male voters	Female voters	Total	Percent
National party (PN)				
Jorge Alessandri	479,104	557,174	1,036,278	35.3
Christian Democratic				
party (PDC)				
Radomiro Tomic	392,736	432,113	824,849	28.1
Popular Unity				
party (UP)				
Salvador Allende	631,863	443,753	1,075,616	36.6

multinational corporations, and representatives of the American government to block congressional ratification, the Christian Democrats joined with Marxist deputies in ratifying Allende's election after he promised to respect the constitutional rules of the game throughout his tenure. Suddenly, the Chilean democracy, which had achieved its reputation for fair play and stability under the leadership of conservative and moderate political parties, found itself with a president determined to execute a bold program of radical reform and income redistribution. It was the ultimate test for democratic politics.

THE REVOLUTIONARY COALITION AND THE RECONSTRUCTED POLITICAL GAME

The manner by which revolutionaries seize power is of interest not only because it tells us about the causes of revolutions but also because it affects the way revolutionaries govern after defeating their opponents. In consolidating its control over the state, the new revolutionary elite makes several critical choices about the treatment of counterrevolutionaries, the organization of its support, the form and degree of political participation in the new scheme of things, and the amount of force used to achieve its objectives. In some instances, these choices are shaped by the ideology the revolutionary brings with him; however, they are also influenced by the conditions created during conquest of power.

How did the Mexicans impose order on a country ravaged by nearly a decade of civil war? How was the new Mexican state organized and who was given control over it? Was democratic government a viable alternative under such conditions, or was the creation of some

kind of autocracy the only way to restore order? Similarly, what were
the political options available to Fidel Castro? Could he accomplish his
social and economic objectives using democratic institutions and procedures? How was he to deal with those who opposed his radical program? And what about the role of the United States? Could its interests be accommodated, or was its exclusion essential to the
implementation of radical economic reforms? Perhaps the most interesting questions involve the Chilean experiment. It might appear
that, unlike the Mexicans and the Cubans, Allende was spared the
travail of political reconstruction because he had agreed to abide by
the rules of a well-established constitutional process. Yet, what about
his program? Could it be implemented in the face of an opposition
majority in Congress? How could he manipulate the rules of the game
to secure his ends without violating the constitutional process? And
what about outside intervention? Would the United States, despite its
opposition to Marxist regimes in the hemisphere, respect Chile's sovereignty because its government was an elected one? In sum, could
Allende demonstrate that political democracy and social and economic revolution were compatible?

Whatever his options, the revolutionary must create new political
rules that help him solve two fundamental problems. The first is the
consolidation of his movement's control over the state. Unlike the
democratic reformer, who wants rules that give all political parties a
competitive chance to win public office, or the military authoritarian,
who wants rules that allow him to dominate the masses, the revolutionary needs rules that bring him the support of the masses and protect him against such enemies as property owners, entrepreneurs,
multinational corporations, and foreign governments. Second, he has
to develop the means for organizing citizens and leading them
through a process of social and economic reconstruction. To rebuild
society, he must penetrate all its institutions, from the family to the
factory. And public apathy and cynical self-interest must be replaced
by hard work and dedication to the achievement of revolutionary objectives. In short, because he seeks to rebuild society, the revolutionary must assert his control over all political institutions and use his
authority to promote an enthusiastic response by the masses.

Because they set out to create entirely new political structures, the
Mexican and Cuban revolutionaries had to confront similar problems
in consolidating their political control and constructing a new society.
The Chilean revolutionaries, in contrast, were saddled with the existing constitutional regime and were forced to pursue their economic
and social objectives by working within it. To understand how revolu-

tionary political games were created in these three cases, it is instructive first to compare Mexico and Cuba and then to contrast both to Allende's unusual experience in Chile.

The consolidation of power in Mexico and Cuba

The first task that faced the Mexican and Cuban revolutionaries was the consolidation of their control over the state. Their military victories over dictatorial rulers did not guarantee them a free hand in creating new governments. Revolutionary upheavals produce political vacuums that must be filled with new political institutions. But their creation of these institutions is made difficult by the fact that revolutionaries do not always agree among themselves about the form the new structures should take. In Mexico and Cuba, for example, conflicts among members of the insurrectionary coalition developed immediately after the old regime had been destroyed and persisted during the first years of the new regime. During those years leaders made the critical political decisions that affected the structure of the revolutionary game for years to come.

The revolutionary generals who emerged victorious from the Mexican Civil War in 1916 were handicapped by several problems at the outset. They had no coherent ideology to guide their reconstruction of the Mexican state; nor were they united behind a single set of revolutionary objectives. As we have seen, they were a disparate group with diverse interests, who fought almost as much with one another as they had with the Díaz regime. In 1916 Mexico was emerging from the chaos of a long and destructive war. Its aspirations had been codified in the 1917 Constitution but the truce was an uneasy one. The constitution allocated formal authority to the president and the legislature, but political power remained in the hands of the many armed leaders whose armies had shared in the victory. Only by establishing practical control over such groups could anyone hope to govern the war-ravaged country.

It is helpful to view the consolidation of power in postrevolutionary Mexico as a series of choices among limited options. There was the question of the fate of the victors and the vanquished. Clearly the old order would never be the same again. The revolution had destroyed the old army, broken the grip of the regional bosses who had enforced the will of the Díaz regime, drastically reduced what was left of the power of the clergy, and weakened the strength of the landed elite. There was no question of restoring the traditional elite to power. Instead the question was: Who, among the revolutionaries, would be included within the governing coalition and how would those chosen distribute power among themselves? Among the potential coalition members were the revolutionary generals, men like Carranza and Obregón and their counterparts in other regions of Mexico, who had at some time during the struggle organized their own armies and taken up the cause of the revolution. Many of them expected to be rewarded for their labors, anticipating that they would be made leaders in the postrevolutionary society. There were also the peasant leaders who, like Zapata, were still seeking the restoration of their lands. Many had seized land during the war, but needed legal recognition of their new titles and the protection of the state. There also was the labor movement, which saw the enforcement of the new labor laws as an obligation of the state. And finally, there were the members of the small middle sector, some of whom saw their economic opportunities enlarged by the destruction of the Díaz regime. But in the end it was a handful of revolutionary generals who made the critical decisions about the role of each player in the new order.

The different kinds of institutions available to the revolutionary generals in 1917 were few. At the outset they recognized the weaknesses of nineteenth-century liberalism, especially in the form it took under Madero in 1910. Mexico required a concentration of government power, rather than its dispersion. Liberal democracy, they feared, would offer an outlet for the conflicts that remained after the revolution without providing any means for resolving them. Moreover, it worked slowly, relying primarily on adherence to procedural norms, often at the expense of rapid social reform.

They also knew that they could not ignore popular demands for the implementation of the reforms contained in the new constitution. The drive for reform in the countryside and factories had gathered too much momentum during the civil war to be delayed by democratic politics after the war's conclusion. Any solution to the political problem had to satisfy such demands by incorporating the players who made them into the new regime. At the same time, control over these players had to be established if the country was to avoid the kind of perpetual conflict between ins and outs that had plagued Mexico during the nineteenth century and most of Latin America since Independence. Some creative and harsh decisions were called for, and between 1917 and 1928 they were made by a handful of revolutionary generals who defeated their rivals and constructed one of Latin America's most powerful and durable political regimes.

A review of Mexican politics during the 1920s lays to rest the fiction that the Mexican revolutionary regime emerged quickly and painlessly after 1917. Consolidation came only after intense and often bloody struggles led by Alvaro Obregón, president from 1920 to 1924, and Plutarco Calles, president from 1924 to 1928. They jailed, bought off, or shot their rivals. Zapata, for example, was ambushed in 1919, Carranza shot in 1920, and Villa assassinated in 1923. The key to consolidation was Obregón's skill as a ruthless but pragmatic political tactician. He created a coalition composed of the revolutionary army, peasant leaders, and labor bosses by offering something to each without allowing any one of them to dominate. He replaced uncooperative rural leaders with ones who supported his gradualist approach to agrarian reform. He helped reorganize the labor movement and, in exchange for union support, rewarded the rank and file with the enforcement of labor legislation. He also expanded the educational system and used it to spread the ideology of Mexican nationalism. In addition, the campaign against the Church was accelerated, especially during the Calles presidency, resulting in its virtual disappearance as a player. And finally, he built a patronage network by rewarding loyal revolutionary generals with sinecures in their home states and positions in the new government.

In Cuba the postrevolutionary consolidation of power came more rapidly than in Mexico, but it too involved a series of strategic decisions by the leaders of the insurrection. The almost complete domination of Fidel Castro and his colleagues over Cuba since the early 1960s should not obscure the severity of the political problems Castro faced when he entered Havana in January 1959. The swiftness of his victory and the involvement of so few Cubans in it had left much of the old political power structure intact. Only Batista and a few thousand army officers, police, and bureaucrats fled the island. Most of the landowning elite, foreign and domestic businessmen, middle-sector professionals, clergy, and other powerful groups remained behind, hopeful that they could survive under a new regime by influencing the course it followed. Castro had to contend with the expectations and power of such players, while at the same time fulfilling his pledge to supporters to create a more just political order and a more equitable economic system.

After the celebration had ended, Cuba's revolutionary leaders turned their attention to the consolidation of their control over the Cuban state and the initiation of a program of radical social and economic reform. Neither could be accomplished without a confrontation with the many players opposed to Castro's revolutionary objectives. Castro needed a strategy for winning that confrontation as quickly as possible. His plan of action emerged gradually through a process of trial and error during the first half of 1959 and involved the isolation of his potential opponents one by one, followed by their forced withdrawal from the new regime. At first glance, Castro's strategy appears to have been inspired by political genius, but in retrospect it is obvious that good fortune and the ineptness of his opponents had as much to do with his success as the brilliance and ruthlessness of his tactics.

Castro's political choices came down essentially to three options: first, he could use his triumph over Batista to propel himself to the head of a broad coalition of anti-Batista groups, and then begin the slow process of creating a new democratic regime that he would likely head as president; second, he could ignore all other players and create a government drawn entirely from the 26th of July loyalists; third, he could take a position somewhere between these two extremes, creating a smaller coalition of those groups who shared his vision of radical reform and using them to consolidate enough control to isolate and defeat his opponents.

He began with the first option, adopted some reform policies, and then, after his enemies had identified themselves through their outspoken opposition to such measures, moved to the third strategy, dropping other players one by one from his coalition until only the 26th of July loyalists and the remnants of the Communist party (PSP) were left in the government. By then, however, he had consolidated his support among the rural and urban masses through a host of popular reform measures and had organized a revolutionary army large enough to defend him from most enemies, both domestic and foreign. What made the strategy so successful was Castro's ability to avoid a confrontation with all his opponents at the same time. By dealing with each separately, he prevented their organization into a united opposition that might have stopped the march of his small band toward the execution of a Marxist revolution.

Castro relied on four fundamental policy decisions to flush out his opponents. First came the use of revolutionary tribunals in early 1959 to judge and then execute approximately 500 members of Batista's police and security agencies. The tribunals not only fulfilled a need for revenge, but also forced many of those who had been associated with the dictatorial regime to seek exile abroad. At the same time, they prompted moderates who were opposed to the crude process of revolutionary justice to disassociate themselves from the regime. Second came the long-awaited announcement of an agrarian reform program in June 1959. Moderates in the cabinet, such as acting president Miguel Urrutia, resigned in protest, taking much of the leadership of the old democratic parties and landed elite into exile with them. And as the moderates began leaving the cabinet their places were taken by 26th of July loyalists, giving Castro increasing control over the bureaucracy. Third was Castro's open alliance with the PSP in late 1959. Castro did not completely trust the PSP and refused to be dominated by it, but he recognized it as a source of political operators who could staff his talent-starved agencies. He also knew that his open association with the Communists would drive the remaining democratic reformers from his regime.

Finally, Castro decided to seek Russian allies, a decision that helped drive the United States from the island. From mid-1959 until the United States broke relations with Cuba in January 1961, Castro skillfully baited the American government and then used its often clumsy reprisals to justify even more drastic anti-American measures. For example, after he signed agreements to import cheap Soviet oil, President Eisenhower ordered American refineries in Cuba not to refine it. Castro retaliated by nationalizing the refineries. Then when Eisenhower terminated Cuba's sugar quota in July 1960, Castro nationalized sugar refineries and most other foreign-owned enterprises. When the cutting of American diplomatic relations with Cuba failed to force any change in Cuban policies, the Americans resorted to the ill-conceived Bay of Pigs invasion a few months later. But in surviving the invasion, Castro increased his following among Cuban nationalists and rid himself of direct American involvement in the country's internal affairs.

Castro's swift consolidation of power was also aided by the small size and relative homogeneity of Cuba in contrast to the larger and more diverse Mexico. It is one thing to gain control over a relatively small island nation and another to dominate a large country plagued by regionalism. Cultural diversity caused by the presence of large indigenous populations and a strong tradition of local political control had long troubled Mexico. As a result, the consolidation of control by the revolutionary generals required the repression of local elites and the neutralization of several hundred rivals to leaders like Obregón and Calles. Cuba, in contrast, despite some racial divisions, was a relatively homogeneous nation. Moreover, Castro did not have to contend with a host of revolutionary generals, but could count on the loyalty of most of the 26th of July movement and the new revolutionary army it created. For him, consolidation was a matter not of uniting the nation but of defeating potential opponents in the Cuban elite and middle sectors, a task that, though plagued by obvious hazards, required less political engineering than the unification of a country as large and diverse as Mexico.

By a process of elimination Castro drove his most likely enemies from the government and quickly consolidated his personal control over Cuba: first Batista and his army, then foreign firms and the rural elite, and then moderates who questioned Castro's ultimate goals. As the ranks of his opponents dwindled, it became easier to identify counterrevolutionaries and jail or exile them. The new regime Castro created was built by those who survived: the 26th of July loyalists, the leadership of the PSP, the new revolutionary army, and the laboring masses whose support Castro cultivated with his charismatic appeal and his economic reforms.

The organization of revolutionary governments in Mexico and Cuba

Three political instruments appear essential to the implementation of revolutionary objectives: an ideology, a mass-based political organization, and a strong and competent bureaucracy. Ideology is used to orient the government and transform the political values of the masses. It instructs citizens about the new rules of the game, motivates them to work for common ends, and gives them a new political ethic for determining right and wrong. The normative values of the ideology, rather than physical force or personal charisma, should become the primary source of the government's authority. A mass-based political organization is needed to spread the ideology, mobilize supporters, and isolate opponents of the regime. The political party is the preferred form of organization, but unlike political parties in liberal democracies, the revolutionary party does not limit its activities to campaigns, elections, and legislative processes. In fact, none of these activities is as important as the mobilization of mass support for the regime. After the party has prepared the way for the revolutionary program by reeducating the masses, the bureaucracy must implement government policy. Working closely with the official party, government agencies carry the burden of reorganizing social and economic institutions and coordinating diverse efforts to achieve revolutionary goals. Because state control over much, if not all, of the economy is essential to the revolutionary's task, state agencies find themselves with more power and responsibility than ever before. How well they use that power determines the fate of the revolution.

The use of ideology. Although it played a minimal role during the Mexican and Cuban insurrections, revolutionary ideology was essential to the formation of new regimes and the execution of policy in both countries. Its symbols gave the revolutionaries and their followers a new sense of identity, and its substance gave direction to their reconstruction of society. It also became an effective instrument of political control, for it contributed to the regimes' popular legitimacy and helped distinguish loyalists from enemies. In substance, however, the ideologies of the two revolutions were quite distinct. They took their ideas from different sources, prescribed contrasting social and economic objectives, and differed in precision and coherence.

The ideology of the Mexican Revolution was created from the political demands of groups who had fought against the Díaz regime. At the outset it lacked coherence and a sense of direction that could guide the government created by the 1917 Constitution. Only after its many parts were brought together and it was used as an instrument in the consolidation of political control by Mexico's first presidents did it take on an identifiable character. What began with President Obregón's efforts to secure the support of peasants and laborers and give Mexicans a new national identity was completed in the 1930s by President Lázaro Cárdenas, Mexico's first president to devote his government primarily to the fulfillment of the revolution's agrarian, labor, and nationalistic objectives.

In addition to setting the goals of the new government, the revolutionary ideology has also set its limits. Although they espoused socialism, the Mexicans created an economy that blends private enterprise with social reform. Since 1920 the country's development has been managed by large private foreign and domestic firms that operate alongside several hundred state-controlled enterprises and a host of large commercial farms that coexist with thousands of peasant *ejido* farms. Instead of being viewed as incompatible, they are all justified as necessary instruments for the achievement of the vague development goals of the Mexican Revolution.

The principal function of Mexico's revolutionary ideology has not been the guidance of economic policy but the maintenance of political control. Through the use of symbols that identify the president and the dominant party with the historic revolt that brought down the old order, Mexican leaders have secured the authority they need to prevail in the national political game. Ideology is, therefore, a way of linking Mexican leaders with the masses by tying both to a glorious past. It has transformed the election from a process involving choices among competing candidates to a means of reaffirming one's inheritance by voting for the candidates who descend from a long line of revolutionary leaders. Opponents of such candidates stand little chance of success because they appear to oppose the national heritage and the candidates linked to it by the revolutionary ideology.

Ideology has played a more central role in the formation of the new Cuban state than it did in Mexico. We shall never know if Fidel Castro was a committed Marxist before he began his insurrection, but we do know that he has built the new Cuban regime on the foundations of a well-developed and well-worn ideology. Castro's adoption of Marxism-Leninism has given Cuba more than a powerful ally in the Soviet Union. It has given the country the direction it needed to create new political and economic institutions. Marxist-Leninist ideology offered a vision of a new society that was the antithesis of what Cubans knew before 1959. Equality was to replace rigid class distinctions, public ownership of the means of production would end the evils of private ownership, and community needs would prevail over individual self-interest. By associating themselves with this vision through the media and public education, Cuba's revolutionary leaders have justified their political authority to the masses.

Fidel Castro has not, of course, had to rely entirely on Marxist-Leninist ideology to sustain his political authority. He has also enjoyed a reservoir of popular support gained from his leadership of the insurrection and his unparalleled ability to communicate with the Cuban masses. Nevertheless, ideology has played a central role in his rule by providing a blueprint for political organization and a set of symbols that could be used to orient and mobilize the masses for the construction of a new society.

The revolutionary party and bureaucracy in Mexico. Simultaneously with their development of a revolutionary ideology, the Mexicans organized a political party and gave it command over a reconstructed bureaucracy. To their credit, they recognized the need to develop the institutional means for enforcing an agreement on the new rules of the political game. Presidents Obregón and Calles had created a strong presidency supported by diverse clienteles with an interest in the implementation of revolutionary policy. But more than presidential skill was required to discipline the country's ambitious politicians and prevent the disorder that would be provoked by open competition for high office. A chain of command respected by all participants had to be created and institutionalized in order to provide smooth successions and avoid disorder. The most efficient way of doing this was through the creation of a political party.

The National Revolutionary party (PNR), created by Plutarco Calles in 1929, was organized geographically around constituencies that selected delegates from the ranks of organized labor, peasants, local revolutionary chieftains, and other groups whose members were willing to subject themselves to the discipline imposed by party leaders. In 1938 the party was reorganized by President Lázaro Cárdenas into a more effective instrument for mass participation in the political process as part of his campaign to revitalize the radical goals of the revolution. Renamed the Party of the Mexican Revolution (PRM), the new organization replaced geographical constituencies with direct sectoral interest group participation similar to that found in corporatist regimes. Within it were represented the *campesinos* through the National Peasant Association, the labor movement through the Mexican Confederation of Labor, a "popular" sector that included public employees and lawyers, and the military. By bringing the masses into the party, Cárdenas not only increased his personal following but also made it impossible for opposition parties to secure the support they needed to defeat the official party. In 1946 the party's name was changed to the Institutional Revolutionary party (PRI), but, with the exception of the separation of the military from it, its structure has remained unchanged.

In addition to its ideology and constituent organizations, the revolutionary party relies heavily on the Mexican bureaucracy to retain its domination over the political game. By increasing the power of the state and making the state the manager of several hundred new enterprises and agencies, Mexican leaders have acquired immense political resources. They control thousands of public jobs, which they can distribute to loyal supporters. Because government employment is a primary route of upward mobility and has fostered the growth of middle sectors with a stake in the maintenance of the status quo, patronage has become one of the regime's most important resources. Moreover, the government's monopoly over public works makes all Mexicans, rich and poor, dependent on its goodwill. By implementing economic policy and social reforms selectively, the president can reward his supporters and punish his enemies. Thus, those who desire essential state services have no choice but to cooperate with the government because opposition guarantees exclusion from its bounty.

If Obregón and Calles set the stage for the contemporary Mexican political game, it was Cárdenas who put it all together by formalizing the ties of the president to the Mexican masses through the creation of the corporatist PRM in 1938. The character of the relationship he established defies conventional categorization. It conforms to models neither of constitutional democracy nor of dictatorship. Instead, it involves a controlled responsiveness by a president who combines some of the powers of a dictator with some of the responsiveness of a democrat. His authority comes not from the constitution alone or from his personal charisma, but from the institutionalized paternalism of the presidency. The clever manipulation of political symbols must be combined with substantive policy benefits in order to sustain the relationship between the president and the masses and continually renew the latter's faith in the president's dedication to the fulfillment of the revolution's promise.

The Mexican president is given immense authority by the constitution, his popular election, and his party's control over the legislature, judiciary, and bureaucracy. The rules of the political game require that he exercise it constantly. He is the initiator of all legislation and the arbiter of all major disputes among party leaders, cabinet ministers, labor and management, and peasants and commercial farmers. He is also the teacher and leader of the masses and the chief manager of a very complex economy. It is his responsibility to maintain public confidence in the ability of the state to meet the minimal expectations of producers and laborers, bureaucrats and entrepreneurs so that Mexico's development can be achieved.

To sustain his political control, the Mexican president must successfully do three things: retain the support of groups affiliated with the revolutionary party, secure the cooperation of groups not in the party, and assure a smooth presidential succession. The first task is managed through patronage, cooptation, and the adoption of policies aimed at satisfying minimal peasant and worker demands. Moreover, through the party organization constituent groups are given the opportunity to ratify government policies, a highly symbolic act aimed at heightening their sense of participation.

The second requirement is more difficult to fulfill. Though the revolutionary party includes representatives of most Mexican groups within its ranks, several very important ones do not belong. For example, there are no representatives of the national business community, foreign investors, or the Church within the party. Yet, the government needs their cooperation, especially that of the first two, if it is to manage the Mexican economy effectively. Because the inclusion of entrepreneurs within the regime would violate the official ideology, informal means of communication and coordination are employed. This is done through a process of mutual accommodation in which the president sets down the rules for economic conduct and foreign and domestic businessmen accommodate to them. The bureaucracy is the enforcer of the agreement, an arrangement that gives bureaucrats immense power over the private sector, often confronting them with irresistible opportunities for graft and corruption.

Mexico's solution to the problem of presidential succession has made it the exception to the Latin American rule of irregular changes of government through direct confrontations between ins and outs involving the frequent intervention of the military. With the exception of a brief interlude after President-Elect Obregón was assassinated in 1928, Mexican presidents have been chosen in regularly scheduled elections every six years with only token opposition from minor Conservative and Socialist parties. What matters in Mexico is not the election itself, whose outcome is a forgone conclusion, but the nomination process through which the PRI presidential candidate is chosen.

The nomination of a Mexican president does not involve primary elections or tough convention contests. Instead, Mexican presidents are chosen through a secretive process by the departing president in consultation with a handful of party leaders. The individual chosen, usually a cabinet minister in the outgoing administration who has been watched closely by the incumbent, is ratified automatically by party delegates at a national convention. Between his nomination and election he visits hundreds of towns and villages throughout the country to reaffirm the relationship between the Mexican presidency and the masses its occupant promises to serve. The presidential campaign is also the means used by party leaders to reconfirm the agreement among members of the revolutionary coalition that holds the one-party system together. The content of this renewable bargain largely determines the policy direction the new president will take. Depending on existing conditions and the demands of the members of the revolutionary coalition, he may veer toward more reform with an emphasis on progressive income redistribution, as did President Echeverría in the early 1970s, or he may chart a more moderate, pro-business course, as did presidents Díaz Ordaz in the late 1960s and López Portillo in the late 1970s.

Finally, there is the matter of the involvement of the Mexican military in the nation's politics. Mexico has been spared direct military intervention largely because of the cooptation of the Mexican military from the outset. After destroying the army created by Porfirio Díaz, the revolutionary generals organized the new regime. Thereafter, the revolutionary military and the new government were one and the same. In fact, until the 1950s each Mexican president was selected from the ranks of the revolutionary generals. Military leadership was eventually deemphasized and with it the involvement of the professional military in national politics. Like all other major institutions, the Mexican military has become a loyal instrument of rule by the revolutionary party.

The revolutionary party and bureaucracy in Cuba. Any discussion of the political organizations and state agencies found in revolutionary Cuba must begin with the role of Fidel Castro, the founder of the revolution and the most influential force in its implementation. Castro's influence must be emphasized not because he has failed to create new political organizations but because he has so completely dominated those he has created. Whatever form they have taken, Cuba's politics have remained under the control of Castro and a group of loyalists from the 26th of July movement.

No organization was more critical to the governing of Cuba in the early years than the revolutionary armed forces that Fidel and his brother, Raúl Castro, created from the remnants of the 26th of July movement. Armed and trained by Soviet advisors, the 300,000-member Cuban military has been as involved in the execution of domestic policy as in the nation's defense. Its officers have staffed government agencies and have played a direct role in the mobilization of the Cuban work force. No organization has been more loyal to Castro and more useful to the establishment of his effective control over Cuban society in the early 1960s. But Castro's is not simply another military regime; the military is only one part of an elaborate set of organizations that has been developed to govern Cuban society and execute revolutionary policy.

Among the first mass organizations created by Cuban leaders were the Committees for the Defense of the Revolution (CDRs). Originally designed in 1960 for security purposes, the CDRs acted as the eyes and ears of revolutionary leaders in each neighborhood, reporting on the activities of counterrevolutionaries and enforcing government policy at the local level. At their peak they numbered 3 million members, but as the counterrevolutionary threat declined in the mid-1960s, they were gradually transformed into smaller organizations responsible for neighborhood ideological education and social organization, communicating government decisions to the masses, and reporting unrevolutionary behavior to authorities.

Neither the military nor the CDRs provided the kind of strong civilian organization needed to transform Cuban society. That task was given to the Cuban Communist party (PCC) in 1965. The party's origins can be traced to July 1961 when Castro formalized his alliance with the existing, prerevolution Communist party (PSP) through the creation of the Integrated Revolutionary Organization (ORI). The ORI was, however, only a transitional organ, which temporarily assisted in the implementation of the initial socialist phase of the revolution. In February 1963 the ORI, which had grown to a membership of 16,000 in two years, was reorganized as the United Party of the Socialist Revolution (PURS). The most important achievement of PURS appears to have been its recognition by the Soviet Union, Cuba's principal foreign ally and financier, as a legitimate Communist party. The final stage of party development began in October 1965 with the creation of the Cuban Communist party, an organization modeled after the Soviet Communist party.

What was the significance of the formation of a Soviet-style Communist party? Initially, very little, for even with the addition of the new party, the basic structure of the revolutionary regime and its leadership remained much the same as before. As the party went through its ORI, PURS, and PCC phases, it never left the control of Fidel Castro and his close associates from the 26th of July movement. Moreover, not until December 1975 did Castro call the first congress of the Cuban Communist party. In the interim the revolutionary elite continued to dominate the state through its control over the bureaucracy and the military.

The Cuban regime has never functioned as smoothly or as effectively as its creators had hoped. During the early years many costly planning and execution mistakes were made, some owing to the revolutionary zeal of Cuba's new leaders, others as a result of the capricious meddling of Castro in the planning process, and still others because of the difficulty of managing a centralized economy. The greatest disappointment came in 1970, when the Cubans failed to achieve a 10 million-ton sugar harvest after an all-out mobilization of the country's resources. The failure, for which Castro personally accepted the blame, was later attributed to the unresponsiveness of Cuba's centralized bureaucracy to economic and social conditions at the local level. Consequently, throughout the early 1970s Cuban officials reassessed their rigid planning and bureaucratic processes in search of ways to make them more effective in implementing revolutionary policy objectives. Their efforts finally yielded an unprecedented plan of political reform that Castro announced at the first party congress in December 1975.

Castro proposed the creation of a new system of popular representation designed to make the bureaucracy more responsive to local conditions. It involved the selection of delegates to municipal, provincial, and national assemblies through competitive elections, and the use of the assemblies to supervise government agencies active within their jurisdiction.

As had been promised, elections were held during late 1976 and delegates to all the assemblies were chosen. The process began at the local level with the selection of 10,743 delegates to 169 municipal assemblies. They, in turn, chose delegates to 14 provincial assemblies (1 for every 10,000 citizens), and to a national assembly (1 for every 20,000 citizens). Each assembly appointed its own executive committee to supervise the day-to-day implementation of government policy. Municipal executive committees, for example, were assigned supervision of schools, hospitals, retail stores, hotels, public utilities, and sports; provincial committees assumed responsibility for intercity transportation and trade.

Whether these reforms will make the Cuban bureaucracy more responsive to local needs or more effective in the delivery of goods and services remains to be seen. The reforms may become window dressing for continued reliance on a system of central control or they may force local bureaucrats to become more attentive to the citizens they are supposed to serve. Much depends on the willingness of Fidel Castro and his associates to relinquish their tight control over the state bureaucracy. Apparent at this date is the fact that neither Castro nor the Communist party has lost influence as a result of the reforms. Of the 481 delegates elected to the National Assembly, 441 are members of the Cuban Communist party. Moreover, the Council of State, which serves as the executive arm of the National Assembly, is chaired by Fidel Castro, assisted by Raúl Castro as first vice-president and five other vice-presidents, three of whom are veterans of the 26th of July movement.

Mexico and Cuba: some essential differences. At this point a brief comparison of the Mexican and Cuban regimes is in order. Clearly there are some similarities in the way the postrevolutionary game has been played in both countries. Both are dominated by strong executives who set national policy and enforce political rules. Each executive is assisted by a revolutionary party and a state bureaucracy. The parties, in turn, use an ideology to mobilize the masses in support of the national executive, the rules of the game, and the implementation of the revolution's goals. Finally, each has transformed the military into a loyal instrument of the state.

Once these similarities are duly noted, we discover some striking differences as well. The Mexicans have created a pluralistic society governed through a corporatist-type party that permits much latitude in individual conduct, especially in the economic arena. The Cubans, in contrast, have tried to create a more homogeneous society governed through the central direction of Fidel Castro and the Communist party. A closer look at the objectives, party structures, and rules of the game in each country highlights these differences.

The ultimate objectives of the Mexican Revolution remain clouded. The official ideology espouses the cause of social justice for peasants and workers, but it lacks a vision of what form the just society should take. As a consequence, Mexican presidents have enjoyed much latitude in their choice of policies, though they have paid for their freedom by having to tolerate a continual debate over the revolution's proper course. The ultimate objectives of Cuba's Marxist-Leninist ideology are less obscure. Moreover, the cumulative experience of other communist nations has given the Cubans concrete examples to follow.

Mexico's revolutionary party is a large, diverse organization that joins separate interest groups in support of the regime. Though the groups owe their existence to the government, they are not totally controlled by it. And as they have demonstrated increasingly in recent years, each has the capacity and independence to provoke minor crises aimed at securing presidential concessions to its demands. The Cuban Communist party, on the other hand, is a tightly organized party whose members form a highly disciplined corps that claims to represent the interests of the entire community rather than separate interest groups.

Mexican treatment of opposition groups also differs from Cuba's. Opposition parties are encouraged though they are never allowed to prevail. More important, many economic interests representing commercial farmers, industrialists, foreign investors, and the like coexist with the official organizations and freely bargain for preferential treatment from public authorities. In Cuba, as Castro has proudly stated, there is no need for an opposition because the only interest is that of the Cuban nation as articulated by its revolutionary leaders and their ideology.

Finally, the Mexicans institutionalized their rules of the game by allocating immense power to the president and making all players dependent on him and his party. By prohibiting presidential reelection they have also assured that political authority will remain in the presidency rather than with the man who occupies it. The Cubans have yet to complete the creation of a new and durable institutional order. They have gone a long way toward that end with the creation of a mass-based party and the involvement of the masses in state administration. Nevertheless, they remain heavily dependent on the leadership and authority of the person of Fidel Castro.

Chile's constitutional Marxist game

What about Allende's experience in Chile? Is it a mere footnote to the revolutionary struggle in Latin America that demonstrates the futility of the constitutional route to economic change? There is no satisfactory answer to this question because the brief experience of a single nation can neither prove nor disprove a theory of revolution. Nevertheless, there are important lessons to be learned from Allende's struggle, especially when his political choices and their consequences are contrasted with those of the Mexican and Cuban revolutionaries.

Allende was a Marxist who wanted to create a socialist society in Chile. He was determined, however, that his methods would be distinctly Chilean. He believed in the ultimate triumph of the proletarian revolution, but was willing to use the procedures of the constitutional regime to transform the capitalist economy and prepare the way for the proletariat's assumption of power. For Allende, socialism was not something to be imposed on Chilean society through the dictatorship of a political party, but rather a goal to be achieved according to the democratic rules of the Chilean political game. Thus, where other Marxists believed the goals of the socialist revolution to be incompatible with the rules of the liberal democratic game, Allende held that within Chile at least this apparent contradiction could be overcome.

If ideology was not primarily a means of political control after 1970, what function did it fulfill for the Popular Unity regime? Its primary purpose, it seems, was to set the direction of government policy and retain the support of Socialists, Communists, Radicals, and others. Allende's initial economic program, as we shall see in Chapter 10, was not as radical as the one adopted by Fidel Castro or as moderate as that of the Mexicans. Instead, it charted a gradual transition to socialism involving the reduction of the power of domestic and foreign entrepreneurs through the gradual expropriation of most of their property, the redistribution of income from the upper to the lower class, and the transformation of the rural social structure through the redistribution of property to peasants and workers. In short, it combined some aspects of the progressive modernization strategy (Chapter 5) with elements of revolutionism.

It was Allende's misfortune that instead of uniting his coalition, his program became the source of continual debate within his administration. Chilean Socialists and Communists had differed frequently in their interpretations of Marxist-Leninist ideology and how it should be applied under Chilean conditions. Many Socialists, most of whom tended to be more doctrinaire and radical in their proposals than the Communists, opposed any compromise with opponents of their revolution and fought vigorously within the cabinet for the acceleration of the socialization of the economy. The Communists, on the other hand, were more pragmatic, willing to accept a moderate course rather than risk provoking the kind of violent opposition that would lead to the government's overthrow by the military. Although the two parties agreed on most of their ultimate goals, their debates over legislative strategy, economic policy, and the mobilization of the masses placed constraints on Allende that would never have been tolerated by Castro in Cuba.

Instead of viewing Salvador Allende as the leader of a typical Marxist party-state, we must see him for what he was: He was a president facing problems common to most leaders of minority coalitions who face stiff legislative opposition. The radical character of his program merely increased his difficulties by mobilizing his domestic opponents and inviting greater than normal intrusions by concerned foreigners into Chile's domestic affairs.

As a political strategist, Allende was quite cautious. He recognized that his electoral triumph had been slim and that he served as a minority president. Although he was anxious to execute his economic revolution, he did not want to antagonize his Christian Democratic opponents and stimulate the kind of civil conflict that could undermine his program. At the outset he was determined to deprive the economic elite of its wealth and power without harming the middle sectors. In practice, this meant a gradual nationalization of elite-owned enterprises accompanied by a prohibition on measures that might deprive the middle sectors of their wealth and property. What made this objective so difficult to achieve, however, was the dependence of many Chilean professionals, technicians, and white-collar workers on the enterprises of the elite for their livelihood. As Allende's critics within his own coalition were quick to point out, nationalization, even if carried out in a gradual manner, would sooner or later threaten all members of the Chilean bourgeoisie and, therefore, the cultivation of their support was a hopeless and self-destructive task. Nevertheless, Allende held firm to his original strategy, guided by the belief that his revolution would be achieved only if he avoided a direct confrontation with potential middle-sector opponents.

No single set of tactics was adequate to Allende's political needs, so he employed several simultaneously. Where possible, he cultivated the legislative support of Christian Democratic senators and deputies. For example, he secured the passage of his copper nationalization bill after attracting Christian Democratic and National party support. When his opponents blocked the passage of other parts of his program, he skillfully used existing laws to promulgate nationalization measures, as when he drew on statutes permitting government seizure of firms that did not produce to capacity. At the same time, he employed Frei's Agrarian Reform Law and accelerated the pace of expropriation. He also sought to build support for his government among middle-sector and lower-class voters so that the Popular Unity coalition (UP) could pick up enough seats to secure a majority in the March 1973 congressional elections. As we can see in Table 9-4, the UP needed to pick up nineteen seats in the Chamber of Deputies and eight in the Senate in order to gain a majority. After Allende's inauguration, Socialist and Communist party organizers launched a major effort to enlist the electoral support of those who had benefited from the government's economic policies in 1971 and 1972. However, in doing this they provoked a joint campaign by the National and Christian Democratic parties to block a UP victory. The election, it turned out, was a standoff, for although Allende's forces managed to increase their share of the popular vote to 44 percent, they gained only six seats in the Chamber of Deputies and two in the Senate.

To make matters worse for Allende, as many of his more radical critics had warned, his programs, despite their relative moderation, provoked the opposition of many Christian Democrats, along with the parties and interest groups that represented the economic elite. The Christian Democrats had accepted some parts of Allende's program, such as the nationalization of the foreign-owned copper companies, the acceleration of agrarian reform, and emergency social welfare measures, but they still opposed the gradual destruction of the capitalist economy. They were also preoccupied by fears that the Marxists would, despite their pledges, abuse the constitution and block Christian Democratic efforts to recapture the presidency in 1976. Under the circumstances there appeared to be three options available to Christian Democratic party leaders: They could continue to support the government's program at the cost of a permanent split in the party between moderates and radicals; they could obstruct the gov-

Table 9-4. *Distribution of seats in Chilean Chamber of Deputies and Senate*

Party	Chamber	Senate
Before 1973 elections		
CODE (PDC-PN alliance)	93	32
UP (Socialists, Communists, Radicals, et al.)	57	18
After 1973 elections		
CODE	87	30
UP	63	20

ernment program in Congress and unite with the National party in a campaign to regain the presidency in 1976; or they could undertake a campaign of total opposition aimed at undermining the government and securing its overthrow by the military. An examination of the behavior of the Christian Democrats in 1972 and 1973 reveals that they began with the first option, soon went on to the second, and after the March 1973 congressional elections turned in desperation to the third.

This is not the place to trace the complex history of Allende's last year in office. Nevertheless, it is worth noting how perceptions – and misperceptions – of violations of the traditional rules of the Chilean political game contributed to the coup that led to Allende's death and the end of constitutional government in Chile on September 11, 1973.

After collaborating in the passage of the copper nationalization bill, the Christian Democrats, fearing Allende was taking the socialization of the economy too far, turned to legislative obstruction of his program. Their principal instrument was a bill – known as the Hamilton-Fuentealba Amendment – which prohibited the nationalization of any enterprise without specific congressional authorization. Allende vetoed the bill in early 1972. There followed a series of negotiations between the government and the Christian Democrats in which the latter tried to extract a promise that the government would abandon its assault on the capitalist system, something Allende could not do without losing the support of critical members of his coalition. Consequently, the negotiations, which lasted until early 1973, finally were dissolved without any resolution of the issue.

Legislative opposition was not, however, enough to halt the government's program, so Christian Democrats turned after March 1973 to more direct modes of obstruction, beginning with the support of strikes in the copper and trucking industries and eventually leading to civil disorder and the provocation of military intervention. Throughout their campaign, they were encouraged and assisted by allies from abroad, especially in the United States, but it would be a gross oversimplification to credit foreigners with stopping Allende's revolution. Most of the credit (or blame) goes to the Chilean political parties and interest groups, who, acting as representatives of the country's bourgeoisie, took advantage of the weaknesses in the government's economic program as well as their own financial resources and organizational strength to bring Allende down.

Chile's constitutional game had worked well as long as no one was forced to relinquish his resources to others. Frei had begun, albeit slowly, to change that, and Allende, determined to create a socialist

Chile, accelerated the transformation. Although he conscientiously adhered to most of the procedures of the democratic game, he violated the unwritten social compact that had made those procedures acceptable to elite and middle-sector players. By mid-1973 Allende had only two choices left: He could compromise with his opponents and limit his objectives, or he could remain adamant and challenge them to violate their own democratic rules by overthrowing him. It was not much of a choice, for if he did the first, he would sacrifice his economic revolution, and if he did the second, he would lose his government.

FURTHER READING

General

Berger, Peter. *Pyramids of Sacrifice*. New York: Basic Books, 1974.
Hagopian, Mark. *The Phenomenon of Revolution*. New York: Dodd Mead, 1974.
Huntington, Samuel. *Political Order in Changing Societies*. New Haven: Yale University Press, 1968, Chapter 5.
Johnson, Chalmers. *Revolutionary Change*. Boston: Little, Brown, 1966.

Mexico

Brandenburg, Frank. *The Making of Modern Mexico*. Englewood Cliffs, N.J.: Prentice-Hall, 1963.
Cumberland, Charles. *Mexico: The Struggle for Modernity*. New York: Oxford University Press, 1968.
Johnson, Kenneth F. *Mexican Democracy: A Critical View*. Boston: Allyn & Bacon, 1971.
Johnson, William W. *Heroic Mexico*. Garden City, N.Y.: Doubleday, 1968.
Padgett, Vincent. *The Mexican Political System*, 2nd ed. Boston: Houghton-Mifflin, 1976.
Reyna, José Luis, and Richard Weinert, eds. *Authoritarianism in Mexico*. Philadelphia: Institute for the Study of Human Issues, 1977.
Tannenbaum, Frank. *Peace by Revolution*. New York: Knopf, 1933.
Womack, John. *Zapata and the Mexican Revolution*. New York: Knopf, 1969.

Cuba

Bonachea, Ramon L., and Marta San Martin. *The Cuban Insurrection: 1952–1959*. New Brunswick, N.J.: Transaction Books, 1974.
Debray, Regis. *Revolution in the Revolution*. New York: Grove Press, 1967.
Fagen, Richard R. *The Transformation of Political Culture in Cuba*. Stanford: Stanford University Press, 1970.
Goldenberg, Boris. *The Cuban Revolution and Latin America*. New York: Praeger, 1965.

Gonzalez, Edward. *Cuba Under Castro: The Limits of Charisma.* Boston: Houghton-Mifflin, 1974.

Guevara, Ernesto "Che." *Reminiscences of the Cuban Revolutionary War.* New York: Grove Press, 1968.

Halperin, Maurice. *The Rise and Decline of Fidel Castro.* Berkeley: University of California Press, 1972.

Karol, K. S. *Guerrillas in Power.* New York: Hill & Wang, 1970.

Ruiz, Ramon Eduardo. *Cuba: The Making of a Revolution.* Amherst: University of Massachusetts Press, 1968.

Seers, Dudley, ed. *Cuba: The Economic and Social Revolution.* Chapel Hill: University of North Carolina Press, 1964.

Suarez, Andres. *Cuba: Castroism and Communism, 1959–1966.* Cambridge, Mass.: MIT Press, 1967.

Thomas, Hugh. *Cuba.* New York: Harper & Row, 1971.

Chile

Allende Gossens, Salvador. *Chile's Road to Socialism,* ed. Joan Garces. Baltimore: Penguin, 1973.

Ayres, Robert L. "Electoral Constraints and the Chilean Way to Socialism." *Studies in Comparative International Development* 8 (2):128–61, summer 1973.

Birns, Laurence, ed. *The End of Chilean Democracy.* New York: Seabury Press, 1974.

Debray, Regis. *The Chilean Revolution: Conversations with Allende.* New York: Pantheon Books, 1971.

Feinberg, Richard E. *The Triumph of Allende: Chile's Legal Revolution.* New York: New American Library (Mentor Books), 1972.

Francis, Michael J. *The Allende Victory: An Analysis of the 1970 Chilean Presidential Election.* Tucson: University of Arizona Press, 1973.

Roxborough, Ian, Phil O'Brien, and Jackie Roddick. *Chile: The State and Revolution.* London: Macmillan, 1977.

Sweezy, Paul M., and Harry Magdoff, eds. *Revolution and Counter-Revolution in Chile.* New York: Monthly Review Press, 1974.

Valenzuela, Arturo, and J. Samuel Valenzuela, eds. *Chile: Politics and Society.* New Brunswick, N.J.: Transaction Books, 1976.

10. The revolutionary game: policy and performance

The experiences of Mexico, Cuba, and Chile demonstrate the diversity of the revolutionary routes to economic development and social justice. The Mexican Revolution occurred in a society that was still in the initial phase of foreign-financed capitalist development. Its leaders sought, not the elimination of capitalism per se, but its reform to meet the needs of Mexicans of all social classes. They abolished the *latifundio* and replaced the traditional elite with a new one composed of government bureaucrats, private entrepreneurs, and peasant and labor leaders. Together, they built a new kind of Mexican capitalism. The Cubans and Chileans, on the other hand, had progressed farther down the road of capitalist development when they began their revolutions. They already possessed many consumer goods industries and public enterprises. And along with their infant industries had come the growth of the middle sectors, an active labor movement, and substantial foreign investment. It was their extensive experience with dependent capitalism that led the Cuban and Chilean revolutonaries to try to erect socialist economies rather than reform their old capitalist ones.

In these three cases we have the results of contrasting approaches to revolutionary social and economic change. The first led to the organization of a system of mixed capitalism with a strong commitment to social reform, the second to the rapid creation of a system of state socialism, and the third to an abortive effort to transform the capitalist economy into a socialist one using democratic means. By comparing the goals of the three revolutions and the diverse ways they tried to achieve the goals, we can discover some of the consequences of revolutionary policy in Latin America.

REVOLUTIONARY DEVELOPMENT PROGRAMS

From its inception, the Mexican development strategy has been plagued by a conflict between its two primary objectives: social reform, especially in the countryside, and industrial development. At first these two objectives appeared quite compatible because the destruction of the *latifundio* and the liberation of millions of peasants were believed necessary to generate the laborers and consumers needed to sustain industrialization. But industrialization also requires the concentration of resources in the hands of investors, either state or private, and in scarce resource situations this often dictates the postponement of social expenditures. Nowhere has the competition between such objectives been more intense than in Mexico since 1940.

Mexican development policy can be divided into two phases. During the first, which lasted from 1920 to 1940, economic recovery and social reform were stressed; industrialization was emphasized during the second, which lasted from 1940 until the mid-1970s. At the outset the new revolutionary elite was preoccupied with political consolidation, a gradual recovery from the devastation caused by nearly ten years of internal warfare, and the initiation of social reform. Structural reforms, which began slowly under Obregón and Calles, was accelerated by Cárdenas during the 1930s. In rapid succession *latifundios* were expropriated, foreign petroleum firms nationalized, labor laws enforced, and educational opportunities expanded. Most important, by breaking down traditional institutions the government freed many Mexicans to join the growing industrial work force.

After 1940 capital accumulation and industrialization were emphasized over social reform. First came the expansion of state investments in economic infrastructure and state enterprises and then the encouragement of private investment. Foreign investors were invited to return to Mexico and tourism was encouraged to increase the supply of foreign exchange and help finance industrial growth. Despite the emphasis on industrialization, agriculture was not neglected during the period. But instead of concentrating only on the redistribution of land to *campesino* farmers, as had been the practice before 1940, the government encouraged the development of large commercial farms in order to feed a growing population and take advantage of food markets in the United States. Government investments in roads and irrigation networks, especially in the northwestern desert region, opened thousands of acres for exploitation by rural entrepreneurs who could afford modern technology and farm management techniques. Of course, land reform and social welfare were not abandoned after 1940. However, both were subordinated to the requirements of industrial growth as government officials became increasingly convinced that the expansion of industrial employment provided the solution to most of the country's social and economic problems.

Where the Mexicans were content to open new opportunities by replacing some traditional institutions with new public and private enterprises, the Cubans were more ambitious, having committed themselves to the construction of a new economic order modeled on the socialist systems of Eastern Europe and the Soviet Union. They began by expropriating nearly all private property. By 1968 all industry and commercial enterprises were in the hands of the state, as was 70 percent of the country's farmland, the remainder having been left in the hands of small farmers closely regulated by the state. The road to socialism has not been a smooth one, however. The socialization of the Cuban economy confronted the country's leaders with a host of difficult decisions regarding the use of central economic controls, the appropriate mix of agricultural and industrial investments, the use of material and moral incentives to raise worker productivity, and the relative importance of capital accumulation and social welfare. Instead of holding firm to one set of solutions to these problems, they have frequently changed course, often forced by miscalculations and project failures to discard one approach in favor of another.

Distributive objectives were stressed in an effort to gain mass support during the first phase of the revolution (1959–60). Driven more by revolutionary ardor than a clear plan of attack, Fidel Castro and his colleagues from the 26th of July movement concentrated their energies on agrarian reform, health care, education, and public housing. As a result of their zeal and inexperience, technical errors, bureaucratic waste, and disorganization accompanied the implementation of most policies. The second phase (1961–2) began with an increase in central control through the emulation of the Soviet model of economic development with its emphasis on economic planning, bureaucratic regulation, capital accumulation, and industrialization. A third phase (1963–7) resulted from a reassessment of the high costs of industrialization and a decision to return to an emphasis on agricultural rather than industrial growth. Again, Soviet planning methods were applied, but now their goals were agricultural production and diversification. The fourth phase (1968–70) saw a shift to more radical methods, such as the use of revolutionary ideology and moral incentives to inspire the Cuban masses to greater effort in the implementation of the government's economic and social programs. This "revolutionary offensive" culminated in an unsuccessful attempt to produce a record 10-million-ton sugar crop in 1970 and a reassessment of the development effort. Since 1970 greater emphasis has been placed on material incentives, more realistic objectives, and the improvement of economic administration through greater popular control over the bureaucracy.

The Cubans' occasional frustrations and constant search for improved modes of economic management have not reduced their determination to make socialism work in their country. As in Eastern Europe and the Soviet Union, disputes among leaders have concerned primarily issues of short-term economic strategy and administration rather than fundamental questions about ultimate purpose. The disputes reflect the frustrations of ambitious revolutionary leaders who must direct an island economy condemned by nature to depend on the production of a few crops and plagued by traditions that have not been easily eradicated during the transition to socialism.

Salvador Allende was as convinced as Fidel Castro of the necessity of socialist revolution. But he lacked Castro's freedom to implement it. Unlike the Cubans, he had to contend with an opposition dedicated to using its economic and political resources to stop him. Nevertheless, Allende and his supporters in the Popular Unity coalition were determined to succeed with their economic revolution before his term expired in 1976. Although they recognized that they could not bring complete socialism to Chile in only six years, they did expect to launch Chile on an irreversible course by transforming most of its economic institutions into instruments of state economic control and using them to transfer resources from the rich to the poor. Moreover, they proposed to do it by adapting Marxist-Leninist principles to Chilean conditions rather than slavishly imitating other socialist countries.

Allende's initial development program had two primary goals: the gradual socialization of the means of production and an immediate increase in mass consumption to build a working class–middle sector alliance. The first was essential if the state was to reallocate society's resources in a more equitable manner; the second was prompted by Allende's determination to secure a majority of the popular vote in future elections as well as protect his government from its upper-class and foreign enemies.

During 1971 and 1972 the Popular Unity government moved swiftly toward the socialization of Chile's capitalist economy. Its immediate objective was the creation of a mixed economy that included three sectors: one controlled entirely by the state, another composed of mixed public-private enterprises where the state was dependent on the private sector's supply of technology, and a third consisting of small private firms involved in retail sales. The government requisitioned some private firms without compensation, using an old law that permitted the seizure of firms that refused to produce at capacity. The local plants of multinational enterprises like Ford, General Motors, and Dow Chemical were among those taken in this manner. Others – for example, all banks, Coca-Cola, Dupont, and Bethlehem Steel – were purchased at book value. And a few, most notably the Kennicott, Braden, and Anaconda copper mines, were nationalized with congressional approval but denied compensation because, according to Popular Unity officials, they had extracted excess profits from their operations. Many foreign firms, however, were left untouched in the initial round because they provided essential goods and services; among these were IBM, Xerox, Mobil, Texaco, Exxon, and RCA. In fact, Allende never went as far with nationalization as his more militant supporters would have preferred or his enemies had feared. Nevertheless, the nationalizations eventually alienated many Christian Democrats who were initially disposed to cooperate with the government; equally important, they also imposed an immense fiscal burden on the Chilean state that heavily taxed its limited resources.

Allende's concern for Chilean workers and the unemployed poor was personal, philosophical, and political. As a medical doctor he was familiar with the condition of the poor, and early in his professional career he had committed himself to the alleviation of their suffering through political action. As a Marxist he also recognized that the proletariat would continue to be exploited as long as it was denied control over the means of production. And as an experienced campaigner and party leader, who had received less than 40 percent of the popular vote in 1970, he knew his hope of electoral victory in the March 1973 congressional elections rested with the mobilization of the urban and rural poor and many in the middle sectors. Consistent with these views, he decreed across-the-board wage increases during 1971, expanded public works programs giving jobs to the unemployed, and froze prices on essential consumer items. He also gave priority to the distribution of scarce foodstuffs to retail outlets that served the urban poor. As a consequence, 1971 became a boom year for Chilean workers, whose real income rose by an average of 40 percent during that year alone.

The Chilean government also had a plan for rural development. The Marxists had blamed Chile's failure to feed itself on the inefficient use of farmland by *latifundistas*. Moreover, the plight of the Chilean poor could be traced, they argued, to the antiquated class structure that prevailed in the countryside. Accordingly, Allende pledged himself to the speedy completion of Frei's agrarian reform program to improve the lot of the *campesino* and foster a higher level of production. Prompted by a wave of land seizures touched off by his campaign and election. Allende expropriated and redistributed twice as much land in his first two years as Frei had done in his last three. In 1965 55 percent of Chile's farmland was held by owners of farms that exceeded 200 acres in size, but by the end of 1972 only 2.9 percent was still left in such large privately controlled units. Expropriated lands were reorganized in several different ways, with some turned into agrarian reform centers or large production units controlled by the *campesinos* who worked them, and others, especially those of a more agro-industrial type such as cattle breeding, run as state farms by government administrators.

Four conditions had to be met for Allende's economic program to succeed. First, economic expansion had to be sustained in order to satisfy the demands of working-class and middle-sector consumers simultaneously. If it was not, shortages would develop, inflation increase, social tensions rise, and support for the government, especially among the middle sectors, decline. Second, the government had to gain enough control over the economy through its nationalizations to capture industrial and financial profits for the treasury and pay for its expansion of public works and other job-creating programs. Without substantially increased revenues, it would be forced to borrow heavily abroad or resort to inflationary Central Bank financing of the deficit. Third, exports, especially high foreign exchange producers like copper, had to be increased to pay for capital and consumer goods imports. This was especially important because Chile could expect little financial assistance from capitalist nations and international agencies who opposed its economic revolution. Finally, a rapid decline in agricultural production due to land expropriation had to be avoided. A drop in food production at a time of rising consumption would lead either to food shortages or increased imports to cover the deficit, neither of which Allende could afford. Obviously, the Allende program was plagued by hazards. If any one of these conditions was not met, serious problems could arise that might undermine the entire effort. Moreover, any failure could be easily exploited by enemies in the elite or from abroad who were determined to stop Allende's socialist revolution.

REVOLUTIONARY PERFORMANCE

The selection of revolutionary goals is not especially difficult, nor is the design of radical development programs. This does not hold true for their implementation, however. No matter how well conceived their programs and how dedicated their designers, the Mexican, Cuban, and Chilean revolutionaries stood little chance of complete success. There are many reasons for this. First, there was the difficulty of transforming institutions and practices that had withstood direct assaults before. Resistance would have to be met and dealt with, and the unpredictable outcomes of such confrontations would likely be different from what the revolutionaries had anticipated. Second, the organization and mobilization of the masses into an attack on the conditions that had oppressed them were unprecedented in their difficulty and plagued by pitfalls. And third, the execution of radical economic programs faced the same physical limitations as reformist or conservative ones. Each country was constrained by its natural resources, and no transformation of ownership could overcome a shortage of critical minerals or a lack of arable land.

The leaders of the Mexican, Cuban, and Chilean revolutions were not especially preoccupied by these difficulties at the outset. Had they been, they probably would not have begun their bold programs. Instead, they ignored most obstacles and set out to effect as much change as possible in four critical areas: land tenure and rural production, industrial ownership and production, national economic independence, and income redistribution. By comparing their performances in each of these areas, we can determine the relative effectiveness of the development programs and how they affected the players of the revolutionary game.

Mexican capitalism

Mexico's leaders are justifiably proud of what their development programs have achieved during the last sixty years. In a hemisphere noted for political disorder and economic crisis, the Mexicans have enjoyed political stability and, until the mid-1970s, continuous and rapid economic growth. They have succeeded by creating their own brand of mixed capitalism under the leadership of a powerful state able to finance and direct the private sector. Through the economic opportunities their policies have opened, several million Mexicans have risen from the depths of poverty to membership in the middle sectors and the new elite.

But not everyone has benefited from the programs of the Mexican Revolution. Most Mexicans still must struggle to survive on incomes below $500 per year. In 1970 the poorest 20 percent of the population received only 4 percent of the national income, whereas the wealthiest 5 percent received 36 percent, 7 percent more than it had in 1960 and a larger share than the same income group in Brazil (27 percent), Chile (30 percent), and Argentina (21 percent) (See Table 7-7). And despite several decades of agrarian reform, nearly one-third of those who live in the countryside remain landless, and their numbers are increasing. Moreover, the government's expropriation of several foreign firms and its tight regulation of foreign investment have not prevented continued dependence on foreign credit and income from tourism. Explanations of these shortcomings, as well as of Mexico's many achievements, must be sought in the policies its leaders have used to deal with rural, industrial, and social welfare issues.

Mexican development policy began with agrarian reform. Even before the revolutionary struggle had ended, Indian communities had begun reclaiming lands that had been taken from them by *latifundistas* during the late nineteenth century. Simultaneously, the revolutionary generals rewarded themselves with landed estates they had confiscated during their military campaigns. Although the rural disorder such action wrought cost the Mexicans dearly by drastically reducing farm production, it set in motion a drive for land redistribution that committed successive governments to the enforcement of one of the revolution's most widely held objectives.

Agrarian reform was also viewed as a necessary step in Mexico's economic development. By gradually redistributing rural property, Mexican leaders hoped to eliminate the rural elite, liberate rural workers for employment in urban industries, and improve the welfare of the peasant recipients of redistributed land. Much of the expropriated land was distributed in the form of *ejido* farms, a traditional mode of tenure in which land is owned by an entire village and farmed either individually or collectively. The process of expropriation, which began slowly during the Obregón and Calles administrations, was accelerated by President Cárdenas during the 1930s. In only six years he expropriated twice as much acreage as had been taken during the preceding seventeen years. Each of his successors has redistributed a lesser amount, though all have made an effort to identify with agrarian reform by turning over land to peasant farmers. As a result, between 1916 and 1972 approximately 2.9 million Mexicans have received 87.2 million hectares of land through the agrarian reform program.

What the Mexicans have created with agrarian reform is, as we can see from Table 10-1, not a rural economy composed solely of *ejido* farmers, but one that combines individual and *ejido* farms. Within each group there are modern, traditional, and subsistence units. Although there is an official 250-acre limit on private farm size, larger

Table 10-1. *Mexican farmland distribution, 1970*

	Modern[a]	Traditional[b]	Subsistence[c]	Total
Number of farms				
(thousands)	201.5	1,140.0	1,479.4	2,815.9
Ejidos	120.3	676.2	1,062.3	1,858.8
Private individual farms	81.2	463.8	412.1	957.1
Percent	7.4	40.1	52.5	100.0
Average income per farm				
(pesos)	79,200	17,200	7,200	

[a]Modern, uses modern technology.
[b]Traditional, cash crops produced without modern technology.
[c]Subsistence, little or no cash crops.
Source: International Bank for Reconstruction and Development. "Mexico: Agricultural Sector." Unpublished paper, 1976, p. 2.

units have been amassed, especially in the northwestern desert regions where large commercial farms were encouraged by the government during the 1940s to supply wheat and soybeans to local markets and cotton and vegetables for export. Meanwhile, the vast majority of *ejido* farmers still lack the capital and technology needed to produce for the commercial market, and therefore, they, along with many small private farmers, must survive at or just above the subsistence level.

Mexican agricultural policy was declared an immense success during the 1960s because it had made the country self-sufficient in basic foodstuffs and produced enough surplus to earn substantial foreign exchange by supplying the United States with fruits and vegetables. But in the early 1970s the country's rising population and accelerating domestic consumption caught up with Mexican agriculture, causing a national food deficit for the first time in thirty years. As most large commercial farms already produce at near capacity, it was apparent that the food deficit could be made up only by raising the production of the *ejidos* and the smaller private farms or by increasing the available farmland. The first alternative requires the infusion of expensive technology and capital into the *ejido* sector, something the Mexican government has tried to achieve, with little success, in recent years. Increasing farmland is an even bigger problem. Only 16 percent of Mexico is currently arable; this amounts to 16.8 million acres, an area slightly larger than the state of Iowa. Though some desert regions in the north and tropical regions in the south could be opened to agriculture, the cost of their development is presently beyond the capacity of the Mexican government.

Another solution would be a program aimed at reducing the country's 3.5 percent annual rate of population growth, one of the highest in the world. Until the early 1970s the population issue was largely ignored by the Mexican government. Recently, the pressures have become so great and their consequences so obvious, especially in the country's overcrowded cities, that reluctant officials have begun to address themselves to the issue. Today, family-planning advice and materials are available in all government hospitals; however, a much more intense effort is needed to reduce the growth rate appreciably, especially in the countryside.

In the industrial area Mexico's performance has been brighter. As early as the mid-1930s Mexican officials recognized that land reform was, by itself, insufficient to sustain the country's economic development. Like many of their neighbors, they concluded that industrialization was essential to the efficient use of the country's abundant labor force and the promotion of long-term growth. But instead of leaving the process primarily to the private sector, they, even more than their neighbors, relied on the state to ignite the country's industrial development. They created state enterprises to exploit the country's petroleum resources and produce iron, steel, petrochemicals, fertilizers, and other essential products. By 1970 the Mexican government was involved in over 400 enterprises, either as the sole owner or as a partner with private interests. It has also invested heavily in economic infrastructure, accounting for 30 percent of the gross domestic investment in the country since 1940. Finally, the government has created several financial institutions that have transferred substantial resources to the industrial sector.

The heavy involvement of the state in the nation's economic development is, of course, not unique to Mexico. In Argentina, Brazil, Chile, and Peru the state also produces many goods, provides many services, and plays a major role in the financing of private investment. What is striking about Mexico is not the level of state economic activity but its enormous range. In no Latin American country except Cuba has the state entered into as many economic arenas. The causes of this spread of state activity are political as well as economic. First, the maintenance of the revolutionary coalition has required the government to assure that certain goods and services are produced and sold at popular prices. When the private sector has not met this need, the state has done so. Second, a desire to prevent the loss of jobs has led officials to rescue failing private enterprises by taking over all or part of their ownership and subsidizing their operations. The government has also taken over some enterprises in order to settle damaging disputes between labor and management. In short, the expansion of the economic role of the Mexican state has been caused as much by the need to retain the support of the members of the revolutionary coalition as by the dictates of underdevelopment. Although its enlarged responsibilities have placed immense financial and administrative burdens on the government, they have also given the government substantial economic power, which it has wielded adroitly as an instrument of political control.

Finally, it should also be noted that the Mexicans have relied more heavily on foreign investment, especially in the industrial sector, than one might have expected so nationalistic a regime to do. To be sure, they have placed many restrictions on foreign investors, including a loosely enforced requirement of 51 percent Mexican ownership of firms in some sectors. But that has not deterred foreign entrepreneurs, for they have found the country's relative economic stability, growing infrastructure, and expanding urban markets very attractive. By the early 1970s it was estimated that foreign firms controlled 35 percent of the country's industrial production and owned 45 percent of the share capital in the 290 largest industrial firms; this amounts to a level of foreign investment that is similar to what exists in other, less avowedly nationalistic Latin American countries.

What has been the result of so much state and foreign investment on the performance of the Mexican economy? Clearly, these investments, along with high tariffs and conservative monetary policies, paid off handsomely after 1940. Largely owing to its industrial growth, the country's per capita gross national product increased at an average annual rate of 3.9 percent between 1940 and 1950, 2.7 percent between 1950 and 1960, and 3.4 percent between 1960 and 1970. This is an impressive achievement compared with the performance of other Latin American nations during this period.

Industrialization has undoubtedly changed the Mexican class structure by creating a new entrepreneurial and bureaucratic elite as well as by expanding the ranks of white-collar workers, bankers, merchants, and skilled laborers. But industrialization has also left the basic problem of mass poverty unsolved. To a large extent, Mexico has become the victim of a development strategy that assumed industrialization would cure most of the country's economic ills. The decision to emphasize capital accumulation after 1940 led to official neglect of the poorest 40 percent of the Mexican population. It had been assumed that agrarian reform would free them to prosper on the land or enter the industrial work force. Many did escape poverty through these two routes, but many more did not.

To make matters worse for the Mexicans, the era of rapid economic growth seemed to have come to an end by the early 1970s. The causes of its demise were many, involving external as well as internal factors. The development strategy followed in Mexico between 1940 and 1970 had relied primarily on the use of price and exchange stability and high tariffs on imported consumer goods to promote import substitution industrialization. As we have seen, this strategy, employed by a strong and stable government, gave Mexico one of the highest economic growth rates in the hemisphere for over twenty years. It did not, however, make most Mexicans affluent, or even comfortable economically. In fact, while Mexico's industries were booming, many other conditions deteriorated. Social inequality increased as income became more concentrated, unemployment rose because only a small proportion of the rapidly growing population was absorbed by new industries, domestic food production failed to keep pace with national demand, and Mexico was forced to increase its dependence on foreign investors and tourism. Meanwhile, the world economy, which had grown at a steady pace throughout the 1960s, went into a sustained recession in the early 1970s. And with recession and surging inflation in the industrial nations came a decline in world demand for Mexico's raw materials and agricultural exports, an unfortunate condition that severely impaired the financing of Mexican economic growth.

President Luis Echeverría tried to bolster the sagging Mexican economy in the early 1970s with a host of new public works projects, the expansion of state enterprises, and the collectivization of *ejido* farms in a desperate effort to increase food production and improve the plight of the rural poor. He also sought to take advantage of the discovery of large petroleum reserves in the Gulf of Mexico by accelerating production and increasing the export of petroleum products. Nevertheless, though many Mexicans profited from this increased state effort, the general economic condition continued to deteriorate. Moreover, increased government borrowing and spending touched off a new wave of inflation – reaching 20 percent in 1974 after two decades of averaging only 2 percent annually – and caused the country's foreign debt to soar to an unprecedented 27 percent of export earnings in 1975. Unemployment also increased when only 300,000 new jobs were created between 1970 and 1976 to meet an estimated need for 800,000 jobs. As a result, in 1976 Mexican authorities were faced with one of the worst economic crises to hit the country since 1917. They had no choice but to announce a humiliating devaluation of the peso, to impose one of the severest austerity programs in the country's history by curbing public investments and social welfare expenditures when such a move could be least afforded, and, like many of their neighbors before them, to secure emergency financial assistance from the International Monetary Fund. Thus, despite a half century of notable economic achievements, Mexico came to share the plight of many other Latin American countries, struggling to cope with economic scarcity, external crises, and the kinds of social tensions they produce. It promised to be the severest test the revolutionary regime had faced since its inception.

Cuban socialism

Cubans take pleasure in comparing their achievements with those of the Mexican Revolution. Their industries are not as numerous or as large as Mexico's and their economy not as diverse, but their dependence on the United States is not as great, illiteracy as widespread, or poverty as common as in Mexico. Of course, their task was less difficult, for Cuba is a smaller country (only 9.5 million inhabitants in contrast to Mexico's 62 million), less diverse ethnically, and less divided geographically. It also enjoyed a higher per capita income before its revolution than had Mexico. But these factors alone do not account for the differences in the results of the two revolutions. Equally important has been the dedication of the Cubans to the redistribution of wealth through the radical transformation of their economy.

The Cubans' most notable achievements have been in the area of social welfare. Universal education, basic health care, housing, nutrition, and the economic status of women have all been improved markedly since 1959. Unlike all other Latin American countries, Cuba now meets the basic physical needs of its citizens. The costs of this effort have not been meager. The achievement has required the destruction of Cuba's capitalist economy and the redistribution of its resources by the state to programs aimed at improving the condition of the masses. Several hundred thousand Cubans have been forced into exile, depriving the country of skilled manpower and many Cubans of their homeland. There has also been a persistent shortage of consumer goods, and rationing continues in the late 1970s, nearly two decades after Batista's demise. By the standards of the urban middle sectors of other countries, most Cubans are not well off. Yet, in comparison with the majority of Latin Americans, they are doing quite well indeed.

The long-term development of the Cuban economy is more problematic. Statistics are scarce and incomplete, but the unevenness of Cuban development since 1959 is apparent. After an abortive attempt to industrialize quickly between 1961 and 1963, Cuban leaders were forced to rely on agriculture once again. Industrialization was not abandoned, but it was pursued at a drastically reduced pace thereafter. During the 1960s the Cubans built for the future by holding down consumption in order to finance infrastructure, agricultural, and industrial investments. As a result, total output, though impressive in such areas as nickel mining, milk and paper production, and electricity generation, has been low in most other sectors. In fact, the production of most industrial goods has remained relatively constant since 1959.

The many successes of the socialist development strategy in China, the Soviet Union, and Eastern Europe must be weighed against the chronic problems that have repeatedly limited its effectiveness. One such problem is its apparent need to impose a very depressed standard of living on the population for an extended period. To be sure, many of those who suffered the most under the old economic system do enjoy an improved living standard, even under socialist austerity. Nevertheless, because a relatively small proportion of the national income is allowed for current consumption during the initial capital formation phase of socialist development, citizens often do without a wide range of consumer goods. Shortages and rationing are common during this phase, which may last for several decades. A second problem is the inefficient use of labor. Socialists are dedicated to full employment and have the power to compel people to work wherever the economic planners believe they are needed. Seldom, however, can they resist the temptation to overallocate labor in order to assure the achievement of high-priority objectives. Waste and temporary labor shortages in other areas often result. Third is the problem of the uneconomical allocation of materials in the production process. The lack of prices that accurately reflect shortages or the real demand for materials, along with the zeal of planners to achieve certain objectives, lead to the overallocation of materials, something that proves costly when resources are already scarce.

These problems, which appear to be endemic to centrally planned socialist economies, have also plagued Cuba. During the first phase of the revolution, for example, materials and labor needed in industry were lavishly allocated to the construction of housing for the rural poor, a noble objective but one that proved costly to the pursuit of the government's other development objectives. Similar misallocations occurred in the industrial sector during the 1961–3 phase, as revolutionary leaders tried to apply the same enthusiasm to industrialization that they had used so successfully in the guerrilla struggle. And, as already noted, the rationing of consumer goods has persisted since the early days of the revolution. During the 1960s rationing could be justified as a necessary price for capital accumulation or as an unavoidable effect of the economic blockade of Cuba by Western Hemisphere nations, but as the Cuban Revolution approached its twentieth anniversary it became increasingly difficult to justify austerity. Undoubtedly, the government will be forced in the years ahead to give greater attention to consumer demand; hopefully, two decades of investments in productive enterprises will allow it to meet that demand. What stands out from the Cuban experience, however, are not such problems as inefficiency and austerity, for they were predictable, but the willingness of public officials to acknowledge their economic errors and change direction. Much more rapidly than the leaders of most socialist countries, the Cubans have responded to their failures with policy reassessments and minor shifts in course. Few leaders, in fact, have been more adept than Fidel Castro at absorbing the political costs of policy failure and, in some instances, even turning failure to his advantage and rallying the public behind each new campaign to overcome the shortcomings of the last one. This capacity for reassessment and absorption of failure does not, of course, prevent waste and inefficiency from occurring, but they are less costly if the government can adapt its program quickly enough to avoid their accumulation.

After nearly two decades of socialist development, agriculture remains the driving force in the Cuban economy. The original agrarian reform of 1959, which authorized the expropriation of all properties over 995 acres, created a dual system of tenure composed of private farms owned by ex-tenant farmers who had been given their land by the state and a cooperative sector composed of expropriated sugar plantations and cattle ranches. In 1963 the second agrarian reform converted most cooperatives into state farms and authorized the expropriation of the remaining large private farms. It left an estimated 200,000 farms of less than 168 acres each – or 30 percent of the country's arable land – in private hands. These private owners, whose prices and marketing are controlled by the state, have been encouraged to join the socialized sector, but few have done so. The anomaly of 200,000 private farms in an otherwise socialized economy continues, it appears, because the government recognizes the private sector's ability to supply badly needed fruits and vegetables to urban consumers and because it is reluctant to seize the land of peasant farmers who acquired their property as a result of the 1959 agrarian reform.

The development of Cuba's rural economy has been hindered repeatedly by administrative and technical difficulties. Nothing illustrates the problems faced by planners and administrators better than the ill-fated campaign to produce a 10-million-ton sugar crop in 1970. Cuba had averaged 5 to 6 million tons of sugar in its annual harvest prior to the revolution. After a decline to only 3.8 million at the end of the intense industrialization campaign in 1963, production rose again to 6.2 million in 1967. To raise it above that level required the reallocation of resources from other activities, a risky endeavor that threatened the production of other goods and offered no guarantee of a 10-million-ton harvest. Nevertheless, Cuban leaders decided to take the risk, and beginning in 1965, they implemented an investment plan designed to modernize the sugar industry in preparation for the 1970 harvest. In addition, they initiated a "revolutionary offensive" in 1968 to mobilize the Cuban people to an all-out assault on the sugar-production problem. Through unprecedented human effort, the heavy involvement of the army in the production process, and the expenditure of record amounts of public funds, the scheme was implemented. Nevertheless, the Cubans produced only 8.5 million tons of sugar in 1970. Administrative problems, technical difficulties, and inflated expectations all contributed to the disappointing results. The experience was a sobering one. Reassessments of the campaign led to the abandonment of several other grandiose plans and the initiation of a more balanced and pragmatic approach to agricultural development.

During the 1970s Cuba's economic fortunes have risen and fallen with the international price of sugar, much as they had before the revolution. Two-thirds of the crop had been committed through trade agreements to the Soviet Union and Eastern Europe at a price of 32 cents a pound, with the remainder being sold on the open market. The sudden rise of the world price to 65 cents a pound in November 1974 gave the Cuban economy its biggest boost since the revolution began. Immediately, the Cubans increased the share placed on the world market to 50 percent of their crop and soon thereafter revised public investment plans upward with the expectation that the added income would accelerate the pace of the country's development. But, alas, prices fell in 1976, descending to only 8 cents a pound, making Cuba once again the victim of its reliance on sugar. As a result, the goals of the ambitious 1976–80 development plan were slashed and proposals for immediately improving the general standard of living postponed.

Cuban leaders did not have to be reminded by collapsing prices of their excessive dependence on sugar exports. Although they have been forced by short-term financial exigencies to return to sugar repeatedly since 1959, they have not given up their campaign for agricultural diversification and self-sufficiency in food production. Since 1970 they have been trying to lay the foundation for a major breakthrough in agricultural production. Thousands of technicians and managers have been trained at home and abroad, experiments in plant and animal genetics have reached advanced stages, and new production processes have been tested successfully. Livestock, dairy, and poultry production have been emphasized under the program. New feeds created from domestically produced molasses and fish meal have been developed to reduce dependence on imported grains, and new breeds of livestock more compatible with the tropics have been developed. The long-term objective of the program is the doubling of livestock, dairy, and poultry production by 1980, an ambitious objective, but one that will not likely be attained. Instead, it appears quite probable that the rationing of some foodstuffs will continue well into the 1980s.

The achievements of Cuban socialism are no longer in doubt. It has not generated affluence, but it has eradicated poverty, provided minimal economic security, and given most Cubans a new sense of dignity. At the same time, its costs have been high. The gains of the Cuban masses have come at the expense of those who owned and managed the economy before 1959. Individual diversity and private competition for economic gain have been replaced by political orthodoxy and conformity to the dictates of a bureaucratic elite. Moreover, Cuba has not overcome some of the economic problems that have plagued the island since Independence. Its leaders still rely heavily on the Soviet Union for the financing of economic projects, its economy is still dependent on a single crop, and consumer goods remain in short supply. The Cuban experience does not offer other Latin Americans a formula for solving all development problems, but it does suggest a way of redistributing the burdens of underdevelopment so that the common people retain some faith in their society.

Chile's abortive revolution

How does one achieve socialist objectives using the institutions and instruments of a capitalist economy? That is the question Salvador Allende must have asked himself after his inauguration in late 1970. Given the system he inherited, it is not surprising that his first policy decisions, as we saw above, took more from the economics of John Maynard Keynes than from either Marx or Lenin. His immediate objective was the expansion of production, wages, and consumption, especially among the urban poor. He had inherited an economy that was coming out of its habitual preelection recession with many industries operating far below capacity. He also enjoyed unusually high foreign exchange reserves of $400 million as a result of high copper prices during the Viet Nam war. Consequently, his first decision was to promote full employment and reward working-class consumers with higher wages and frozen prices.

In the short run Allende's expansionary policies were an immense success. In fact, 1971 was a boom year for the Chilean economy and a record year for working-class income. Unemployment was reduced to near zero, the gross national product grew by nearly 9 percent, and prices rose by only 20 percent, slightly below the annual average of the Frei years. Despite expropriation and the controversy it caused, copper production also rose slightly during the year. By taking a pragmatic approach to the Chilean economy rather than the more doctrinaire one recommended by radicals within his coalition, Allende had, it seemed, achieved the kind of economic growth and reallocation of income that would boost his political fortunes without inducing a violent reaction from his opponents.

But Allende's policies, it soon became apparent, were neither as bountiful nor as moderate as they first seemed. Cracks in his economic edifice, which began to appear in 1972, widened rapidly during the first half of 1973. Some were of his own making; others were helped by his foreign and domestic opponents. Hidden from view in 1971 were several disturbing facts. Although consumption rose, gross domestic investment declined by 5 percent as private firms responded

Table 10-2. *Chilean economic performance, 1971–3 (annual growth rates)*

	1971	1972	1973	1960–73
Gross national product at constant prices	8.9	1.0	−5.0	3.5
Gross domestic investment at constant prices	−5.0	1.6	−5.5	3.6
Retail price index	20.0	77.5	353.5	43.5

Source: World Bank. *World Tables 1976.* Washington, D.C., 1976, pp. 74–5.

negatively to the threat of expropriation and the state, already heavily involved in spending to increase consumption, did little investing. Moreover, the fiscal and monetary policies followed at the end of 1971 differed substantially from those proposed by Allende after his inauguration. First, public revenues were much less than intended (owing in part to the refusal of opponents in Congress to authorize tax increases), and expenditures were much greater. This forced Allende to increase the money supply by 100 percent to cover a fiscal deficit that was 71 percent larger than planned. Second, the balance of payments took a turn for the worse, accumulating a $315 million deficit in 1971 after a $91 million surplus in 1970. An overvalued exchange rate, increased imports to meet consumer demand, the accelerated flight of financial capital, and a 30 percent drop in copper prices all contributed to the deficit. To make matters worse on the supply side, agricultural production began to fall during the 1972–3 harvest as the effects of low prices, a lack of seed and fertilizer, and administrative bottlenecks began to be felt. Finally, although the government managed to contain the inflationary effects of its programs in 1971 with price controls, prices began to rise rapidly in late 1972 and continued into 1973, increasing 190 percent during the first nine months of the year alone.

Inflation and shortages were not new to Chile, and governments had survived such conditions in the past. What made Allende's situation different was both the severity of the economic difficulties he faced in 1973 and the determination of his enemies to exploit them. Two of the latter were the United States government and the multinational firms with investments in Chile. The administration of Richard Nixon was opposed to Chile's Marxist government and was determined to secure its demise through any means short of direct military intervention. One tactic was to limit the flow of financial assistance to Chile. Allende had been careful to make payments on Chile's foreign debt in order to keep his country's good credit rating. The United States government was, however, determined to undermine that rating by cutting off new credit to Chile and forcing Allende to request moratoriums on the payment of Chile's debt, something he reluctantly did in late 1971. As part of its campaign to isolate Chile financially, the United States disbursed only $15.5 million in previously authorized loans in 1971, while Chile was repaying $51.3 million in old debts. At the same time, the United States maintained a generous program of aid to the Chilean military as well as covert assistance to several opposition groups. Pressure was also exerted by the American-owned copper companies, which, displeased with Allende's refusal to compensate them for their expropriated enterprises, tried to block the delivery of Chilean copper in United States and European ports. The Chileans succeeded in bypassing some of the foreign embargoes and locating other sources of credit; nevertheless, the American blockade reduced Allende's policy options considerably.

The Popular Unity government might have survived the economic impediments placed in its path by foreigners, but it could not overcome those imposed by an increasingly intractable and effective opposition within Chile. We have already seen how Allende was faced by a choice between compromising with the Christian Democrats (PDC) in 1972 or pushing ahead with his program and risking increased opposition from the Chilean bourgeoisie. Allende sought some kind of compromise that would reduce the constant attacks on his government, but he steadfastly refused to meet the PDC demand for a halt to the nationalization of private firms. When it became apparent that he would not give in to their demands, the PDC and its National party allies initiated their all-out campaign to bring the Popular Unity revolution to a halt whatever the cost.

After searching throughout 1972 for areas where the government was most vulnerable, the opposition settled on the copper and trucking industries in early 1973. By encouraging strikes that could bring the copper industry to a halt, they hoped to intensify the country's growing foreign exchange crisis. The potential effects of strikes in the trucking industry were even more devastating because most Chilean goods in internal commerce were transported by truck. Without food or other consumer items the urban middle sectors could be counted on to lead an open rebellion against the government, as they had done during a brief truckers' strike in October 1972.

In April 1973 miners and technicians at the El Teniente copper mine went on strike. Despite their ideological sympathy for the Popular Unity government, they initially refused to accept its decision to grant less than the wage increase they had been promised. A month later a settlement was reached and most of the miners returned to work. However, a hard core of white-collar workers and technicians, encouraged by the PDC, remained on strike until July and did substantial damage to the production of copper. But the critical blow was struck by the trucking industry from June through August. Chile's truckers, most of whom are small independent operators, had gone on strike once before in October 1972 to protest a government proposal to absorb them into a state trucking company. Backed by a sympathy strike of retailers, they had forced Allende to declare a state of siege, admit military officers to his cabinet, and eventually withdraw the proposal. When they went on strike again in June 1973 they were acting as part of a well-conceived opposition campaign to force the government to halt its program of nationalization, admit Christian Democrats to the cabinet, and chart a more gradual course. There is general agreement that the truckers' strike, which lasted until the coup of September 11, was the single most important factor in paralyzing the Chilean economy and fomenting political chaos during July and August 1973.

In the end, it was the military, encouraged by Conservative and Christian Democratic leaders and provoked by rising civil strife and economic chaos, that abruptly brought Chile's brief socialist experiment to a close. The Chilean military, known since the 1930s for its restraint in political matters, had been divided in its assessment of the Popular Unity government and its program since Allende's inauguration. Some officers were willing to give the government their support as long as it carried out its revolution in a constitutional manner; members of this group, whose support Allende deliberately cultivated and whom he trusted until the day of the coup, went so far as to join Allende's cabinet in order to help him deal with the civil violence encouraged by his opponents. Others in the military opposed Allende and his attack upon Chilean capitalism from the outset, but did not undertake to overthrow him until 1973, when increasing civil unrest and the encouragement of the Christian Democrats made the organization of a coup feasible. By then, Allende's frantic last-minute efforts to deal with his collapsing economy and work out a compromise with his opponents were not enough to stop a military determined not only to evict Marxists from the government but also to end constitutional democracy in Chile.

What conclusions can we draw from the economic performance of the Allende regime? It is difficult to assess the program entirely on its own merits because its performance was affected by forces and conditions beyond Allende's direct control. To argue that it was a failure because it did not withstand the attacks of its opponents ignores the issue of whether Chile could have been developed under a socialist program had there been no interference from abroad or civil strife at home. Nevertheless, it is apparent that Allende's unorthodox blend of Keynesianism and socialist consumerism was more costly and less well programed than planned, yielded damaging inflation, drained the treasury, and drastically reduced capital formation.

Much of Allende's difficulty stemmed from the unusual nature of the task he had undertaken. Unlike most revolutionaries, who first seize power through military or insurrectionary means, then consolidate their political control and use it to implement drastic economic reforms, Allende, because he came to office through electoral means without majority support, lacked sufficient power to impose his will on Chilean society. As a result, he had to devote his economic policies to the acquisition of more power through the cultivation of the support of working-class and middle-sector voters and the winning of future elections. But in dedicating his economic policies to the pursuit of political popularity he contributed to an economic crisis that helped the elite mobilize many in the middle sectors against the UP government. In retrospect, it seems that Allende was the victim of an apparent contradiction in his strategy: He could not gain the support of the middle sectors and build a socialist society at the same time. One or the other had to give sooner or later. On September 11, 1973, it was the socialist revolution that did.

LESSONS FROM THE REVOLUTIONARY
EXPERIENCE

What can we learn from these three attempts at revolutionary change? It is apparent that no single generalization will accommodate the diverse Latin American revolutionary experience. The means used to seize power differed widely, ranging from Mexico's multifaceted and prolonged civil war to Cuba's concentrated insurrection to a reliance on conventional electoral practices in Chile. The manner in which political control was consolidated and new regimes created can also be contrasted. The Mexicans had to go through a series of power struggles among the revolutionary generals before the new regime was firmly established; the Cubans quickly expelled their rivals and consolidated their control through the charismatic appeal of Fidel Castro; the Chilean revolutionaries never did gain full control. Each revolution produced a different set of political rules as well. Mexicans use electoral rituals and a corporatist-type party to legitimize their very strong presidency; Cuba is still struggling to make the transition from rule by Fidel Castro and a small bureaucratic elite to a one-party regime that is responsive to the needs of the masses; the Chileans relied on traditional democratic rules and were undermined by them.

There is some similarity on the economic front, however. All three began with a determination to improve the lot of the masses by destroying the rural elite through agrarian reform, by expelling foreign investors through the expropriation of their enterprises, and by asserting state control over vital production processes. Nevertheless, the ultimate forms of the three economic systems were quite different. Mexico never progressed beyond an innovative system of mixed capitalism; Cuba became one of the most socialized economies in the communist world; and the Chileans were stopped after combining conventional expansionary economic policies with gradual socialization.

The diversity of Latin America's revolutionary experience has important implications for those seeking to develop a strategy that could propel them to the head of revolutionary transformations in other parts of the region. One is that there appears to be no single strategy that assures victory – or even a high probability of it – in all cases. This does not mean that every situation is unique and therefore without relevance to others. But before one tries to replicate the tactics of one revolution in another circumstance, he must recognize that to a large degree Latin America's few successful revolutionary seizures of power were acts of creative invention in response to local conditions and opportunities. General economic and social conditions may appear much the same throughout the hemisphere, but the particular circumstances that are relevant to the success or failure of revolutionary tactics vary from one setting to another, and so, therefore, must the strategies followed.

Another implication of the Latin American experience is the importance of preparing the revolutionary regime to withstand the counterattacks of its opponents during its formative years. The means used to consolidate power are critical, for it is during this process that the new regime is most vulnerable. It is not hard to understand why revolutionaries prefer authoritarian rules and methods. These facilitate political consolidation by a few leaders and make it easier to deny opponents the opportunity to counterattack. The failures of Allende in Chile reinforce this conclusion. In fact, one of the greater ironies of recent Latin American experience stems from the fact that by exploiting democratic rules to undermine Allende, his opponents may have reinforced the revolutionary's belief in the necessity of authoritarian methods.

The current appeal of revolution to many Latin Americans seems attributable more to the shortcomings of other forms of development than to the achievements of the region's few revolutions. Aspiring revolutionaries see conservative modernizers as leaders who have achieved high economic growth rates at the cost of greater dependence on foreigners and the continued impoverishment of the masses. And although they may acknowledge that progressive modernizers have opened some opportunities to the poor, they are distressed by the reformer's concessions to traditional elites and his willingness to sacrifice the more radical elements of his program. When contrasted with these experiences, revolution cannot help but retain some of its appeal to those who are frustrated by the status quo.

But revolution too has its limitations. Clearly, Latin America's revolutionary regimes are plagued by the same kinds of natural resource problems that have constrained nonrevolutionary regimes; moreover, they have yet to escape their vulnerability to the world economy. Revolutionary change also exacts some high costs. Once a blueprint for the new society is selected, it must often be imposed by force at the cost of lives and liberty. Some people must suffer for others to gain from revolutionary change. It may be the rich yielding their resources to the poor, but it also may be the masses succumbing to the dictates of a bureaucratic elite.

Most striking is the fact that despite the failure of traditional and reformist elites, continued political corruption, and exploitation, there have been few true revolutions in modern Latin America. Prevailing institutions have proved very resistant to the attacks of revolutionaries. Elites and their middle-sector allies have amassed immense economic and military strength and have secured powerful foreign allies who have helped them withstand revolutionary attacks repeatedly. This does not mean that the cause of revolution is hopeless. The Cuban success alone is grounds for the rejection of such pessimism. It does indicate, however, that revolution is no easier today than it was in Mexico in 1910, Cuba in 1958, or Chile in 1970.

FURTHER READING

Mexico

Glade, William P., and Charles W. Anderson. *The Political Economy of Mexico.* Madison: University of Wisconsin Press, 1963.

Hansen, Roger. *The Politics of Mexican Development.* Baltimore: Johns Hopkins University Press, 1971.

Reynolds, Clark W. *The Mexican Economy: Twentieth Century Structure and Growth.* New Haven: Yale University Press, 1970.

Tannenbaum, Frank. *Mexico: The Struggle for Peace and Bread.* New York: Knopf, 1956.

Vernon, Raymond. *The Dilemma of Mexico's Development.* Cambridge, Mass.: Harvard University Press, 1965.

Wilkie, James. *The Mexican Revolution: Federal Expenditure and Social Change Since 1910.* Berkeley: University of California Press, 1967.

Cuba

Bonachea, Rolando, and Nelson Valdes, eds. *Cuba in Revolution*. Garden City, N.Y.: Doubleday (Anchor Books), 1972.

Dumont, René. *Cuba: Socialism and Development*. New York: Grove Press, 1970.

Is Cuba Socialist? New York: Viking Press, 1974.

Horowitz, Irving Luis, ed. *Cuban Communism,* 2nd ed. New Brunswick, N.J.: Transaction Books, 1972.

Huberman, Leo, and Paul Sweezy. *Socialism in Cuba*. New York: Monthly Review Press, 1970.

Mesa Lago, Carmelo. *Cuba in the 1970's: Pragmatism and Institutionalization*. Albuquerque: University of New Mexico Press, 1974.

Revolutionary Change in Cuba. Pittsburgh: University of Pittsburgh Press, 1974.

Radosh, Ronald, ed. *The New Cuba: Paradoxes and Potentials*. New York: Morrow, 1976.

Chile

Boorstein, Edward. *Allende's Chile: An Inside View*. New York: International Publishers, 1977.

De Vylder, Stefan. *Allende's Chile: The Political Economy of the Rise and Fall of Unidad Popular*. New York: Cambridge University Press, 1976.

North, Lisa. "The Military in Chilean Politics," *Studies in Comparative International Development* 11(2):73–106, summer 1976.

Petras, James, and Morris Morley. *The United States and Chile: Imperialism and the Overthrow of the Allende Government*. New York: Monthly Review Press, 1975.

Roxborough, Ian, Phil O'Brien, and Jackie Roddick. *Chile: The State and Revolution*. London: Macmillan, 1977.

United States Congress, House, Committee on Foreign Affairs, Subcommittee on Inter-American Affairs. *United States and Chile During the Allende Years, 1970–1973*. 94th Congress, 1st Session, 1975, pp. 1–677.

Senate, Select Committee to Study Governmental Operations with Respect to Intelligence Activities. *Covert Action in Chile 1963–1973*. 94th Congress, 1st Session, 1975, pp. 1–62.

Valenzuela, Arturo, and J. Samuel Valenzuela, eds. *Chile: Politics and Society*. New Brunswick, N.J.: Transaction Books, 1976.

11. Points of departure

It is now time to pause and review what we have learned so far and then to look to the future, identifying the remaining unanswered questions that merit further inquiry. We began by viewing Latin American politics as a kind of game, not because we saw it merely as a recreational activity – which it obviously is not – but because the game concept provided a useful model of the real world that helped us begin to understand the structure and dynamics of Latin American politics. We discovered that the Latin American game has acquired its particular character from repeated failures to resolve basic issues involving fundamental political rules. This is not because no one has attempted to secure lasting agreements on rules, but because so few of those who tried have convinced their countrymen of the merits of the rules they proposed. As a result the game has been characterized by the continuous use of multiple political resources by those who contend for the right to create governments and influence the selection of officials to direct them. Elections, for example, have been held with great frequency, but their results have sometimes been nullified by the intervention of the military or by popular uprisings against elected officials. Moreover, the electoral process itself has often been abused by players whose desire for political power has exceeded their respect for electoral rules. In such settings one does not learn a great deal about politics by focusing exclusively on constitutions and formal government procedures; instead, the informal norms and political practices that shape the way the game is played must also be studied.

We next examined several players, focusing on their political interests and resources. Our analysis revealed not only the diversity of their interests and the variety of resources they can bring to bear in the national political process, but also the deep conflicts over development policy issues and political rules that divide them. Wealth, physical force, patron-client relationships, expertise, and popular followings are used by players to contest issues of income distribution, agrarian reform, workers' rights, foreign investment, and the like. Disputes that might be resolved quietly in more affluent societies often acquire a high level of intensity in Latin America, where great disparities in wealth exist and where long-standing feelings of exploi-

309

tation and injustice prevail. Intense conflict over development policies in turn helps reinforce disagreements over the rules of the game, as each player comes to view particular sets of rules as giving unfair advantages to others in the contest for wealth, status, and power.

To complete our introduction to the Latin American game, we reviewed the economic strategies Latin American leaders have employed to affect the outcomes of the political game. We learned to distinguish different strategies according to their objectives, instruments, and likely consequences. Most strategists begin with assumptions about the causes of underdevelopment and build their theories and their policy prescriptions from those assumptions, trying to promote development by rewarding those who contribute to the attainment of official objectives and depriving many of those who do not. For example, some take land away from unproductive *latifundios* and redistribute it to needy peasants. Similarly, foreign-owned enterprises may be expropriated by the state in order to promote nationalistic objectives that benefit native entrepreneurs. Whereas these decisions about the winners and losers of the development policy game are made ostensibly on economic grounds, implicit in them are important and often controversial political judgments about who deserves to profit from the actions of the state.

Using what we learned about the rules of the game, players, and economic strategy, we turned in Part II to the examination of four of the political games found in postwar Latin America. We identified their origins, examined the rules they followed, studied the structure of the coalitions they created and the nature of the opponents they faced, and assessed some of their achievements as evidenced in their economic and social policies.

We saw how the Populists arose in response to social changes that accompanied industrialization and urbanization after 1940. They opened the political process to the urban masses, whom they mobilized and controlled in a paternalistic manner. They also expanded the power of the state, but in doing so they increased its financial and administrative burdens without generating the resources needed to handle these burdens. As a result, many of the Populists' initial achievements did not endure. Neither did the political regimes they created. Something more than the mobilization of the masses, clever opportunism, and the manipulation of political rules was needed to develop the political consensus required to sustain a new political order.

The populist experience taught aspiring democratic reformers that industrialization and social welfare programs directed at urban consumers could not, by themselves, generate sustained economic development. Growth-retarding structural obstacles also had to be removed, beginning with the antiquated *latifundio* system and foreign control over critical economic activities. The reformers were convinced they would succeed with their program of modernization and structural change if they could build a broad coalition of peasants, laborers, industrialists, intellectuals, and bureaucrats to support them. Yet, despite their adroit use of democratic procedures to mobilize support for their reforms, many democratic reformers were forced by their conservative opponents to compromise their principles and limit their objectives. To make matters worse, their ambitions often exceeded their ability to finance and administer their programs, and they had to abandon many projects in midstream. As a result, those reformers who were fortunate enough to survive the attacks of their opponents have had to lower their sights and accept very modest achievements, while the less fortunate have been compelled to withdraw to the sidelines and watch the military reshape politics to its liking.

The military authoritarian regime was created by conspirators who had grown impatient with economic instability and intolerant of the games played by civilian politicians. They were also preoccupied with mass disaffection with the existing political order and the threat of radical change. Their methods were harsh, but their political solutions were often simple, usually involving the imposition of public order and then the harsh enforcement of controversial economic policies. The short-term performance of military authoritarian regimes has been notable: They have demonstrated repeatedly an ability to repress political conflict and impose temporary economic stability. Over the long haul their achievements have been less impressive, however. They have proved incapable of generating popular support for their regimes or creating institutions that can be maintained without widespread repression. More often than not, the military authoritarians were victims of an illusion about politics and its effects on economic development. The simple repression of political activity does not lead to sustained economic development, no matter how effective one's initial economic policies. And promises of future gains are seldom enough to generate support for military government policies, especially when the promises are contradicted by regressive economic measures that increase the concentration of wealth and make economic security appear even farther beyond the grasp of the masses.

Given the obvious shortcomings of populist, democratic reformist, and military authoritarian paths to development, it is tempting to conclude that the revolutionary alternative, with its promise to transform social and economic structures, offers the surest way of curing the region's development ills. But such a judgment would be premature. The region's revolutionary experiments have been too few, and the revolutionary experience too inconsistent, to permit conclusive assessments of their outcomes; moreover, the performance of the region's revolutionary regimes has been mixed, at best. In Mexico and Cuba, for example, the revolutionaries did demonstrate a capacity for eliminating players from the game, redistributing resources, and building mass support through the use of ideology and mass organizations. But their schemes have been costly in terms of human lives, physical and psychological dislocation, and increased regimentation. More important, the revolutionaries have yet to demonstrate that they can generate the kind of well-being coveted by their peoples and escape heavy dependence on foreign suppliers of financial resources. The point that needs to be made is not that the revolutionary regimes have failed, but that before we can judge them successful, we must weigh their gains carefully against their costs, just as we must do with every other mode of development.

Where, then, has our examination of postwar Latin American development taken us? Clearly, our inquiry has not generated a strategy that can quickly cure all the region's development ills. All known forms of politics and economic strategy have their limitations. How we judge them depends not only on our assessment of their ability to achieve their objectives but also on our agreement or disagreement with their goals. The critical issue is not whether a particular kind of government can carry out agrarian reform but whether agrarian reform itself is desirable. One has to decide, for example, which is most valued, the welfare of the few or the welfare of the many, individual liberty or economic equality, national autonomy or reliance on foreigners. How these judgments are made by Latin Americans and those who influence their conduct will determine the destiny of the countries in this much-troubled region in the years ahead.

SOME UNANSWERED QUESTIONS

It is appropriate to end an introduction to the study of Latin American politics with a series of questions in need of further investigation. In the preceding chapters you learned many things about Latin America. A great deal, however, remains to be discovered about the region and its political life. This book cannot provide a detailed introduction to all the Latin American countries and their current governments. Political conditions change rapidly, and governments come and go. What should endure from this inquiry are not only the descriptions of four different political games and the players involved in them, but the concepts and methods used in the study. Games, rules, players, economic strategies, and policy outcomes – these are the tools that can serve as points of departure for the further study of Latin American politics. To them you can add other approaches and methods as you develop more comprehensive inquiries.

In building on the foundation laid down in previous chapters, you will need to develop at least two kinds of knowledge. First, you will want to increase the depth of your understanding. We have only scratched the surface of available information. More intensive study of the region's history as well as its economic and political institutions, processes, and behaviors is required to comprehend the details of Latin American politics. Second, you will want to increase the breadth of your understanding by developing general theories that explain Latin American political behavior. The systematic explanation of political phenomena should be familiar to you by now. Throughout this book explanations of several aspects of Latin American politics have been suggested. For example, in our discussion of the rules of the game in Chapter 2, the frequent unscheduled changes of government that have occurred in many Latin American countries were attributed to, among other things, fundamental disagreements over the rules of the political game that arose after Independence and have continued under the pressure of an intense competition for political power among players representing different social classes and economic groups. We also accounted for the fates of several different political regimes. For example, the failure of the Populists to establish durable forms of government was explained as a result of their personalistic, ad hoc political processes and their cynical use of multiple sets of rules to divide and defeat their opponents. Most of the explanations we offered were limited to a narrow range of phenomena. But broader, more generalized ones can be developed through the systematic comparisons of Latin American nations.

It is tempting to confine ourselves merely to describing Latin American politics, taking refuge in its complexity and the idiosyncrasies of individual nations. Yet, Latin American countries do have many things in common that can serve as a basis for theory building. More than one Latin American country has experienced industrialization, foreign penetration, military coups, popular insurrections, democratic reformism, military authoritarianism, and revolution. As a result, Latin America offers an interesting real world laboratory in which to develop explanations of political life using the comparative method. It supplies a wide range of political phenomena: One finds, for example, many different party systems, interest groups, governmental institutions, and public policies. At the same time there are similarities of heritage, political culture, and social structure that allow us to hold some conditions relatively constant while we search for relationships among others.

The diversity of Latin American life should not deter us from developing generalizations that apply to more than one country. We can begin by seeking out relationships that hold for only a few countries that appear to share certain economic or political characteristics, and then testing our findings against the experience of other countries. We can also compare the kinds of political changes countries have experienced at different points in their histories. For example, even though organized labor entered the political game at different times in separate countries, we can learn something about political change by comparing the manner of its entrance and its effects on politics and economic policy in different settings. A brief look at some current efforts to develop theories of Latin American politics will illustrate what this search for theory and explanations entails.

THE POLITICAL CONSEQUENCES OF SOCIOECONOMIC CHANGE

Few questions have commanded as much attention from students of comparative politics as the one that asks about the effects of socioeconomic change on political life. Some inquiries into this issue have focused on particular forms of economic change and explored their effects on the political process, looking for changes in rules or power structures. Using this approach, one might begin with industrialization and then analyze how it affected the rise of the middle sectors and the urban proletariat and how they, in turn, changed the political game and its outcomes. Other investigators have moved in the opposite direction, beginning with a particular political phenomenon, such as the creation of new political regime, and then searching for its origins in the kinds of social and economic changes that preceded it. One might, for example, search for the causes of populism in the rise of the industrial bourgeoisie and urban working class during the initial phase of import substitution industrialization.

One of the first concrete issues examined by those interested in the effects of socioeconomic change on politics was the relationship between capitalist economic development and the rise of democratic government. Preoccupation with the empirical investigation of this rather narrow relationship began in Western industrialized nations, where social scientists sought to discover the socioeconomic origins of their own liberal democratic governments; later it spread to the less developed nations, where concern centered on the problem of creating and sustaining democratic regimes. Investigators wanted to know whether industrialization and rising affluence had anything to do with the expansion of political participation, increasing electoral competition, and widespread acceptance of the democratic rules of the game. Their initial mode of inquiry was to compare several countries, looking first at the form of government and then at the social and economic conditions that prevailed at the time. This exercise uncovered what appeared to be a convincing relationship between a country's level of economic development (as measured by its per capita income and other indexes of wealth) and whether it had a democratic government. Simply stated, the higher a country's level of development, the more likely it was to be democratic. This finding came from the discovery that most of the wealthier nations of the world – located primarily in Western Europe and Anglo-America – had democratic governments, whereas the poorer nations, with very few exceptions, were ruled by some form of authoritarianism.

Several inferences were drawn from this finding. One concentrated on the process through which this relationship developed, arguing that industrialization touched off a series of socioeconomic changes leading to urbanization, social mobilization, increased wealth, popular political participation, and the acceptance of democratic rules. A second, and more instrumentally oriented, inference was that one could actually increase the probability of the emergence and survival of democratic government in a country by accelerating the process of capitalist economic development. The first inference represented an attempt to build a more comprehensive theory from the discovery of the simple association between economic development and democratic politics; the second involved the more questionable enterprise of engineering a particular form of political change. The latter would not be especially significant were it not that such thinking greatly influenced American foreign assistance programs to Latin America during the 1960s. Although much more than the encouragement of democratic government was involved in such programs as the Alliance for Progress, the assumption that increased economic development would help promote democratic politics was influential in their design.

But what about the relationship between the level of economic development and democratic politics within the laboratory of contemporary Latin America? If one had compared the Latin American countries at any time during the 1950s or 1960s, an apparent association – albeit a weak one – between level of economic development and democratic government could have been found. The countries that had democratic governments of some kind were, on the average, more developed economically than those that did not. Examined more closely, however, the relationship is less convincing, because there are some conspicuous exceptions that need to be taken into account. Take Argentina, for example. The most affluent nation in Latin America for several decades, it is also one of the most prone to military interruptions of democratic rule. At the other extreme is Costa Rica, one of the least affluent but most democratic countries since 1948. A few exceptions do not invalidate relationships that apply to several countries, but there is a second fact that has been even more damaging: the recent decline in the number of democratic regimes in the hemisphere at a time when the per capita incomes of the Latin American countries have been rising.

These discoveries forced investigators to question not only the validity of the relationship itself, but also the method by which it was originally established. The method used was to take all countries at one point in time, rank them according to their level of economic development and the degree of democratic politics they enjoyed, and then correlate these two sets of rank orderings. This is the cross-sectional method of comparison. In essence, it developed inferences about the process of socioeconomic and political change by comparing differences among countries at a single point in time. Because the more developed countries were also more democratic, it was assumed that economic development had led to their democratization. But is this the case? Moreover, if our objective is to understand a process that involves gradual economic and political changes that occur over several decades, would it not be more appropriate to focus on change as it occurs instead of making inferences about it using the cross-sectional approach?

Many students of political change have done just that, turning from comparing several countries at one point in time to examining the process of change as it has occurred over time. Their findings have prompted a reexamination of the relationship between economic development and democracy and have suggested explanations for the rise of various nondemocratic forms of government in Latin America. Three examples will illustrate where these efforts to develop new theories might take us.

The destabilization hypothesis

What does the examination of the process of socioeconomic change in developing nations teach us? The destabilization hypothesis suggests that instead of discovering a positive relationship between capitalist economic development and the creation of stable democratic governments, we will find that increasing instability and political conflict usually accompany rapid socioeconomic change. The reason for this is not hard to find. If we examine industrialization in developing countries, we discover a very complex process through which traditional values and social institutions are gradually transformed. Industrial development uproots people and relocates them in strange environments. Attitudes change, aspirations rise, frustrations with the status quo increase, and social conflicts among newly emergent groups multiply. Disputes over the allocation of societal resources that were resolved easily in traditional societies suddenly take on new meaning in the context of industrialization. New groups emerge to contest with traditional groups for a piece of the economic pie, producing conflicts that embyronic democratic institutions do not always survive. Whether they survive depends not just on the level of economic development but also on the adaptability of political elites, the permeability of the social structure, the intensity of ethnic, racial and linguistic divisions, and the rate at which wealth and new opportunities for social status increase. In many instances democratic governments are overwhelmed by development-induced social conflict and give way to some form of authoritariansim as political elites try to impose order on their divided societies. Applied to Latin America, the destabilization hypothesis might, for example, explain the collapse of reformist democracies by arguing that social conflicts that arose during the early stages of industrialization undermined insecure democratic institutions.

The destabilization hypothesis raises many questions that merit further investigation within the context of Latin America. For example, what about the relationship between industrialization and social conflict? Does it involve a linear process in which conflict continually increases with industrialization, or will conflict subside at some point? Or do only certain forms of industrialization, such as that dominated by foreign-controlled enterprises, produce social and political conflict? And will conflict always threaten democratic government? Some types of conflict may actually be conducive to bargaining and peaceful resolution using constitutional processes. What kinds of institutions usually emerge during the process of industrialization, especially when that process is heavily dependent on foreign capital and technology, as it has been in Latin America? Do traditional institutions adapt and survive or are they eliminated under the pressure of change? And what is the impact of socioeconomic change on political party and interest group systems? Under what conditions do single-party, multiparty, or no-party systems emerge? In sum, how much can we learn about Latin American politics by testing the destabilization hypothesis?

The imperialism hypothesis

A theory that has received renewed attention of late is one that seeks to explain Latin American underdevelopment and political conflict by viewing both as products of a world economic system dominated by the industrialized capitalist nations. Many different versions of the theory have been put forward. The most conventional form argues that the dominant fact of Latin American life is its exploitation by European and North American imperialism. The imperialists have dictated the course of the region's development, deliberately keeping it weak and poor so they could extract its resources at the lowest possible price. Imperialism has also perpetuated a rigid class structure through which traditional elites and the urban bourgeoisie dominate and exploit the rural and urban masses. Politically, the system is characterized by the manipulation of national elites by the foreign traders and investors who represent the industrialized capitalist nations within the region. Unless this historical relationship between industrial capitalism and Latin American development is understood, it is argued, one cannot comprehend the region's politics or its poverty.

A revisionist version of the theory – one that is informed by postwar economic experience – suggests that the rise of the multinational corporation has led to a new international division of labor that has altered the form of the relationship between the capitalist developed nations and the underdeveloped ones. Economic penetration is no longer confined to the extraction of minerals and the purchase of agricultural commodities; through the efforts of the multinational corporations, it has been extended to manufacturing as well. As a result, a relationship that was once limited to extractive enterprises and the perpetuation of economic stagnation has been transformed into one that now encourages industrialization and the sale of locally manufactured products within the region. It is this promotion of economic growth within selected urban enclaves that distinguishes the new imperialism from the old. Yet, as the revisionists are quick to point out, even though the form of imperialist domination has changed, the basic fact of domination has not. Like the more traditional forms of imperialism, the new one perpetuates the exploitation of the masses, only now the relationship between the imperialist nations and Latin America is more complex than ever before, involving a host of new technological, financial, organization, and market connections.

The politics of the new imperialism is characterized by the collusion of the multinationals, Latin American militaries, the managers of state enterprises, and a Latin American bourgeoisie that has accommodated itself to the new international division of labor. Within this context, the hypothesized relationship between economic development and democracy examined above becomes irrelevant because in the imperialist system it is not the form of the government that matters but the fact of economic and political domination by the agents of international capitalism. Whether the game is populist, democratic reformist, or military authoritarian makes little difference because real power continues to be held by the same players. How else, it is asked, can one explain the persistence of underdevelopment and exploitation throughout the region despite the application of a host of different economic and political strategies aimed at alleviating such conditions?

Unfortunately, the imperialism hypothesis and its many variants are not easily tested by conventional empirical methods. The hypothesis uses very general concepts to describe large aggregations of people, such as the bourgeoisie, the proletariat, and the imperialists. It also relies primarily on the dialectical method of analysis rather than causal logic. Focusing on dynamic relationships between foreign and domestic economic structures and social classes rather than political parties, interest groups, and voting behavior, it generates sweeping generalizations about economic and political domination and its consequences. They are, however, generalizations that merit closer scrutiny, for they have major implications for our understanding of the region's politics. We can begin with the relationships the imperialism hypothesis posits between the world economy and Latin American development. We must ask, for example, how has the world economy conditioned the development of Latin America? What options did it make available to Latin Americans, and how did Latin Americans select among them? And to what extent have the structures of the Latin American economies been shaped by foreigners rather than by the region's traditions and resources? The domestic manifestations of imperialism also require investigation. What is the process through which the imperialists rule? Is the domestic bourgeoisie a monolithic force that has accommodated itself to the imperialists? Or does it enjoy some capacity for autonomous action? Have its role and the alliances it has made changed over time or remained the same? The function of the state also merits further analysis. Does the increasing economic power of the state make it more or less responsive to the imperialists? How does one explain the recent assertion of state control over foreign enterprises? Is it evidence of the end of imperialist domination or only of minor adjustments in existing economic relationships? If we are to move beyond the blind acceptance or rejection of the imperialism hypothesis, we must find answers to these questions.

The scarcity hypothesis

Another hypothesis that addresses the relationship between economic development and politics emphasizes the permanence of fundamental economic conditions that make the creation of affluent, mass consuming societies and the kind of pluralistic, competitive politics thought to be associated with them unlikely in Latin America in the foreseeable future. This pessimistic view of the region's prospects has grown out of widespread disillusionment with the failure of industrialization to transform Latin American society.

Since the early 1940s Latin American leaders have experimented with a variety of economic development programs aimed at improving the welfare of the region's peoples. Their efforts have produced accelerating growth rates and in many countries the doubling of per capita income. Nevertheless, they are far from creating the mass consuming societies to which they aspired. Poverty remains a massive problem in many countries, and income disparities between those involved in the modern and traditional sectors continue to grow. Import substitution industrialization, agricultural modernization, regional integration, the nationalization of foreign enterprises, and the redistribution of rural land have yielded benefits for many Latin Americans, but they have not significantly altered the fundamental fact of poverty for a majority of the region's people. In 1975, 40 percent of the population of Latin America were still rural dwellers, 30 percent still suffered from malnutrition, and a majority lived at or just above the subsistence level.

The scarcity hypothesis argues that the region's underdevelopment will persist not because of domination by imperialists but because of limited resources and rapidly expanding populations that make it impossible to increase production rapidly enough to improve the welfare of the masses in any significant way. This hypothesis points, for example, to the fact that arable land is in very limited supply, a fact that cannot be changed by agrarian reform. Moreover, the barriers imposed by the region's mountains and tropical lowlands make the expansion of farmland unlikely given current levels of technology. One of the most disconcerting statistics in this regard is the fact that during the past five years Latin America, the traditional exporter of cash crops, has increased its importation of food at the rate of 10 percent a year. Nor does the region's mineral wealth offer a much brighter picture. A few countries are blessed with highly valued minerals, but most are not. There are, for instance, three countries that import petroleum for each one that exports it. To make matters worse, it now appears that industrialization was a false panacea. Although the regional industrial product has been increased substantially, unemployment continues to increase throughout the region, cities are becoming crowded with the poor, and urban services have fallen far below demand. Not even the revolutionary reallocation of resources will change this condition, it is argued. Neither Mexico nor Cuba has overcome the problem of scarcity; the best they can do, it appears, is allocate scarce resources more equitably within their societies.

What is the implication of the scarcity hypothesis for the study of politics? If it is correct, it makes the association between economic development and democratic government irrelevant because it argues that a high level of development is beyond Latin America's capacity. The forms of government found in the region are not products of rapid growth and spreading affluence but of permanent underdevelopment. Such an assertion obviously merits serious investigation. In particular we must examine the political consequences of the kinds of scarcities it forecasts. Will the intensification of competition for increasingly scarce resources accelerate economic conflict and spill over into the political process? Can such conflicts be contained or will they undermine any government forced to deal with them? Does scarcity mean that all conflicts must take on a zero-sum character in which the gain of one player always comes at the expense of another? Or is there some room for mutually beneficial exchanges? What political institutions (e.g., political parties, interest groups, the military) are best able to mediate scarcity-induced conflicts? Does their mediation require authoritarian government or will democracy do? And what about the role of the more affluent nations? Does increasing scarcity give them greater opportunity for dominating the Latin American economies or will they be compelled to share their wealth with Latin Americans in order to avert world conflict?

There is no easy way to answer these very important questions or those raised by the destabilization and imperialism hypotheses. Nevertheless, we must try to answer them using all methods at our disposal. It is hoped that this book has opened the door to the kinds of careful and informed inquiries that are needed to increase our understanding of Latin America and its people.

FURTHER READING

Ayres, Robert. "Development Policy and the Possibility of a 'Liveable' Future for Latin America." *American Political Science Review* 69(2):507–25, June 1975.

Cardoso, Fernando Henrique. "Associated-Dependent Development: Theoretical and Practical Implications," in Alfred Stepan, ed., *Authoritarian Brazil: Origins, Policies and Future.* New Haven: Yale University Press, 1973, pp. 142–78.

"The Consumption of Dependency Theory in the United States," *Latin American Research Review* 12(3):7–24, 1977.

Chilcote, Ronald. "A Critical Synthesis of the Dependency Literature." *Latin American Perspectives* 1(1):4–29, spring 1974.

Dahl, Robert. *Polyarchy: Participation and Opposition.* New Haven: Yale University Press, 1971.

Duff, Ernest, and John McCamant. "Measuring Social and Political Requirements of System Stability in Latin America." *American Political Science Review* 62(5):1125–43, December 1968.

Frank, Andre Gunder. *Latin America: Underdevelopment or Revolution.* New York: Monthly Review Press, 1969.

Lumpen-Bourgeoisie and Lumpen-Development: Dependence, Class and Politics in Latin America. New York: Monthly Review Press, 1972.

Hopkins, Raymond. "Aggregate Data and the Study of Political Development." *Journal of Politics* 31(1):71–94, 1969.

Huntington, Samuel. *Political Order in Changing Societies.* New Haven: Yale University Press, 1968, Chapter 1.

Lipset, Seymour Martin. *Political Man: The Social Bases of Politics.* Garden City, N.Y.: Doubleday, 1960, Chapter 2.

Martz, John. "The Place of Latin America in the Study of Comparative Politics," *Journal of Politics* 28(1):57–80, February 1966.

Needler, Martin. *Political Development in Latin America.* New York: Random House, 1968.

O'Donnell, Guillermo A. *Modernization and Bureaucratic-Authoritarianism: Studies in South American Politics.* Berkeley: Institute of International Studies, University of California, 1973, Chapter 1.

Schmitter, Philippe. "New Strategies for the Comparative Analysis of Latin American Politics." *Latin American Research Review* 4(2):83–110, summer 1969.

Stepan, Alfred. "Political Development Theory: The Latin American Experience." *Journal of International Affairs* 20(2):223–34, 1966.

Appendix

Appendix Table 1. *Latin American demographics*

Country	Area (square miles)	Population (1976) (millions)	Population growth rate (annual average, 1965–73)
Argentina	1,072,000	25.7	1.5
Bolivia	424,000	5.8	2.6
Brazil	3,286,000	110.2	2.9
Chile	292,000	10.8	2.0
Colombia	440,000	23.0	3.2
Costa Rica	20,000	2.0	2.9
Cuba	44,000	9.4	1.8
Dominican Republic	19,000	4.8	2.6
Ecuador	109,000	6.9	3.4
El Salvador	8,000	4.2	3.3
Guatemala	42,000	5.7	2.1
Haiti	11,000	4.6	1.6
Honduras	43,000	2.8	3.0
Mexico	762,000	62.3	3.5
Nicaragua	50,000	2.2	3.1
Panama	29,000	1.7	3.1
Paraguay	157,000	2.6	2.6
Peru	496,000	16.0	2.9
Uruguay	72,000	2.8	1.2
Venezuela	352,000	12.3	3.3

Sources: World Bank. *World Tables 1976*. Washington, D.C., 1976. Overseas Development Council. *The United States and World Development: Agenda 1977*. New York: Praeger, 1977.

Appendix Table 2. *Latin American economic and social conditions*

Country	Per capita GNP, 1974 (U.S. dollars)	Physical quality of life index[a]	Percent of labor force in agriculture, 1970
Argentina	1,520	84	15
Bolivia	280	45	66
Brazil	920	68	44
Chile	830	77	21
Colombia	500	71	41
Costa Rica	840	87	43
Cuba	640	86	34
Dominican Republic	650	64	55
Ecuador	500	68	54
El Salvador	410	67	47
Guatemala	580	53	63
Haiti	170	31	80
Honduras	340	50	65
Mexico	1,090	75	40
Nicaragua	670	53	51
Panama	1,000	81	39
Paraguay	510	74	55
Peru	740	58	45
Uruguay	1,190	88	17
Venezuela	1,970	80	22

[a]Index, developed by the Overseas Development Council, combines measures of life expectancy, infant mortality, and literacy.

Sources: Overseas Development Council. *The United States and World Development: Agenda 1977.* New York: Praeger, 1977. World Bank. *World Tables, 1976.* Washington, D.C., 1976.

Appendix Table 3. *Latin American distribution of public expenditures, 1974*
(U.S. dollars per capita)

Country	Military	Education	Health
Argentina	22	37	12
Bolivia	8	12	4
Brazil	20	33	2
Chile	20	32	18
Colombia	5	10	5
Costa Rica	4	44	16
Cuba	37	32	12
Dominican Republic	10	9	16
Ecuador	10	15	5
El Salvador	5	13	5
Guatemala	4	12	7
Haiti	2	1	1
Honduras	5	10	4
Mexico	6	28	6
Nicaragua	10	16	16
Panama	1	61	39
Paraguay	8	8	2
Peru	26	31	8
Uruguay	34	45	20
Venezuela	37	80	44

Source: Ruth Leger Sivard. *World Military and Social Expenditures, 1977.* Leesburg, Va.: WMSE Publications, 1977.

Appendix Table 4. *Latin American military expenditures and assistance, 1975*

Country	Total military expenditure (millions of constant U.S. dollars)	Percent of GNP	Armed forces per 1,000 population	Military assistance from United States, 1946–73 (millions of U.S. dollars)
Argentina	787	2.32	6.17	174.5
Bolivia	54	2.73	3.70	35.5
Brazil	2,230	2.21	4.25	430.2
Chile	303	4.32	10.39	184.4
Colombia	151	1.22	5.86	141.6
Costa Rica	0	0.0	0.0	1.9
Cuba	360	6.14	12.97	12.4[a]
Dominican Republic	42	1.43	3.67	33.1
Ecuador	68	1.87	2.84	63.2
El Salvador	19	1.16	1.94	7.8
Guatemala	40	1.26	2.15	30.3
Haiti	9	1.20	1.19	4.1
Honduras	17	1.78	3.74	10.3
Mexico	483	0.88	1.60	14.0
Nicaragua	29	2.04	2.21	16.6
Panama	14	0.84	4.78	6.4
Paraguay	21	1.48	5.84	16.9
Peru	568	4.80	6.13	142.9
Uruguay	67	2.40	8.17	59.8
Venezuela	493	2.08	4.29	132.9

[a] Before 1959.

Sources: United States Arms Control and Disarmament Agency. *World Military Expenditures and Arms Transfers 1966–1975.* Washington, D.C., 1977. United States Agency for International Development. *U.S. Overseas Loans and Grants 1945–1973.* Washington, D.C., 1974.

Index